Brand Luther

Brand Luther

1517, Printing, and the
Making of the Reformation

ANDREW
PETTEGREE

PENGUIN PRESS
NEW YORK
2015

PENGUIN PRESS
An imprint of Penguin Random House LLC
375 Hudson Street
New York, New York 10014
penguin.com

Illustration credits appear on page 369.

ISBN 978-1-59420-496-8

Printed in the United States of America
1   3   5   7   9   10   8   6   4   2

Designed by Amanda Dewey

Contents

Part 4. BUILDING THE CHURCH

PREFACE

I N 2017 WE MARK the five-hundredth anniversary of one of the seminal moments in Western civilization: the inception of the Protestant Reformation. From small beginnings, a theological quarrel in eastern Germany, emerged a tumultuous movement of renewal and reform; questioning, defiant, and ultimately utterly divisive. Within a generation the whole concept of reform had changed its meaning. Advocates of the movement now known as Protestantism had separated themselves from the Western Catholic tradition; the division was permanent and, as it turned out, irreconcilable. Over the next two centuries Europe divided into warring churches, fractured families, and hostile states. Enmity between Protestant and Catholic shaped European politics and ignited wars of murderous hatred. Christendom turned against the enemy within. All over Europe state power was enlisted to execute as heretics or traitors those who repudiated the local religion, whether this was Protestant or Catholic.

These bitter, brutal divisions would prove enduring. In 1685 the king of France would demonstrate his piety by expelling his remaining Protestant subjects: perhaps as many as nine hundred thousand were forced to leave their homes forever. Three years later England expelled its king for the offense of being Catholic; a subsequent law disqualifying anyone from inheriting the crown if he or she married a Catholic was repealed only in 2013. The divisions and corrosive loyalties of Old Europe were also transported across the Atlantic: it was only in 1960 that the United States elected its first Catholic president, and then by the narrowest of margins.

The event chosen by history to mark the beginning of these transforming events is, set in this context, astonishingly mundane. We now date the Reformation from the day, October 31, 1517, when a little-known German professor proposed an academic disputation—an event so routine in sixteenth-century universities that no one at the time thought it worth recording whether the propositions for debate were printed and posted up on the normal university billboard, the door of a local church. The professor, of course, was Martin Luther, and his propositions, the ninety-five theses against indulgences, set off an unexpectedly lively debate. Within five years the German church was in turmoil, and Luther was a condemned heretic and the most famous man in Germany.

How an academic quarrel in northeastern Germany became the seed of a great movement takes some explaining. It will not be accomplished here by offering another biography of Luther, and this is not my intention. Luther was, as will be seen, a remarkable man, a person of courage and talent who met his moment of destiny with extraordinary skill and resourcefulness. His life and works have been the subject of study and reappraisal since his own lifetime to the present day, and the anniversary will be the opportunity for a further stocktaking. The purpose of this book is rather different. What will concern us here is how, in the very different communication environment of five hundred years ago, a theological spat could become a great public event, embracing churchmen and laypeople over a wide span of the European landmass.

None of this was as it should have been. In 1517 the church hierarchy was very confident of its ability to close down the hubbub around Luther. The usual channels, a confidential letter to persons of influence, underpinned by a judicial process in Rome, should have sufficed to silence a turbulent priest. There was no reason that the criticism of indulgences, fairly commonplace already in intellectual circles, should become a toxic public event. Most of all, there was no reason to believe that Electoral Saxony, a medium-sized state far from the main centers of European power politics, could incubate an event of European importance.

To understand how this came about we need to investigate a very strange alignment of events and circumstances that allowed Luther to capture the public imagination, but first of all to survive. Luther, like most of the great figures in history, was also very lucky. He was fortunate in the protection he received from influential patrons, and in the fact that they could see how protecting him could suit their purposes. He was fortunate in his friends. He also chose his moment well. When Luther first spoke out against indulgences, Europe was beginning to embrace, albeit with some caution, a new and powerful communication process, the printing press. It was sixty years since Johannes Gutenberg had announced, to general applause, the success of his experiments printing with moveable type, but the long-term consequences of this technological development were still decidedly uncertain. Those who enthusiastically embraced the new medium found it was remarkably difficult to make money producing printed books: most of the first printers lost money and many went bankrupt. Chastened, the second generation took refuge in conservative subjects. It was by no means clear how or why printing could serve a great movement of change. Printers, in fact, discovered that the most reliable profits lay in servicing the needs of traditional religion. They would need some persuading to abandon this steady, established business.

It was thus far from certain exactly how print would be relevant to the rumbling ecclesiastical spat in the north German churches. Wittenberg, Luther's base in Saxony, had no printing press at all until 1502; the whole of the half century of experimentation and growth since Gutenberg had passed it by. Luther himself had reached his maturity, and a position of modest responsibility and respect in his local order, without publishing a book. Yet within five years of penning the ninety-five theses, he was Europe's most published author—ever. How he achieved this was the most extraordinary of the Reformation's multiple improbabilities. It is also the story of this book.

It is a story that sees Luther blossoming almost overnight as a writer of extraordinary power and fluency, a natural stylist in a genre that had not to that point particularly valued these skills. In the process Luther created what was essentially a new form of theological writing: lucid, accessible, and above all short. Crucially, at an early stage of the furor caused by the criticisms of indulgences, Luther made the bold and radical decision to speak beyond an informed audience of trained theologians and address the wider German public in their own language, German. This decision to move beyond the language of scholarship, Latin, was deeply controversial, but it allowed complex theological ideas to be presented to a nonspecialist audience. It also put his opponents at a disadvantage from which they never fully recovered. Certainly it vastly increased the potential market for Luther's books; Germany's printers responded with a hungry enthusiasm.

Luther's writings electrified Germany, but they also transformed the dynamics of the printing industry. By the time of the Reformation the European geography of print had achieved a fairly fixed state, and it was an infrastructure that should have had no place for little Wittenberg. The principal publishing hubs were all established in Europe's largest commercial cities; Wittenberg, in contrast, was small and remote, and miles away from any of the large markets necessary to sustain major book production. Luther realized very early that this had to change: Wittenberg had to develop a book industry capable of sustaining the vast demand for his works, one that would also do justice to the potency of his call for fundamental Christian reform.

To accomplish this, and from very early in the period of his notoriety, Luther intervened directly and forcefully in the management of the press. Until 1517 Wittenberg had only one not very competent printing press. By the time of Luther's death the town's production matched that of Germany's mightiest cities. Over the sixteenth century as a whole, Wittenberg was Germany's largest printing center. This was Luther's achievement, and it was a very personal one. Luther was no distracted intellectual, but a man of great practical skill. He understood and relished the practicalities of turning words and ideas into a printed artifact. Luther's father had made his living in the copper-mining industry, and young Martin would have experienced firsthand the opportunities and perils of a life wrestling precious metal from a harsh and unforgiving landscape. Once he became a writer, he put this experience to very good use.

Luther spent his life in and out of the print shops, observing and directing. He had very firm views on how his books should look, and imposed exacting standards. Most of all, Luther understood the aesthetics of the book. He appreciated that the quality and design of the printed artifact that presented his message was itself a visual totem to its respectability and truth. In 1519 Luther took a crucial initiative to bring to Wittenberg an experienced printer who could keep up with the demand for his work, and from that point on he took a leading role in directing production within the city. Most important, he took pains that his own precious, original writings were spread around the growing number of print shops to ensure that they all remained viable.

This is a crucial part of the story of Luther's Reformation, and it is one not often told. It was not just about the sheer volume of demand for Luther's work, though this was also impressive. Luther was sufficiently popular to put bread on the table for publishers throughout Germany, not just in Wittenberg. It was also the case that, working with his printers, Luther transformed the look of the book. In this he had the crucial support of Lucas Cranach, court painter in Wittenberg and a significant force in the book industry as well. It is arguable, in fact, that Cranach's most significant contribution to the Reformation came not with the iconic portraits of Luther that spread the reformer's image and fame around Germany, but with his part in the development of a new brand identity for Wittenberg's Reformation pamphlets. His designs clothed Luther's works in a new and distinctive livery, immediately recognizable on a crowded bookstall. The result was the development of a form of book that was itself a powerful representative of the movement—bold, clear, and recognizably distinct from what had gone before. This was Brand Luther, and its success lay at the heart of the tumultuous events that convulsed his homeland in the years after 1517. It lies at the heart of Luther's success, and of the transforming impact of the Reformation.

LIST OF ILLUSTRATIONS

LIST OF ILLUSTRATIONS

Part 1

✳

A SINGULAR
MAN

A Small Town in Germany

IKE MANY OF HISTORY'S most commanding personalities, Martin Luther was gregarious by nature. He was interested in people and loved to be in company. That was certainly a mercy, for in the second half of his life he was seldom alone. From the point in 1517 when he first registered on the consciousness of his fellow Germans, Luther was a controversial, divisive, charismatic, and inspiring figure; to some extent, he has remained so ever since. Those who came into his company seldom forgot the experience. Even in his early career the intense young monk attracted the interest of a number of influential figures who discerned in him a special talent. In later life, among his intimates, he inspired a passionate devotion. Thousands flocked to Wittenberg to hear him preach, or in the hope of attending his lectures. Those admitted to his circle of friends enjoyed the particular privilege of joining him at table, where Luther would relax and hold forth.

This was Luther's especial domain. The day's labors past, he would sit with his friends and talk. Fueled by his wife's excellent beer, conversation would become general, discursive, and sometimes unbuttoned. Often one of the more eager of his dinner companions would make a record of his master's pronouncements; Luther, a university teacher for thirty years and used to being surrounded by note-takers, thought little of this.

Not all of what passed at table reads particularly well today. Luther was among friends and relaxed; he sometimes spoke to shock, and delighted in the outrageous. His jokes don't always amuse us. But the *Table Talk* is also full of profound, though unstructured, theological observations and acute perceptions of contemporary society.[1]

It is curious that, in this great mass of words, Luther said so little about his own movement, the Reformation. Between 1517, when Luther first attracted public attention, and his death thirty years later, Luther and his followers reshaped their world. Western Christianity was split in two, as it turned out, permanently. Families, cities, and nation-states were forced to choose sides: whether to remain with the old church, or to follow Luther into schism and new patterns of worship and belief. All this Luther accepted with remarkable calm. His actions had been dictated by God: the path he had taken was shaped by a higher power. In that respect the remarkable life he had led was not of his own making, but the consequence of patient obedience to God's command.

So it is left to us, in our more secular age, to reflect on the magnitude of Luther's achievement; but also, the sheer improbability of it all. Luther's career was a monument to a towering talent, but it was also a pyramid of multiple improbabilities. There was nothing in the first thirty years of his life to suggest that here was an individual who would convulse a continent. It was extraordinary that a man who had built a steady and, for someone of his background, remarkably successful career within the church should suddenly repudiate both the institution and its spiritual leadership. It was even more extraordinary that he should survive to tell the tale.

When, at the height of the "Luther affair" in 1521, Martin journeyed across Germany to face the judgment of the German Empire at the Diet of Worms, he did so under guarantee of safe-conduct. Luther would be allowed to arrive and depart unharmed. But there were those among the emperor's entourage who urged him to repudiate this promise and have Luther arrested and executed.[2] Such had been the fate of another heretic, Jan Hus, a century before, and it was the fate that many of Luther's friends expected for him. Luther himself did not expect to leave Worms alive. That he had reached this climactic moment at all he owed to the stolid support of his own local ruler, Frederick the Wise, a devout Catholic who never left the old faith. He also, incidentally, owned one of Europe's finest collections of relics, the sacred remains that lay at the heart of the theology of indulgence that Luther denounced with such vehemence. Curiously he had never met his turbulent professor; it may have been at the Diet of Worms that he cast eyes on Luther for the first time. Many contemporaries found Frederick's protection of him unfathomable. Certainly without it Luther's career as a reformer would have been stifled very quickly.

Luther owed his notoriety during these years to another of the Reformation's extraordinary improbabilities: that a monk who into his thirtieth year had published nothing, and who shared the conventional education of other churchmen, should somehow reinvent himself as a writer and polemicist of astonishing power. More than that, in an age that valued prolonged and detailed exposition, complexity, and repetition, it was astonishing that Luther should have instinctively discerned the value of brevity. Luther in effect invented a new form of theological writing: short, clear, and direct, speaking not only to his professional peers but to the wider Christian people. This revelation of style, purpose, and form was at the heart of the Reformation, as it will be at the heart of this book.

And Luther achieved all this from a thoroughly incongruous place, a small, inconsequential market town on Europe's eastern periphery, a place that to this point had scarcely figured in the annals of European history: Wittenberg. This was in many ways the greatest of all the improbabilities of the Reformation, for which Renaissance Europe had no precedent. Europe in the sixteenth century was a society of rising nation-states, full of intellectual vitality. Its cities, with their churches, universities, and the new printed books, were one of the greatest adornments of this culture. But little of this cultural and economic Renaissance had reached the sandy, underpopulated plains of northeastern Germany. When Martin Luther first made his way to Wittenberg in 1508, he was not impressed, a sentiment shared by most of the small number of people who recorded their recollections of this tiny border settlement.

Yet this is how it turned out. From the time that Luther settled permanently in Wittenberg in 1511, his fate and that of his new home would be permanently intertwined. Wittenberg would become Luthertown (Lutherstadt), a title it formally adopted in the twentieth century. Wittenberg was the heart of the Reformation, and it shared and mirrored Luther's own transformation.

ON THE WHITE MOUNTAIN

When Luther first walked through the gates of Wittenberg, he would have found a modest settlement of some two thousand souls.[3] The great cities of Germany were up to thirty times this size; even in the locality, Wittenberg was dwarfed by Leipzig, the local trading hub, and Erfurt, the lively university city where Luther had spent his formative years. Wittenberg had first emerged as a settled place in the twelfth century, after a brutal struggle to eradicate the local Slavic population. To the settlers from the flatlands of Flanders called to repopulate the region, the gentle hills close to the Elbe seemed formidable enough. So they called their new home White Mountain, the Wittenberg, after the white sand of the hill and on the banks of the river, sufficiently shallow at this point for a ford. Over the next two hundred years this became a walled city, strong enough to defy a Hussite army during the Bohemian Revolt. But it never quite threw off the feeling of a frontier settlement, standing sentinel against the alien hordes. Significantly the largest cities in this part of Germany, Erfurt and Leipzig, were to the south and west, angled toward the cultured southern heart of the German Empire.

It was from Erfurt that Luther had been dispatched to join the Au-

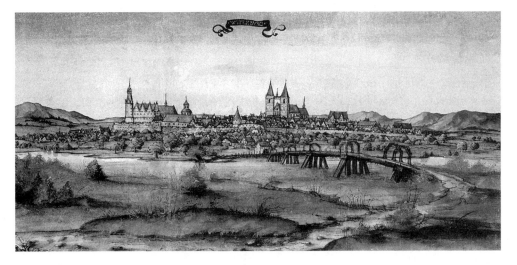

WITTENBERG

Seen from the south, and the far bank of the river Elbe, we can pick out the castle complex to the left, the parish church in the center, and the Augustinian cloister on the far right.

gustinian cloister at Wittenberg, and he never quite forgot these daunting first impressions. He had found Wittenberg, he reflected some years later, on the edge of civilization, *"in termino civilitatis."* Had it been only a little farther east it would have been *"in mediam barbariam,"* in the middle of the barbarians.[4] Other visitors were equally unflattering. According to one traveler who experienced Wittenberg at about the time of Luther's arrival, it was a poor, unattractive town, with old, small, ugly wooden houses, more like a village than a town.[5] Not surprisingly, when Luther's views had stirred notoriety, these were sentiments his enemies were eager to echo. According to Johannes Cochlaeus, an early and dogged critic, Wittenberg was:

> A miserable, poor, dirty village, in comparison to Prague, hardly worth three farthings: yes, in fact, it is not worthy to be called a town of Germany. It has an unhealthy, disagreeable climate; it is without vineyards, orchards or fruit bearing trees of any kind . . . dirty homes, unclean alleys; all roads, paths and streets are full of

filth. It has a barbarous people who make their living from breweries and saloons, and a body of merchants not worth three cents.[6]

George, Duke of Albertine Saxony, enemy and rival to Luther's own patron, Frederick the Wise, put it more succinctly. "That a single monk, out of such a hole, could undertake a Reformation, is not to be tolerated."[7] Indeed, one of the reasons opponents so underestimated Luther at first was because they simply could not conceive anything of importance emerging from such a place.

NEW WEALTH AND NEW INVENTIONS

The comparative backwardness of Wittenberg in this era was all the more glaring because the German cities were regarded, with some justice, as among the greatest jewels of European civilization. In the fifteenth century Germany had become one of the powerhouses of the European economy. While the emerging nation-states of Spain, France, and England expended their gold in dynastic conflict, Germany enjoyed comparative peace. Germany had its emperor, a member of the Habsburg family, who certainly aspired to expand his authority; but the Habsburg lands were too dispersed, and crucially, the emperor's own position depended not on heredity succession, but on election by a college comprised of the rulers of seven of Germany's larger states. These were the elite among the three hundred rulers of Germany's patchwork of small and tiny territories. Their borders were in constant flux. Saxony, where Wittenberg lay, could have been one of the largest but for a family tradition of partible inheritance that led to frequent divisions. Some of the grandest territories were held by bishops, true princes of the church such as the archbishop of Mainz, Albrecht of Brandenburg, a man who would play a large part in Luther's story.

By the fifteenth century many of the largest cities had successfully repudiated the authority of any neighboring prince: these were the imperial free cities. Nuremberg, the greatest of them all, had a considerable territory of its own; in southern Germany it coexisted in friendly rivalry with Augsburg, center of the German banking industry. Augsburg was also southern Germany's major news hub, a crucial staging point on the imperial post road linking Germany, Italy, and the Low Countries.[8] To the north lay Hamburg and Lübeck, leaders of the venerable Hanseatic League of Baltic trading towns; to the west Cologne, Strasbourg, and Basel were strategically located on the Rhine, the great communication and transport artery that linked the rich trading towns of Flanders with Italy to the south. It was the connection with Italy across the perilous Alpine passes that was the lifeblood of Germany, for Italy was the gateway to Asia and its precious cargoes of spice and silks. The greatest benefits of this international trade were confined to the imperial cities of the south and west; at the turn of the sixteenth century very little of this luxury trade would have found its way to the chilly northern plains of Thuringia and Saxony, where fish and grain dominated the local markets.

In the second half of the fifteenth century the sophisticated markets of Flanders, Italy, and southern Germany began to deal in a new branch of trade: the commerce in printed books. When in the mid-1440s a dogged Mainz entrepreneur called Johannes Gutenberg began to experiment with new ways to mass-produce books, it was by no means clear that this was an invention the world really needed. Europe already had a highly developed book trade, volumes lovingly hand-copied from manuscript to manuscript. Consumers and collectors would seek out their manuscripts from the best and most famous copy shops, or take their texts to the local scribe: this was a very flexible market. The trade in manuscripts would continue to flourish for many years after Gutenberg first exhibited pages of his printed Bible at the Frankfurt Fair in 1454.[9] Gutenberg's Bible certainly attracted a great deal of attention and quickly sold out. But it also bankrupted him. It was the last major project in which he would be involved.

Gutenberg's story, one of technological fascination and financial failure, would be disturbingly characteristic of the first seventy years of printing.[10] As news of his great achievement spread, princes, bishops, or town councils all wanted to have a press in their territory. Printing spread quickly through Germany, Italy, and France, and thence more haltingly to Europe's periphery: Spain, England, and Scandinavia. But most of these ventures, unsuitably located in small cities away from the major centers of population, closed after publishing only a handful of titles. It took some time for the fatal flaw in the business model to become apparent. It was comparatively simple to print some three hundred, five hundred, or even a thousand copies of a printed text. But the manuscript book trade, essentially a retail business linking one text with one purchaser, gave no hint of how such quantities could be sold in a marketplace spread all over Europe.

The answer, painfully derived after thirty years of expenditure and failure, was to be guided by those who had this sort of experience: the wealthy merchants who dominated Europe's transnational luxury trades. These were the men who knew what was necessary to make the new trade work: raising capital for the necessary investment and transporting books in bulk to major markets, where they could be traded, often by exchange, for other consignments of books. They knew how to arrange storage for many hundredweight of paper until an edition could be disposed of, and how to handle the complicated loans and exchange transactions necessary in any capital-intensive industry.

So the book trade contracted. Although books were at some point in the fifteenth century printed in more than two hundred places around Europe, two thirds of them were produced in only twelve cities. All of them were large commercial centers, strategically situated in Europe's major trading places: six in Germany, four in Italy, and two in France.[11] This iron geography of book production would prove remarkably enduring. Of the twelve great printing towns of fifteenth-century Europe, none was smaller than thirty thousand inhabitants. This was true also of the two sixteenth-century latecomers to the printing elite, London and Antwerp.

It was a world that should have had no place for little Wittenberg. And initially this was exactly how it turned out. The experimental age of printing, the fifteenth century or incunabula age, passed Wittenberg by altogether. Such books as the inhabitants of the small city required, and these were not many, could have been purchased in nearby Erfurt and Leipzig, both of which had a lively early printing industry. The first printing press was not established in Wittenberg until 1502, as a service to the new university. Most university towns had a press of their own, but this was hardly a flourishing venture. It was probably only the determination of Wittenberg's ruler, Frederick the Wise, that his capital should have the appropriate accoutrements of cultural sophistication that allowed it to stagger on.

Yet within the next fifty years Wittenberg would defy all the rules of the new print economics and become a center of the book world. This was almost entirely due to Martin Luther: his notoriety, his passionate following, and his uncommon talent as a writer.

This book tells the story of how a new revolutionary movement was incubated in a tiny, remote city and quickly took Germany by storm. It is not just a story about books. Luther and his friends used every instrument of communication known to medieval and Renaissance Europe: correspondence, song, word of mouth, painted and printed images.[12] Many people adhered to the new movement when they first heard Luther speak; others were led to the evangelical message by those who emerged as leaders in the hundred or more German cities that adopted the Reformation. The Reformation took wing largely because its advocates grasped that the pulpit could be one of the most powerful organs of public information and persuasion available in sixteenth-century society. All that said, the Reformation could not have occurred as it did without print. Print propelled Martin Luther, a man who had published nothing in the first thirty years of his life, to instant celebrity. It was his genius to grasp an opportunity that had scarcely existed before he invented a new way to converse through books. In the process he changed Western religion and European society forever.

He also changed Wittenberg. Wittenberg, a town that had no printing at all before 1500, would become a powerhouse of the new industry, trading exclusively on the fame of its celebrity professor. And Wittenberg was not an isolated case. In many medium-sized and small German towns, the Reformation galvanized an industry that had withered after the first flush of overexuberant experimentation.[13]

All this Germany owed to Luther, and in this respect Wittenberg was a microcosm of a larger transformation. But it was in Wittenberg that it began, and began rather slowly, for at first the sleepy little settlement found it difficult to grasp the enormity of what was unfolding in its church and university. Luther, whose intuitive understanding of the power of print was one of the most remarkable aspects of his extraordinary personality, would have to intervene personally to ensure that Wittenberg developed a print industry that could match the huge demand for his work.

But that is for the future. Let us first take a little time to become acquainted with the city that Luther made, and that made Martin Luther. The best way to do this is in Luther's company, for he was a congenial soul, though perhaps more so as the paterfamilias of mature years than as the intense young professor we first find hurrying through the streets of Wittenberg in 1513.

WALKING WITH LUTHER

In 1513 Luther had been definitively settled in Wittenberg for two years. Our walk with him will take the same path of a more famous walk that occurred four years later, as Luther strode through the town to pin up on the castle church his ninety-five theses: the event that would ignite the Reformation.

Or so tradition would have it. Fifty years ago a mischievous Catholic theologian suggested that the posting of the ninety-five theses was, in fact, a myth, a fable that grew up only when Luther became famous.[14] There were indeed no contemporary witnesses, or at least none that thought the event important enough to record.[15] This unwelcome intervention, not surprisingly, set off a storm of controversy. In one recent poll of the German public, the posting of the theses was voted the third most important event in German history, so it would be disconcerting indeed to think it did not take place. Personally I am inclined to believe the posting of the theses did take place, and to settle the question I will introduce evidence that emerged some years after Erwin Iserloh lobbed his hand grenade into the calm waters of Luther studies.[16] We will come to that in due course. In 1513 indulgences were far from Luther's mind, and certainly he had no wish to challenge the church in which he was making a promising career.

Luther was just approaching his thirtieth birthday. The first contemporary images show a lean, earnest young man, dressed in the habit of the Augustinian order that he had joined eight years before. He lived in modest quarters on the third floor of the Augustinian monastery, at the very eastern end of the city. The community housed some thirty monks, many of whom studied or had teaching duties in the university.[17] It was an intense, intellectual atmosphere, which no doubt suited Luther well, for he, too, was notably cerebral. In 1512 he had been promoted to professor, a distinction that earned him the important privilege of a heated room.

Luther's destination this morning was the university, situated in the castle church at the farthest western end of Wittenberg. It is a walk of about half a mile from one end of Wittenberg to the other. This walk took in Wittenberg's two main streets, which run parallel to the Elbe River on its northern shore and which then, as now, shaped the topography of the city. As he hurried to his duties, there would have been little to detain him. Luther was not at this point well-known to Wittenberg's citizens; it was only in the following year, 1514, that he would begin regularly to preach to the townsfolk in the parish church. Wittenberg's one parish church lay a few yards behind the main street, where the city broadened out to the north. This was the dwelling place of Wittenberg's artisans and craftsmen, modest enough men who nevertheless dominated the city's town government. For unlike the great imperial cities of Augsburg, Nuremberg, and Strasbourg, Wittenberg had no patrician elite of international merchants. This was a small community serving a modest agricultural commerce. Its beating heart was the marketplace, through which Luther would now quickly pass. Here, as elsewhere, this was a crowded place of market stalls, a hubbub of bawling tradesmen, live animals, and impatient customers.

Opposite the marketplace, on a corner of the road leading to the castle, was a building site. Here, on a huge corner plot, stretching back to the gate to the river Elbe, the artist Lucas Cranach was building a residence fit for Wittenberg's most distinguished inhabitant. Cranach was one of a number of major figures drawn to Wittenberg by commissions to decorate the city's most striking new building projects: the castle and castle church. But unlike Albrecht Dürer, Hans Burgmair, and others, Cranach had remained in Wittenberg as the elector's court painter. This was only one of a number of ventures pursued by this enterprising and driven man, who in 1513 was well on the way to being Wittenberg's major employer. At this point, he and the young professor striding past his new building would have had little connection. In the years to come, their partnership, built on a profound mutual respect and friendship, would shape the Reformation.

Luther was now five minutes from his destination, the castle church, where much of the formal instruction of the university was held. Or perhaps he was heading for the university library, recently settled in the castle itself. The castle was another new building, only completed in 1509, a monument to the determination of Wittenberg's ruler, Frederick, to build a residence appropriate to his status as a prince of the Empire.

Frederick's passion for building can be traced back to a crisis in the ruling dynasty at the end of the fifteenth century. In 1485 the lands of

FREDERICK THE WISE

Luther's essential protector, though the two men may never actually have spoken to each other. Frederick's tenacious loyalty to his turbulent professor was always something of a mystery, even to Luther.

the Wettin Saxon dukes had been divided between two brothers, Ernest (Frederick's father) and Albert. According to the strange Saxon custom, the elder brother, Ernest, decided how to divide the territories, and the younger, Albert, then chose which portion to take. Not surprisingly Albert chose the richest territories around Meissen, which also encompassed Saxony's largest city, Leipzig. The inheritance of Ernest was more awkward, a long thin strip of territory with no natural center, and with Wittenberg the only town of any size. But it was Ernest who received the real prize: the electoral title that made him one of the seven hereditary electors whose privilege it was to select the Holy Roman Emperor.

When his son, Frederick, inherited these Ernestine lands in 1486, he determined to make something of this. Frederick was scrupulous in his attendance at every major meeting of the German assembly, the Diet. And he decided to make of Wittenberg a place fit for an electoral capital.

In 1486 the old residence was razed to the ground, and a new castle and church built in its place. This was a monumentally expensive project that would take twenty years to complete, for Frederick wanted a statement: a princely home built in the best Renaissance fashion, and a church to house his enormous and fast-growing collection of relics.

The church in which Luther now found himself would have been a cluttered place, home not only to the university but to a teeming array of altars and religious offices. Even before Frederick's rebuilding, the All Saints foundation of the castle church possessed a precious distinction, a very rare indulgence that offered general remission from sins for all those who made an act of worship there on All Saints' Day.[18] Such indulgences, which offered the prospect of forgiveness in the hereafter for sins that might otherwise impede the progress of a soul to paradise, would in due course attract Luther's ire, but in the centuries before, they were wildly popular, both as a means of raising funds for local churches and among those who bought them. When the new castle church was dedicated in 1503 by Cardinal Raymond Peraudi, the pope's roving emissary, he graciously bestowed new indulgences on the church and its visitors. The pope obligingly played his part, urging Germany's cathedrals and churches to offer some of their relics for Frederick's increasingly impressive collection. Relics—fragments of the bones of saints and other holy memorabilia—were another pivotal aspect of medieval piety, and the pious pilgrim earned further indulgence by gazing upon them. It is one of the real curiosities of the Reformation that Frederick the Wise, at the same time that he stubbornly protected Luther from the consequences of his criticisms of medieval spirituality, also continued to add to his collection of relics. By 1520, when the latest inventory would be taken, it had reached 18,970 individual objects and was one of the largest in Germany. The most precious, rare items, such as a vial of the breast

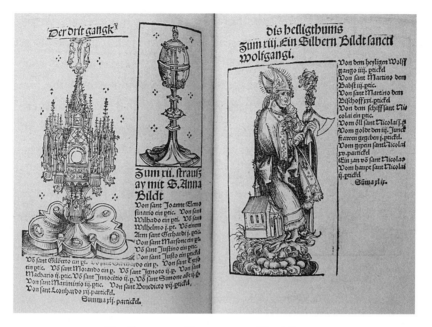

THE CATALOG OF FREDERICK THE WISE'S RELICS,
WITH ILLUSTRATIONS BY LUCAS CRANACH

*The collection, already large when this catalog was published in 1509, would continue to grow
massively even as Luther's protest against indulgences and the cult of saints gathered pace.*

milk of the Virgin Mary and a twig from the Burning Bush, would be
preserved in beautiful gold or silver cases.[19] When laid out for the benefit
of pilgrims, the collection crammed eight aisles of the castle church.
There would have been little teaching on All Saints' Day, as pilgrims
flocked to avail themselves of the 1.9 million days of indulgence that the
assiduous visitor would gain from seeing them all. From 1509 there was
a catalog, with 124 woodcut illustrations by Lucas Cranach, to guide
them through the treasures.[20]

Even when the relics were not on display, this would have been a
busy place. In 1517, as the accounts show, nine thousand masses were
said at the various altars; forty thousand candles were lit in honor of the
dead.[21] This was big business, and if Luther had stopped off in the town
church on his way home, he would have found things much the same.

For the citizens of Wittenberg, however modest their houses and despite the sneering disregard of passing intellectuals, were not prepared to let the electors have everything their own way. Over the course of many years the town council had doggedly asserted its rights over the local countryside. Wittenberg had bargained and wheedled, taking advantage of the ebb and flow of ducal power to purchase important privileges: the right to mint coins, the power to exercise justice. Its trade guilds had poured money into their own institutions, not least the sacred societies that sponsored masses for the souls of dead members. So Wittenberg's parish church was also full of altars and side chapels, employing a small horde of priests praying continuously for departed souls.

This, in 1513, was Luther's world: a town of 384 dwellings, far away from the main centers of culture and sophisticated urban life in Germany, Flanders, and Italy. Its new university, founded in 1502, was scarcely one the brightest lights in Europe's intellectual firmament, like the venerable medieval institutions at Paris and Bologna, Louvain and Cologne. This was actually the smallest place in which Luther had ever lived, and he never quite shed a sense of its essential provincialism. But both the town and the university, profiting from the patriotic pride of the elector, had a fierce sense of identity. This was not a city torn apart by the sort of tensions between patricians and urban craftsmen that would so complicate the urban Reformation in much of Germany. Though Luther might sometimes yearn for the greater sophistication of larger cities, Wittenberg, in fact, provided an extremely sympathetic environment for his years of intellectual inquiry. When his cause became notorious, both the town and its rulers would cleave to him with a dogged loyalty.

THE INDUSTRY OF EDUCATION

Luther could not have made a Reformation—indeed he could not have survived—without the support he received in Wittenberg: from his fiercely protective elector, Frederick the Wise; from his colleagues in the university; from the citizens who from 1514 were the first to appreciate the extraordinary power of his preaching. Over the course of Luther's life this loyalty would be richly rewarded. As Luther became the most famous man in Germany, so Wittenberg became a magnet for those throughout Germany and beyond who saw Luther as their spiritual leader and protector. Countless thousands bought his published writings. By the time of Luther's death in 1546, Wittenberg was transformed.

We will appreciate the scale of this transformation if we accompany Luther on a second walk through the town that he had now, perhaps reluctantly, come to see as home. The year is 1543, and Luther still lives at the Augustinian house. But there are now no monks: they were cleared out within a few years of Luther's repudiation of the pope, victims of a new theology that denied the existence of purgatory and thus cut the spiritual roots of the monastic life of prayer. The rulers of Germany's cities and princely states laid greedy hands on the monastic property that had previously dominated the landscapes and townscapes of Europe; in Wittenberg, a grateful elector passed the entire Augustinian house over to its most famous inhabitant. Today it is still the Lutherhalle, home to the magnificent museum devoted to Luther's life and movement.

For some years Luther lived there alone, but by 1543 the house was once again teeming with life. In 1525 Luther, no longer bound by his monastic vows, had taken a wife. This event, the marriage of a former monk to Katharina von Bora, a former nun, had scandalized Christendom, and confirmed all the worst fears of Luther's growing band of critics. Had the unity of the Western Church been sacrificed to the lusts of one man? But this scandalous union brought Luther enormous personal happiness. Children followed, and Luther found contentment as well as new spiritual insights in his role as paterfamilias. Katharina also proved an astute manager, presiding over a household now filled with students and lodgers, the more privileged of whom would join Luther at table, drinking in his conversation.

Luther's progress through the town on this occasion is unlikely to have been as rapid. The lean, purposeful monk of 1513 is a distant memory; Luther's figure is a testament to years of sedentary occupation and hearty food (Katharina ran a very successful market garden as well as her brewery). Besides, Wittenberg is now a crowded place, crammed with students and the professors who instruct them. It is unlikely Luther could have traveled far without someone stopping to greet him. A few yards along College Street is the home of his friend Philip Melanchthon. Luther ranked it among his greatest achievements to have lured Melanchthon to Wittenberg. For years he fretted that another university might tempt him away, and in the years after the storm first erupted over indulgences he reproached himself bitterly that his impetuosity might have allowed Leipzig, the despised local rival, to induce the temperamentally conflict-averse Melanchthon to move on. But Melanchthon was a loyal friend as well as a brilliant scholar. This partnership of opposite temperaments was the foundation stone on which the churches of the Reformation would be built.

At the end of College Street Luther would find himself once again back in the marketplace. Here the transformation wrought in Wittenberg is most visibly apparent. As Luther enters the square, on the southeastern corner, he would pass the Eagle, a substantial inn established in 1524 to house and refresh the host of merchants and distinguished visitors for whom Wittenberg was an essential part of their itinerary.[22] At the southwest corner Lucas Cranach's large factory dwelling was now complete, an immense complex of eighty-four rooms. Between, at Markt 4, lay another Cranach residence, the present day Cranach House, a magnificent structure on four floors in the new Renaissance style.

The Cranach House looked down on a scene of busy commerce. On the other side of the square lay the new town hall, the Rathaus. The old, rather modest building familiar from Luther's first years had been demolished in 1521, and a new larger civic center constructed, as the town reinvested the first fruits of its new prosperity. In some respects the town elders acted too hastily, before the full extent of Wittenberg's commercial renaissance had become clear. This new town hall lasted less than fifty years, and was replaced in 1573 by the more confident and monumental structure that dominates Wittenberg's central square today. Now this is an impressively open space; in 1543 it would have been filled with market stalls, including a row of semipermanent booths erected between the town hall and the parish church.

For by 1543 Wittenberg was packed; in fact, it was seriously over-crowded. The influx of tradesmen, merchants, and especially students was almost more than the city could bear; in some years students made up a third or even half the population.[23] The result was a significant in-crease in the prices of food, clothing, and accommodation. Property owners remodeled their houses and built extra stories to meet the de-mand for additional rooms. The open spaces within the city walls were now largely built over, and wooden houses had been rebuilt in stone. Like most communities, Wittenberg was happy to flaunt its new wealth.

Most likely Luther would have been happy to slip away from the hubbub of the market and take refuge in the nearby parish church. This, rather than the castle church at the other end of town, was now his spiritual home. It was here, in 1514, that he had first begun to assert his extraordinary influence over Wittenberg's citizens, in sermons of mes-merizing power and passion. In 1543 he now shared these preaching du-ties with his great friend, Johannes Bugenhagen.

To Wittenberg's older residents the church would have been virtu-ally unrecognizable from thirty years before. Particularly in its interior architecture, the impact of Luther's Reformation was quite unmissa-ble. Gone were the numerous side altars, with their priests celebrating Mass and the constant mumbling of propitiatory prayer. Instead all spiritual energy was concentrated on the central worship service. The church's furnishing was remodeled to reflect the new shape of congrega-tional worship, built around prayer, Bible reading, the singing of hymns, and preaching. Since Wittenberg, rather unusually for a town of this size, had only one parish church, the Sunday worship service would in effect have been a gathering of the whole community. Here they would have heard Luther preach as many as four thousand times in his thirty years as their minister. A privilege for which admirers would journey many miles was part of the everyday experience of Wittenberg's citizens. It helps explain the remarkable influence Luther exercised in his own community.

Luther's role as city preacher to some extent eclipsed the importance of the castle church, particularly when the elector was not in residence. Frederick the Wise had passed away in 1525, still stubbornly clinging to both his traditional Catholic faith and his celebrity professor. But under Luther's influence his wondrous collection of relics was quietly packed away; from 1522 they were no longer exhibited, and pilgrims were forced to go elsewhere for the promise of salvation. Frederick's successors, his brother John (who ruled from 1525 to 1532), and nephew John Frederick (from 1532 to 1547), were if anything even firmer in their support for Luther; in this he had been fortunate indeed. By 1543 Luther's trips outside Wittenberg were usually concerned with service to the electoral family or with preaching to them in their other residences.

So leaving the parish church Luther would have been unlikely to have bent his steps to the castle; he might instead have turned right, away from the river and into the residential area to the north. This was where most of Wittenberg's printers had established their premises. Luther took a keen interest in the publication of his books, and nowhere was the transformation of Wittenberg more dramatically demonstrated than in the teeming mass of printers, booksellers, and bookbinders that filled the workshops of this busy quarter.

In 1513, when we first followed Luther through Wittenberg, he would not have had to go far to visit Wittenberg's printers, since the university print shop was situated in the immediate vicinity of the Augustinian monastery. This was the only printing press in operation at that time. That year, it published just ten works, all in Latin, and all for the students and professors of the university: copies of orations, textbooks, and the like.[24] Even though the printer, Johann Rhau-Grunenberg, was notoriously slow, the surviving books would not have kept his press busy for more than a small portion of the year.[25] In 1543, in contrast, Wittenberg sustained six busy shops, between them responsible for some eighty-three editions. Of these, half were in German and half in Latin; most of the copies would have been destined for export. With the swarm of ancillary workers involved in the trade, wholesalers, bookbinders, carters, and merchants responsible for the complex monetary transactions of long-distance commerce, publishing was undoubtedly one of the largest industries in this thriving city. Its most successful figures, such as the publisher Moritz Goltz, were among the richest inhabitants of the town.[26]

The bare statistics capture only a part of this transformation, but they are nevertheless striking. Between 1502 and 1516, five successive printers published a total of 123 books, an average of 8 a year.[27] All were in Latin and most very small. None of the printers seem to have made much of a living out of this. This was an industry teetering on the brink of viability, probably sustained only by direct subsidy from the elector and the university.[28] Between 1517 and 1546, on the other hand, Wittenberg publishers turned out at least 2,721 works, an average of 91 per year.[29] This represents around three million individual copies, and includes many of the milestone works of the era, not least multiple editions of Luther's German Bible.

This vast blossoming of what was essentially a new industry was entirely due to Martin Luther. One in three of all the books published during these three decades were Luther's own works and another 20 percent were those of his Wittenberg colleagues and followers.[30] Even in 1543, when the passions of the first years were a distant memory, half the books published were written by either Luther or Philip Melanchthon. And the Luther effect proved enduring. Even after his death, the industry continued to grow, reaching 165 new editions in 1563 and over 200 annually in the last decade of the century. Wittenberg was now Germany's largest publishing center, eclipsing established centers of the book trade like Strasbourg and Cologne, overtaking even mighty Augsburg and Nuremberg.[31]

Thanks to its favorite son, Wittenberg had subverted the iron economics of publishing, the apparent requirement that major production centers could only be located in Europe's principal commercial cities. This was a transformation that seemed to many contemporaries quite miraculous, among them Luther himself, who could never quite fathom his own extraordinary popularity as an author. Naturally he gave the credit to the direct intervention of a beneficent deity: printing, he believed, was technology heaven-sent to spread God's word and banish error. In fact, as we shall see, the emergence of Wittenberg as a publishing giant was far from straightforward. For several years after Luther's bold challenge first sent shock waves through Germany, most of his works were published elsewhere. Wittenberg's printers—in the first instance, Wittenberg's sole printer, Rhau-Grunenberg—were seemingly overwhelmed by the astonishing appetite for their local prophet. It took several years, and Luther's direct intervention, before an industry could be constructed to ensure that the publication of Luther's works could be marshaled within his own city. In the process these newcomers helped develop the distinctive look that forever shaped the image of Luther in the wider world and radically changed the readership of the book industry.

This transformation, essentially the story of this book, is in reality three transformations: of Luther, the intense monk, into a best-selling author; of the book industry, shaken from its roots in a scholarly, Latinate book world by the emergence of a mass market; and of Wittenberg. For this was the town that Luther made, and the electric bolt to the local economy would be replicated by a rippling echo of smaller transformations as other of Germany's cities shared in the booming demand for a new type of literature.

Martin Luther was a theologian of great insight, a charismatic leader and preacher, a writer of great passion and skill. But he was also, without any doubt, the chief motor of the Wittenberg economy. Nothing else could have made this small, peripheral city into the print capital of Gutenberg's homeland; but this, for around eighty years after 1517, was Wittenberg's unlikely fate. It is these two stories, the spiritual and theological, and the economic and commercial, that need to be woven together to understand the extraordinary impact of the Reformation. In this way, Wittenberg, the small border town perched on the edge of civilization, would share with Luther responsibility for igniting one of the great transforming movements of the last millennium.

2.

THE MAKING OF
A REVOLUTIONARY

ARTIN LUTHER'S FIRST YEARS in Wittenberg were a period of discovery and exploration; his subsequent celebrity was in no way preordained. If we require proof of this we need look no further than a remarkable document compiled in 1515 by an unknown humanist author: a list with biographical sketches of 101 professors associated with the universities of Leipzig, Wittenberg, and Frankfurt-an-der-Oder.[1] None of these institutions was in the front rank of Europe's universities. Leipzig was a medieval foundation, but Wittenberg and Frankfurt-an-der-Oder were very recent, both established in the last twenty years. The list, never actually published, was probably drawn up as part of a student recruitment campaign for the three universities in northeastern Germany. Yet even in this relatively undistinguished company there was no place in the top one hundred for Wittenberg's professor of biblical theology: Martin Luther.

The reason for this neglect is not far to seek. In 1515 Luther, although an established fixture on the Wittenberg University faculty, had published nothing. His first tentative steps into print came only the following year, 1516, the year before the indulgence controversy. Yet within four years of this, Luther would be one of the most famous men in Germany: revered, or reviled, for the bold, defiant pronouncements that had thrown his church into turmoil and the German Empire into constitutional crisis.

The speed and sheer improbability of this transformation have been a continuous challenge for historians from the time that Luther's own followers first began to offer their interpretations of this extraordinary life. In particular Luther's early years, his intellectual formation, and the genesis of his revolutionary theology remain a difficult study. Luther's halfhearted promise to write an autobiographical introduction to the planned collected edition of his works fell prey to other commitments and his declining health.[2] The friends who shared his table concentrated on recording the constant flow of words rather than asking probing questions about his upbringing. One of the first contemporary biographies was compiled by a dogged opponent, Johannes Cochlaeus, who naturally put an unsympathetic construction on Luther's rejection of his monastic vows and his former loyalties.[3] This at least was the work of a scholar; though the author's repetition of the fable that attributed Luther's birth to his mother's coupling with the devil in a bathhouse did him no particular credit.

In truth, the known facts of Luther's upbringing provide little clues to his tumultuous impact on German society. The first thirty years of his life are remarkably conventional: the product of a loving, relatively prosperous family, set on a course for a secure if relatively unassuming career. Having decided on a career in the church, Luther exhibited a determined commitment to institutions that had provided him with significant opportunities to develop his talents as a teacher, if not yet, as we have seen, as a published author. We will not explain the extraordinary eruption of passionate, creative energy of the years after 1515 by an investigation of the surprisingly fragmentary details of Luther's upbringing. What we may see, however, are the building blocks that would shape Luther's worldview and sustain him through his time of maximum vulnerability: the thorough grounding in the learning of his day; the network of friends and patrons who saw in him an unusual talent and were prepared to stick by him through his whirlwind spiral of controversy and confrontation; most of all, his university.

Luther's commitment to Wittenberg was by no means immediate. When he was first sent to lecture at the new university, he returned to Erfurt after a year with little regret. The definitive transfer in 1511, at the urging of his friend and patron Johann von Staupitz, could easily have seemed like an uncomfortable exile from the more sophisticated company of Erfurt. But in the years that followed, Luther committed himself wholeheartedly to the project of the university, and to its ethos. It was here that his unexpected genius as a creative thinker was first unlocked. It was in the university's cause that he first sought out controversy, and first began to gather a following. It was in championing the University of Wittenberg that Luther first became a leader, and posed his first challenge to the theological orthodoxies of the day.

YOUNG MAN LUTHER

Martin Luther was born in the small German town of Eisleben, almost certainly in November 1483.[4] Although by a strange coincidence Luther also died there, Eisleben would play only a minor role in Luther's personal itinerary, since the family moved on shortly after he was born. This was a relatively prosperous home; Luther's father, Hans, had been born into a family of independent farmers from Möhra (now Moorgrund), near Eisenach in Thuringia. His wife, Margarethe Lindemann, came from a family that had recently moved to Eisenach from Bad Neustadt in northern Bavaria, about sixty miles away. The Lindemanns were on sufficiently good terms with Hans to provide capital for his business ventures.

At the time of Luther's birth Hans was preparing to embark on an ambitious but potentially perilous enterprise.[5] In 1484 he would move his young family to Mansfeld, further up in the Harz Mountains, where

LUTHER'S WORLD

Hans intended to try his hand in the mining industry. At this time the county of Mansfeld boasted some of the richest seams of copper in all of Europe. The copper ran in a thick rib through the hills, sometimes close to the surface, sometimes many hundreds of feet below. The extraction and smelting of this precious metal required both skill and substantial investment, and at this point the mines of Saxony and Thuringia were attracting investment capital from some of Germany's most substantial banking and merchant families. Hans Luter (as the family name was then given) did not have this sort of money, and he was forced to borrow heavily to set himself up.

This was a lucrative but precarious trade. A seam of copper could plunge impossibly deep, a mine could collapse or flood. It was a hard, dangerous life, requiring strong nerves even of those who, like Hans, remained above ground. Since he leased rather than owned the mining rights, he could only operate his mines and furnaces by continually renewing lines of credit.[6] The family remained heavily exposed throughout his life, and Hans only finally paid off his debts in 1529, the year before his death. So although his business flourished—he was elected to the Mansfeld city council, and the family lived well—this prosperity was fragile. The young Luther would have learned both the great gains to be won by industry, and their unpredictability.

The importance of this unusual background, at a time when very few of Europe's population were engaged in primary industries such as mining, is not always recognized in studies of Luther's intellectual formation. In later life Martin would recall a household where parenting was strict and children were taught the value of money. But attempts to interpret the crucial turning points of Luther's life as a reaction against a cold and distant father, or mother, tell us more about the era in which they were written (the 1960s and 1970s) than about Luther.[7] Martin was conscious that he came from a loving home; he honored his parents and in turn would be a devoted and doting father. But in an age when industry was in its infancy, few academics would have experienced so closely the particular context of life in a household dependent on the golden harvest of precious metals. This experience would stand Luther in good stead when in his middle years he interested himself in another fledgling industry requiring strong nerves and heavy investment, the printing trade. When Luther walked into a printing shop, he did not do so as the naive academic who imagined that the creative process ended with the completion of his manuscript, but as a practical man, well-grounded in the harsh economics of profit and loss, and the disciplines and dangers of a business run on credit. This would be, from the standpoint of the Reformation, a lesson well learned.

For the moment the Luters prospered. Although the family contin-

LUTHER'S PARENTS

Painted by Lucas Cranach toward the end of Luther's parents' lives, these pictures capture the impact of a long tough career in the mining industry. Though his upbringing was strict, young Martin was the product of a loving home, and always remembered it as such.

ued to grow (Martin was one of eight children, though only four lived to adulthood), there was enough money left to send Martin to school. His education probably began at the local *Trivialschule* in Mansfeld. By the age of thirteen he had made sufficient progress with his letters to be sent away to school, for a year in Magdeburg, then to Eisenach. Here he was under the supervision of his mother's family, and Martin would remember these as happy years. By 1501, just short of his eighteenth birthday, he was ready to make the relatively short journey to Erfurt, to be enrolled in the university. It was at this point that an extra letter was added to the family name, and Martin became Luhter, and later Luther.

At this time Erfurt was a large and thriving city, one of the largest and most sophisticated in northern Germany. Its population of twenty thousand was served by more than one hundred ecclesiastical institutions: as much as 10 percent of the population were monks, priests, or nuns. The two thousand students who attended the university found lodging around the town or, in the first years, in dormitories in the university's own quarters.

Erfurt was the largest place in which Luther had ever lived, and he took a little time to find his feet. At the end of his first year he was ranked thirtieth in a class of fifty-seven, but by the time he completed his MA in Liberal Arts he ranked second in a class of seventeen.[8] Now, at the insistence of his father, Luther applied himself to the study of law. There was never any question that Martin would follow his father into the mining business. For his clever son, Hans had in mind a profession that might lead to lucrative fees, perhaps even a place in the administration of one of the region's princely courts and a career of distinction and influence. Martin dutifully supplied himself with the necessary texts, but it soon became clear that he had no taste for this new life. Within a few months he had abandoned his father's careful plan, sold his law books, and applied to join the local chapter of the Augustinian Hermits, the so-called Austin Friars.

This first turning point in his life was one for which Luther did, in years to come, provide a detailed explanation. As the story goes, Luther was returning from a visit to family in Eisenach when, four miles short of Erfurt, he was caught in a thunderstorm. The terrified Luther feared for his life and swore that if he was spared he would abandon the world for the monastic life. Two weeks later he was as good as his promise.

There is no reason to doubt the essence of this narrative, but it is unlikely to be the whole truth. For four years Martin had lived in an atmosphere saturated with the religious culture of one of Germany's richest ecclesiastical cities and its university. He had proved an apt pupil, and dry legal texts held no appeal. The inescapable calling, the unanswerable intervention of an all-knowing deity, resolved a career dilemma with which Luther had probably been struggling for some time. The unmissable allegory of the most powerful conversion narrative of the New Testament, Saul on the road to Tarsus, also provided a means to short-circuit awkward discussions with a pious but understandably furious parent who had invested so heavily in a brilliant future for his son.[9] In the event, the breach between the two was of short duration. When Martin was ordained a priest in Erfurt in 1507, his father made a rather ostentatious

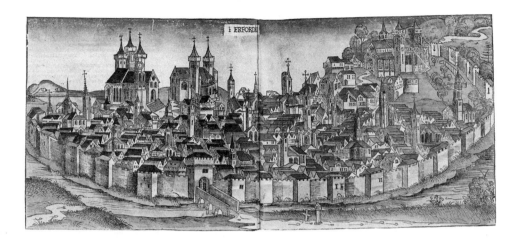

ERFURT

One of Germany's great cities, and the largest place in which Martin Luther ever lived.

appearance, accompanied by twenty mounted companions. He also made a substantial donation to the Erfurt Augustinian house.

Luther had opted for a hard and austere life, a life of constant study punctuated by the monastic round of frequent collective prayer, the daily offices. He slept in a small, unheated cell, ten feet by seven, equipped only with a straw bed; further decoration was forbidden. Coping with the transition from the gregarious, companionable aspects of student life was not easy, and Luther experienced periods of self-doubt and low spirits that would continue to afflict him intermittently throughout his life. But he accepted obediently the life he had chosen, and it was not long before his evident talent marked him out for offices of responsibility within his house and order.

Life in the Erfurt Augustinian monastery may have been hard, but the institution was also rich, well-endowed with property and possessed of a fine library. It also maintained close links with the university, where Luther was able to continue his theological training. From 1502 the Erfurt Augustinians had also begun to develop connections with the newly established university in Wittenberg. To add luster to the new institution, Frederick the Wise had been keen to secure the assistance of Johann von Staupitz, a rising star of the order and from 1503 vicar of the German Reformed chapter of the Augustinian Hermits. From 1503 Staupitz was formally seconded to Wittenberg as the university's first professor of biblical theology. Staupitz was also heavily involved in encouraging other Augustinian houses to adopt the austere standards that characterized Erfurt and those houses that had adhered to reform. He would be the first of a number of influential public figures who would play an important role in promoting Luther's career. When, in 1508, the lecturer in philosophy at Wittenberg took a brief sabbatical to prepare for academic promotion, it was Luther whom Staupitz summoned to fill the vacancy.

This unlooked-for promotion caused Luther some difficulties on his return to Erfurt the following spring. Staupitz's efforts to recruit the other Augustinian houses in Germany to the cause of reform were proving increasingly controversial. In 1507 a way forward was proposed whereby the reform congregations would merge with other houses of the Saxon province. This could be interpreted as either a great victory for Staupitz or a possible dilution of the reforming agenda; the members of Luther's Erfurt house chose to take the latter view. Two delegates, Johann Nathin and Luther, were dispatched to Rome to plead this case. This journey, in 1510–1511, was the longest Luther ever undertook, and it made a deep impression on the young monk. Even before crossing the Alps, he passed through some of Germany's most wondrous cities, Nuremberg, Ulm, and Memmingen. In Italy the two brothers journeyed on via Milan, Siena, and Florence. But it was the glories of Rome, its churches and places of pilgrimage, that most attracted Luther's admiration. For Luther, Rome represented an unexpected opportunity to celebrate his church in the fountainhead of its authority; his instinct was to take full advantage of the spiritual benefits offered by Rome's numerous sites of special indulgence. His parents were still alive, so Martin could do nothing for them, but Luther gladly scaled the Santa Scala on his knees to free his grandfather from purgatory. Luther's experience of Rome also left a certain ambivalence. He was shocked at the casual cynicism he witnessed among Rome's enormous clerical population; the sheltered life he led in Erfurt's reformed house had not prepared him for the experience of hearing priests cracking jokes about the Eucharist. Luther's impressions are confirmed by another visitor, Erasmus of Rotterdam, who had visited Rome five years previously. "With my own ears," Erasmus would recall, "I heard the most loathsome blasphemies against Christ and his apostles."[10]

These more negative recollections would return to Luther in later years, when his writings brought him into conflict with the pope. For the moment, though, he was more concerned with the mission on behalf of his order, which had achieved nothing, so on Luther's return Staupitz attempted to settle the question by negotiation. An agreement was reached that would preserve the special status of reformed institutions while largely absorbing the other houses. Presented to the reformed houses for ratification, a majority of the Erfurt brothers still favored rejection; but Luther joined a minority that supported Staupitz. Luther's decision to follow his patron rather than the majority of his own house was a hard one, and it cast a shadow over relations within the cloister that never really lifted. In these circumstances a further period in Wittenberg presented a tactful opportunity to allow tempers to cool. Luther was not to know that the Augustinian house in Wittenberg would be his home for the rest of his life.

LEUCOREA

When Luther returned to Wittenberg it was understood that he would resume his teaching duties in the university. This represented a considerable opportunity for a man of his intellect, now restlessly searching for a way to apply his rapidly expanding theological knowledge. For the university founded by the determined elector had made a promising beginning; Luther was only one of a number of talented men who had committed themselves to the new institution.

The establishment of a university in Wittenberg was a logical part of Frederick the Wise's determination to bring distinction to his new capital.[11] The partition of 1485 had placed Saxony's only university, Leipzig, in the territories of the Ernestine branch. The emperor's tactful and supportive hint that all of Germany's electoral territories should have a university only served to confirm Frederick's determination to create an institution worthy of his status in the Empire. The elector set to with characteristic energy. Offering the university quarters in his new castle complex gave a clear signal of sustained commitment to its success, and Frederick also purchased other properties around the city to serve as lecture theaters and dormitories. In the meantime, the castle church served as its chief teaching space, and the church door as its bulletin board. Here notices of forthcoming academic events, such as disputation theses to be defended, would be posted. The church door must have been crowded with academic paperwork long before Luther published his famous theses against indulgences and affixed them with the rest.

The foundation of the university broke new ground in several respects. It was, in its first years, a secular establishment. Frederick obtained authorization for the new university from the emperor rather than the pope, a charter letter granted by Maximilian in June 1502. It was only five years later that the pope gave his blessing, awarding special privileges to the university that permitted it, usefully, to apply income from the All Saints Church to university purposes.[12] The new institution also proposed a clear and relatively daring intellectual agenda. The letter of invitation to the grand opening on October 18, 1502, written unusually in German, announced that the new university, besides traditional subjects, would also teach the humanities. The commitment to the new humanist learning was symbolized by the adoption of the name Leucorea, from the Greek for white and mountain.

These eye-catching statements attracted a great deal of interest among German scholars. The poet Hermann von dem Busche traveled to Wittenberg to perform the opening oration, and several other luminous figures accepted positions on the faculty. Johann von Staupitz was the first dean of Theology; the first rector was the accomplished astronomer Martin Pollich von Mellerstadt. Nikolaus Marschalk, a committed humanist who had published in Erfurt the first Greek primers printed in Germany, joined the Faculty of Arts. Among the early professors of law were three trained in the finest Italian schools: Petrus of Ravenna, Johann von Kitzscher, and Christoph Scheurl.

Not all found the transition from established centers of learning easy. In 1505 Christoph Scheurl had made a particularly expansive oration at the University of Bologna, celebrating the German nation's contribution to letters. The new university at Wittenberg was singled out for special praise.[13] Scheurl extolled the achievement of Frederick the Wise, who he claimed (perhaps unwisely, as he had never been there) had turned his capital from a town of brick into a city of marble. In the event even brick proved slightly optimistic. Three weeks after his arrival Scheurl was longing for the sophisticated Italian companions he had so recently goaded with the perfections of Germany. Wittenbergers, in contrast, he found to be drunken, quarrelsome, and crude.[14]

Scheurl was a decent man, and quickly got over this culture shock. Soon he would be guiding his new university as its rector. Students also responded to the new regional institution with enthusiasm. When the university first opened its doors in 1502, 416 students matriculated, with a further 258 the following year.[15] This represented an extraordinary injection of energy into a town of only 2,000 inhabitants. After this, enrollments tailed off, and in 1506 the university faced its first crisis, an eruption of plague that necessitated temporary evacuation to Herzberg. Since this coincided with the foundation of the university of Electoral Brandenburg at Frankfurt-an-der-Oder, there was good reason to believe that students, a notably fickle crowd used to the principle of the *peregrinatio academica,* might desert Wittenberg for good.

It was in this context that Mellerstadt persuaded a colleague, Andreas Meinhardi, to pen a work advertising Wittenberg's many charms.[16] The dialog introduces us to two students, Reinhard and Meinhard, one headed

CHRISTOPH SCHEURL

Scheurl was one of the most talented recruits drawn to the new University of Wittenberg. In an oration in Bologna Scheurl had heaped extravagant praise on the culture of the German north; when he arrived, Wittenberg was something of a culture shock.

to Wittenberg, the other to Cologne. Reinhard is so impressed by what he hears that he decides to revise his plans and join Meinhard in Wittenberg. Their arrival is well-timed, allowing them to visit the castle church on All Saints' Day and see the relics exhibited. The remaining chapters complete the walking tour with frequent classical allusions in which Wittenberg is compared, rather ambitiously, to Rome. In this respect the dialog demonstrates the danger of treating humanist puff pieces as documentary evidence; but it also shows the energy and commitment that the first generation of pioneers manifested in their new institution.

Scheurl's arrival, in 1507, proved something of a turning point. The plague receded, and students could return. New colleagues were recruited, among them (though at first only as a stand-in for a brief winter semester) Martin Luther. In 1508 Frederick invited Scheurl to draw up new statutes for the university. With characteristic panache Scheurl modeled them on those of the greatest of the Italian universities, Bologna, and a more recent foundation in Germany, Tübingen. Scheurl continued to boost the university in a series of widely circulated orations before moving on, in 1511, to new duties in Nuremberg. The time was ripe for a new generation, supplied by the shrewd patronage of Johann von Staupitz, who in 1511 transferred both Luther and his friend Johann Lang from the Augustinian house in Erfurt. In 1512 the two friends were joined by Georg Spalatin, who took charge of converting the elector's extensive book collection into a new university library. Spalatin, Frederick's secretary and confidant, would subsequently play an enormously important role as Luther's emissary and advocate to the electoral court.[17] In the next years these three friends, Luther, Spalatin, and Lang, would combine to reshape the university around a more aggressive and confrontational intellectual agenda.

FIT FOR PURPOSE

Frederick's new capital required one other statement of purpose: the provision of a printing press. Thankfully, this needed no great exertion on the elector's part since the solution lay easily to hand. One of the first teachers of the university, Nikolaus Marschalk, was in possession of a press, and he brought it with him from Erfurt. The first books printed on this press appeared in the year of the university's foundation, 1502.[18]

Despite these promising beginnings, printing in Wittenberg did not flourish. Marschalk operated the press for only two years before he left Wittenberg. The press stayed behind, in the hands of Marschalk's colleague, Hermann Trebelius. He was, if anything, even less successful, and published only a few titles before he abandoned the venture. Two more printers would come and go before in 1508 the press passed finally

NIKOLAUS MARSCHALK

A crude woodcut decorating one of Marschalk's early Erfurt publications. Marschalk was a significant intellectual force in the newly established Wittenberg University; that he operated his own printing press was a further incidental benefit.

into the hands of a man who would stick to the task, Johann Rhau-Grunenberg. For a period from 1506 to 1507, after the departure of Trebelius, Wittenberg seems to have been without a press altogether.

The reasons for the repeated failure to create a going concern in Wittenberg are not difficult to discern. Before the foundation of the university in 1502 there had been no printing press in Wittenberg; this was now a full fifty years after printing was first established in Mainz. The new invention had made its way to northeastern Germany, to Erfurt and Leipzig, relatively quickly, but not to Wittenberg.[19] In these intervening fifty years the industry had come a long way. The first generation of pioneers were often closely associated with local universities (as in the case of Paris) or religious houses (Subiaco, near Rome). But by 1500 the industry had passed into the hands of experienced businessmen and artisan craftsmen. In this respect the Wittenberg press, operated by scholar amateurs, was something of a throwback.

The first products of the press sadly bear this out. The concentration of the printing industry into larger, capital-intensive ventures in Europe's major commercial cities had allowed for considerable investment to refine both the process of production and the aesthetics of the printed page. The larger print shops could marshal a range of typefaces in different styles and sizes. These were used to lead the reader through complex texts, differentiating the text body from notes, signaling section breaks and significant places in the argument.

The products of the early Wittenberg press exhibited none of these characteristics. None of the earliest Wittenberg printers were particularly accomplished, and they had at their disposal only a limited range of types. Marschalk, operating his press as a private concern and essentially as an extension of his scholarly work as a teacher of Greek, possessed some Greek type. This had most likely been obtained through the good offices of Wolfgang Schenk, the Erfurt printer with whom he had worked before coming to Wittenberg. But this veneer of sophistication could not disguise the relative poverty of the range of fonts available to Wittenberg's first printers.

Nor was there any immediate prospect of the investment necessary to bring any alteration to this situation. In its first fifteen years (if it survived at all) the Wittenberg press was destined to play only a limited role, supplying the local needs of the university's professors and students. It would print largely the day-to-day necessities of academic life: announcements, a statement of theses to be defended in academic examinations, celebratory orations, and the like.[20] Any more substantial publications, including the standard textbooks required in class, were supplied from elsewhere. It made no sense for Wittenberg's printers to attempt to compete in this long-established and smoothly functioning market. Nor was there much future in the publication of vernacular literature for local citizens: the size of the town was too small for this sort of speculative commercial publishing.

This all amounted to a fairly obvious recipe for business failure, and this indeed was the fate of Wittenberg's first printers. A press was only sustained because Frederick considered it a matter of personal prestige to maintain a local printing house. The most substantial early Wittenberg publications, such as the catalog of the castle relic collection, were almost certainly paid for directly by the elector.[21] But even this substantial volume was unlikely to have kept the press active for more than a few months (the largest expense would have been the woodcuts supplied by Lucas Cranach). No purely commercial printer would have been prepared to make his home in Wittenberg for the promise of such intermittent work. In these circumstances the university authorities might have thought themselves lucky to attract a new printer with at least a rudimentary experience of a working commercial press: Johann Rhau-Grunenberg.

Rhau-Grunenberg was lured to Wittenberg from Erfurt, where he had worked in the printing house of Wolf Sturmer. He was not an uneducated man, and had evidently attained some sort of university qualification.[22] It was probably this that brought him to the attention of Staupitz, who persuaded him to leave Sturmer and take up the vacant position of university printer in Wittenberg. The university did everything in its power to smooth his path. Rhau-Grunenberg was furnished with the printing materials left by Marschalk and Trebelius, and provided with a workshop and residential space on university property. In 1512 he moved into new quarters close to the Augustinian house, where he would have been a near neighbor of Martin Luther.

Over the years Luther developed very mixed feelings about Rhau-Grunenberg. He recognized that he was pious and well-intentioned. In the difficult years after 1517 Rhau-Grunenberg would offer Luther unwavering support, and this was the sort of loyalty that Luther felt a duty to repay. But fondness was often balanced by exasperation. Rhau-Grunenberg was notoriously slow, and in the furious pamphlet exchanges that followed the indulgence controversy, that put Luther at a real disadvantage. His work was also functional and unimaginative. This might have been passable for a student who required a cheap broadsheet or pamphlet for a necessary academic examination, but it was painful to someone of Luther's refined aesthetic sensibilities.

In September 1516 Luther reported to Spalatin that faculty colleagues wanted him to publish his lecture notes on the Psalms; they were suggesting he give them to Rhau-Grunenberg. Luther was not keen to surrender this work to the press at this point, but at least if they went to Rhau-Grunenberg, he wrote, the work would be nothing fancy, because they would then be printed in a rougher typeface.[23] This may seem a little grand and lofty from someone who to that point had published virtually nothing, and he would indeed entrust his first work, his modest introduction to sections of Johannes Tauler's mystical work, the *Theologia Deutsch,* to Rhau-Grunenberg in this same year.[24] But you only have to examine a sample of Rhau-Grunenberg's work to realize that Luther had a point. Take a typical early product of his press, an oration given by Filippo Beroaldo.[25] The book was a small quarto of twenty-four leaves, a steady week's work for a well-managed press. The text is presented as an undifferentiated mass in a medium Roman type. There are no decorated initials; rather, the first capital is a small character in the same font used for the rest of the text, set in a space that would normally be assigned to a woodblock initial (as if, as in the first years of print, it would subsequently be painted over by an illuminator). The text is poorly aligned and heavily abbreviated. Rudimentary side notes cling awkwardly to the text body. The title page is two simple lines in the same text type, again in a style more reminiscent of the 1470s. It is as if the intervening forty years of title-page development had simply not taken place.[26]

This was published in 1508, shortly after Rhau-Grunenberg arrived in Wittenberg, but the next ten years registered no substantial improvement. This in itself was unusual, because printers learned their craft and improved the quality of their work by studying and adopting features they found in other books. By this point there were circulating in Wittenberg plenty of books printed in Europe's leading centers of typographical design, as we will see when we examine the university library. But Rhau-Grunenberg seemed content just to plod along. As the proprietor of the only press in Wittenberg, he could rely on at least a modicum of work from the university to keep his press active.

Yet only up to a point: for the more status conscious of the faculty, Rhau-Grunenberg's work was not of an acceptable standard. The most telling judgment on the quality of Wittenberg printing in these years can be found in the number of those associated with the university who looked elsewhere when they had texts to put to the press. Christoph Scheurl was in every other respect a passionate advocate of Wittenberg, but he would not consign his works to the rude attentions of Rhau-Grunenberg. A second edition of the Bologna laudation published after his arrival in Wittenberg was instead dispatched to Martin Landsberg in Leipzig.[27]

A series of orations given in Wittenberg by Scheurl and others was also sent to Landsberg for publication, a round trip for manuscript and printed copies of almost a hundred miles.[28] In November 1508 Scheurl gave an oration in honor of two recently promoted scholars, which begins with a long dedication to Lucas Cranach, Wittenberg's most distinguished artistic adornment. It continued with praise of the elector, before embarking on a long and fulsome description of the glories of Wittenberg and its castle church. Yet even this (perhaps especially this) could not be entrusted to the local printer.[29] Most incongruous of all was the use of Landsberg for Andreas Meinhardi's promotional dialog extolling the virtues of Wittenberg and its new university: a new Rome, perhaps, but not in its printing culture.

During these years the elector was assembling his own distinguished book collection. In 1512 this would be made over to the university, for the use of its scholars and students. Georg Spalatin was entrusted with the task of enhancing the collection, and considerable sums were made available for this purpose.[30] It almost goes without saying that none of the books Spalatin wished to acquire were printed locally. Spalatin sought out the best editions, published in the most distinguished print shops all over Europe. Books were purchased from the bookshops of Erfurt, and from the fairs in Leipzig and Frankfurt. In March 1512, emboldened by the elector's generosity, Spalatin wrote directly to Aldus Manutius in Venice, asking that Manutius send a catalog of his books in print. Aldus was

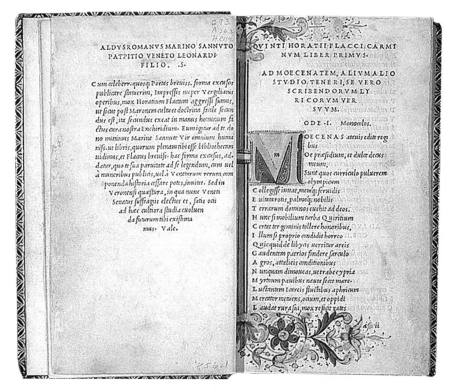

ALDUS MANUTIUS, HORACE (1501)

Aldines were the benchmark of quality for any sixteenth-century collector who aspired to build a library. The contrast with the quality of locally produced books would have been telling and obvious.

at this point Europe's most famous printer, his books (now universally known as Aldines) a benchmark for elegance and editorial rigor. Any aspiring collector wanted to have examples in his library and Frederick was no exception. But securing the books from faraway Venice proved difficult. Spalatin's inquiry and then a second letter failed to elicit a response, so a third was dispatched, this time signed personally by the elector. This explained the sort of library that Frederick wanted to create, and the important part the products of this famous shop would play in building its reputation. A follow-up letter from Spalatin shrewdly asked Aldus to note with a cross the books in his catalog he kept in stock at his branch office in Frankfurt, from where they could be more cheaply transported to Wittenberg.

It is rather extraordinary that despite this battery of correspondence it would be March 1514 before Aldus would reply, rather unconvincingly pleading that earlier letters had vanished in the post. The order was placed and the books supplied. The Aldines were the jewel in an increasingly precious collection, a priceless resource to the local professors and a standing rebuke to the quality of the local press. In the circumstances one can perhaps forgive Luther's frustration at Rhau-Grunenberg's stolid indifference to aesthetic considerations, turning out the utilitarian works that to the more sophisticated reader screamed provincialism. It was a jarringly discordant note in Frederick's otherwise highly successful campaign to create a northern cultural capital. Certainly no one handling Rhau-Grunenberg's rudimentary offerings could ever have imagined Wittenberg's future as a major print entrepôt.

STRUGGLES

Luther's return to Wittenberg in 1511 was the result of a shrewd deal between Staupitz and the elector. Luther would take over Staupitz's chair in Biblical Studies, and Frederick would sponsor the necessary fees for Luther's promotion to a doctorate.[31] Luther was only twenty-nine years old when he assumed these daunting duties, following in the footsteps of his academic patron. The next five years would be a time of diligent study and significant intellectual development as well as sometimes heated controversy. During this time Luther was every bit as much a student as a teacher: his heartfelt engagement with biblical scholarship can be followed in his two great lecture series in these years, on the Psalms and Paul's Epistle to the Romans.

Understanding Luther's state of mind during these important years is to a large extent bedeviled by what comes after. We know that between 1517 and 1520 he would repudiate his church and build, on the basis of startlingly original biblical premises, a new understanding of man's relationship with God. Almost from that day to this, theologians have sought to identify the origins of this Reformation breakthrough, the precise moment at which Luther came to the decisive theological insights. Luther's own contribution to this debate, a brief reminiscence of 1545, is not particularly helpful, as he described a long period of spiritual wrestling leading to a decisive revelation of God's righteousness: "Now I felt as if I had been born again: the gates had been opened and I had entered Paradise itself."[32]

One can see why toward the end of a dramatic and turbulent life, Luther would choose to see his early spiritual maturity in this way, as strenuous wrestling with obdurate theological problems leading to a decisive moment of revelation. This is certainly a reconstruction that does justice to the momentousness of the eventual consequence for his life, his world, and his church. This narrative of strenuous engagement has become a fixed point in the Luther drama, the period of *Anfechtungen*, struggles, driving the intense young monk almost to the point of despair.

This stress on the struggle through long periods of intense study before Luther reached his central theological insights has one other important function. From the perspective of 1545 Luther sought to differentiate his own spiritual journey from more radical thinkers who, inspired by his scriptural principles, had reached their own surprising revelations of God's purpose.[33] Luther had now had twenty-five years to regret his too-casual proclamation of a "priesthood of all believers," as the enthusiasts he would angrily denounce as fanatics presented their own versions of the social gospel. So this retrospective presentation of a Reformation breakthrough balanced two elements, patient study and sudden understanding, with subtle care.

The reality is probably far less dramatic than this carefully constructed narrative would suggest. Through five years of teaching and study, Luther moved beyond a solid grounding in traditional theology toward an exposition of the Christian life based on an intense and continuous engagement with Scripture. The most immediate struggle of this period was of a rather different nature: a determination, shared with initially doubtful colleagues, to incorporate these new theological insights into the curriculum at Wittenberg. This led to a tense altercation, in which Luther took an increasingly leading role: a dress rehearsal for the controversy that would erupt over indulgences in 1517.

The maturation of Luther's theological understanding can be divided into two key elements: the turn toward Augustine, and his understanding of the centrality of Scripture. Both can be followed in texts richly annotated in Luther's own hand. The awakening to Augustine began as early as 1509, while Luther was still in Erfurt. Luther's thorough study of Augustine's *City of God* and *De Trinitate* (*On the Trinity*) is revealed by copiously annotated texts now in the Ratsschulbibliothek in Zwickau. From this point on Luther would draw Augustine to the heart of his theological understanding. The result was a revulsion against Aristotle, the Greek scholar whose works dominated both the university curriculum and the Scholastic method; in time, this hostility to Aristotle would become almost pathological.

More immediately Luther had to master new tasks that became progressively more numerous and demanding. In October 1512 he was promoted to Doctor of Theology in a ceremony from which his Erfurt brethren remained ostentatiously absent. Luther had been initially reluctant to assume these responsibilities, and it required all of Staupitz's eloquence to persuade him. In future years he would have cause to bless his patron's persistence, as in the controversies with his ecclesiastical superiors after 1517 he frequently referred to his status as a doctor and professor as proof of his competence to debate adversaries in the church hierarchy. His first major lecture series in his professorial role, on the Book of Psalms, began in the autumn of 1513. Luther's method involved a careful verse-by-verse exposition of each psalm in sequence; for preparation he used a specially prepared Latin edition of the text with wide spaces between the lines, in which he made copious manuscript notes.[34] In 1515, before he began his lecture series on Romans, Luther commissioned Rhau-Grunenberg to produce a similar wide-spaced edition for his use and that of his students. Luther's own copy survives in the library at Berlin.[35]

These teaching duties had to be balanced with his responsibilities to the Augustinian monastery, where he was now subprior, and to the local town church. Luther was already preaching regularly to his monastic brethren when in 1514 he was asked also to take on similar duties in the parish church.[36] This was the beginning of a pastoral responsibility to the people of Wittenberg that would continue to his last years. What may have at first seemed like one commitment too many would come to play a critical role in shaping Luther's vocation. The cerebral and to this point rather introspective scholar monk was required to wrestle with the problem of how his new spiritual insights could be made relevant to a diverse congregation of his fellow citizens—and how he could hold their attention. Luther gradually grew into this role. The parish church unlocked in him a talent for the homely simile that sweetened the forthright and powerful message of repentance. This preaching experience was also something on which he would draw when, in the years after 1517, he first tried his hand at writing in the vernacular.

The growing self-confidence and intellectual authority can be seen in the course of the two great series of academic lectures of 1513 to 1516. Luther began his lectures on the Psalms in 1513 with frank reflections on his own spiritual struggles. This allowed him to develop his important insight that the critical obstacle to understanding Scripture was man's inner resistance to God's will. By the time of the lectures on Romans Luther was ranging far more widely, offering sharp criticism of those princes of the church who abused their trust with an extravagant and godless lifestyle.[37]

In all this frantic activity Luther did not neglect the business of the university. The intense professor was by this time developing a following both in his order and in the academic community. In 1514 Georg Spalatin wrote to ask Luther's opinion of the Reuchlin affair, the hot-button topic that divided modernizers and conservatives. Johann Reuchlin had been the one prominent scholar to object to the wholesale confiscation and destruction of Jewish books, deemed by its advocates necessary to the Jews' eventual conversion to Christianity. This had made Reuchlin himself the subject of a campaign of public denigration, but humanists, many of whom would later play a prominent role in Luther's affairs, rallied to Reuchlin's cause.[38] In this case Luther sided decisively with the friends of innovation, as he did in 1515 when his friend Johann Lang made a bold attack on Occam, Duns Scotus, and the Scholastics.[39] Thus were the fault lines drawn between the old learning, associated with Scholasticism and the great medieval theologian Thomas Aquinas, and the new. In 1516 Luther was one of the first eager readers of the Greek New Testament of Desiderius Erasmus; for all his later reservations about Erasmus he immediately recognized this as a milestone of biblical scholarship. Not all of Luther's Wittenberg colleagues were as comfortable with the direction of travel. The conflicting visions of scholarship came to a head when one of Luther's pupils, Bartholomäus Bernardi von Feldkirchen, defended a set of dissertation theses that strongly affirmed the supremacy of Augustine over Thomism. The ripples of this controversy reached as far as Erfurt, and Luther was forced to take up his pen to mollify both his former Erfurt brethren and Wittenberg colleagues such as Andreas von Karlstadt, who viewed with alarm these increasingly radical curricular developments in the Wittenberg Theology Faculty. Yet after a trip to Leipzig to secure a scholarly edition of Augustine with which to refute Luther, Karlstadt declared himself converted to Luther's point of view. Henceforth he would be Luther's most fervent supporter. By May 1517 Luther could report triumphantly to his friend Lang that the tide had turned:

> Our theology and St. Augustine are continuing to prosper and reign in our university through the hand of God. Aristotle is declining daily and is inclining toward a fall which will end him forever.[40]

By this point Luther had committed himself to a full frontal assault on Scholasticism, in the context of a fundamental renovation of the university curriculum. For the next eighteen months this would be Luther's first preoccupation, in his mind of much more fundamental importance than the secondary issue of indulgences, until events proved otherwise. Over the summer Luther penned the manifesto of this new reform movement: ninety-nine theses against Scholastic theology to be debated at the degree ceremony of one Franz Günther of Nordhausen on September 4, 1517. These theses bear all the hallmarks of the later, more famous theses on indulgences—forthright, probing, and provocative.[41] For many years the first published version of these theses was thought to be lost, until in 1983 a copy was rather sensationally discovered interleaved among the pages of a quite different book in the Herzog August Bibliothek in Wolfenbüttel.[42]

Survival rates for early printed broadsheets are notoriously low, and many of the examples that do survive have come down to us as mere fragments, many recovered from the bindings of other books, where they were used as printer's waste. In cases like these, after the necessary sheets had been distributed, any surplus stock was sold by the printer to bookbinders, who used the wastepaper as packing between the pigskin used for the outer cover and the inner board of the binding. Most of the fragments unearthed during restoration work of this sort are relatively unremarkable;[43] to find an unknown work of Luther was a discovery of a wholly different order, particularly a work so critical to the reconstruction of the operation of the Wittenberg press at the beginning of the Reformation. So we know from this discovery that the original publication of the theses against Scholastic theology was a single-sheet broadside, no doubt intended for exhibition on the church door and for distribution to those attending. It is printed in the no-nonsense typefaces of Johann Rhau-Grunenberg. To assist the reader, or those attending the disputation, Rhau-Grunenberg divided the theses into four groups of twenty-five. Although they appear to make up four full groups, one hundred in total, in the first group the numbering jumps from seventeen to nineteen, reducing the total to ninety-nine. This sort of error was also quite common, as we will see when we discuss the printed editions of the theses on indulgences. But we now know categorically from this example that Rhau-Grunenberg was printing theses in broadsheet form, and was doing so for Luther only eight weeks before the theses on indulgences were published.[44] This, as we will see, is a discovery of some importance for the debate that has raged on the posting of Luther's more notorious theses on indulgences.

The irony is that when Luther penned the theses on Scholastic theology he probably regarded them as a far more daring and potentially controversial statement than the later theses on indulgences. Certainly Luther did everything in his power to bring these earlier theses to wider public attention. Copies were dispatched to Johann Lang and to the Erfurt Augustinians. On September 11, Luther dispatched a copy to Christoph Scheurl in Nuremberg.[45] Despite these efforts, the hoped-for public debate never took off. None of Luther's anticipated disputation partners took the bait. Despite, as he saw it, the importance of the subject, the theses sank without trace; as we have seen, none of those who read them thought them important enough to keep them among their other papers.

This was Luther's first systematic attempt to spread his reputation beyond Wittenberg, and it had failed completely. Although he would remain fully committed to curriculum reform, Luther had received a harsh lesson in his capacity to command public attention, as a modestly published professor from a provincial university. There is little doubt that this discouraging experience would have had an impact, and probably shaped his expectations of the likely resonance when, eight weeks later, he proposed another set of theses, this time on the subject of indulgences Nothing, certainly, could have prepared him for the storm they would unleash, or the impact they would have on his life, his religion, and his adopted city.

3.

INDULGENCE

HEN LUTHER TOOK AIM against indulgences in his ninety-five theses, he was attacking a hugely important institution, a cornerstone of popular devotion and a mainstay of the church economy. That is well-known, and would certainly have been perfectly clear to Luther himself. What is less widely appreciated is that the attack on indulgences also threatened an extremely lucrative part of the printing industry. From the first days of printing, publishers had alternated large projects with jobbing tasks that took less time and assisted their cash flow. These included many commissions for ecclesiastical customers: tracts, brochures, ordinances, and indulgence certificates. Among the few surviving prints authentically attributed to Johannes Gutenberg are two certificates of indulgence, one in thirty lines and one in thirty-one.[1] These would have been the certificates handed out to pious donors, confirming their donation and the terms and length of remission from purgatory attached to their pious act. Both these indulgences survive in surprisingly high numbers, and in several other editions.[2] Another of Gutenberg's early works was the so-called *Türkenkalender*, a pamphlet poem drumming up support for fund-raising for a crusade against the Turk.[3] This was big business, both for the ecclesiastical institutions who benefited from the grant of an indulgence, and the printers who turned out thousands of copies of the sermons, brochures, handbooks, and certificates that accompanied any indulgence campaign.

At the time that Luther first made his fateful protest against indulgences, such considerations would have been far from his mind. He was more focused on ensuring that his views received attention, dispatching copies to his friends and other interested parties, as he had with the theses against Scholastic theology. But it was the printing press that made Luther's theses a public matter and would rapidly make of their author a controversial and notorious figure. In the process printers were richly compensated for any lost business through the suppression of demand for indulgences. Luther's movement opened up a new era in the history of cheap print. It was a commercial as much as a theological revolution.

THE ECONOMY OF SALVATION

The Catholic practice of indulgence developed gradually during the Middle Ages, and from relatively modest beginnings.[4] Indulgences derive from the priestly power to absolve a penitent sinner. By pronouncing forgiveness the priest restores the link with God threatened by sinful acts; only then could a Christian be assured of salvation. As part of the healing process the priest would prescribe for the confessing sinner a carefully weighed punishment, or penance. From the eleventh century onward the church occasionally allowed that a measured part of this penance could be rescinded in return for noteworthy pious acts. Some of the first indulgences, for instance, were offered to those prepared to join a Crusade. Others involved acts of charity, the giving of alms, donations to support the building of churches, or attendance at the consecration of a new church.

In this respect the granting of an indulgence was never a simple financial transaction. A confessant must first convince the priest that he is penitent, then confess his sins and accept the prescribed penance. Only the third part of this, the punishment, can be replaced by indulgence.

But there is no doubt that with indulgences the financial aspect loomed ever larger in the calculations of both the penitent and the church authorities.

The doctrine and practice of indulgence developed enormously throughout Europe in the two centuries before 1500. This had two main causes: a decisive intervention of the church hierarchy to bring order to the rapid proliferation of indulgences, and the emergence of purgatory as a distinctive element of church doctrine. Already by the time of the Lateran Council in 1215 concern at the disorderly growth of indulgences brought a stipulation that bishops and archbishops should limit remission to forty days. Only the pope could offer a full (plenary) remission for all sins. The value of this privilege was demonstrated when Pope Boniface VIII proclaimed the year 1300 a special jubilee: pilgrims who journeyed to Rome in this year would receive forgiveness for all their sins. The success of the jubilee, and its impact on the local economy, led to the proclamation of further jubilees at rapidly decreasing intervals, first fifty, then twenty-five years.

Indulgences were also frequently proclaimed to raise armies for crusading against the Turk; these continued long after the Holy Lands had passed definitively into the hands of the infidel in the thirteenth century. Indeed, with the fall of Constantinople in 1453 the battle with Islam took on a new urgency, with repeated calls for funds to raise new armies to turn back the Ottoman advance in the eastern Mediterranean.

The crucial, perhaps fatal, development in the theology of indulgence was the papal declaration that indulgence could be purchased on behalf of another. This would normally be a dead relative, suffering in purgatory and thus beyond the reach of confession and absolution. The emergence of purgatory as a sort of holding station for those ultimately destined for paradise was a defining feature of late medieval Catholicism. The ultimate salvation of souls in purgatory was assured, but the time of uncomfortable waiting could be stretched out indefinitely. In 1476 Pope Sixtus IV allowed the application of indulgence to the relief of these suffering souls, opening the floodgates for a mass of penitential acts and donations. It was such a devotion that Luther performed for the relief of his dead grandfather in Rome, and it was the fear of the sorrows of purgatory that ensured the fame of vast collections of relics such as those of Frederick the Wise.

In view of the later notoriety of indulgences it bears emphasis that in the overwhelming number of cases the pope did not benefit directly. Most grants were for the support of pious projects, the building or rebuilding of churches, or the performance of a stipulated pilgrimage.[5] Those that did raise money for papal funds, campaigns against the Turk, and the notorious St. Peter's indulgence of 1515, were rather the exception than the rule. Luther's Augustinian community in Erfurt was granted indulgence in 1502, and again, to support the building of a library, in 1508. The reconsecration of the All Saints Church in Wittenberg in 1503 was accompanied by a further grant of indulgence.[6] But it was the great international fund-raising campaigns that caught the eye, particularly, in the later fifteenth century, the repeated series of appeals for a new crusade against the Turk.[7]

The high point in this fund-raising effort came with the three great campaigns in Germany led by Cardinal Raymond Peraudi between 1486 and 1504.[8] Peraudi was the great impresario of the indulgence trade, bringing to the economy of salvation both logistical brilliance and a real sense of theater. The campaigns were planned like the military operations they were ostensibly intended to fund. Towns that Peraudi proposed to visit on his preaching tour were contacted in advance, and detailed contracts agreed for the division of the sums raised (generally one third to the local church and two thirds to Peraudi and his team). Peraudi was also the first to devise a specific tariff for donations that linked the size of the expected gift to the financial resources of the donor—a sort of spiritual progressive taxation.[9] In places that lay beyond Peraudi's itinerary a delegate might be appointed: the Dutchman Antonius Mast led the campaign in Sweden, for instance, and Michael Poyaudi in Finland.[10] The money gathered during these campaigns was very substantial. In 1491 Peraudi was able to loan Emperor Maximilian ten thousand guilders of the money collected in Sweden. That same year he received a receipt for twenty thousand gold ducats collected in Scandinavia and dispatched to the Curia.[11] It was Peraudi, too, who performed the reconsecration of the All Saints Church in Wittenberg, proclaiming a new indulgence for this already richly endowed church.

Peraudi died in 1505, but this brought no letup for the citizens of Germany. Between 1503 and 1510 a crusade indulgence for the German order in Livonia and its struggle against the Tatars was preached in almost every church province. Between 1513 and 1519 indulgences were proclaimed for major building projects in Constance, Augsburg, and Trier.[12] This sustained fund-raising formed the essential backdrop for Pope Leo X's momentous initiative: the appeal for support to rebuild the fountainhead of the Western Church, St. Peter's in Rome.

A VIRTUOUS TRADE

"As soon as a coin in the coffer rings, the soul from purgatory springs." This, according to Martin Luther, was the depths to which the trade in indulgences had by 1517 been reduced: a crude financial transaction making a mockery of the careful requirement of real repentance. This characterization, of course, is Luther's, articulated in the twenty-seventh of his ninety-five theses.[13] We have no direct evidence that such words were used by those hawking the indulgence for St. Peter's in towns near Wittenberg, and the caricature is one that suited the reformers well. But there is no doubt that the whole process had by this point been thoroughly monetized. This was not all bad. The proceeds from indulgences enabled many churches to embark on rebuilding programs that would otherwise have been beyond them. The precious certificates brought comfort to many sincere Christians anxious for the fate of their own souls and those of their departed relatives. Among the greatest beneficiaries were those who supported this great industry with the necessary publications: Europe's printers.

The great late medieval boom in indulgence preaching coincided neatly with the invention of printing. Europe's printers were soon heavily involved in producing the various publications generated by the preaching of indulgences. Johannes Gutenberg, as we have seen, was happy to print indulgences; so, too, was William Caxton, the first printer of England.[14] All the major indulgence campaigns generated a blizzard of print.[15] For one relatively modest campaign, in aid of the collegiate church in the small Swabian town of Urach, we can count over two dozen printed documents spread over six years. It required six different printing houses to cope with the workload.[16]

Most precious of all was the contract to print the certificates of indulgence: the formal document attesting to the donation and the spiritual relief provided. On May 2, 1452, the papal legate of Germany, Nicholas of Cusa, authorized the prior of St. Jacob's Church in Mainz to have two thousand indulgences ready for sale to the citizens of Frankfurt by the end of the month.[17] If these were to be handwritten the copy shops of Mainz would have been very busy; two or three years later Gutenberg could have fulfilled this order in a few days. But an order of this size, enormous for a printed book, was quite modest for indulgences. We know of one contract for 130,000 indulgence certificates. Another, for the monastery of Monserrat in Catalonia, was for 200,000 copies.[18] Orders of this size would no doubt have been divided among several printing shops, speeding completion and spreading the benefit around the trade.

This was ideal work for a printer. An indulgence was a single sheet of paper printed on one side only. So long as the printer could source the required paper, it was a straightforward job. Furthermore, this sort of work had the priceless advantage that here the printer was working for a single client. He simply had to fulfill the order and deliver the whole stock to the sponsoring church, bishop, or indulgence commissioner. There were none of the complex problems of distribution and sale connected with the retailing of books. Nor were there endless middlemen, carters, wholesalers, booksellers, and money brokers, who in

AN INDULGENCE CERTIFICATE FROM 1504

The sale of indulgences was big business for the church, and provided steady work for printers. This was one of the simplest and most lucrative assignments a printer could take on, and the size of the order was often huge.

the normal course of the book trade would take their cut and erode the printer's margins.

This was the most ephemeral of all print. Many indulgences are known today from a single copy. Others have clearly disappeared altogether, and we know of them only from surviving contracts with printers. But of the identified printed works published during the fifteenth century, the first age of print, around 2,500 (10 percent) are single-sheet items. Of these over a third are indulgence certificates.[19] Given what we know of the very high print runs of these works, this must represent at least 2 million precious certificates: simple to produce, but each representing to the sponsoring church a substantial donation.

To assess their value to the print industry in Germany let us return to the towering figure of Raymond Peraudi. Moving swiftly from city to city, Peraudi ordered new stock as he went. So he provided work for most of the major print centers in Germany: Mainz and Cologne, Leipzig and Erfurt; Memmingen, Würzburg, and Ulm in the south; Nuremberg, Augsburg, Speyer, Basel, and Strasbourg.[20] It was probably in Lübeck that Antonius Mast sourced the twenty-five thousand certificates with which he was supplied for the Scandinavia campaign.[21] And in addition to the certificates, Peraudi also required a mass of other print: summaries of the papal bull authorizing his campaign; a printed handbook for confessors (that offered both instructions for preaching the indulgence and stipulated the prices to be charged); a copy of Peraudi's own letter of appointment.[22]

In the years following Peraudi's death none could quite match the cardinal for this systematic exploitation of the medium of print. For all that, the traffic in indulgences continued to provide good business for Germany's printers. The campaign for the rebuilding of St. Peter's in Rome from 1515 to 1517 was a case in point.[23] Among those who produced the various printed artifacts accompanying this campaign were some of Germany's most accomplished printers. They included Melchior Lotter in Leipzig, Silvan Otmar in Augsburg, Adam Petri in Basel, and Friedrich Peypus in Nuremberg. Within four years all of these men would be heavily involved in printing Luther; Adam Petri indeed would be one of the first to print Luther's ninety-five theses against indulgences. There is little room for sentiment in commerce. The church had been an excellent client, until Luther became a better one.

POISONED CHALICE

The trade in indulgences was now big business, and brought profit to many. Not all, however, could witness the increasingly brash commercialism without misgivings. Even before Luther registered his own reservations, a number of voices had been raised in criticism of the indulgence trade. Although by no means numerous, or even particularly influential, these critics did create an important context for the debate that followed Luther's disputation theses. It meant that when Luther's views first attracted attention, many were inclined to give him a hearing, even if they would not all ultimately follow him down the road that led to a complete break with the church hierarchy.

Critics of indulgences in the period before 1517 can be divided into three groups: intellectuals, many of them either senior churchmen or committed humanists; Germany's rulers, worried at the money draining out of Germany; and discontented buyers. Of the three, it was the intellectuals who were initially most vociferous, and ultimately most deceived in their expectations of Luther.

Skepticism about the practice of indulgence was not new. The decisive intervention of the Lateran Council of 1215 was recognition that the unregulated development of such a practice would bring potentially undesirable consequences. Once firmly under papal direction, however, there were remarkably few voices raised against the principle of indulgence in the latter part of the fifteenth century. The range of church institutions that benefited from the practice, combined with its rampant popularity among the faithful, sufficed to still any dissent. In his second great campaign Peraudi was reputed to have disposed of fifty thousand letters of indulgence in one place, Vorau in the Austrian Steiermark.[24] Only one brave voice, that of the Würzburg cleric Dr. Dietrich Morung, was raised in protest. Morung used his pulpit to question the pope's power to offer relief to those in purgatory.[25] This, as we have seen, was a very recent doctrine, but Peraudi reacted with crushing force. Morung was excommunicated and incarcerated for ten years. After this, others kept their counsel.

It was only in the course of his last great campaign that Peraudi seems to have sensed a significant ripple of dissent. In March 1502 he lashed out angrily against "murmurers and detractors." The cardinal was sufficiently riled to defend the theology of indulgences in an open letter.

This seems to have been sufficient, and the results of the campaign were certainly spectacular: a reputed four hundred thousand gulden for papal coffers.[26]

Peraudi's death brought a subtle change. In the second decade of the sixteenth century a number of respected and influential figures began to express reservations about the apparently relentless sequence of fund-raising ventures. In Würzburg, Constance, and Augsburg, local clergy warned against the dangers of the substitution of indulgence for true penance.[27] Most eye-catching was the intervention of Johann von Staupitz, Luther's first patron and a senior figure in the Augustinian order. In a series of sermons preached at Nuremberg during Advent 1516, Staupitz condemned the excesses of indulgence preachers in terms that would find many echoes in Martin Luther's later writings. In the early months of 1517 these much admired sermons were published in both Latin and German.[28]

These criticisms were not confined to Germany. In the Reformation narrative the Theology Faculty of the University of Paris, the Sorbonne, is normally cited as a bastion of orthodoxy, but in March 1518 it, too, expressed its reservations about indulgences. The Sorbonne censured the proposition that "whoever puts a teston, or its value, in the crusade chest for a soul in purgatory, frees the said soul immediately."[29] This phrase offers a remarkably close echo of the infamous jingle cited by Luther, and apparently something of the sort had been circulating in Paris since the 1480s.

The churchmen who now made their reservations known seem to have been emboldened by a rising tide of criticism among Germany's rulers. Although happy to petition the pope for indulgences for their own purposes, local authorities certainly recognized the potential damage if huge quantities of specie were withdrawn from the local economy to be sent to Rome. All early modern societies were cash poor; many everyday financial transactions were conducted by barter.[30] Indulgence certificates, however, had to be paid for in coin, and this resulted in large sums being taken out of the German economy. These concerns

SILVER THALER OF FREDERICK THE WISE, 1522

Early modern Europe suffered from an acute shortage of specie, particularly of coins in small denominations. While many transactions relied on barter and credit, indulgences could only be paid for in cash, draining money out of the economy.

were laid bare in a spectacular altercation between Peraudi and the Emperor Maximilian, a rare occasion on which the proud cardinal was comprehensively worsted.[31] During the course of Peraudi's last campaign the emperor had made plain his intention to retain in Germany a greater share of the monies raised by Peraudi's industry. The cardinal was appalled and took to print to denounce this violation of his papal privilege.[32] But Maximilian was unmoved; the money was not released. Repeated attempts to shame Maximilian into compliance achieved nothing and Peraudi was ultimately forced to retreat to friendly Strasbourg for fear Maximilian might be goaded to reprisals by the intemperance of his press campaign.

Other German authorities took note. In 1516 the imperial free city of Nuremberg found itself simultaneously resisting the promotion of the Empire-wide Holy Spirit indulgence, while appealing to the pope for a new indulgence for its own church. This may not impress in terms of intellectual consistency, but the council's explanation of their opposition was a significant straw in the wind: they regarded the pope's indulgence, they said, "more as a deception of the common folk, than serving as nourishment for their souls."[33] Here the council was responding to an unmistakable sense of indulgence fatigue. There is some indication that this may have set in as early as Peraudi's last campaign, though the evidence is ambiguous. In Nuremberg receipts fell by a third between the campaigns of 1488 and 1502, though in Strasbourg they registered a modest increase (here, as elsewhere, receipts were most buoyant where Peraudi preached in person). By the second decade of the sixteenth century the trend was unmistakable. The great city of Speyer had contributed 3,000 gulden in 1502; the campaign of 1517 raised just 200. In Frankfurt in 1488 Peraudi had raised 2,078 gulden; in 1502 he grossed just half of this; the St. Peter's indulgence of 1517 brought in a mere 304 gulden.[34]

The problem was fairly clear. With repeated campaigns over almost thirty years for both local and international causes, most pious souls had by now purchased the precious certificates and were, therefore, reluctant to fork out again. This problem was recognized in the papal Curia, and brought forth an unpopular and highly controversial resolution: with the promulgation of each new indulgence, previous grants were suspended and the effectiveness of previously purchased indulgences placed in abeyance. In the case of the St. Peter's indulgence this hiatus was set at eight years.[35] For those close to death, or who looked to the assurance of previous pious investment, this was especially bitter. Resentment at this maneuver was specifically alluded to in Luther's eighty-ninth thesis: "Since the pope seeks the salvation of souls rather than money by his indulgences, why does he suspend the indulgences and pardons previously granted when they have equal efficacy?"[36]

The effect of these incremental grievances was not lost on those charged with promoting new indulgence campaigns, among them Albrecht of Brandenburg, archbishop of Magdeburg and newly promoted archbishop of Mainz. It was the sordid financial transaction underlying this promotion that added gas to the fire lit by Luther. In return for one of Germany's richest ecclesiastical prizes, and for permission to hold the two sees simultaneously, Albrecht would pay the pope twenty-three thousand ducats, a huge sum. To help Albrecht meet this obligation it

ALBRECHT OF BRANDENBURG, PRINCE OF THE CHURCH AND PATRON OF ART

It was this print that Dürer sent to Cranach as a possible model for his portraits of Luther. Despite their differences Albrecht retained a sneaking regard for Luther, sending him a generous gift on his marriage in 1525.

was agreed that half of the proceeds of preaching the St. Peter's indulgence in his diocese could be set against this debt.

One did not have to be a radical critic of the church to believe that with this transaction the commerce of devotion had gone too far. Albrecht, in fact, agreed, and his initial instinct was to refuse.[37] He was under no illusions as to the difficulties he would face in raising this money in a part of Germany that had witnessed two major indulgence campaigns in the previous five years. At least the money raised in these instances had been for German causes, whereas in the case of the St. Peter's indulgence all the money would be sent to Rome. Surely the pope should look to his own resources; or, as Luther put it in the remarkably bold and tactless thesis number eighty-six:

> Why does not the pope, whose wealth is today greater than the wealth of the richest Crassus, build this one basilica of St. Peter with his own money, rather than with the money of poor believers?[38]

Albrecht's misgivings were fully justified. Perhaps he should have shown the prudence of another German prince, Albrecht of Brandenbach-Ansbach, who when offered a similar bargain refused point blank to be involved. It was clear, he replied, that the St. Peter's indulgence was not popular among the common folk.[39] More telling still was the refusal of the German Observant Franciscans to undertake preaching of the indulgence. The Franciscans were the order traditionally associated with indulgence preaching, and on this occasion they were specifically tasked by Leo X to work with Albrecht of Mainz in the organization of his campaign. But this assignment was declined. According to Friedrich Myconius, then a member of the order, the indulgence was too associated in the public eye with "Roman luxury." Albrecht was forced instead to turn to the Dominicans, contracting with the fifty-year-old Johann Tetzel to lead his campaign. It would prove to be a fateful choice.

THE CHURCH DOOR

As we have seen, indulgences were not a major concern of Luther's during his first busy years in Wittenberg. They rate only occasional treatment in the course of his two major lecture series between 1513 and 1516. In the lectures on the Psalms in 1514 Luther refers to indulgences as one of the means by which people are led to believe that the Christian life is easy; he criticizes churchmen for their willingness to take part in the trade.[40] By the time of the lectures on Romans in 1516, as was typical of the series as a whole, Luther is more trenchant and hard-hitting. Now he condemns indulgences as ostentatious and meaningless works that lead to neglect of the unglamourous works of Christian charity. For the first time he also offers pointed and direct criticism of the Church hierarchy: "The pope and the priests who are so generous in granting indulgences for the temporal support of churches are cruel above all cruelty, if they are not even more generous or at least equally so in their concern for God and the salvation of souls."[41]

Despite this ominously direct language, it was only in 1517 that Luther began to engage with the issue in any sustained way. For now his Wittenberg congregation was beginning to experience at firsthand the impact of Tetzel's campaign in the diocese.

The St. Peter's indulgence was never, in fact, preached in Wittenberg, or indeed in Electoral Saxony, since the elector withheld his consent. This was not because Frederick had been persuaded by the criticism of indulgences, but for baser financial considerations. The sale of indulgences was likely to diminish the impact of his relic collection, which by now carried a dazzling panoply of spiritual benefits; in addition Frederick saw no reason to oblige Albrecht, a member of the rival house of Hohenzollern, not least because the bishopric of Magdeburg, to which Albrecht had been appointed, had previously been occupied by members of his own family.

So Tetzel stayed out of Saxony. But when he preached at Zerbst and Jüterbog he was close enough to its long, straggling border for citizens of Wittenberg to go and hear him, returning with the precious certificates.[42] Luther was apparently riled when in confession proud owners showed him their certificates and asked for lighter penances. He would also have been deeply troubled at reports of the unrestrained manner in which the indulgence was preached, throwing off all subtlety in the search for souls. The text of one sermon attributed to Tetzel tells its own story:

You priest, you nobleman, you woman, you virgin, you married woman, you youth, you old man . . . [r]emember that you are in such stormy peril on the raging sea of this world that you do not know if you can reach the harbor of salvation. . . . You should know: whoever has confessed and is contrite and puts alms in the box, as his confessor counsels him, will have all of his sins forgiven. . . . Do you not hear the voices of your dead parents and other people, screaming and saying: "Have pity on me, have pity on me . . . for the hand of God hath touched me" (Job 19.21)? We are suffering severe punishments and pain, from which you could rescue us with a few alms, if only you would.[43]

Luther's frustrations bubbled to the surface in a sermon on February 24. Preaching on the text, "Come unto me, all who labor and are heavy laden," Luther rounded on those who sought refuge from their sins; indulgences are to be deplored because they teach us to fear punishment more than sin. Luther, whatever he thought of Tetzel, was not above a bit of theater himself. "Oh, what dangerous times! Oh, snoring priests! Oh, darkness worse than Egyptian! How careless are we in the midst of all our evils!"[44] A further sermon a few days later returned to the subject with a sustained treatment that placed at its heart the central dilemma of penance: indulgences alleviate penalties only for the truly contrite, but the contrite accept punishment rather than seeking alleviation.

Luther's thinking developed further in the course of the summer, when he composed his first sustained writing on the subject.[45] This tract was not immediately published; its role seems to have been to help him order his thoughts for the subsequent disputation theses. Luther asked himself the crucial question that underpinned the commerce in indulgences: Could an indulgence ensure passage to heaven? His answer was an emphatic no. The imperfectly contrite have no right to indulgence; the perfectly contrite have no need of it. Here lies a hint of the radicalizing influence of Luther's developing new doctrine of salvation.

The manuscript treatise on indulgences shows Luther shaping his views into a measured and coherent rejection of both the practice and theology of indulgences. In the autumn of 1517, by now aware that his call for a debate on Scholastic theology had gone unheeded, Luther determined to make these criticisms a public matter. This would have two strands: a renewed call for scholarly debate (the ninety-five theses), and a direct appeal to Archbishop Albrecht to rein in the excesses of the preaching being undertaken in his name.

The form of the scholarly disputation—a series of independent yet linked propositions—allowed Luther to range widely around an issue that he now clearly regarded as critical to the spiritual health of his church. Many of the theses articulated themes that he had enunciated in his earlier lectures and in the manuscript treatise of the summer, but the more provocative populist statements of the last sections reflected his genuine anger at his recent experience of the preaching of the St. Peter's indulgence in the surrounding territories. A powerful series of ten theses replicated what he records as "the shrewd questions of the laity," such as: "Why does not the pope empty purgatory for the sake of holy love and the dire need of the souls that are there if he redeems an infinite number of souls for the sake of miserable money with which to build a church?"[46] This topicality is one strong feature of the theses; another is the direct and unflinching way in which the developing theology of indulgences is associated directly with papal power. The pope or the papacy is directly referenced in forty-four of the ninety-five theses. Some of the more provocative we have cited already; one in particular anticipated his own later reaction to the developing crisis and the attempt to bring him to obedience:

90. To repress these very sharp arguments of the laity by force alone, and not to resolve them by giving reasons, is to expose the church and the pope to the ridicule of their enemies and to make Christians unhappy.

THE DOOR OF THE CASTLE CHURCH

The catalog of Frederick the Wise's relic collection contained this woodcut of the castle church. Many of the university's classes took place here, and the door was the university's customary billboard.

It was this—the decision to proceed against him by force rather than persuasion—that, more than any other consideration, would lead to Luther's ultimate repudiation of papal authority.

If the normal practice was followed the theses would have been sent to the university printer and set to the press. They would then have been affixed to the door of the castle church, the university's normal bulletin board. This, according to Philip Melanchthon's later account, occurred on October 31, less than eight weeks after the failed call for a debate on

Scholastic theology and the same day that Luther dispatched his letter to Archbishop Albrecht.

As we have seen, whether, in fact, the theses were posted in this way has been the subject of a prolonged, if rather contrived, debate.[47] It is pointed out that no eyewitness ever recorded having seen Luther at work with his hammer and nail. This is hardly surprising: the posting of formal academic documents is never a thrilling sight; no one at that point could possibly have imagined the sensational consequences. The historic record of the early part of the Reformation is often, as we have seen with the details of Luther's early life, frustratingly incomplete. In 1516 Luther reported to a friend that he was so weighed down by correspondence that he could have kept two secretaries continuously employed.[48] Yet for the thirty-four years of Luther's life before 1517 only forty-seven letters survive. Luther was not a famous man; his letters were not at this point worth saving. On several occasions in this book we will find ourselves discussing publications of which no one thought to retain a copy.

This was certainly the case with the first published version of the ninety-five theses if, as seems likely, it emanated from the local print shop of Johann Rhau-Grunenberg. Yet even if we lack specific contemporary documentation, the circumstantial evidence for the posting of the theses is overwhelming. We know that the Wittenberg press had been established largely to serve the interests of the university, and academic ephemera of this sort dominated the output of the first print shops.[49] We can also call in evidence the relatively recent discovery of Rhau-Grunenberg's September printing of the theses on Scholastic theology.[50] This provides critical evidence for the existence of a Rhau-Grunenberg broadsheet prototype of the ninety-five theses on indulgences. For the earlier broadsheet Rhau-Grunenberg used what was clearly his house style, dividing the theses into blocks of twenty-five. This was precisely the form in which the Nuremberg and Basel reprints of the ninety-five theses on indulgences were presented, suggesting they were set up on the basis of a lost Wittenberg original. This really crucial piece of evidence—the existence of a broadsheet edition printed in Wittenberg of theses proposed by Luther only eight weeks before the theses on indulgences—was unknown when the whole posting debate was initiated; one is tempted to think that if the volume in which it was discovered had been examined thirty years earlier, then this discussion would have been rendered largely redundant.

We also know that knowledge of the theses spread very quickly locally, as could only have been the case had they been exhibited publicly. Crucial evidence here is a letter to Luther of no later than November 5 from Georg Spalatin. Spalatin wrote to complain that he had not been sent a copy of the theses; clearly even at this early point they were an object of discussion at the court.[51] Finally, we have the clear statement of Philip Melanchthon, who arrived in Wittenberg a year later and was in a position to have spoken to many people who knew exactly how the controversy had begun, including Luther's academic colleagues in the university. So almost certainly the indulgences were posted up on the door of the castle church, as the accepted narrative would have it, most probably in a now lost printed edition of Johann Rhau-Grunenberg.

So far, so ordinary. But there were a couple of circumstances that would have suggested to early observers that this would not be a mundane academic event. First, the choice of date was enormously provocative, for October 31 was the eve of the greatest day in the Wittenberg calendar, All Saints', when the elector's vast collection of relics was exposed to public gaze. As Luther strode through the town to affix his theses, the town would have been filling with pilgrims preparing to process through the same door where Luther's denunciation of indulgences would soon be displayed. Luther was not naive on this point. In an illuminating retrospective commentary on the whole controversy, he revealed that he had, in fact, preached at the castle on indulgences, and the elector had made his displeasure known.[52] Frederick was, as everyone was aware, enormously proud of his church and its collections. Although the ninety-five theses were squarely aimed at Tetzel and Albrecht, Frederick's foe, if the elector had chosen to take offense, as well he might, Luther was finished. This is the first hint of the almost willful heedlessness that would characterize Luther's actions in the next two years, a source of both great strength and huge peril.

For a careful academic reader the theses also held surprises. A long list of propositions does not necessarily make a coherent argument; this is not the point. But the shift in voice, the mix of carefully considered general propositions and blisteringly direct utterances placed in the mouth of the laity, was very unusual for what purported to be a formal academic exercise. The effect was rather discordant. When subjected to close examination by unsympathetic authorities the theses would have exuded a distinct whiff of danger; the demotic explosions gave many hostages to fortune. Clearly many of the first readers did not quite know what to make of this. Luther, looking back on these events, did not take any great pride in the ninety-five theses. Had he had any sense of their likely impact, he told a later correspondent, he would have taken far more care with them.

For now, Luther was keen to give the theses the widest possible circulation. As with the theses on Scholastic theology, copies of Rhau-Grunenberg's printed version were dispatched to his usual circle of friends, with the request that they circulate them further. But first he had a letter to write to Albrecht of Brandenburg. Although couched with a degree of the deference appropriate to their two very different stations in life, the letter is remarkably forthright. After cursory compliments Luther comes straight to the point:

> Under your most distinguished name, papal indulgences are offered
> all across the land for the construction of St. Peter. Now, I do not so
> much complain about the quacking of the preachers, which I have
> not heard; but I bewail the gross misunderstanding among the
> people which comes from these preachers, and which they spread

everywhere among common men. Evidently the poor souls believe that when they have bought indulgence letters they are then assured of their salvation.[53]

In this letter Luther focused his criticism on the printed instructions for the preaching of the indulgences, which Luther asked Albrecht to withdraw.[54] He enclosed a copy of his manuscript treatise on indulgences, and almost as an afterthought (he mentioned it only in a postscript), the ninety-five theses.[55]

The weeks stretched by without reply. This was not entirely Albrecht's fault. Luther's letter was probably dispatched first to Magdeburg. Remarkably, the original survives, so we know it was only opened on November 17, and then sent on to Albrecht at his palace in Aschaffenburg.[56] He seems not to have been aware of it before the end of November, by which time news of the proposed disputation in Wittenberg was circulating quite widely.

Albrecht was already not in the best of tempers. The receipts from the preaching of the indulgences had thus far been quite modest, and certainly far from sufficient to meet his obligations to Rome and his bankers. The refusal of Frederick the Wise to allow the indulgence to be preached in his lands was already a provocation; then came this presumptuous attack from one of Frederick's professors. In the circumstances, the archbishop's response was remarkably measured. On December 1 he passed Luther's communication to the Theology Faculty at Mainz with the request for an opinion; he wrote again on December 11 to urge the doctors to make haste. The answer when it came was a masterpiece of equivocation. The Mainz theologians defended the right of the University of Wittenberg to stage such disputations. At the same time they felt that issues of this sort were best left to the pope. Albrecht did the sensible thing and forwarded the theses to Rome.

Luther, meanwhile, was doing what he could to make the theses known. He wrote to his diocesan bishop, the bishop of Brandenburg, who advised him to leave the whole issue alone. Otherwise his correspondents were familiar friends, Lang in Erfurt and Christoph Scheurl in Nuremberg. Scheurl in particular responded enthusiastically, sharing the theses with friends in the city patriciate and intellectual community.[57] Scheurl may also have taken a role in arranging for the theses to be reprinted in Nuremberg, an absolutely decisive step in ensuring their wider public impact. Further editions were published in Leipzig and Basel. These were a study in contrasts. The Leipzig edition (probably based on an unofficial manuscript copy) was muddled and misnumbered: a reader would have thought Luther had written eighty-seven theses.[58] The Basel edition, in contrast, was a neat and elegant pamphlet, like the Nuremberg edition dividing the theses into three groups of twenty-five and one of twenty. In keeping with Basel's reputation as a sophisticated cultural capital the numbering was in Roman numerals. With this pamphlet Luther's theses entered the bloodstream of the European intellectual community. It was this edition that, in March 1518, a curious Desiderius Erasmus sent to his great friend Thomas More in England.[59]

The dissemination of the ninety-five theses took Luther into uncharted waters; the same, to a considerable extent, was true of the printing industry. In the course of the sixteenth and seventeenth centuries Europe's printers would put out many thousands of academic disputations. The publication of dissertation theses was an essential part of progress to any higher academic degree, and very few had a purpose or value that lasted beyond this formal academic occasion. If they survive, they are seldom consulted today. In fact, academic libraries possess many thousands of these dissertations that have never actually been cataloged.

This sort of academic ephemera seldom attracted any notice outside the university where the disputation took place; I am struggling to think of any examples where dissertation theses found a sufficient audience to merit a new edition elsewhere. Yet in Luther's case his theses on indulgences were reprinted three times, in three separate cities, including one (Nuremberg) that did not have a university. According to Luther's correspondents the Nuremberg press also published the theses in a German translation, though if this was the case no copies have survived.[60] This,

The 95 Theses

Here in the broadsheet edition published in Nuremberg by Hieronymus Höltzel (USTC 751649), note the division of the theses into three groups of 25 and one of 20, presumably following the model of the lost Rhau-Grunenberg original.

again, would be totally unprecedented. Something very unusual was going on.

Martin Luther certainly thought so. "What is happening is unheard of," he told a correspondent in May 1518, and he was certainly correct. The printing of the ninety-five theses had given them a new life, totally separate from the planned disputation, which, of course, never took place. This restricted academic event was now completely forgotten, for thanks to print the indulgence controversy had become a public matter. And not all who read the text could afford to allow Luther's criticisms to go unanswered.

TETZEL

In all the many thousands of books written about the Reformation, virtually no one has had a good word to say about Johann Tetzel, Albrecht of Mainz's commissioner for the sale of indulgences in the diocese of Magdeburg. Tetzel is the pantomime villain of the Reformation: frequently portrayed as crude and unscrupulous, prepared to make the wildest of claims to extract money from the credulous. This is something of a travesty. Tetzel was certainly flamboyant and a showman, but then so, too, was Raymond Peraudi; so were many of the great medieval preachers who drew vast crowds on their peripatetic preaching tours. He was an educated man, and a sophisticated and thoughtful theological writer, as the indulgence controversy would prove. He was also good at his job. And while his superiors were slow to react to Luther's challenge, Tetzel recognized the seriousness of the threat. He was the first to articulate a response to Luther's criticism, earning further abuse for his pains. Tetzel was savagely treated partly because Luther and his friends recognized him as a formidable adversary; which is why they set out to destroy him.

Tetzel's appointment as indulgence salesman was hardly a desperate last resort for Albrecht. Although Albrecht had been disappointed in obvious candidates to lead the indulgence campaign, Tetzel offered a wealth of relevant experience. He was educated at the University of Leipzig and had taught theology at the Dominican school in the city. Since 1509 he had been the inquisitor, or master of heretics, for Poland. He also had considerable experience in the preaching of indulgences. Not surprisingly, given the lack of enthusiasm of other candidates for the position, Tetzel could command a decent salary for his services. He was paid a stipend of eighty gulden a month, a considerable sum; in addition he and his subcommissioners claimed expenses of three hundred gulden a month. Albrecht complained angrily at this lack of economy, but given the frenetic pace of Tetzel's itinerary, and the distances covered, it is hard to see how this could have been achieved without cost.

Tetzel was also at the heart of the first coherent effort to rally conservative forces against Luther. This occurred at a meeting of the Dominican chapter in Frankfurt-an-der-Oder, home to the new university of Electoral Brandenburg. In a demonstration of support for their Dominican brother, a series of theses were prepared in defense of indulgences, to be debated by Tetzel. As was often the custom in Germany the theses were written by someone else, in this case Konrad Koch, known as Wimpina, the university's senior theologian.

This closing of ranks in the Dominican order was also highly significant. It reinforced the already evident tribal element of the conflict, Dominicans against Augustinians, Wittenberg University against Leipzig and now Frankfurt. From this point on the Dominicans became identified as Luther's most determined pursuers, and they crop up with increasing frequency in the judgment of his case. To Martin Luther's baleful Augustinian eye they seemed to be particularly well entrenched in Rome. In the short run this perception may even have helped Luther. From the time that the Dominican chapter wrapped Tetzel in its protective embrace, Luther's Augustinian brethren were inclined to give him the benefit of the doubt. This gave him crucial breathing space to make his case. This was important, because Luther was about to do something that would make many of his fellow churchmen distinctly uneasy. Luther had decided that Tetzel's theses required a reply. But he would make it not in Latin, the language of scholarly debate, but in German.

First, however, came an episode that would cause Luther considerable embarrassment. Tetzel's countertheses were brought to Wittenberg from Halle, with instructions that they should be distributed among the students. But before this could be achieved the bookseller found himself surrounded by a hostile crowd. The whole consignment of broadsheets, apparently eight hundred copies, was taken from him and burned.[61] Although the desire to defend their own professor against a rival university played its part, this was not something that could be dismissed as a student prank. The repercussions were potentially profound; for Luther it was the first sign that his protest would raise forces he could not control and take the movement in directions he would not approve. Luther was forced to assure his friend Lang that he had had nothing to do with it; his turn burning books would come in 1520.[62] These riotous Wittenberg students do, however, remind us that in the violent and destructive culture wars set off by the Reformation, it was the evangelicals who were the first to commit their opponents' works to the fire.

Tetzel's stout defense of indulgences prompted a major change of direction in Luther. Previously he had been highly skeptical about taking theological debate outside the academy. Now he decided to embrace the wider public whose interests and loyalties had become increasingly engaged by the dramatic conflict unfolding around them. Luther would make a public defense of his theses on indulgences: in print, as Tetzel had responded to him in print, but now in the vernacular.

This was a signal moment for Martin Luther, and indeed for the Reformation. Up to this point Luther could plausibly have drawn back and laid the controversy on indulgences to rest; he could argue that he had merely proposed theses for debate, provocative and speculative, as the genre demanded. He could have acknowledged that some of his propositions had been imprudently expressed. His opponents could in turn accept that he had raised issues of importance. The carefully measured provisional response of the Mainz theologians seemed to point the way to just such a resolution. The closing of ranks around Tetzel, denying any validity in Luther's criticisms, had raised the stakes dramatically. If this was to be a public scandal, Luther would address the public. But by doing so, taking the debate out of the academic theater and the formal process of the dissertation, he also abandoned the protection of his status as a professor. From this point on Luther would be a marked man.

Luther began working on his German treatise early in March 1518; it was published toward the end of the month. The *Sermon on Indulgence and Grace* offered a succinct and trenchant defense of his teaching. But, as was always the way with Luther, he also moved the debate forward. For the first time, in the introductory contextual propositions, Luther questioned the traditional teaching on penance, which he here associated with the proponents of Scholastic theology. But it is also noteworthy that in addressing a lay audience Luther significantly reins back his criticism of the church hierarchy. The St. Peter's indulgence is specifically mentioned—in the circumstances it could hardly be ignored—but the tract largely avoids the technical questions of authority raised in the ninety-five theses. Instead it is addressed directly to the lay Christian faced with practical dilemmas of salvation and the temptations of indulgences. The reader is given precise, practical guidance in short pithy sentences: It is a grievous error for anyone to think that he can make satisfaction for his own sins (thirteenth proposition). Indulgence helps no one improve but tolerates people's imperfection (fourteenth). It is much better to benefit someone in need with a good work than to give to a building (sixteenth).[63]

In itself the *Sermon on Indulgence and Grace* would not be a major contribution to the ongoing theological debate, or the emerging clash of authority. But it was an instant publishing sensation. Rhau-Grunenberg published two or possibly three editions; by the end of the year it had been reprinted in Leipzig four times, and twice each in Nuremberg, Augsburg, and Basel.[64] This set a pattern that would be followed for almost all of Luther's vernacular works for the following years of controversy: an instant, insistent demand for the Wittenberg originals, followed by immediate republication in the major citadels of German print. In this way Luther swiftly made his way into the homes of thousands of his fellow citizens, who had probably never before owned the work of a living German author. The decision to address a wider public had been his own; but it was print that had made him a national figure.

The *Sermon on Indulgence and Grace* alerted the German printing industry to Luther's potential value. But what is perhaps most remarkable about this modest, unassuming work is what it reveals about Luther's completely unexpected facility as a vernacular writer. This was his first serious foray into vernacular writing, yet it can only be described as a work of intuitive genius. Luther replaces the ninety-five propositions of the Latin theses with twenty short paragraphs, each developing a single aspect of the question. None is more than three or four sentences long; the sentences are short and direct. The whole work is a mere fifteen hundred words. It fits perfectly into an eight-page pamphlet.

This was a revolution in theological writing. For this was not an age that in general valued brevity, as the 95 theses of Luther and 106 of Tetzel made clear. Luther's colleague Andreas von Karlstadt, ever a man of extremes, even contrived 406 theses on one occasion.[65] Nor was it any different with the spoken word. Luther's choice of "Sermon" in the title almost seems to mock the genre, for as any attendee would attest, sermons were usually of interminable length. The sermon was a theatrical event, with repetition, exhortation, and rhetorical virtuosity, an endurance test for preacher and audience alike. In an age of strenuous devotion, this was rather the point. Luther, in contrast, had produced a sermon that could be read, or read aloud, in ten minutes, and still engaged the heart of the question.

With the German sermon, Luther had truly burned his boats. This was no longer a matter that could be resolved among academic theologians, but would now be played out in a public theater. One of the first to realize this was Johann Tetzel. As his ecclesiastical superiors grappled with the issue of how, and by whom, Luther would be brought to book, Tetzel took up his pen: and he, too, would write in the vernacular.

His *Rebuttal Against a Presumptuous Sermon of Twenty Erroneous Articles* is courteous and persistent, avoiding any of the personal vituperation that would characterize future exchanges between Luther and his Catholic opponents.[66] Tetzel also became the first of Luther's opponents to make a connection between the criticism of indulgences and the heresies of John Wyclif and Jan Hus, a parentage that at this point Luther would have found acutely embarrassing. Tetzel's work, published in a neat Leipzig edition, deserves to be better known, not least because it demonstrated that Luther's opponents could, if they chose, compete very effectively in such a vernacular exchange.[67] Mostly, of course, they chose not to, a tactical error that left the field largely open for Luther's supporters.

Luther had Tetzel's work in his hands very quickly. Branding it (quite unfairly) "an unparalleled example of ignorance," he set about a reply. This second pamphlet was, again, extremely succinct, and another publishing success, with nine editions in 1518.[68] Tetzel's *Rebuttal*, in contrast, largely failed to find an audience. The first edition was not reprinted; for his further and last contribution to the debate he reverted to Latin. This work Luther simply ignored.

Tetzel was by this point a much diminished figure: tired, humiliated, and ill. For his own protection he had taken refuge in the Dominican house at Leipzig; the public had turned against him and his career as an indulgence salesman was at an end. So, too, was his usefulness to the Catholic Church. Although his local Dominican brethren continued to offer him sanctuary, the church hierarchy preferred to throw him to the wolves. When the pope's delegate Karl von Miltitz came to Germany in the autumn of 1518 to attempt a solution to the Luther problem, he made it abundantly clear that Tetzel was expendable, that he was prepared to "butcher the black sheep." By denouncing the commissioner's excesses and irregularities, the doctrine of indulgences could perhaps survive unscathed. In a personal interview in Leipzig the aristocratic von Miltitz subjected Tetzel to a calculated public humiliation.

That meeting would be Tetzel's last appearance on the public stage. He died in July 1519, broken and defeated. In the years that followed, the reformers continued to heap opprobrium on a man whose career conveniently symbolized the worst excesses of the indulgence trade; few voices were raised in his defense. Later Luther would rather shamefacedly claim that he had written to Tetzel in his last days to offer him spiritual comfort. If this is the case, the letter has not survived.

The Reformation would make and break many reputations; in due course the conflicts and passions generated by the division of the churches would claim many lives. But there is little doubt that Johann Tetzel, theologian and defender of indulgences, was its first victim.

Part 2

✳

THE EYE
OF THE STORM

4.

THE EYE OF THE STORM

I N THE TWO YEARS 1518 and 1519 Luther's world changed out of all recognition. He became a public figure. He became, to his distress, the enemy of the church he had served so faithfully for his first thirty-five years. He began to attract passionate devotion beyond the small number of intimates who had thus far shared his cause. And he became a best-selling author.

It was during these years that Germany's rulers were gradually awakened to the potentially momentous consequences of the *causa Lutheri,* the Luther affair. Luther, meanwhile, met every twist and turn of the gathering controversy with new theological revelation. For two years he wrote and wrote. German readers devoured every work; each new text was instantly reprinted and sold in huge numbers. Wittenberg's fledgling printing industry struggled to keep pace. That, too, was a problem that had to be addressed.

These were also years when Luther was obliged to travel out of Wittenberg very frequently—more than he would ever do in his life again. In the three years between March 1518 and March 1521 Luther undertook three long and demanding journeys, to Heidelberg, Augsburg, and Worms, as well as shorter but still stressful trips to Leipzig and Altenburg. The trips to Augsburg and Worms were undertaken at considerable peril. To protect him from likely papal retribution it had been necessary to obtain safe-conducts, but neither Luther nor his anxious friends could be certain these would be honored.

These journeys were also of great importance to the development of Luther's public persona. Luther was on the road for several months. He covered most of the almost three hundred miles to Heidelberg on foot, staying with friends and in Augustinian houses. The journey to Worms three years later was undertaken in very different circumstances and became the occasion for dramatic demonstrations, as a fascinated public scurried to catch a glimpse of the notorious heretic friar, and supporters orchestrated noisy demonstrations in his favor. Crucially, in all of these travels the way stations along the route provided the opportunity for Luther to make his case, initially on indulgences, later on other aspects of his developing theology. He sat down with sympathetic members of his order, senior theologians who could not be persuaded, and curious and influential patrician intellectuals like Willibald Pirckheimer. Most of these conversations involved people meeting Luther for the first time. Many remembered it as a life-defining encounter with an exceptional mind and an extraordinary personality.

The strain on Luther must have been intense, as he was introduced to a bewildering variety of new friends and potential allies at the end of an exhausting day on the road. We must remember, too, that many of these conversations were undertaken under the shadow of the looming ordeal of a formal audience in hostile territory that had the potential to end his career and his incipient movement. That he conducted himself with such cool confidence is, in the circumstances, extraordinary, as indeed was his physical and mental stamina. Luther had to grow very quickly, not least as he adapted to carrying the hopes and expectations of the increasing numbers who had committed themselves to his cause. As with his blossoming activity as a writer and public theologian, this was another challenge for which Luther's previous life had provided little preparation. But all of these encounters played a critical role in building the Reformation.

ROME

In 1518 responsibility for settling the Luther affair moved to Rome.[1] The Curia was aware of Luther's criticisms of indulgences by January 1518, and from this time on German matters loomed increasingly large in the pope's calculations. The fact that it would take a further two years before Luther's definite condemnation may give the impression of slow deliberation, even indecision and delay. This was not really the case. The Curia was immediately aware of the need to shut down Luther's protest. But this had to be done in such a way as not to inflict further damage on the indulgence trade, if possible with the full cooperation of the local powers. This was seen, therefore, as much as a diplomatic as a theological problem. And here lay the difficulty. It was relatively easy to recognize the dangers in Luther's criticisms of indulgences, and to reaffirm traditional teachings. It was quite another matter to lay hands on him.

In this dilemma lay the key to the very different approaches to the events of 1518 and 1519 favored by Luther's opponents and his friends. In Rome it was immediately clear that it would be best if the resolution of the Luther affair could be conducted through diplomatic channels, and behind closed doors. It followed, equally, that Luther's best chance of survival lay in ensuring that his cause remained in the public eye. The oxygen of publicity was, quite literally, a matter of life and death.

Given Luther's criticisms of the papacy in his ninety-five theses, it was inevitable that Rome would be the proper locus of judgment in his cause. It was sensible, therefore, for Albrecht of Brandenburg to forward to Italy the bundle he had received, written as he put it by "an impudent monk of Wittenberg." This summary and rather contemptuous judgment set a bleak tone for the Roman procedures against Luther. There was never any possibility that the papal authorities could have acceded to Luther's demands for a radical rethinking of the teaching on indulgences. To have suspended, or in any way undermined, the preaching of the St. Peter's in-

AETHERNA IPSE SVAE·MENTIS SIMVLACHRA LVTHERVS
EXPRIMIT·AT VVLTVS CERA LVCAE OCCIDVOS·

M·D·X·X·

LUTHER IN 1520

The first of Cranach's iconic portraits of the reformer, this was deemed too confident and provocative for public circulation.

dulgence at such a time would have ruined Albrecht, and fatally weakened the economy of the church. It was unlikely such a possibility was ever seriously considered. The earnest writings of an unknown Augustinian and a call to debate in a distant and obscure university hardly constituted a significant threat. The Roman Curia had adequate procedures for dealing with such minor squalls; there was nothing to suggest that the impudent monk would have been more than a minor item in a crowded agenda.

The Luther materials were passed to Silvestro Mazzolini, known as Prierias, a capable theologian (and a Dominican), to judge. But even before he had a chance to examine them, the pope dispatched a letter to Gabriele della Volta, general of the Augustinian Hermits, requesting him to take measures to silence Luther. Della Volta was in Venice, so passed the instruction to the German regional superior, who was, of course, Luther's friend and patron Staupitz. It was only in May, when it became clear that the German Augustinians would not cooperate, that the process in Rome moved forward. Prierias was now asked to prepare an opinion. According to his later rather incautious boast, it took Prierias only three days to determine that Luther's theses were heretical. In the matter of indulgences it fell within the authority of the church to establish true doctrine; therefore: "Whoever says regarding indulgences that the Roman church cannot do what it *de facto* does, is a heretic."[2]

On the basis of this opinion Luther was summoned to Rome to answer for his opinions. This judgment was communicated to Luther in Wittenberg in early August; he also had access to Prierias's determination, which had been published as a pamphlet in Rome and swiftly reprinted in Augsburg and Leipzig.[3] It was immediately clear to Luther that to obey this summons would have been potentially fatal. Happily, the stars had aligned to make such an outcome improbable. In August the assembly of the German nation, the Imperial Diet, had gathered in Augsburg. Here they were joined by the pope's representative, Tommaso de Vio, Cardinal Cajetan. Cajetan would be one of the most interesting figures to engage himself with Luther. Although another Dominican, which Luther did not find reassuring, he was an exceptionally gifted theological thinker, measured and unflappable. He was also far from being an uncritical admirer of indulgences. Cajetan had actually addressed the issue in an important treatise, written at the invitation of a fellow cardinal (Giulio de' Medici, the future Pope Clement VII). While avoiding any mention of the issue of papal authority, Cajetan made clear that he wished to rein back the exuberant growth of indulgences. He frankly recognized that they were not to be found in Scripture or the church fathers. The recreation of a true doctrine of penitence would have no need of them.[4]

So while Cajetan came to Augsburg as the pope's agent, he was far from being an uncritical advocate of the status quo. He would also have been made aware of the mutinous temper of the German Estates, faced with new financial demands to combat the ever-present Turkish threat.[5]

Cajetan was swiftly convinced that Luther should be heard in Germany, not Italy, and this recommendation was transmitted to Rome.

The pope was prepared to accept this advice, but by this time the process against Luther had moved on. A letter from the Emperor Maximilian, which included a forthright denunciation of Luther, spurred a change in the nature of the judicial process against him. A new summary procedure was initiated, in which Luther was to be treated as an obstinate teacher of heresy. This decision had been reached, it should be noted, by August 23, 1518, when it was communicated to Cajetan; this was two years before Luther's final condemnation in the famous bull *Exsurge Domine*. From this point on, Luther was faced with a bleak alternative: recantation or excommunication.

This established a difficult context for Cardinal Cajetan's fateful meeting with Luther at Augsburg in October 1518. Although Cajetan was fully capable of an articulate and fruitful debate—indeed, only his subtle diplomacy had brought matters to this point—his hands were tied by the nature of the process already concluded in Rome. It placed him in a situation that would tax the equilibrium of even this normally genial man.

LOW BLOWS AND MISUNDERSTANDING

While these events were played out in Rome, back in Wittenberg Luther was forced to grapple with the consequences of his unexpected celebrity. The year 1518 had gotten off to a good start. Luther had seen off the first substantial criticism of his theses on indulgences and achieved a major publishing success with his first major vernacular writing, the *Sermon on Indulgence and Grace*. But it is clear he did not immediately understand the magnitude of the change in his life. Reading his correspondence presents an eerie illusion of normality; Luther's concerns seem surprisingly parochial. He continued his work on the reform of the Wittenberg curriculum, alert to the possibility that the rival faculty at Leipzig might seek to exploit his notoriety and stir up trouble for him.[6] During the course of the year what seems to have given him the greatest pleasure was securing the services of Philip Melanchthon as professor of Greek; amidst all his other cares he took enormous pains to ensure that Philip was made comfortable and adequately provided for.[7]

The challenge to his critics was rather different. They had seen the public reaction to Luther's criticism of indulgences; they had also witnessed the success of the *Sermon on Indulgence and Grace*. But it was not immediately clear how best to respond. Tetzel had tried and been swatted away. How could one conduct a debate when one party (Luther) had deliberately stepped out of the normal structures of academic discourse? The difficulty in coming to terms with this shifting landscape accounts for much of the frustration, anger, and the charges of bad faith that characterized the increasingly testy exchanges of these years.

The news that Luther was under investigation in Rome cast a considerable cloud in Wittenberg. Since della Volta had been ordered to resolve the matter within the Augustinian family, Luther was summoned to attend the next chapter of the German Observants in Heidelberg, in April 1518. Luther was obliged to request a leave of absence from his university duties; he took the opportunity of writing to the elector to ask also for a safe-conduct, which would protect him as he traveled the nearly three hundred miles to Heidelberg, passing through multiple political and ecclesiastical jurisdictions, many potentially hostile. Frederick was happy to oblige. Not only did he provide the requested letter, he also wrote independently to two of the leading rulers along Luther's route, the bishop of Würzburg and the Count Palatine, asking them to give him protection in their territories. Though Luther was not to know this, Frederick the Wise had embarked on a course from which he would never subsequently deviate, to the bafflement of the pope and most other diplomatic observers. The effort to turn Frederick would occupy a great deal of time and fruitless ingenuity over the next two years, and probably significantly delayed Luther's final condemnation: for Frederick could, at a stroke, have effected the discreet removal of the Luther problem, which the ecclesiastical hierarchy would greatly have preferred. But this stubborn, careful man had decided to stand by his professor and his university, for reasons he never fully revealed, and he remained steadfast to this determination, heedless of all threats and oblivious to all blandishments. Luther was lucky, in this, perhaps above all else.

Frederick was also thorough. To his letters he now added a further instruction to Staupitz, noting that he had released Luther from his professorial duties only very reluctantly, and insisting he be sent straight back after the congregation. So the option of sending him from Heidelberg to Rome was foreclosed. In the event, neither Frederick nor Luther should have worried, as the Heidelberg gathering was a triumph. The Observant Augustinians closed ranks, as had the Dominicans around Tetzel. Luther was given the opportunity to expound his new theology to an appreciative audience. One of those present, Martin Bucer (a Dominican interloper), recorded his first impressions:

> [A]lthough our chief men refuted him with all their might, their wiles were not able to make him move an inch from his propositions. His sweetness in answering is remarkable, his patience in listening is incomparable, in his explanations you would recognize the acumen of Paul, not of Scotus; his answers, so brief, so wise, and drawn from the Holy Scriptures, easily made all his hearers his admirers. On the next day I had a familiar and friendly conference with the man alone, and a supper rich with doctrine rather than with dainties. He lucidly explained whatever I might ask. He agrees with Erasmus in all things, but with this difference in his favor, that what Erasmus only insinuates he teaches openly and freely. Would that I had time to write you more of this. He has brought it about that at Wittenberg the ordinary textbooks have all been abolished, while the Greeks and Jerome, Augustine and Paul are publicly taught.[8]

Bucer had approached the occasion a skeptic: he starts this letter by reporting that Luther was "not one of our number." He left the congregation a disciple—in due course he would become a leader of the Refor-

Ein Freiheit des Sermons Päpstlichen Ablaß

Luther's second reply to Tetzel, here in an Augsburg reprint by Jörg Nadler (USTC 643353). At this stage of the controversy it was in Luther's interest that his works were circulated as widely as possible by reprints of this sort.

mation in his own right, in the critical Rhineland city of Strasbourg. Print could only do so much; for people to devote their lives to this young movement, Luther's personal magnetism played a vital part.

On his return to Wittenberg Luther published a brief summary of this meeting. This, intended for a clerical audience, was in Latin; the second reply to Tetzel, *Ein Freiheit des Sermons Päpstlichen Ablaß*, he published in German. At the same time Luther was working on what he regarded as his most critical task, the promised full explanation of his views on indulgences for his ecclesiastical superiors; it would be published, in the summer, with a respectful dedication to Pope Leo.[9] This was the most considerable text that Luther had yet consigned to Rhau-Grunenberg's press, and the backlog of work that developed as the printer gave it his painstaking attention would cause Luther considerable difficulties. On

May 16 Luther had preached in the town church at Wittenberg a pro-vocative sermon on the validity of excommunication. Possibly anticipat-ing the future course of his own case, Luther argued that the church's ban could not impact on a Christian's inner relationship with God. This was incendiary stuff, but became more so when churchmen in the con-gregation circulated in manuscript a series of theses drawn from it, which naturally threw into sharp relief the more provocative statements. Since Wittenberg's only press was fully occupied, Luther had no oppor-tunity to place into the public domain the full text of the sermon; the hostile summary thus became, for some critical months, the only known version. It was this document, when placed in the hands of the Emperor Maximilian, that induced him to write to Rome demanding that immedi-ate action be taken against Luther. Even Spalatin was misled when he read this text, and urged Luther to moderate his language. The sermon was subsequently published, but too late to undo the damage.[10]

Luther had other trials to face in these months; some, again, caused by the failure on both sides to control the distribution of texts not originally intended for immediate publication. After Tetzel, the first to attempt a full response to Luther's ninety-five theses was Johann Eck, chancellor of the University of Ingolstadt.[11] As this lofty office would imply, Eck was a gifted theologian, and his manuscript offered a root-and-branch dissection of Luther's propositions. Eck's treatise had been compiled at the request of the bishop of Eichstätt and was clearly not intended for publication. Eck called his text "Obelisks," or daggers, after the signs used in the critical study of ancient literature to denote spuri-ous portions of a text marked for removal. This set the tone for an exco-riating dissection, in which Eck dismissed Luther as simpleminded and unlearned. Like Tetzel he also made the connection between Luther's rash denunciation of papal power and the Hussite heresy.

The text began to circulate widely among scholars, ultimately reach-ing the hands of one of Eck's academic foes. Sensing mischief, he so-licitously passed it to Johann Lang, who forwarded it to Luther. Here Eck's daggers hit their mark. Luther was sorely wounded, not least because Eck had previously been seen as a likely friend of reform. He was sufficiently one of the Nuremberg circle to have been on the list of those to whom Christoph Scheurl had circulated Luther's theses in November 1517.[12]

Luther poured out his sense of grievance in a letter to a friend, dated March 24: "What cuts me most is that we had recently formed a great friendship"; in May he replied to Eck directly.[13] To Eck's daggers he opposed his asterisks (stars): these were the critical signs that marked the most valuable texts. This, however, was the only playful part of the exchange. Luther now had little time for his former friend: "as far as I can see, you know nothing in theology but the husks of scholasticism." Any hope this exchange would remain private was dashed when Karlstadt, as so often rushing in with more enthusiasm than judgment, published his 380 theses against Eck's "Obelisks" (later extended to 406).[14] Eck was obliged to reply; the battle lines were drawn.

One more of Luther's writings during this period must be mentioned, his short exposition on the Ten Commandments. This was a different sort of Luther from the cantankerous, unforgiving disputant of the exchange with Eck. This was Luther as the healing pastor, the father of his Wittenberg congregation, and, through the wonders of print, the citizens of Germany. This was the first time in these years that Luther stepped out of the controversial arena to address the concerns of the lay Christian, and at a length they could engage with: a mere eight pages in quarto. It was also very successful, with at least eight editions before 1520.[15] This was a Luther who struck a chord with many lay Christians disinclined to follow the twists and turns of academic controversy but eager for spiritual comfort in troubled times. It was a strand of Luther's writing that would play an important role in the years to come in building his public following.

AUGSBURG AND LEIPZIG

During the spring and summer of 1518 Luther was obliged to summon up new reserves of energy and courage. Penning the various defenses of his ninety-five theses was only a small part of the multiple obligations that now competed for his time. Correspondence occupied a huge amount of time, keeping in touch with friends, pleading his cause, and soliciting information on the play of events on the larger stage, as news was sometimes frustratingly difficult to come by in Wittenberg. All this, of course, was in addition to his normal duties as pastor and professor.[16] On August 7, Luther received his formal summons to Rome; there then ensued several long weeks of anxious waiting until he was informed that the hearing had been transferred to Augsburg. Even this journey was not without peril: Luther was well aware that condemnation and death might be the ultimate price. His friends in Nuremberg, where he rested briefly on the route, made strenuous efforts to persuade him to turn back to Wittenberg. Luther remained stoical, even fatalistic, but this second long journey in six months had taken its toll. He arrived in Augsburg on October 7, exhausted and suffering from stomach troubles.

When Luther first appeared before Cardinal Cajetan he was not aware of the recent turn of events in Rome: that his views had formally been condemned as heresy, requiring of him now an unambiguous act of contrition, otherwise sentence of excommunication would be pronounced. These new constraints had been conveyed to Cajetan, who wisely had chosen not to share this bleak turn of events with Luther's protector, Frederick. It meant, however, that Luther brought to his interview with Cajetan utterly unrealistic expectations of what could be achieved by their discussion.

This was a tragedy for the church, which thus passed up the last slim hope of reconciliation. But it was doubly a tragedy for Cajetan, who of all Luther's opponents was best equipped to engage with this curious man, who now, on their first meeting, prostrated himself at the cardinal's feet, as convention demanded. Discussion began in a cordial enough tone, but soon the hopeless impasse was revealed. Luther asked the cardinal to elucidate the reasons behind the church's rejection of his propositions; Cajetan insisted on obedience and submission.

This was a shattering encounter for Luther that stripped away much of his remaining faith in the church hierarchy. Their last meeting having ended with angry words on the cardinal's part, Luther lingered for some days in increasing anxiety lest his safe-conduct be revoked. Finally, on the evening of October 20, Luther slipped away, taking leave of the cardinal by letter. His formal appeal against Cajetan's proceedings was posted on the door of Augsburg Cathedral two days later by a friend. Luther arrived back in Wittenberg on October 31, the first anniversary of the posting of the theses. How utterly his life had changed in these twelve tumultuous months.

For the moment Luther was safe, but for how long? He was pursued back to Wittenberg by a letter from Cajetan, requesting the elector to hand Luther over to be conducted to Rome. It was only in December that Luther became aware that Frederick would refuse. He occupied the time by writing a short account of the meeting in Augsburg; on November 18 he also formally appealed the pope's anticipated judgment to a meeting of the general council. The general council, an assembly of cardinals and other leading churchmen that had met intermittently over the preceding centuries, had played the decisive role in ending periods of schism during the medieval era, and was still evoked by reformers as an alternative source of authority to an increasingly imperial papacy. It would, of course, ultimately be such an assembly, the Council of Trent, that would take the crucial steps toward a reformed and revitalized Catholicism. But the general council could only be summoned by the pope, and it was wholly implausible to imagine that such a gathering would be convened to hear Luther's case. Initially Luther's appeal was most likely conceived as a legal maneuver to strengthen the elector's position in defying a clear instruction from the pope's representative. But in the years to come this assertion of the primacy of the authority of the general council, a relic of the conciliarist dispute of past centuries, became an increasingly important aspect of Luther's gradual rejection of papal power. In due course the hopes of a reforming general council would be a fixed point in the agenda of reconciliation fitfully pursued by Catholics and evangelicals after the decisive Protestant breach. Both the *Acta Augustana* and the text of Luther's appeal (*Appellatio*) were swiftly published in Wittenberg, then in Leipzig and Basel; in the case of the *Appellatio*, Luther claimed, prematurely and against his will.[17] While he normally denounced Rhau-Grunenberg for his slow work, in this case Luther claimed he had jumped the gun; he had given the text to the printer but had intended it to be distributed only after news arrived of his formal excommunication.[18] This has the whiff of scapegoating, an explanation cooked up by Luther when friends taxed him that the appeal was premature and possibly counterproductive.

For affairs in Rome had reached a delicate stage. Rather than proceed to immediate judgment—pointless while Luther was safely tucked away in Wittenberg—Rome embarked on a new round of diplomacy. This new mission was entrusted to Karl von Miltitz, a vain and not especially subtle papal councillor, whose attempt to broker a solution in his native Saxony occupied much of the winter and the early months of 1519. Frederick and Luther were happy to engage with von Miltitz, not least because his arrival in Germany had convinced the envoy of the genuine sympathy for Luther's cause. Luther was prepared to cooperate in the draft of a letter of apology to the pope, which mostly, however, skirted around the theological questions at issue. At this point political perspective altered dramatically, and decisively in Luther's favor. On January 12, 1519, the Emperor Maximilian died. In the election to choose his successor, his grandson Charles of Spain would be the strong favorite. But nothing was certain, and Frederick, as dean of the electoral college, would play a vital role.

Suddenly the matter of Frederick's protégé appeared in a different light, particularly as Pope Leo had his own reasons for wishing another candidate to succeed to the imperial throne. On March 29, 1519, the pope wrote directly to Luther, addressing him as "beloved son" and rejoicing in his willingness to recant (in this Leo was misinformed). No longer was Luther the "insolent monk" or "son of perdition" whose case was already closed.

The maneuvers surrounding the imperial election won Luther a six-month respite, an interval he would occupy with further writing and teaching. It was in this period particularly that Luther developed his pastoral role with a series of short treatises on subjects of immediate concern to lay Christians: on the Lord's Prayer, on the body of Christ. All were swiftly reprinted in numerous editions. Luther also occupied himself with revising his lecture series on Galatians from the academic year 1516–17 as an academic commentary. This was handed over to the Leipzig printer Melchior Lotter in May, though it did not appear until September.[19]

During this comparatively tranquil interlude it was left to Luther's German opponents to pursue the theological quarrel. Foremost among them was Johann Eck. Still smarting from Luther's reply to his "Obelisks," Eck had little doubt that the public exposure of Luther's teaching would reveal the full extent of the emerging Wittenberg heresies. Luther's loyal but impetuous Wittenberg colleague, Andreas von Karlstadt, had provided the opening with his 406 theses against the "Obelisks." In his published response Eck challenged Karlstadt to a public disputation, with Karlstadt to choose the venue. Originally set for April 1519, in due course the disputation was fixed for Leipzig in June.

This put Luther in something of a bind.[20] He was aware, of course, that he was the real target. He was also uncertain how effectively Karlstadt would plead his cause. When Eck published a set of twelve theses as the basis of the debate, Luther published countertheses of his own; he also proposed himself as the appropriate disputant. This change in arrangements could not, however, be made without the agreement of the hosts: the University of Leipzig, and ultimately Duke George. The duke had no real wish to provide a platform for Wittenberg's new phenomenon and took his time to reply. It was only after the contending parties had actually arrived in Leipzig that Luther received formal permission to take part.

By this time Eck had succeeded in widening the scope of the discussion, focusing critically (and for Luther dangerously) on the issue of papal obedience. Luther had raised the matter of the historical basis of papal authority in his countertheses, greatly to the distress of several of his friends. Karlstadt, who still intended to take part in the disputation, pointedly reasserted his obedience to papal authority. Luther, typically, made a virtue of his isolation, publishing, in advance of the debate, his research on the question of papal authority as a separate pamphlet.[21]

Not surprisingly, with such a dramatic and contentious prehistory, the event itself was eagerly awaited throughout Germany. Leipzig prepared itself for the expected influx of visitors and spectators. While Eck had slipped into town unobtrusively, the Wittenberg delegation arrived together, two hundred strong, bolstered by a large number of students. Not to be outdone, Jerome Emser, a former secretary of Raymond Peraudi now attached to the court of Duke George, ensured that Eck would receive a guard of honor from the students of Leipzig on the first day of formal proceedings.[22] During the disputation the Wittenberg students made a thorough nuisance of themselves, not least with a noisy demonstration outside Eck's lodgings, so it was something of a relief when the debate began to bore them and many slipped off home.

The debate finally got under way on June 27, though Luther only entered the lists on July 4, after Eck had debated with Karlstadt. The humanist poet Petrus Mosellanus, having delivered a lengthy opening address, went on to record his impressions of the protagonists.

> Martin is of medium height with a gaunt body that has been so exhausted by studies and worries that one can almost count the bones under his skin; yet he is manly and vigorous, with a high clear voice. He is full of learning and has an excellent knowledge of the Scriptures, so that he can refer to facts as if they were at his fingers' tips. . . . In his life and behavior he is very courteous and friendly, and there is nothing of the stern stoic or grumpy fellow about him. He can adjust to all occasions. In a social gathering he is gay, witty, ever full of joy, always has a bright and happy face, no matter how seriously his adversaries threaten him. One can see that God's strength is with him in his difficult undertaking. . . .
>
> Eck . . . is a great, tall fellow, solidly and robustly built. The full, genuinely German voice that resounds from his powerful chest

sounds like that of a towncrier or a tragic actor. . . . His mouth and eyes, or rather his whole physiognomy, are such that one would sooner think him a butcher or common soldier than a theologian. As far as his mind is concerned, he has a phenomenal memory. . . . In addition, he has an incredible audacity which, however, he covers up with great craftiness.[23]

Luther gets very much the better of this comparison, and may, for the neutral observer, have made the more favorable impression. But there is no doubt that Eck was the more formidable debater. With wily persistence he pinned Luther back to his most controversial position, his denial of the historical roots of papal primacy. Gleefully he called attention to the most notorious progenitor of Luther's view, the Czech heretic Jan Hus. Technically it fell to the universities of Paris and Erfurt to adjudicate the result, but rather than wait both sides rushed to place their own presentation of events in the public domain. Philip Melanchthon inevitably made Luther the victor, while Jerome Emser spoke up for Eck.[24] Emser's contribution called for a sharp, dismissive retort from Luther, who also published his own explanations (*Resolutiones*) of his Leipzig theses.[25] Eck, for his part, offered his own account, in response to Melanchthon, and a justification against Luther.[26] Europe's scholarly community, never so entertained nor so conspicuously in the public eye, relished every thrust and counterthrust. Leipzig's printers, kept ceaselessly active by this rush of Latin pamphlets, reveled in their brief moment upstaging Wittenberg as the chief locus of the Reformation conflict.

Leipzig was a decisive moment for Martin Luther. It was characteristic of the man—and not always to his advantage—that he would never step back from a position once taken. Eck had pushed him further than most of his supporters would have wished on the matter of papal authority and in his affirmation that the notorious Hus had in many respects been a true Christian. As the sound and fury of Leipzig receded Luther would build these positions into the bedrock of his emerging ecclesiology. Leipzig was also a defining moment for many in the first

SERMO DE TRIPLICI IVSTICIA
R. PATRIS MARTINI LVTHER
AVGVSTINIANI VVIITEN•
BERGENSIS.

AN EARLY LUTHER WORK PRINTED BY RHAU-GRUNENBERG

Rhau-Grunenberg had done a reasonable job as a printer of simple Latin texts for the university, but when he continued in the same style with Luther's writings, the relative crudity of his work was all too apparent.

generation of the Reformation, the point at which they defiantly affirmed the Wittenberg positions or definitively stepped back. It was also the Reformation's first great moment of public theater. The traditional esoteric rituals of academic discourse had found a large new audience that went far beyond the theologically informed. Not just Germany, but the wider international scholarly community began to see that something very profound was stirring in the north.

THE FORTUNES OF TRADE

In 1515, we will remember, Luther did not rate a mention in a list of the top one hundred professors of three rather obscure German univer-

sities. In the two years 1518 and 1519 he became Europe's most published author. His fame, and for the first time his image, was spread
around Europe in numerous published works, in Latin for the international scholarly community, in German for the new audience Luther was
building for his unique mixture of theological controversy and pastoral
instruction. In these two years Luther had written 45 original compositions: 25 in Latin and 20 in German. No wonder by the time he appeared
at Leipzig he seemed to have been reduced to skin and bone; the work,
and the nervous tension of constant danger, had worn him away. But he
had done what was necessary to grasp his moment of opportunity; the
printing industry, and the popularity of his writings among an expanding
reading public, had done the rest. The 45 works published by Luther
translated into a total of 291 editions by the time German printers had
met the huge public interest with instant reprints and the first anthology
volumes; and then, of course, there were the works of friends and adversaries.[27] It is worth pausing to consider the impact of this great rush of
print on the German printing industry: how indeed it could cope with
such a sudden new demand for works of urgent topical interest.

In 1515 and 1516 German print shops turned out something over
eleven hundred titles. This was already impressive, and far in excess of
the output of both France and Italy, the other two major European
centers of print activity. The print trade in these other markets was struc-
tured rather differently. Although in France and Italy, Paris and Venice
played a dominant role, in Germany production was far more widely
dispersed. Only Leipzig, and less reliably Strasbourg, would be responsible for more than one hundred titles in any one year.

This, as it turned out, created the ideal conditions for the rapid dissemination of Luther's writings. Generally the first edition would be put
to the press in Wittenberg, in the single then-operating print shop of
Johann Rhau-Grunenberg. It would then be rapidly reprinted in Leipzig,
fortuitously close, and home to several well established publishing
ventures. From there the text could be relayed on to Nuremberg, Augsburg, and thence onto the great cultural capital of the Rhineland, Basel.

In some respects it served the movement well that Wittenberg, at this point, was simply too small to cope with the extraordinarily rapid increase in demand for Luther's works. Rather than centralizing production in one place, and facing the complex tasks of distributing stock over large distances, it made far more sense to dispatch a single copy to new markets, where a new edition could be printed off. This was particularly the case with small books, as the capital investment required to publish a small pamphlet was relatively modest. With large books, the risk of two presses embarking on competing editions and having large amounts of unsold stock tipped the balance in favor of centralized production. And many of Luther's works, as we have seen, were very short, allowing them to be reprinted very quickly. A well-organized print shop could print five hundred copies of an eight-page pamphlet in a day.

What was so remarkable was how quickly, instinctively, Luther adapted his writing to optimize benefit for the printing trade. Of his forty-five writings of these years, twenty-one were eight pages long or less. The demand and public interest meant that they often sold out very quickly. Printers got an immediate return for minimum investment. Luther, it very quickly became clear, was a safe bet for the printing industry.

The impact of the Reformation on a local printing industry can be very well illustrated with the example of Augsburg.[28] Augsburg was one of Germany's proudest and most sophisticated cities, a major center of commerce and international finance. It was also a major information crossroads, the only one of the free cities that lay on the route of the imperial postal service. But in 1517 its printing industry experienced something of a hiatus, publishing only 37 titles in the whole year. Augsburg had no university, so lacked that important local market. In the years that followed, the Luther affair sparked a major regeneration. Overall production rose to 89 titles in 1518 and 117 in 1519; Luther accounted for 41 of these extra editions. In 1520 Augsburg's printers would publish a staggering 90 editions of Luther's works.[29]

The case of Basel was rather different; this rich, cultured city embraced Luther in a much more measured way. Whereas the largest portion of the Augsburg Luther editions were in German, Basel's main contribution was a series of reprints of Luther's Latin books, including, as we recall, the first edition of the ninety-five theses in pamphlet form.[30] This was the work of Adam Petri, who would go on to publish over a hundred Luther editions in the next ten years. In the first years, however, the crucial contribution was made by Johann Froben, Erasmus's long-term collaborator. In October 1518 the enterprising Froben published an anthology of six of Luther's Latin works on the indulgence controversy. This was enormously successful: Froben sent copies all around Europe and claimed to have disposed of the best part of six hundred in Paris alone.[31] His initiative was rapidly plagiarized by Matthias Schürer, in Strasbourg, another western city extremely well-placed for international sales. Schürer's editions offered much the same selection, with the addition of the *Acta Augustana*.[32] Froben might have been sore at this raid on his market, but the absence of copyright protection in the patchwork of political jurisdictions that made up the German Empire actually helped greatly in assisting the rapid spread of Luther's work. There was nothing to prevent a printer in one city or state from republishing the work of a printer in another, and, of course, Luther as author received nothing from the sale of his works. Froben would later recall rather ruefully that his Luther anthology was his most successful title, somewhat to the chagrin of Erasmus, who insisted that Froben abandon publishing Luther if he wanted their own relationship to continue.[33]

The impact of the Luther controversies on the print industries of Augsburg and Basel was indicative of a more general revival of printing in the German lands. The interest in Luther allowed printers to make quick profits, which they could then reinvest in other projects. Overall the number of titles published doubled between 1517 and 1520, reaching a new peak in 1523: at this point German presses published three times the number of books printed in France and Italy combined.[34] This raises the question of how it was possible for the industry to expand production so very rapidly. Undoubtedly, in 1515 there was spare capacity, with many presses rather underemployed. Where new print shops were established, or existing businesses expanded, the capital costs involved were relatively modest: a wooden press could be constructed very quickly and was a relatively simple piece of machinery. The principal bottlenecks would have been the casting of new type and the supply of paper. With respect to type, Germany was lucky in possessing Europe's most advanced metalwork industries (in which Luther's father, we will remember, had made his living).

With respect to the supply of paper it helped that the industry was so dispersed, and so could rely on several major areas of paper manufacture. But this was certainly a major concern: it is revealing that when Lucas Cranach, Wittenberg's canniest businessman, decided to invest in the printing industry, he bought his own paper mill so that he could be assured of adequate stock.[35] Other major publishers made similar investments; for those with more modest resources paper could often be obtained by exchange—taking so many reams of paper in return for half as many printed sheets, which the paper barons could then sell. This reflected the customary calculation that paper represented about 50 percent of the cost of the finished book. It is also the case that the increased demand for paper would have been rather lower than the raw figures for number of editions published would suggest. Many of Luther's works, and those published by his colleagues and adversaries, were very short. A sixteen-page pamphlet in quarto would require only two sheets of paper per copy, a thousand sheets for an edition of five hundred. So a great deal of the apparent increase in output could be accounted for by displacing work on larger books to publish Luther.

This was an extremely attractive proposition for book-trade professionals. Publishing large books could be extremely risky. A Latin tome of five hundred pages required an enormous stock of paper, and might take up to a year before the printing was complete and the first copies could be sold. A printer had to have good credit to meet these costs (and those of wages and maintaining the print shop) before sales could recoup any of the investment. Worse, it was by no means certain that the copies would sell; the publisher had to allow for heavy discounts to move the stock, and heavy costs in transporting the texts to a widely dispersed readership. Each new book was a risky business: underestimate demand and the work of resetting the text for a new edition would take another year; overestimate demand and one might never make back the costs, with a large portion of the expensively printed sheets rotting in storage for years.[36] With a Luther pamphlet, the job was ready for sale in a couple of days, sale was virtually assured, and with German titles the market was largely local. All the complexities of the trade, which brought financial embarrassment to so many publishers, seemed to have been resolved. It was no wonder that printers came to love Luther, and Luther came to transform the German printing industry.

OLD MAN RHAU

The question remained how much of this buoyant market could be reserved for Wittenberg. By 1518 the inadequacies of the local industry were all too obvious. In any circumstances one press would have been insufficient to meet the enormous demand for Luther's work. That this press was in the hands of Johann Rhau-Grunenberg was a recipe for embarrassment and frustration.

As we know, Luther had always had problems with the quality of Rhau-Grunenberg's work. In these years of controversy and rapid pamphlet exchanges this was further compounded by Rhau-Grunenberg's inability to work at anything other than his own stately pace. In 1518 matters began to come to a head. The time Rhau-Grunenberg took to publish Luther's full statement of his views on indulgences, the *Resolutiones,* had had calamitous consequences, as the maliciously constructed version of his sermon on excommunication was allowed to circulate without reply. Rhau-Grunenberg could not make space to publish the true text until several months later, at which point the damage was done. Rhau-Grunenberg might protest that the *Resolutiones* needed to be published with care, since it was destined to pass into the hands of senior churchmen, but in this case slow did not mean better. Luther thought the quality of the final product embarrassingly deficient.[37] Significantly, Luther attributed this to his long absence at the meeting with Cajetan in Augsburg, the implication being that in normal circumstances Luther took care to exercise close supervision over the printing process. This was not unusual for authors in this period: by far the best way to avoid irritating errors in the texts was to check the proof sheets oneself, but since the sheets were set up one at a time this demanded almost daily attendance at the printer's shop.

With Rhau-Grunenberg overtaxed, Luther was forced to send a number of original texts to Leipzig for publication.[38] This, though, had its own drawbacks. It was dangerous, since a manuscript could be lost on the road or fall into the wrong hands. In this case, too, Luther could not be on hand to check the accuracy of the printer's work. The logical solution was to persuade a further printer—or printers—to open a business in Wittenberg. And this, in addition to all his other responsibilities, Luther now decided to pursue.

His choice fell on Melchior Lotter, one of the best established of the Leipzig printers.[39] Lotter was by now a veteran of the German print world, having first published books in Leipzig as long ago as 1495. He had built his business steadily, and by 1517 he had almost five hundred titles to his name. This in itself would not have been enough to account for Luther's preference. The even more prolific Martin Landsberg also plied his trade in Leipzig, and had an established relationship with Wittenberg University: between 1507 and 1511 he had published a number of works for Christoph Scheurl and other of the Wittenberg literati.[40] It was a third Leipzig printer, Jakob Thanner, not Lotter, who had published the Leipzig edition of the ninety-five theses, though he had made such a poor job of it this may have ruled him out of contention.

The most substantial obstacle in the case of Lotter was that he had a perfectly satisfactory relationship with the old church. It had been Lotter who, in 1516, had published the manual for confessors for the indulgence campaign that had so offended Luther.[41] In 1517 he published two

Pſalteriū ſummi tū
ditoris et Egregij cytharedi Daui
dis pphete excellētiſſimi filij Jeſſe:
ſoli⁹ ſpuſſancti inſtinctu ſine omni exteriori adminicu
lo editū:Et per Diuū Aureliū Auguſtinū in tres
quinquagenas ſagaciter diuiſum:oibus cæ
terox pphetarū libris præferendū:ad
laudem cunctipotentis dei accura
te impreſſum

AD LECTOREM EPIGRAMMA

Contudit immanem:funda ſtridente:Goliam
Ieſſeus cythara/Dauid agebat oues.
Carminibus ſuperū placauit numina ſacris
Votis ſupplicibus:prẹmia magna:tulit.
Ergo auditor ades/fraudes ſi vincere cures
Hoſtis/et exculta voce placere deo.
Si Iouis ardentem ſuperi placare furorem
Sydera ſi poſcis:vel Stygis antra fugis.

Lipſiae ex aedibus Melchioris Lottheri:

MELCHIOR LOTTER SENIOR IN LEIPZIG

The superior quality of works published in Leipzig, the established center of printing in the German northeast, was clear for all to see, which is why Luther hoped to lure Lotter to Wittenberg.

editions of Jerome Emser's life of St. Benno, a great local focus of traditional devotion; in 1518 he would publish the first Catholic attack on Luther, Tetzel's *Rebuttal,* and two editions of the Roman condemnation of Luther's teaching on indulgences.[42] Yet a few weeks later he was publishing for Luther.

This was essentially a pragmatic alliance. What seems to have attracted Luther was Lotter's reputation as a publisher of serious works of Latin scholarship. It was here that Rhau-Grunenberg's work was most seriously deficient. His plain, undecorated, and utilitarian work reeked of provincialism—precisely the impression Wittenberg could not afford to give now that the university aspired to a leading role in curriculum reform, and Luther's works found readers in the wider intellectual community. Lotter, in contrast, had years of experience in precisely this sort of work: 475 of the 511 books he had published before 1518 were in Latin.

In the summer of 1518, when Rhau-Grunenberg's press was hopelessly clogged, Luther was forced to turn to Lotter to get his reply to Prierias into the public domain. At this point Lotter preferred to cover his bases; he published Luther's text, but in a joint edition with Prierias's original. That way he could be seen not to have taken sides. On the other hand it could not have escaped his attention that Luther was very good business; this dual edition was printed three times in the first year.[43] While the good Catholic in Lotter might have disapproved, the businessman was definitely interested.

In May 1519 Lotter made a first visit to Luther in Wittenberg. It was clear he was now seriously considering opening a branch office there; shrewdly he wooed Luther by exhibiting a sample of the typefaces he would be employing in any putative Wittenberg books. Luther was enthusiastic: to his well-tutored eye, these typefaces bore comparison with those of Froben, the Basel printer whose edition of Luther's collected works had made such an impression on him. What a boon it would be, Luther rhapsodized to Spalatin, to have works printed with a Wittenberg imprint with types of this quality. With Lotter's help Wittenberg would

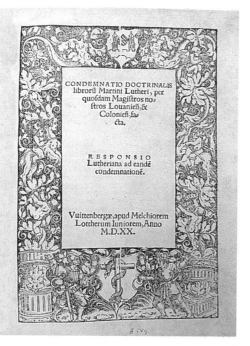

CONDEMNATIO DOCTRINALIS
librorũ Martini Lutheri, per
quosdam Magistros no-
stros Louanien̄,&
Colonien̄,fa-
ĉta.

RESPONSIO
Lutheriana ad eandẽ
condemnatione.

Vuittenbergæ,apud Melchiorem
Lottherum Iuniorem,Anno
M.D.XX.

Melchior Lotter Junior
in Wittenberg

*Transposing the technical experience
and design quality of a major Leipzig
press to Wittenberg was a priority for
Luther in 1519. As we can see here, he
was not disappointed.*

SPECTABILIBVS ET PRAECLARISSIMIS VIRIS MA-
GISTRIS NOSTRIS, DECANO ET FACVLTATI THEO-
LOGIAE LOVANIEN. AMICIS TANQVAM FRATRI-
BVS E. P. V. AMICVS ET CONFRATER A. CAR.
DERTVSEN.

Pectabiles præclariſſimi Magiſtri no
ſtri, amici chariſſimi , literas v̄ras,vii.
nouembris ad me datas,xxvi.eiuſdem
accepi,quihus plane explicatis,quæ ſit
vobis erga Chriſtũ affectio, & quis erga ſanctiſſimã eius fidem zelus. Vidi er
rores quos ex diuerſis ſcriptis & traĉtatibus Lutheri
ſacræ theologiæ magiſtri annotatos,ad me miſiſtis, q
ſane tam rudes , ac palpabiles hæreſes mihi præ ſe ferre
videntur,vt ne diſcipulus quidem theologiæ,ac prima
eius limina ingreſſus , ita labi merito potuiſſet . Et ex
hoc maxime hæreticum ſe probat, ꝙ paratum ſe pro-
fitetur ignem,ac mortem pro illis ſubire.& omnẽ con-
tra ſapientem , hæreticum eſſe. Taceo cauſas,quibus
de ſingulis articulis declarari poſſet,quemadmodum
hæreſim cõtineant,vt prolixitatẽ vitẽ in re nõ ambigua
nec neceſſaria, Miror valde,q̄ hõ tam manifeſte, tanꝗ
pertinaciter in fide errans , & ſuas hæreſes omniquaꝗ
diffundens,impune errare,& alios in pernicioſiſſimos
errores trahere impune ſinitur.Vos certe bene ac lau-
dabiliter facitis,ꝙ peſtiferis hominis dogmatib9 (ꝗtũ
in vobis eſt) obuiam itis,doĉtrinalis condemnationis
antidotũ illis opponendo,ne illius errata etiam vos in-
uoluant,ne ve rei ſitis apud dominũ animarũ, quæ oc-
caſione peruerſæ eius doĉtrinæ pereunt,quemadmodũ
fieret,niſi eiuſdem doĉtrinæ falſitatem ac perniciem cẽ-
ſura veſtra ac veritatis manifeſtatione monſtraretis.
Iuxta illud ſaluatoris.Qui non eſt mecum,contra me
eſt,& qui non colligit mecum,ſpargit. Sed illud in pri-
A ij

even be able to contemplate printing in all of the scholarly languages, Greek and Hebrew included.[44]

The two men were able to build their working relationship during the Leipzig Disputation, when Luther was lodged in Lotter's substantial workshop residence.[45] For Luther, used to Rhau-Grunenberg's much more modest print shop, this busy office must have been a revelation. It was in these weeks, too, that Lotter was engaged in bringing out Luther's commentary on Galatians, and Luther would have been able to examine its pages as they emerged. This, too, would be a conspicuously successful publication.[46] It was probably during the last days of the Leipzig Disputation, when Karlstadt was again the principal disputant on the Wittenberg side, that the deal with Lotter was sealed.

Lotter was now too well established in Leipzig to move to Wittenberg himself. But he contracted with Luther to establish a branch office in Wittenberg, under the direction of his son. The deal brought with the press a portion of Lotter Senior's types; others were obtained from Basel, citadel of German humanism and quality printing.[47] The press was up and running by December 1519, having been found space in Lucas Cranach's capacious factory at Schloβstrasse 1; it was fully operative from the early months of 1520.

The relationship worked well, and indeed, in years to come, as the supply of work dried up in Leipzig, Lotter Senior may have regretted not moving to Wittenberg himself. In all of this Rhau-Grunenberg was not forgotten. Luther would occasionally allow his frustration to boil over, and Rhau-Grunenberg was a convenient scapegoat. But Luther was not one to abandon a loyal friend, and Rhau-Grunenberg continued to receive a fair portion of Luther first editions.

Most of all, Wittenberg was now beginning to assemble the capital and technical infrastructure to deal with the vastly expanding demand for Luther's works. This was just as well, because the following years would see the interest in Luther, heretic, visionary, or German hero, reach new heights.

5.

OUTLAW

MARTIN LUTHER PUBLISHED his first work in 1516, a modest introductory essay to the *Theologia Deutsch* of Johannes Tauler. Four years later, at the end of 1520, he was the most prolific living author since the invention of printing seventy years before. This was a primacy that he would retain until the end of the sixteenth century, by which time his works had been published more frequently than any known author in the history of Western letters. This achievement goes beyond the mere statistical. To understand the full extent of Luther's impact on the book industry, one needs to appreciate how very difficult it had been for living authors to win a hearing at all. The most published authors of the first age of print were almost all historic figures: classical authors such as Cicero or Aristotle, medieval churchmen, and the early church fathers. This stranglehold of the departed was much resented by the new generation of aspiring authors, which is why those who did make the breakthrough, such as Battista Spagnoli and Desiderius Erasmus, were so much admired. But these were both literary men; Luther had somehow made a breakthrough in the most conservative of genres, theology.

Luther owed this extraordinary renown to his own facility as a writer, his versatility, and his willingness to ignore all attempts to silence him. And it is a profound comment on this phenomenon that this public explosion of interest, incubated in the years 1518 and 1519, reached new heights in 1520 and 1521, the period when Luther was officially pronounced excommunicate and outlaw, officially removed from society and beyond redemption. That such a man should be embraced by a new reading public signaled a profound shift in public consciousness. It also brought into sharp relief the extent of the difficulties the church now faced in bringing him to heel.

GOOD WORKS

In the six months after Leipzig, Luther penned sixteen new works. The year 1520 would pass in a similar blaze of creativity. Friends marveled that he could keep up this relentless program of writing, and certainly it took its toll. But Luther, as he confessed to a friend, never struggled to find words for the task in hand. "I have a fast hand and rapid memory. As I write the thoughts just naturally come to me, so I do not have to force myself or ponder over my materials."[1] Once he had committed his thoughts to paper, he seldom revised or made corrections. The manuscripts of his work that have survived show little sign of significant second thoughts.

For all that, 1520 did see a perceptible reorientation of his literary activity. The fury of the polemical exchanges that had characterized the months before and after Leipzig for the time receded, and Luther could turn his mind to other tasks. The pastoral and pedagogic writings that had proved so popular continued. And Luther also found space to take stock of the tumultuous change that had been wrought in his faith: his attitude to his church, his perception of his extraordinary place in the unfolding national crisis, the huge reorientation of the theological foundation stones of his belief. From this great work of mental recalibration would emerge the monumental works of theology and ecclesiology for which the year 1520 has been known.

We now associate the Luther of these years with the three great writings in which he set out the new Reformation agenda: *To the Christian Nobility of the German Nation, The Babylonian Captivity of the Church,* and *The Freedom of a Christian Man.* Contemporaries, it must be said, would not have immediately recognized these as being of a different order from the twenty-five other writings published during the year. Many would have been distracted by the multiple dramas that rumbled through the year, as charge and countercharge followed the fallout from Leipzig, and the pope and Germany's political powers wrestled over Luther's fate. In the short term Luther owed his growing public renown as much to his works of pastoral theology, his careful exposition of a healing Gospel, which struck an increasing chord with the German public.

This reorientation after the dramas of Leipzig was one that many of Luther's friends quietly welcomed. Luther was not at his best in the white heat of controversy. The intensity that he brought to the cut and thrust of academic debate might impress those who witnessed these occasions, but as Leipzig had demonstrated, a wily opponent could lead him in directions where a more politic spirit would not have ventured. Luther was all too inclined to dismiss opponents as ignorant blockheads, where, as Eck had shown, they were anything but; and once driven into dangerous terrain, he would embrace the new radical expression with obstinate defiance. He was not an easy man to follow, as even his most loyal friends were beginning to discover. Particularly in his letters Luther would maintain a running commentary on the polemical exchanges: his mighty efforts to smite his opponents and their feeble replies, their weasel words, poor faith, and cunning, the laughable poverty of their reasoning matched only by their duplicity and witless twisting of his own words. No doubt this was a necessary tension relief at a time when Luther never knew when the next tumult would erupt, or which former friend might speak against him. But for the tight band of his inner circle of confidants these letters often made uncomfortable reading.

So the more subtle among his friends began to lead Luther toward writing tasks that would engage his best qualities. In the summer of 1519

Frederick the Wise had fallen dangerously ill. It was suggested to Luther that the prince would appreciate a comforting meditation, and Luther obliged with a series of beautiful reflections known in Latin as his *Tessaradecas Consolatoria* (*Fourteen Consolations*).[2] Other similar assignments were soon put his way.

Another obvious outlet for Luther's boundless energy was the spiritual needs of his congregation. One remarkable letter from these years explains why he found it so difficult to make time to translate his explanation of the Lord's Prayer into Latin. He certainly wanted to do this, he wrote, but he had his lectures and his preaching, his duties to the university, seeing another publication through the press; and in addition "each evening I expound to children and ordinary folk the Commandments and the Lord's Prayer."[3] Every evening. At this time he usually also preached three times a week. These relatively mundane pastoral tasks mattered to Luther enormously, and from this experience, enriched by his constantly evolving theological understanding, came some of the richest writings of these years.

One such was *The Treatise on Good Works;* among all the mass of texts that Luther penned during these years he himself regarded it as the best thing he had written.[4] Once again the initiative came from Spalatin, though when Luther began it he apparently intended nothing more than the preparation of a sermon for his Wittenberg congregation. In the event the task took him two months, and the brief homily became a substantial and fundamental work. Luther's intention was to spell out clearly, for a lay audience, the practical implications of his rejection of good works as a means to earn salvation. Luther set out the alternative with his usual uncompromising clarity: "the first and highest, the most precious of all good works is faith in Christ."

Note for yourself, then, how far apart these two are: keeping the first Commandment with outward works only, and keeping it with inward trust. For the last makes true, living children of God, the other only makes worse idolatry and the most mischievous hypocrites on earth.

Here Luther sanctified the faithfulness of the everyday, the dutiful performance of the obligations of one's calling, as opposed to what he called self-elected work, such as "running to the convent, singing, reading . . . founding and ornamenting churches . . . going to Rome and to the saints, curtsying and bowing the knee." The search for God's purpose in the everyday was the human healing consequence of justification by faith, the theology of salvation that Luther would expound in its definitive form later in the year in *The Freedom of a Christian Man*.

The dedication of *The Treatise on Good Works*, to the elector's brother and heir, Duke John, also contains a short but moving defense of Luther's vocation as a vernacular writer.

And although I know full well and hear every day that many people think little of me and say that I only write little pamphlets and sermons in German for the uneducated laity, I do not let that stop me. Would to God that in my lifetime I had, to my fullest ability, helped one layman to be better! I would be quite satisfied, thank God, and quite willing then to let all my little books perish. Whether the making of many large books is an art and of benefit to Christendom, I leave for others to judge. But I believe that if I were of a mind to write big books of their kind, I could perhaps, with God's help, do it more readily than they could write my kind of little discourse.

I will most gladly leave to anybody else the glory of greater things. I will not be ashamed in the slightest to preach to the uneducated layman and write for him in German. Although I may have little skill at it myself, it seems to me that if we had hitherto busied ourselves in this very task and were of a mind to do more of it in the future, Christendom would have reaped no small advantage and would have been more benefitted by this than by those heavy, weight tomes and those *questiones* which are only handled in the schools among learned schoolsmen.[5]

The reading public obviously agreed. *The Treatise on Good Works* was an immediate success, with four editions from Melchior Lotter before the end of the year, and reprints in Augsburg, Nuremberg, Basel, and Hagenau. Luther's *Sermon on the Mass,* tutoring the laity on another key aspect of his new theology, went through ten editions in 1520 alone.[6] If we are seeking an explanation of why so many Germans were drawn to Luther, despite the wild, extravagant denunciations of the established church and the bitter, angry polemic against his critics, we have to recognize that this was not the Luther that many readers saw. Rather they embraced the patient, gentle expositor whose explorations of the Christian life offered them comfort and peace.

DUE PROCESS

At the Leipzig Disputation both parties had agreed that formal judgment should be rendered by the universities of Paris and Erfurt. Neither university viewed this charge with any great enthusiasm. Erfurt would eventually decline to take a position, while Paris delayed a response for two years, by which point events had moved on. It was left to others to fill the void, informed not only by the protocols of the disputation, but by the rancid charge and countercharge of the ensuing pamphlet war. On August 30, 1519, the University of Cologne issued a public proclamation condemning a number of teachings found in Luther's works. The basis of this condemnation seems to have been the second collective edition of Luther's works, published in Strasbourg on the basis of Froben's Basel prototype.[7] The Cologne articles were then delivered to the Faculty of Theology of the University of Louvain, who in November issued their own judgment. These statements, from two distinguished institutions somewhat removed from the partisan hurly-burly of Erfurt and Leipzig, were important and influential, and played a critical role in marshaling conservative opinion against Luther. The published texts of these judgments would also guide the renewed deliberations of Luther's cause in Rome.

A published version of the universities' judgments was soon in Luther's hands, and he fired off a reply.[8] He also engaged in a polemical exchange with the bishop of Meissen, who had taken up the cudgels on behalf of Duke George, the host of the Leipzig Disputation and now emerging as a dogged defender of the established way. Clearly, though, resolution of the matter required a definitive verdict from Rome, where the initially swift engagement with Luther's heresy had been hopelessly sidetracked by the complex politics of the Empire in 1519. In January 1520 the process against Luther was formally reopened. Even now the required sense of urgency seemed decidedly lacking. Commissions were formed, dissolved, and reconstituted. It was only with the arrival of Johann Eck, summoned by Pope Leo as the acknowledged champion of orthodoxy and Luther expert, that matters moved forward. In May 1520 Eck had prepared a draft for discussion in consistory, and in June this was finally issued as the papal bull *Exsurge Domine*. The bull, like all such documents, took its name from the first words of the text: in this case the words of the psalmist, "Arise, oh Lord, and judge thy own cause."

This was very much Eck's document, a much more comprehensive condemnation of Luther's teaching than had been favored by others in the Curia. It ranged far beyond the original issue of indulgences, with forty-one articles of condemnation drawn from the whole range of Luther's writings. It declared Luther to be in error in the matter of penance, the Lord's Supper, excommunication, the power of the pope, good works, free will, and purgatory. It was a manifesto of Luther's movement in reverse. If not recanted, all of the errors listed here would bring Luther, his allies, and his protectors under the penalties of excommunication and interdict. It was a hugely influential statement of where the church would stand in all the major issues of doctrine, church practice, and government raised by Luther in the escalating conflict, anticipating many of the doctrinal positions affirmed by the Council of Trent forty years later.

The bull was also a legal document, and formally at least held out the hope of repentance and reconciliation. Luther was allowed sixty days to signal his return to obedience, this grace period to begin at the point when the bull had been formally posted on the cathedral doors in Rome and the three local German dioceses of Brandenburg, Meissen, and Merseburg. The honor of formally serving this document was given to Johann Eck. This proved to be a far more difficult assignment than marshaling the commission in Rome. Eck's return to Germany was anything but triumphant. The posting of the bull in Rome had been accompanied by a burning of Luther's books, but an attempt to replicate this ceremony in Mainz caused such public anger that the town executioner abandoned the task. In Leipzig Eck was greeted with mocking satirical verses and forced to take refuge in the monastery of St. Paul. He left without having accomplished his task; when the university did, on Duke George's insistence, post the bull, it was smeared with mud and defaced. This was also the case elsewhere in the vicinity, such as Torgau; in Erfurt students tossed copies of the bull into the river.[9] Although Eck did, through various means, succeed in distributing the bull as its terms stipulated to the major cathedrals, not a single copy of the original broadsheet version—the version that would have been posted in this way—has so far been traced today.[10] In many jurisdictions the local church authorities preferred to avoid public disturbances by delaying publication, or avoiding it altogether.

With the formal promulgation of the bull so comprehensively disrupted it was left to Germany's printers to fill the gap. In addition to the official broadsheet version of the bull it had, like Luther's ninety-five theses, also been issued as a pamphlet, and this became a European best seller. The original Rome version was reprinted in Paris, Antwerp, and Krakow. In Germany it was printed in the loyally Catholic jurisdictions of Cologne, Ingolstadt, Würzburg, and Bamberg.[11] These were not

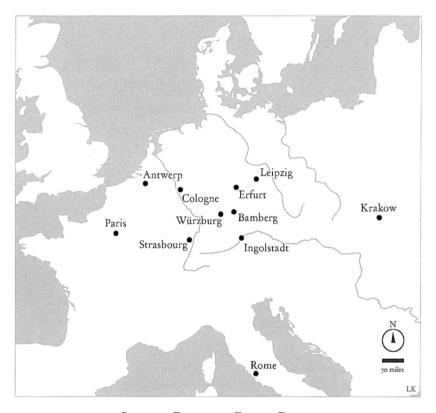

PUBLISHED EDITIONS OF *EXSURGE DOMINE*

places where Luther's works had been extensively printed, but the bull was also published in places that had eagerly embraced Luther, like Leipzig, Erfurt, and Strasbourg. Once again printers were happy to hedge their bets. Johann Schott of Strasbourg published the papal bull a matter of weeks after he had enjoyed a runaway success with Luther's *Babylonian Captivity*. His colleague Johann Prüss published both the bull and Luther's *Freedom of a Christian Man*. The Leipzig edition was published by Martin Landsberg, a printer with a long-established Wittenberg connection.[12]

Of course, there was every reason why Germans would have wanted to see this text, whether they sympathized with Luther or his opponents. Many even of those who deplored Luther's uncompromising positions were still, like Erasmus, made uneasy by the sweeping nature of the bull's condemnations. Others were simply curious. It is notable that in addition to the dozen pamphlet versions of *Exsurge Domine,* there were also at least two editions in German: an Ingolstadt edition in a translation supplied by Johann Eck, and another published by Peter Quentel in Cologne.[13] This represented a significant change in strategy, quite possibly conceived on Eck's own initiative. While in Rome it seems still to have been preferred to treat Luther's case as a judicial matter, to be settled according to the church's established procedures, in Germany at least there was a dawning recognition that it would be necessary to fight fire with fire.

Luther's own response was not slow in coming. He was aware of the bull's main provisions long before a copy reached him, through several pairs of hands, in Wittenberg on October 10. The rector of the university would protest at this irregular delivery "in a thieving manner and with villainous cunning," but Eck's reluctance to send his own messenger to Wittenberg is understandable, given its reception elsewhere. Luther's first reaction was to treat the bull as a personal concoction of Eck, and he taunted his opponent for his failure to deliver it personally. He followed the same line in a Latin pamphlet, *Against the Execrable Bull of Antichrist,* also published in a German version.[14] These partisan efforts served to rally supporters, but they were clearly not sufficient. In December 1520, and at the urging of Frederick the Wise, Luther penned a more substantial and considered defense of the articles condemned in the bull.[15] But with the delivery of the bull to Wittenberg the clock was ticking on the sixty-day grace period for Luther's formal response to Rome. For this he planned a more dramatic gesture.

MANIFESTOS

The extraordinary dramas and tensions of these months had kept much of Germany transfixed: from the frantic local conflicts that erupted around the posting of the bull, to the urgent private political discussions where Luther's fate was debated and bargained over. Yet somehow, amidst all this sound and fury, Luther found the energy and mental space to compose the three great works that have come to define his movement. These three writings were *To the Christian Nobility of the German Nation, The Babylonian Captivity of the Church,* and *The Freedom of a Christian Man.* Although sometimes considered as three components of a program or agenda, they were, in fact, very different, all responding, as was Luther's way, to different aspects of the situation in which he found himself: the complex problems of authority and jurisdiction; the profound implications of his soured relationship with the church hierarchy; and the fundamental theological reflections on which Luther based his new understanding of the Christian relationship with a merciful God.

By the beginning of 1520 Luther was clear enough how things would end in Rome; his definite condemnation was only a matter of time. His appeal to a general council was a deft legal maneuver, but no more than that; successive popes had definitively pronounced against any such appeals, and Luther's attempt to invoke a general council would form one more article in the condemnation of his heresies in *Exsurge Domine.* So in the summer of 1520 Luther decided to preempt papal condemnation by inviting the new Emperor Charles V to take in hand the long-delayed reform of church abuses within the German Empire.

In making this appeal, Luther could associate himself with a long tradition of church criticism that had recently taken on a profoundly nationalistic tone. A large part of the resentment of indulgences had been the perception (not always rooted in reality) that large sums of money were in this way being drained from Germany to enrich Rome. Complaints of this sort were regularly aired among the grievances (*gravamina*) submitted by the German Estates at meetings of the Imperial Diet.

In his address *To the Christian Nobility of the German Nation* Luther set out to show that the necessary reform of the church could only be addressed by the German people acting independently.[16] The Roman Church had become so irredeemably corrupt that it lay beyond reform. In making the case, as ever, Luther deepened and broadened the theological precepts on which he made this appeal. To empower the German laity, Luther had first to demolish the ring of fortifications behind which lay the claim to papal primacy. These included the pope's claim to be the final and infallible interpreter of Scripture, and the assertion that only a pope could call a general council. Most critical was the first line of defense: the pope's claim to superiority over any secular power. Luther's demolition of this claim was based on a challenge to the radical separation between the lay and clerical estates that had been a fundamental organizational principle of medieval society. Luther, on the contrary, denied that the distinction between priest and layman had any scriptural validity. Rather, all baptized Christians were, by virtue of their baptism, members of a priesthood of all believers.

The manifesto went on to say a great deal more. There was a long and eloquent denunciation of the total corruption of the papacy, which had turned Rome into a giant bazaar:

> At Rome there is such a state of things that baffles description. There is buying, selling, exchanging, cheating, roaring, lying, deceiving, robbing, stealing, luxury, debauchery, villainy, and every sort of contempt of God that Antichrist himself could not possibly rule more abominably. Venice, Antwerp, Cairo are nothing compared to this fair and market at Rome, except that things are done there with some reason and justice, while here they are done as the Devil himself wills.

Was Luther here recalling the bewildered young monk, amazed at the cynicism and worldliness he encountered on his trip to Rome in 1510? As he warmed to his theme, he enrolled the sympathies of all who had experience of the multitude of fees that smoothed the way of the church and civil government.

> What has been stolen, robbed, is here legalized. Here vows are annulled. Here the monk may buy freedom to quit his order. Here the

clergy can purchase the marriage state, the children of harlots obtain legitimacy, dishonor and shame be made respectable, evil re-
pute and crime be knighted and ennobled. Here marriage is allowed
that is within the forbidden degree, or is otherwise defective. Oh
what oppressing and plunder rule here! So that it seems as if the
whole canon law were only established in order to snare as much
money as possible, from which everyone who would be a Christian
must deliver himself.[17]

The tract closed with a potpourri of radical recommendations: that
all the mendicant orders should be combined into one; that clerical celibacy should be abolished; that masses for the dead should be discontin-
ued; that usury should be prohibited. But it was the "priesthood of all
believers" that would be the radical time bomb ticking away at the heart
of this work, a loose phrase that Luther would have plentiful opportunity to regret.

Published in August 1520, *To the Christian Nobility* was an instant sensation. Lotter, no doubt working on more than one press, contrived an
edition of four thousand copies, quite unprecedented for this sort of
work. Even so it sold out within a fortnight. Luther was able to make
some modest additions for a second edition, which appeared before the
end of the month. A remarkable ten further editions spread the message through Germany through the now customary chain, Leipzig,
Augsburg, Basel, and Strasbourg.[18] Luther was aware that not all approved the sharply polemical tone, but it hit its mark with the first intended audience, Germany's princes and civic leaders. Luther had deftly
associated himself with their cause, and with their long-standing grievances about the financial power of the church. They could warm to his
neat encapsulation of these sentiments, without necessarily seizing the
radicalism of the underlying theological precepts. At a time when Luther's fate was being actively debated among those preparing for the next
crucial meeting of the Imperial Diet, this was a vital constituency.

Even before *To the Christian Nobility* was published, Luther had turned his attention to the second of these three great works, *The Baby-lonian Captivity of the Church*.[19] The title alone reflects his sense of utter alienation from the institutional church. The Christian people were, like the people of Israel, held in tyranny and bondage by the Roman hierarchy. This was a complex work, written in Latin for a scholarly audience. Luther began rather sensationally by repudiating some of his early writings, which he now found overly timid. For Luther's restless search for fundamental truths had led him to a root-and-branch reassessment of the Roman sacramental system. Of the seven sacraments that underpinned the Christian life, Luther was now prepared to recognize only three: the Eucharist, baptism, and (with reservations) penance. It was in his treatment of the Mass that Luther most stunned his readers. The Church had surely erred in denying the laity the cup: in this, he now calmly proposed, the Bohemian Hus had been correct. But the core of the issue lay in his denial of the central sacrificial act that lay at the heart of the Mass, transubstantiation.

In asking his clerical readers to repudiate their whole sacramental system, Luther offered his most shocking view of his new theological program. The Mass lay at the heart of the clerical office. By paring back the sacraments from seven to three, Luther had demolished the church's role as a sacramental institution, nourishing the Christian from cradle (baptism) to death (extreme unction). No wonder many of its readers regarded this as the most scandalous of all Luther's writings.

The Freedom of a Christian Man took a different tone altogether. After the excoriating, unsparing exposition of reform in church and society, this was Luther describing his personal revelation of salvation that awaited all true Christians. The freedom of the Christian man was the liberation that comes to a Christian justified by faith. With this, the last of Luther's major expository works of 1520, Luther brought to its conclusion the reflections on the Christian life so powerfully begun with *The Treatise on Good Works* some six months before. Luther freely affirms that the true Christian will live a life of service to his fellow believers, moved by God's love and love for his fellow men. But the good works that flow from Christian charity will never win salvation, for that salvation is already assured. Accepted in faith, the message of Christ brings assurance to all Christians without further demonstration of piety. Thus is the whole penitential system of the church overthrown, though, without the theatricals of Luther's other major writings in this period, the radical impact of this new theology may well have escaped the first generation of readers.

The Freedom of a Christian Man has the most complicated publication history of the three great treatises of this year. The German edition, probably completed first, was dedicated to the mayor of the city of Zwickau, Hieronymus Mühlpfordt. The Latin edition was prefaced instead by an open letter to the pope.[20] This represents a last, rather resigned response on Luther's part to the incessant and increasingly frantic diplomatic activity of Karl von Miltitz. In August von Miltitz had informed the elector that he would pursue another attempt at mediation. Luther was skeptical, especially when he learned that *Exsurge Domine* had already been published. But he agreed to meet von Miltitz and was persuaded that no harm might come of a letter assuring the pope that their quarrel was not a personal one. This Luther duly appended to the Latin text, praising Leo for his personal piety and denouncing those that surrounded him. Leo, he assured the pope with fraternal concern, was merely the sheep among wolves. Quite what anyone would have made of this in Rome is hard to imagine, particularly if it had arrived with copies of Luther's *To the Christian Nobility,* with its vivid tour of the domain of Antichrist, or the *Babylonian Captivity.* But if it helped present Luther to the more important audience gathering for the Diet as a man eager for peace, then it would have served some purpose.

Both Latin and German editions of *The Freedom of a Christian Man* were published on November 20, the climax of an extraordinarily fertile period of literary creativity. In the space of one year Luther had written twenty-eight different works, which ranged across the gamut of pastoral instruction, pungent works of polemic, appeals for reform, and fundamental works of theology. Only the continued publication of his lectures

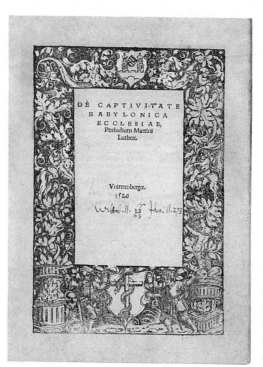

TWO MAJOR MANIFESTOS OF 1520

De captivitate babylonica ecclesiae (The Babylonian Captivity of the Church)/Von der freyheyt eynes Christen menschen (The Freedom of a Christian Man).

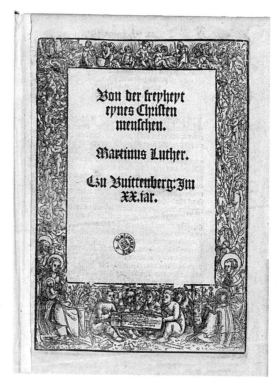

Already the combination of Melchior Lotter's craftsmanship and Cranach's new revolutionary title-page designs was transforming the look of Wittenberg books.

and commentaries was squeezed out by the pressing obligations of this crowded year. Once again Germany's printers were the beneficiaries, turning out over three hundred editions of Luther's works, along with a considerable number written by others drawn into the controversies on either side. But the time had surely come for resolution. As *The Freedom of a Christian Man* left the print shop, Luther had three weeks left to make his reply to *Exsurge Domine*. He had conceived a special ceremony to mark the occasion.

WORMS

On December 10, 1520, Philip Melanchthon posted on the door of the university church the invitation to colleagues and students to witness "a pious and religious spectacle, for perhaps now is the time when Antichrist must be revealed." This was to take place not in the customary place of academic debates, but outside the Holy Cross Chapel, at the east end of the town, near the stockyards, where cattle were butchered and the clothes of those who had died of plague were burned. Here a pyre had been erected, and once the solemn gathering had assembled and the fire had been lit, Luther cast into it a range of representational texts of the old church: papal decretals, a copy of the Canon Law, and some of the polemical works of Eck and Jerome Emser. Luther kept a list, which he defiantly shared with Spalatin in a letter later that day.[21] At the last moment Luther plucked from his cloak a copy of the papal bull, and that, too, was hurled into the flames.

In many respects this was the most unfortunate of the dramatic set-piece events of the Reformation. Several of Luther's colleagues had misgivings about the burning of Canon Law; his defense, after all, had to this point relied on due process, and this seemed out of keeping with Luther's insistence on appeals to his professorial status and the authority of the general council. The original intention had been to include in the pyrotechnics a copy of Duns Scotus, as representative of the despised

Scholastics, but none of the Wittenberg professors had been willing to sacrifice their copy of such a valuable book.[22] It is surprising indeed to find Philip Melanchthon associated with such a gaudy occasion, but the loyal Philip had long recognized that Luther was a force of nature not to be contained. Needless to say the students present reacted with exuberant enthusiasm, adding their own offerings to the blazing pyre, and the professors were obliged to retreat with what could be mustered of their dignity.

This tawdry act of theater ultimately achieved very little, beyond providing an opportunity to relieve some of the pent-up tension of the long period of waiting for papal judgment. On January 3, 1521, the grace period for Luther's submission having expired, a new bull declared Luther's final excommunication. In practice, though, the crucial event had occurred two months previously when Frederick the Wise had met the papal legate, Jerome Aleander, in Cologne. Frederick made unambiguously clear that he would not enforce the bull against Luther. The conflict, if it were to be resolved at all, would only be resolved politically.

So for Luther life went on much as before. Although formally released from his monastic vows, Luther had no immediate plans to abandon his black habit or to leave the monastery. He did, however, welcome release from the obligation to perform the monastic devotions, with which he had fallen hopelessly in arrears. The greater impact was on the wider Wittenberg community. While Luther had had many months and years to prepare for a life outside the Roman obedience, his colleagues suddenly had to face a future in a university now identified as a rogue institution radically separated from the wider Germany and international intellectual community. Perhaps indeed this was the real purpose of the book burning of December 10, a public act of separation on behalf of the community. Not all approved: in 1521 Wittenberg would witness a sharp fall in student enrollments, as parents considered the implications of committing their children to an institution now effectively in schism. But those who remained lost none of their enthusiasm for Luther. In the days before Lent the students integrated into their traditional revels pointed mockery of the pope and his cardinals. And it was in these same months that Lucas Cranach embarked on his definitive pictorial representation of the separation of the churches, the *Passion of Christ and Antichrist*.[23] Thirteen paired sets of woodcuts depicted on one side Christ and his disciples, and on the other, the pope in his pomp. While Christ preaches and performs acts of mercy, the pope feasts; while Christ drives the money changers from the Temple, the pope gathers money into his indulgence chest. As so often, the Wittenberg movement met Luther at his most radical and scandalous and embraced the consequences.

While these events were played out in Wittenberg, the Imperial Diet was locked into an angry trial of strength over Luther's fate. The young Emperor Charles V was insistent that he would not allow Luther to appear at the Diet; the Estates, in turn, refused to allow Luther to be condemned unheard. Only after weeks of wrangling was a compromise of sorts achieved. Luther was to be summoned to answer for his writings, but without any disputation: Worms was not to be a platform for the heretic to make his case. On March 6, Charles put his reluctant signature to the letter of summons, and the imperial herald set off to bring Luther from Wittenberg. For the duration of the hearing he would be under the emperor's protection.

The herald arrived in Wittenberg on March 26; within a week Luther had departed, accompanied by three colleagues and the good wishes of the city council, which provided a generous sum toward travel expenses. It rapidly became clear that this financial support would be largely superfluous, as Luther was warmly welcomed at every staging post: at Leipzig, Naumburg, and then at Erfurt, where he was conducted by a large civic delegation to his former home at the Augustinian house. The following day, a Sunday, Luther preached, as he would again in Gotha and Eisenach later in the week. Everywhere Luther appeared he was surrounded by curious and sympathetic crowds. Forewarned by the angry reactions to attempts to exhibit the papal bull, those who did not support Luther kept a low profile. Yet this rapid trek across Germany,

PASSION OF CHRIST AND ANTICHRIST

Cranach's wonderfully realized image of the pope personally supervising the indulgence trade was as evocative and hard-hitting as any modern cartoon.

constantly in the public eye, took its toll on Luther. By the time his party had reached Frankfurt he had fallen sick. There was little time for recuperation, since two days later he was in Worms.

Three years before, he had made his way to Heidelberg and then to Augsburg largely unknown. Now in Worms the city trumpets were sounded to herald the arrival of a distinguished guest; one hundred horsemen rode out to escort him through the gates; as he descended his carriage a monk reached down to touch his hem. This was all witnessed by informants of the incredulous papal legate, who had counseled against the emperor receiving Luther.[24] Aleander's own arrival had been very different: despite liberal supplies of money he had been unable to secure anything but a small, unheated room, and he was forced to endure gibes and threatening gestures when he ventured forth on the streets. He noted, too, that all the booksellers' stalls were crammed with Luther's writings and exhibited his picture for sale. Aleander was used to conducting his business behind closed doors; now he had seen at firsthand just how forcefully Luther's cause had engaged the German nation, and he was badly rattled. "Now the whole of Germany is in full revolt," he reported to Rome; "nine tenths raise the war cry 'Luther,' while the watchword of the other tenth who are indifferent to Luther is 'Death to the Roman Curia.'" And Luther had clearly struck a chord with his appeal for a general council: according to Aleander, "All of them have written on their banners a demand for a council to be held in Germany, even those who are favorable to us, or rather to themselves."[25]

After his triumphant entrance Luther's actual appearance before the Diet may have seemed somewhat anticlimactic. In the late afternoon of the following day Luther was summoned to the crowded room where the Imperial Estates were gathered. Here he was confronted by a pile of his books. The imperial spokesman, Johann von der Ecken, now asked whether Luther would acknowledge that he had written them, and whether he would renounce the heresies they contained.[26] At the request of Luther's lawyer the titles of the books were read and Luther acknowledged his authorship; but, to general perplexity, he asked for more time to consider his reply to the second question. This was grudgingly granted, so the next day Luther returned, and managed, despite interruption, to repeat his denunciation of the papacy while differentiating other of his writings that dealt with practical Christian morality. After a brief adjournment von der Ecken pressed for a direct answer: Would Luther recant? This last hope of reconciliation and compromise Luther now definitively repudiated:

> Unless I am convinced by testimonies of the Holy Scripture or evident reason (for I believe neither in the pope nor councils alone, since it has been established that they have often erred and contradicted themselves), I am bound by the Scriptures adduced by me, and my conscience has been taken captive by the Word of God, and I am neither able nor willing to recant, since it is neither safe nor right to act against conscience. God help me. Amen.[27]

The young emperor was scandalized, but many of those present believed that Luther had handled himself well; they insisted that a small commission should be established to examine him further. To the emperor's frustration and humiliation, three days were set aside for these discussions, but it was Luther who brought them to an end. On April 26, he left the city, escorted again by the imperial herald. In his absence the wrangling continued, and it was only on May 26 that the emperor finally got his way and Luther was placed under the imperial ban.

Long before this Luther had disappeared. The evidence of both popular enthusiasm and support for Luther among his fellow princes may have emboldened the elector to pursue the dangerous course on which he had now determined. Rather than give Luther up, he would be spirited away to protective custody. Thus without open defiance of the emperor, Luther would be protected from the consequences of the imperial interdict. So it was that in the Franconian Forest beyond Eisenach, Luther and his companions were intercepted by a band of mounted knights. Luther was taken, dressed as a knight, to an isolated castle, the Wartburg.

SECLUSION

Luther would remain at the Wartburg for ten months. At first his location, even the fact that he was alive, was a closely guarded secret: in Wittenberg only Melanchthon, Spalatin, and Nicolas von Amsdorf, another stalwart friend, knew of his whereabouts. But the steady stream of messengers, letters, and books must have brought an ever-widening circle into the elector's confidence.[28] If they did not know precisely where he was, many must have known Luther was alive from the evidence of his continuing literary activity.

The months at the Wartburg were not easy for Luther. He had lived the last four years in a fury of action, surrounded by people, shaping events. Now he was alone, more alone even than his first months in the monastery, and without the monastic offices to shape and guide his devotions. Luther appreciated the irony of this, telling one correspondent, "I have no more news, since I am a hermit, an anchorite, truly a monk, though neither shaved nor cowled."[29] In his letters to Wittenberg friends—a real lifeline—Luther insists so frequently on his patient obedience to God's will that the effort this required of him is palpable. He also had to believe that in his absence his movement, his case, and his university were all in safe hands. He hated being out of the swing of things, passing on such snippets of news as came his way and yearning for more. But at least he could still write, and this he did, incessantly. The messengers from Wittenberg brought news, supplies, and sometimes proof sheets for correction; they departed back with new manuscripts for the press.

Initially, at least, he occupied himself with the reverberations from Worms and the papal condemnation. In June Luther penned a refutation of the Louvain theology professor Jacobus Latomus, who had offered a considered justification of the faculty's condemnation of Luther's teachings. Luther also took the first opportunity to reply to the adverse

THE WARTBURG

After the excitements of Worms and four years at the center of events, it was not easy for Luther to endure the isolation of the Wartburg.

judgment of the Paris Sorbonne.[30] The delivery of Jerome Emser's latest contribution to their rather fruitless exchanges also merited reply.[31] But Luther's removal from the hurly-burly of the pamphlet wars in due course had the rather positive consequence that the polemical aspect of Luther's writing steadily receded. There was also the practical point that all of the correspondence to and from the Wartburg passed through Georg Spalatin, who could, therefore, exercise some prudent control over the texts that should be passed to the printer. A sharp denunciation of Albrecht of Mainz, who had announced a new indulgence for his relic collection in Halle, fell under this embargo.[32]

For the most part Luther was happy to turn to less pungent tasks. For his absent congregation he offered a long reflection on confession and several smaller meditations on the Psalms. He cleared away the last stages of a German translation of the *Magnificat* that had been interrupted by the journey to Worms. By the summer he was ready to embark on the two major projects that would occupy much of his time at the Wartburg. The first would be a sequence of postils, or homilies on the Epistles and Gospels prescribed for the Sundays and festival days of the church year. These could be used either for private devotion or as models for sermons.

One of the cruelest deprivations of Luther's months at the Wartburg was his inability to preach. He was by now deeply rooted in Wittenberg. He fed off the devotion and affection of his Wittenberg congregation, who provided a vital sounding board by which he could measure the clarity and coherence of his lay theology. In this time of separation Luther could at least provide spiritual comfort, and he bent himself to the task with his usual sense of purpose.

This major project would stretch over several months and involved several changes of mind on Luther's part. These were dictated partly by the difficulty of securing the necessary reference texts from Wittenberg; there was also the perpetual problem of the quality of Wittenberg printing. By this point Luther had finally recognized that Rhau-Grunenberg could not be trusted with complex projects. In the period immediately before Lotter's recruitment from Leipzig, Rhau-Grunenberg had got himself into serious difficulties publishing Luther's second lecture series on the Psalms, having printed far too many copies of the first sheets. Clearly he had miscalculated the print run, and probably the paper necessary for such a big book. The solution, which would also be adopted for other substantial projects, was to publish in segments or fascicules, purchased on a subscription basis and then bound together by the owner when the work was complete. This served to salvage Rhau-Grunenberg's work on the Psalm lectures, though Luther hinted darkly that he would insist on a reprint "in a more distinguished typeface" on the Lotter press.[33] But with Luther at the Wartburg and unable to supervise the press in person, the relationship with Rhau-Grunenberg came close to total collapse. For some reason, and against all experience and logic, Luther had assigned the printing of the postils to Rhau-Grunenberg. But when he saw the proof sheets of Rhau-Grunenberg's work on his book on confession (*Von der Beicht*) he could contain himself no further.[34] The resulting tirade to Spalatin is worth quoting at length:

> I have received the second and third set of printed sheets of the book *On Confession* from you; I had previously received them from Philip, too, along with the first set. I cannot say how unhappy and disgusted I am with the printing. I wish I had sent nothing in German. It is printed so poorly, so carelessly and confusedly, to say nothing of the bad typefaces and paper. John the printer is always the same old John and does not improve. For goodness sake, under no circumstances let him print any of the German postils! What I have sent of them should be stored away, or rather returned to me so that I may send it somewhere else. What good does it do to work hard if such sloppiness and confusion causes other printers [who may reprint from this first edition] to make more mistakes that are worse. I do not want the Gospels and Epistles to be sinned against in this way; it is better to hide them than to bring them out in such a form. Therefore I am sending you nothing now, although I have finished almost ten large manuscript sheets of the [postil]. I shall send nothing more until I have seen that these sordid money-grubbers, in printing books, care less for their profits than for the benefit of the reader. For what does such a printer seem to think except, "It is enough that I get my money; let the readers worry about what and how they will read it."[35]

Having thus skewered Rhau-Grunenberg he added rather ominously, "Philip has sent me three sets of printed sheets of the *Latomus*, which I like very much." This, of course, was printed by Melchior Lotter.[36] Luther also seems to have ensured that responsibility for publishing his work *On Confession* was passed to Lotter after Rhau-Grunenberg's unsatisfactory first edition. Lotter reprinted it twice in 1521.[37]

Allowance should obviously be made here for Luther's state of mind. He was at this point suffering seriously from constipation. The packages from Wittenberg also brought medicines, with which he was obliged to dose himself regularly. He chafed at the lack of exercise, and attempts to cheer him by the occasional ride out with his hosts achieved nothing, since he had little interest in hunting ("this bittersweet pleasure of heroes . . . a worthy occupation indeed for men with nothing to do").[38] The regime in the Wartburg was taking its toll, both physically and mentally. His previous weekly bulletin had complained bitterly that part of one of his texts seemed to have been mislaid, and that the *Magnificat* was taking such an inordinate time to appear.[39] It is clear from this that Luther very much missed his day-to-day involvement in the work of the press. He was used not only to exercising close supervision over the quality of Rhau-Grunenberg's work, but also to managing the work flow through the printers' shops. On August 6 he told Spalatin, "I wish [the printing] of this *Defense* of Philip's postponed until such time as the presses are idle, unless you think otherwise. The same should have been done with Psalm *Exsurgat,* because there are other things that are more necessary and urgent."[40] And after calming down, he did allow printing of the postils to continue: "But I do want it to be printed on folio paper with Lotter's typefaces, since it will be a large book. I would divide it into four parts of the year, from quarter to quarter, so that it will not be too heavy and expensive."[41] This was a recurring theme. Earlier in the summer he had told Spalatin that he would be shifting some of the material from one volume of the postils to another, to keep down the price: "I am doing this so that not too big a book frightens readers and buyers."[42]

Of course, and rather paradoxically, it is only because he is away from Wittenberg that one has this positive proof of the true extent of Luther's everyday involvement with the nuts and bolts of the printing process. He has, in his absence, to articulate instructions that normally he would have conveyed in person, in the print shop, talking to Rhau-Grunenberg or Lotter. But these letters do provide very precious evidence of Luther's keen understanding of the technical and practical disciplines of bringing his works into the public domain. Of his fellow authors perhaps only Desiderius Erasmus showed such a close appreciation of how important it was to be directly engaged with every stage of the work.

The winter of 1521 brought other trials. Luther had cause to be increasingly concerned about the loyal but wayward Karlstadt and his influence over the university in Luther's absence. In the fury at Luther's condemnation and nervousness over his fate it was dangerously evident that the reform movement might get out of hand. In December Luther paid a brief, perilous, and clandestine visit back to Wittenberg to confer with allies as to what should be done. Returning to the Wartburg he devoted himself to a new task, the translation of the Bible into German. He began with the New Testament, and within eleven weeks had completed a first draft, though it was always intended that this would be thoroughly revised, with the help of colleagues, on his return. This, it was clear, could not be much longer delayed. The plan had been that Luther would remain out of sight at the Wartburg until Easter, but the news of the confusion in the churches of Wittenberg and turbulence in the university faculty was ever more alarming. Luther would not have been comforted to know that Melanchthon had despaired of restraining Karlstadt and was considering leaving Wittenberg altogether. Ignoring the elector's firm instructions that it was not yet prudent for Luther to be seen in public, Luther left the Wartburg at the end of February, resurfacing in Wittenberg, to general astonishment, on March 6, 1522. The age of protest was at an end. Now began the harder work of creating a new church.

6.

BRAND LUTHER

WHEN LUTHER RETURNED FROM the Wartburg in March 1522 he had been a public figure for four years. An increasingly fascinated German public had followed every twist and turn of his dramatic life: his confrontations with authority, his bold defiance, his improbable escapes from terrible disaster. Needless to say his reappearance in Wittenberg after ten months of seclusion was a major public event. His sudden disappearance on the road from Worms had been the subject of anxious, even anguished, speculation among his followers. Albrecht Dürer was not the only one who suspected he had been secretly done away with; Dürer thought they would come for Erasmus next.[1] So when Luther reappeared, hale and hearty, his followers rejoiced that once again he had defied the odds and triumphed against the forces massed against him.

For Luther's enemies, also increasingly numerous, came the dawning realization that the best chance to lay hands on Luther and put an end to his defiance had now passed. For the rest of his life he would be living, and increasingly rooted, in Wittenberg. As an excommunicated heretic and outlaw the protection that could be afforded by the electors of Saxony was strictly circumscribed; any longer journeys would now be freighted with risk. So while Luther would continue to minister to his

Wittenberg flock for another twenty-four years, for those elsewhere in Germany, his allies and his printed books would have to stand surrogate for his commanding presence.

By the end of 1522, nearly five years after he first addressed a German public in the *Sermon on Indulgence and Grace,* Luther had published some 160 different writings. About a third of these were in Latin, and these texts were important for, as we shall see in the next chapter, persuading clerical colleagues to join his crusade for a reformed Christianity and played a vital role in the success of his movement. But what made Luther truly exceptional was his willingness to step outside his own clerical caste and reach out to the Christian people of Germany. They responded with an interest and enthusiasm unprecedented in recent history. By the end of 1522, his German works had been published in 828 editions. The next eight years would see the publication of some 1,245 more, an estimated total of some two million copies.[2] The production, sale, and distribution of these books was a mammoth undertaking. In the process Luther and his friends had recast both the German publishing industry and the reading public.

To understand the full extent of this transformation, it is helpful to cast our eyes back to the state of the book industry before Luther. In the first age of print, roughly the seventy years before the Reformation, the archetypal book would have been long, expensive, and in Latin.[3] In choosing books to publish, the first printers took their cue from what they knew of the book market before print was invented. Most customers were churchmen, scholars, or students, with a smattering of rich collectors from the nobility. Consequently the first printers aligned their production to the established best sellers in these customers' favored fields: religion, academic texts, chronicle histories, and so on. Books became more plentifully available, but remained expensive. A personal collection of more than thirty titles was still very unusual.

The Reformation put books into the hands of many purchasers from outside these established groups. Many of these new readers would never previously have owned books. Even if they had one or two, these would have been treasured family possessions, a Book of Hours or a chronicle; for the same price they could now buy several dozen Reformation *Flugschriften*. And many people did precisely this; ordinary citizens for whom books had previously been a comparatively marginal phenomenon were now repeatedly exposed to the literature of the Reformation, in a wild profusion.

Engaging this new public would ultimately be hugely lucrative for Germany's printers, but the challenges of this expanding market were not insignificant. Capturing new readers required both ingenuity and innovation: a new movement required a new sort of book. In mastering these design challenges, Germany's printers gradually settled on a look that was distinctive and instantly recognizable. This was Brand Luther, and it was one of the great unsung achievements of the Reformation.

THE TECHNOLOGY OF IMITATION

The first of Luther's works published in Wittenberg were in design terms very little different from what Rhau-Grunenberg had published in the previous ten years. Examining these books, potential purchasers would certainly not have known that something extraordinary was afoot. This was Rhau-Grunenberg's way. Although an educated man, he was something of a printing novice when he came to Wittenberg. His apprenticeship in Erfurt was brief, and he had absorbed none of the more sophisticated working practice of the larger Erfurt houses. Nor did he show any inclination to change an established formula.

It quickly became clear that the demand unleashed by the Reformation had overwhelmed Rhau-Grunenberg's little shop. Luther grumbled that he was slow and inaccurate; but it was also the case that the new money flowing into the shop from sales did not inspire him to the reinvestment that could have transformed the look of his books. A tract published for Andreas von Karlstadt in 1518 still looked exactly like something he might have produced for a student's dissertation defense when he first became the university printer.[4] Something clearly had to change.

The first hint that the Reformation could offer something better came when Luther's works were taken up in Germany's larger printing centers. The pamphlet version of the ninety-five theses published by Adam Petri in Basel is a quite beautiful piece of work.[5] The text is spread through eight quarto pages, in neatly balanced groups of twenty-five and twenty. The numeration is crisply aligned in the margin. Careful use is made of indentation to distinguish the separate theses. The use of white space to guide the eye is elegant. So, too, is the woodcut initial at the head of the texts. (As we have seen, Rhau-Grunenberg seems not to have equipped himself with a set of these larger initials.)

The chain of connection between Basel and Wittenberg ran through Leipzig and Augsburg. Leipzig, rather fortuitously, was at this time the largest center of book production in Germany. Its long established and experienced printing houses employed a far greater range of typefaces than Rhau-Grunenberg. Early Leipzig reprints of Rhau-Grunenberg's work offered a master class in how different fonts of type could be used to differentiate text and supporting matter, side notes, and references. Melchior Lotter Senior, one of the first to print Luther in Leipzig, also used decorative blocks to create a border surrounding the text of the title page.[6] This was a useful way of drawing the customer's eye to a particular item laid out on the bookseller's stall, though not particularly new: we see the same framing device in editions of the sermons of Savonarola published in Florence in the last decade of the fifteenth century. Augsburg printers also contributed early Luther editions of great elegance and professional competence. Augsburg was unusual in the history of printing, in that almost from the beginning of print, vernacular, rather than Latin works, had dominated its output.[7] This long experience in the publication of German-language works was now put to the service of Luther's movement.

Luther would have been aware of the vast superiority of the editions of his works published elsewhere in Germany, not least from copies sent back to him by friends or grateful printers. We know that when Johann Froben of Basel wrote to Luther in 1518 to inform him of the success of the anthology of his works, he enclosed a copy of this volume, and some volumes of Erasmus.[8] Luther would also have had opportunities to examine the books published in Augsburg, Leipzig, and Nuremberg during his various trips out of Wittenberg in the years 1518 and 1519. The Wittenberg University library also contained examples of some of the best workmanship available in the European book world, thanks not least to the elector's assiduous courtship of Aldus Manutius.[9]

Martin Luther was a man of refined aesthetic sensibility. He knew that the books published in Rhau-Grunenberg's shop hardly did Wittenberg justice. He complained early and often of the quality of the workmanship, the frequency of errors, the slow pace of production. Persuading Melchior Lotter to send his son to Wittenberg was an important step toward remedying this situation.[10] Melchior Junior turned out to be extremely able. He brought to Wittenberg the efficiency and competence of his father's well-capitalized print shop; he also had access to a wide range of his father's types.

The look of Wittenberg Luther editions improved immeasurably. Here we see what was becoming quite distinctive of the Reformation *Flugschriften,* the vernacular pamphlets published in Leipzig, Augsburg, Basel, and now also Strasbourg. All would be in the quarto format used for most everyday publishing in Germany.[11] They were usually very short, eight or sixteen pages, which would have been one or two sheets of paper, printed and then folded into four (hence quarto). Using so little paper, they were always very cheap. Customers took to purchasing large numbers, which they then bound together in impromptu anthologies (which is how many of them have come down to us). These *Flugschriften* usually had a neat, orderly title page, spelling out the subject and in Luther's case naming the author. This was important, for it was not universally the case that the title page would include the author's name (particularly if the author was a living person, rather than one of the great classical or medieval authorities). In Luther's case his name would appear, since he was an important selling point. The title page would also, as in Melchior Lotter's examples, often make use of decorative woodblocks to encase the text.

The printer's world was very much one of imitation and shameless borrowing; when printers saw that a trade rival had adopted a new feature that seemed to work, they would simply incorporate that feature into their own work. In this way there gradually emerged the features that we associate with the Reformation pamphlets, and we see these replicated in many hundreds of individual titles. Wittenberg was now able to play a full part in this trade. But what Melchior Lotter brought to Wittenberg was essentially the proficiency and style of Leipzig; indeed, his works are stylistically quite close to works published in his father's shop, still fully operative in Leipzig. There was nothing very distinctive to Wittenberg about these books. To create a specific Wittenberg style, the city's printers had to make use of their greatest latent asset. For Augsburg and Leipzig might have had greater capital resources, the longer printing heritage, and the better-established print shops. But Wittenberg had Lucas Cranach.

LUCAS

Cranach was born Lucas Maler (Painter), in the small Franconian town of Kronach, midway between Erfurt and Nuremberg.[12] As the name suggests, his father also worked in the trade that would make his son famous. Young Lucas's artistic education took place in southern Germany and Vienna. Of the major German painters of this period, Cranach was the most prominent never to have visited Italy. What he imbibed of the Italian Renaissance was learned at second hand, from studying the works of others and especially Albrecht Dürer, the yardstick against which all artists of the northern Renaissance have been measured, then and now. But Cranach remained very much his own man. A master technician, his work remained quintessentially German, without the self-conscious obei-

ÆTATIS SVA · LXXVII
· I 5 5 0 ·

LUCAS CRANACH

One of Luther's closest allies in the Wittenberg elite, Cranach would play a crucial role in presenting Luther to the wider world. He also played an instrumental role in the Wittenberg publishing industry.

sance to Italian style characteristic of celebrated contemporaries. This is most obvious in his depictions of the human form, and in the magnificent landscapes in which many of his works are framed.

Cranach was already a mature force of established reputation when he joined other distinguished contemporaries in Wittenberg, to work on the decoration of Frederick's mammoth building projects. But whereas Dürer and others came and went, Lucas was content to remain in Saxony; in 1505 he succeeded the Venetian Jacopo de' Barbari as Frederick's court painter. This was a role that called above all for versatility. Cranach was obliged to turn his hand to anything that took the elector's fancy: religious art, portraits, hunting scenes, or wall painting. He orchestrated court festivities and the necessary banners and decorations; on one occasion he even designed a nut grater for the elector's young nephews.[13] These multiple assignments taught Cranach efficiency in the dispatch of work, a skill that would come to characterize his whole career. Cranach was an exceptionally effective manager and an astute businessman; he also worked extremely quickly. He was already famous among contemporaries for this speedy painting style, a pragmatism that has not always found favor with the more fastidious modern connoisseurs.

His new patron was evidently delighted with Cranach's work. For his diverse responsibilities Lucas was well rewarded. He received a salary of one hundred gulden a year, double that of his Venetian predecessor.[14] He was also given a horse and an apartment in the castle. All his artistic materials were paid for separately. Crucially, although his responsibilities to the elector took priority, Lucas was also free to take on work for other patrons. Since he was by far the most distinguished painter in northeastern Germany, these commissions came in a steady flow, and Cranach continued to take on work for a large variety of institutions and individuals throughout the rest of his long life.

In contrast to Martin Luther, who scarcely ever came into the elector's presence, Cranach's relationship with his patron was close. In 1508 Frederick may have raised some eyebrows by granting his relatively low-born court painter a coat of arms. This same year Cranach was dispatched to represent the elector on a diplomatic mission to the Low Countries. The ambassadors had been sent to negotiate a marriage alliance between the imperial house and the elector's own family. Although this did not materialize, Cranach was able to immerse himself in the extraordinary achievement of the Flemish artists on this trip. This was his first major sortie out of the Germanic lands, and it would not be repeated.

During these early years in Wittenberg, Cranach had also mastered the art of the woodcut. Woodcuts—where the image was carved into a block of wood, from which a printed impression could be taken—played an important role in the book industry. The woodcut could be laid on the platen alongside text, and then printed off in the same impression. This was not the case with engraving, another illustrative technique beginning to make its mark, since the metal engraved plate had to be passed through a different, cylindrical press. This meant that combining engraving and text in moveable type on a single sheet required the paper to be passed through two separate presses, and careful alignment; the insertion of woodcuts into a page of type posed no such complexities. Woodcuts were by this point heavily used for decorative material, such as initial letters and bordering, for playing cards and for illustrations, printed either separately on broadsheets or on the pages of books.

It was in Germany, and precisely in these years, that the art of the woodcut reached its peak.[15] In the years before the Reformation the woodcut form found its most refined expression in the great Passion series of Albrecht Dürer, but Cranach's series of fourteen woodcuts on the same theme (1509–1511) certainly bears comparison.[16] Cranach was also required to undertake more mundane tasks in this genre, such as the more than one hundred illustrations required for the published catalog of Frederick's great relic collection.[17] With so many and varied responsibilities, Cranach was by this time of necessity a major employer. Between 1510 and 1512 he shifted his operations from the increasingly cramped quarters in the castle to a new site in the center of town. Here, after massive building works that lasted the best part of a decade, he would gradually create a vast artistic factory, a workshop on the scale we associate with the greatest of the northern artistic entrepreneurs, Peter Paul Rubens or Rembrandt. At Schloßstrasse 1 Cranach presided over the production of artistic work in industrial quantities. We know of one order, from 1532, for sixty paired portraits of the elector, John the Constant, and his late brother, Frederick the Wise.[18] These were manufactured in the workshop by a small army of assistants, for the elector to distribute to favored citizens and foreign dignitaries. The iconic portraits of Luther, of Luther and his wife, Katharina, or of Luther and Melanchthon, were manufactured in similar quantities.[19] Not all of these workshop pieces were of the highest quality, but they played an important role in building the iconography of the Reformation.

With the factory on the Schloβstrasse Cranach had embarked on the first of a series of acquisitions that would in due course make him the owner of nine separate properties around Wittenberg. One was a second substantial house on the market square at Markt 4; it was here that Cranach lived between 1513 and 1517 while the major building works were under way fifty yards away. (The house at Markt 4 is now the location of the Cranachhaus Museum.) This beautiful building, which he also remodeled in the finest Renaissance style, had been purchased from Martin Pollich von Mellerstadt, first rector of Wittenberg University and Frederick's personal physician. Von Mellerstadt had negotiated a lucrative privilege to operate an apothecary business, and Cranach made sure that he inherited this also. This may seem an unusual diversification, but for Cranach it made perfect sense. There were good profits to be made from the supply of herbs and spices to the students, professors, and local inhabitants, and Cranach, in addition, also had a monopoly on the sale of sweet wines in the city. An apothecary shop was an important place of information gathering. Citizens would come by seeking remedies for trifling or more serious afflictions (or send their servants to fetch them). While they were waiting for these potions to be mixed, they would stop and gossip. Customers would also consult the apothecary about the most likely remedies for pain or debilitating conditions. So the proprietor of such a business held the community's most intimate secrets, and in this case his boss was Wittenberg's most shrewd and substantial businessman.[20] In a world where almost all major business transactions functioned on credit, the apothecary shop provided priceless nuggets of information about who might be in failing health, who had a secret affliction not yet revealed to creditors, and whose business might soon be available for purchase. Quite apart from its generous profits (always good for cash flow), the capacity this business gave its proprietor to measure the pulse of the city made this one of Cranach's shrewdest investments.

By 1517 Cranach was one of Wittenberg's most substantial citizens. A decade later his tax assessment placed him among Wittenberg's three wealthiest inhabitants, and certainly he was its most active and energetic business entrepreneur. In 1519, like Luther's father in Mansfeld, Cranach took his place on the city council, the beginning of a thirty-year involvement in municipal politics, during which he would serve three times as the city's *Bürgermeister*. Inventive, versatile, and where occasion demanded quite ruthless, Cranach was a force to be reckoned with. When in the early 1520s he turned his attention to Wittenberg's expanding printing industry, the impact was immediate and transformative.

THE GODFATHER

It is not known when Cranach and Luther first became acquainted. In their first years in Wittenberg the two men moved in very different circles. Cranach was by some distance the more distinguished of the two, constantly in the elector's presence and from 1512 permanently established in the center of the town and its most eye-catching dwelling. But sometime around 1518 the two men became friends. Cranach would have attended Luther's sermons in the town church. From his court connections he would have known of the reverberations that followed the austere professor's provocative theses. He was impressed—and fascinated; at an early stage Cranach would become a committed and important supporter of Luther's new movement.

This support came with limits. For all his loyal service to the Reformation, Cranach never ceased working for Catholic clients, including Albrecht of Mainz.[21] If Luther objected, then on this occasion he sensibly kept his counsel. In other respects the two friends were well matched. They were roughly of the same generation (Cranach was born in 1472, eleven years before Luther) and both had now reached their full maturity. Both were powerful, driven men, who took easily to positions of responsibility: both knew how to inspire loyalty and to command obedience. Both, too, came to married life relatively late, Cranach in 1512, at the age of thirty-nine, and both would become devoted parents: between 1513 and 1520 Barbara Cranach became the mother of five children, two of whom would follow into their father's business. Luther was honored to be chosen as godfather to one of the children; in due course Cranach would return the compliment, after Luther's own far more controversial marriage in 1525. Cranach was, in fact, one of the very few present at this discreet ceremony. This was a relationship of mutual respect, mutual affection, and mutual benefit. Cranach gave the Reformation some of its most memorable images; Luther in return would take a strong line against the radical rejection of pictorial art promoted by some of his Wittenberg colleagues. Cranach, civic leader and artistic entrepreneur, would be one of the rocks on which the Wittenberg Reformation would be built.

Cranach's first signal service to the Reformation came in fashioning the three iconic portraits of Luther that made his physical features known beyond the relatively narrow group of those who had encountered him in person. The initiative for the first portrait—an engraving—seems to have come, curiously enough, from Albrecht Dürer. A passionate admirer of Luther from his first reading of Luther's works, Dürer regretted the lack of a true likeness of the reformer. He wrote suggesting that such a likeness be created, enclosing copies of his magnificent woodcut portrait of Albrecht of Brandenburg as a model.[22] Cranach studied the portrait of Albrecht carefully before embarking on his own rendition of Luther. The result was a triumph, simultaneously a magnificent propaganda piece and a wondrously lifelike rendering of the reformer at this seminal moment of his career (1520).[23] Cranach makes of Luther exactly what the occasion demanded, the simple monk, lean but not gaunt, staring calmly outward, resolute and monumental in the face of adversity: the very picture of the simple man of God, strong against the marshaled forces of the institutional church. It is a fascinating portrait of simplicity in strength and determination.

This image, in fact, was not destined for immediate circulation. In the months before Luther's appearance at the Diet of Worms, there were those at the elector's court who feared that this portrait of heroic resolution might strike the wrong note. Asked to respond, Cranach produced a second image that, while capturing Luther's inner essence in exactly the same way, gives the appropriate hint of humility.[24] Luther, now shown within a wall niche, places a hand across his heart in a traditional sign of friendship and sincerity; in his other hand is an open book. Once again he wears the monk's habit.

The third early portrait captured the historical moment when, holed up in the Wartburg, Luther made a brief trip back to Wittenberg to prevent his movement from taking a disastrous turn in his absence. This whole incident reveals much about the intimacy between painter and reformer that had been established by this date. After his condemnation at Worms, the danger to Luther was very real; the success of his removal to protective custody depended on the secret of his whereabouts not being revealed. So it is a measure of the trust that existed between the two men that on a rest stop on the perilous ride to the Wartburg Luther sent an urgent message to Cranach telling him he was in safe hands: "I shall submit to being 'imprisoned' and hidden away, though as yet I do not know where."[25] It was Cranach who wrote to alert Luther of the likely consequences if Karlstadt was allowed to introduce radical change in Luther's absence, and Cranach whom Luther consulted on his secret trip back to Wittenberg on how to prevent the incendiary acts of iconoclasm that Karlstadt seemed to intend. During these urgent and secret consultations, the painter snatched a moment to sketch Luther bearded in his disguise as a German knight, the portrait of Junker Jörg that has become an important milestone in creating the Luther legend. It was also one of Cranach's first renderings of Luther on a panel painting, the first of a series in which Cranach captured the staging posts of Luther's life and career.[26] There is the harrowed, hunted figure of 1525, Cranach's most shocking and evocative psychological portrait;[27] the serene pastor of mature years (the most copied of all his images); the grumpy patriarch of the 1540s. More than any other, this, Cranach's Luther, is how

LUTHER AS JUNKER JÖRG

Sketched by Cranach on Luther's fleeting first return from the Wartburg, this was the artist's first panel portrait of him. It was widely disseminated as an equally striking woodcut.

history has come to see him. It is an extraordinary portrait sequence of a man who, in any other circumstances, could not expect his true likeness to be known to history.

The representation of Luther to the wider world is essentially Cranach's achievement, and virtually any other contemporary representation, and many after his death, in some way reaches back to this personification by Cranach. So it may seem perverse in the circumstances to suggest that in many respects this was not even Cranach's greatest service to the Reformation movement. Here we have to take into account a far less heralded achievement of his artistic imagination, combined with his extraordinary gifts as a business entrepreneur. For if we are to identify the greatest contribution of the Cranach workshop to the promotion of the evangelical movement as a whole, it probably lies not in this portrait art, nor even in the iconic designs created by Cranach to encapsulate the new Reformation theology, but in his contribution to the Wittenberg book industry. The distinctive look of the Reformation *Flugschriften* as they emerged from the print shops of the 1520s owed everything to the design brilliance of Lucas Cranach. It was Cranach who would be the authentic creator of Brand Luther.

BRAND LUTHER

Lucas Cranach became directly involved in the Wittenberg printing industry at the end of 1519, when he became a vital component of the transaction that brought Melchior Lotter to Wittenberg. Cranach was already well-known in Leipzig and to Melchior Lotter Senior, to whom he supplied some of the first of his prototype decorative title pages.[28] So part of the deal was that the son would be provided with work space in Cranach's cavernous factory at Schloβstrasse 1; Cranach and his partner, the goldsmith Christian Döring, were from the beginning investors in the business. Sometimes Lotter would publish in his own name, on other occasions the press would publish under the imprint of Cranach and Döring. Döring was another of Luther's closest friends among the citizenry and one of Wittenberg's wealthiest merchants: it was Döring who had loaned the horses and carriage that had carried Luther and his companions to Worms.[29] He also had a large trucking business, so could handle the distribution of the consortium's books to other places of sale. At around the same time, Cranach also invested in the purchase of a paper mill: this way he would control the whole of the production process, and through Döring, distribution also. It was a typically bold and decisive intervention in an industry that, thanks to Luther, seemed to promise healthy profit.

The publishing arm of the business was something that Cranach pursued only for a very few years. Perhaps the profits were disappointing, but in truth, this was only likely to be a relatively marginal part of his engagement in the book industry. For Cranach possessed one asset that made him quite indispensable to all of Wittenberg's printers: a monopoly on the production of illustrative and decorative woodcuts.

It was this that allowed Cranach to play a dominant role in the Wittenberg book trade for three decades; it also allowed him to transform the look of Wittenberg books.[30] To this point Wittenberg imprints had mostly been associated with the spare, utilitarian texts of Rhau-Grunenberg. Printers outside Wittenberg had improved the look somewhat, using decorative borders to frame the title. Cranach offered a radically new solution: a title-page frame, made up not of separate panels but a single woodcut. Here the illustrative features were blocked around a blank central panel into which the text of the title could then be inserted. It was a masterpiece of design innovation, with one step solving the complex problem of integrating text and decorative material while allowing space for imaginative artistic expression on the front of the book.

It was a major and decisive breakthrough in the history of the book, never before applied to texts of this type. Until this point, grand woodcut title-page designs would have been confined to the largest, most expensive books. Cranach's exquisite work now adorned pamphlets that might sell for no more than a few pence. And what frames these are. Cranach brought to this new engagement with book design the accumulated experience of one of Germany's most capable and imaginative artistic entrepreneurs. The result is a whole series of masterpieces in miniature, bringing to the title pages of Wittenberg's Reformation *Flugschriften* a balance, poise, and sophistication that they had to this point entirely lacked. Stylistically this was the part of Cranach's artistic oeuvre that most self-consciously adhered to the principles of Renaissance art. A statement was being made: that the message of the Reformation, Luther's message, deserved to be arrayed in magnificence. In the process,

BRAND LUTHER

Here all the elements of marketing Luther are included: the highlighting of name and place, and Cranach's distinctive title frame.

and thanks to Cranach's decisive intervention, the Wittenberg book was catapulted from the back to the front of the pack in terms of aesthetic appeal.

What Cranach had achieved with these new title-page designs was not easy: it required the combination of Cranach's skills as a pragmatic, practical spirit and his enormous artistic imagination. To this point in the history of art, narrative images were most effectively achieved within a landscape format, where the story could flow naturally across the canvas. A book inevitably required an upright, portrait format. Furthermore, the design had to be fitted around a central block of empty space, where the title text could be inserted. This was a unique problem in the history of visual art. Cranach's solutions were ingenious, with broad blocks at the top and bottom, allowing room for vertical figures up the sides and decorative putti around the corners. This use of corners was, of course, impossible when a framing border was created from four separate blocks. The extensive use of landscape foliage and animals from the hunt drew on Cranach's experience painting hunting scenes for Frederick's court. Other title-page designs use classical motifs such as the judgment of Paris (another favorite subject for his workshop) or Pyramus and Thisbe. The title-page borders by and large make no allusion to the pamphlet's contents, and were indeed frequently reused for different titles. The exceptions were those occasions when Cranach designed biblical scenes as title-page decoration: the blinding of Saul (for an edition of the Epistles and Gospels), Samson and the lion, David and Goliath (for an edition of the Psalms).[31] Cranach also took the opportunity to incorporate into his title pages one of his true masterpieces, The Law and the Gospel.[32] This was one of the most innovative pieces of religious iconography generated by the Reformation, an original composition of Cranach's contrasting the old Law (of Moses and the Old Testament) with the new covenant of Christ. The two are divided by a tree, blasted on the side of the old Law, green and flourishing on the side of the new. Complex and intricate in its original manifestation as a panel, to reconfigure this as a title page, with blank central space for the title, was one of the great design achievements of the age.[33]

The accumulation of this portfolio of ornate title-page woodcuts occupied the Cranach workshop for the best part of two decades, and in the process they totally changed the appearance of Reformation *Flugschriften*. Wittenberg's printers embraced them without hesitation; not just Melchior Lotter, who worked on Cranach's premises (but with whom the painter soon fell out), but other newcomers to the Wittenberg printing industry: Joseph Klug, Georg Rhau, Nickel Schirlentz, and Hans Lufft. Even Rhau-Grunenberg embraced the new style. At last Wittenberg books could face the world in a livery that expressed the dynamism, sophistication, and optimism of the new movement.

Printers elsewhere soon sat up and took note. It was in the nature of the industry that such a radical innovation could not easily be confined to Wittenberg. Cranach's design breakthrough was soon being carefully examined by other industry professionals wherever Wittenberg books were sold. This was the way the book world worked—in fact, the way it had worked since the first proof sheets of Gutenberg's Bible had been exhibited at the Frankfurt Fair in 1454. Many printers attended the regular book fairs in Frankfurt and Leipzig not because they needed to do so to sell their books, but so they could cast a professional eye over the work of their competitors and see what looked new and interesting. As a result of this scrutiny, Cranach's most successful designs were soon being shamelessly copied in both Augsburg and Nuremberg.[34] Cranach was no doubt relatively phlegmatic about this; he knew how the game was played. This was an age with no real concept of intellectual property, and the protection of a monopoly was only as good as the jurisdiction in which it was issued. The overall impact of this rampant copying, however, was undoubtedly to improve further the design coherence of the Reformation *Flugschriften,* as Cranach's innovative designs were copied into new markets.

The distinctive look provided by Cranach's title-page designs was the final component of a puzzle that had been taxing Germany's printers since the early days of the Reformation: how to make the most of their most marketable property—the new phenomenon that was Martin Luther. This resolution was not reached without a certain number of false starts. One was the use of Luther's image in book art. The first attempt to incorporate an image of Luther on a title page appears on a pamphlet account of the Leipzig Disputation; it, therefore, predates Cranach's iconic portraits. Perhaps for this reason it cannot be counted a success. The representation of Luther in a doctor's cap is no more than a cipher without real recognizable features. The overall effect is not helped by the fact that the lettering in the surrounding inscription is reversed, and can only be read with a mirror. This was clearly rushed out to cash in on Luther's new notoriety. Between 1520 and 1522, rather more successfully, a Strasbourg publisher, Johann Schott, used locally cut copies of Cranach's representation of Luther in his monk's garb, one on the title page of a pamphlet and the other on the inside cover.[35] But this, too, failed to catch on. A movement that articulated the primacy of the Word was never entirely comfortable with the promotion of any sort of personality cult around Luther. One of the Strasbourg pamphlets captured this dilemma perfectly by portraying Luther with the nimbus of sainthood, a particularly inappropriate image given Luther's criticism of the cult of saints.[36] No book published in Wittenberg during these years ever included a portrait of Luther on the title page, and this early attempt to popularize the reformer's image alongside texts of his writings soon spluttered and died.

Luther's name was a different matter. In the design of the Reformation title page we also see printers gradually waking up to the potency of Luther's personal reputation as a writer and teacher. Very early works often buried Luther's name in the midst of a dense block of text; not infrequently his name was split over two lines of text (Lu- / theri) if that was what was dictated by the blocking. This simply obscured the book's most obvious selling point, as printers quickly recognized. Soon they had learned to move the name, "Mart. Luthers," "Martin Luther," "Doct. Martin Luther," into a line of its own, often separated from the main body of the title. The name is often in a bold type of larger size, in a manner calculated to spring off the page, catching the eye of purchasers surveying a mass of titles piled up on the bookseller's stall.

The last element of brand identity was Wittenberg itself. In most parts of Europe it was now common practice for the printer's address to be printed in a neat, small type at the bottom of the title page. Not so in Wittenberg. Here the printer's name was mostly relegated to the end (the colophon) or omitted altogether. Instead the city was given pride of place, often on a single line at the bottom, separated by an inch or more of white space from any other text.

That Wittenberg was now an essential part of the brand—the seal of quality and authenticity—is demonstrated by the number of times this strategy is employed even on pamphlets printed elsewhere. A number of Augsburg printers, for instance, took to printing "Wittenberg" starkly on the lower part of their title pages. Perhaps, being charitable, one could suggest that the printers were simply advertising the fact that the text itself was from Wittenberg, or that it was the work of Martin Luther of Wittenberg. Either way, whether calculated to deceive or intended to inform, it makes the point that within a few years, thanks largely to Lucas Cranach, Wittenberg had thrown off the clumsy provincialism that had marred Luther's first publications. Now Luther's city could offer finished products worthy of their contents: pamphlets that in their design and appearance confidently proclaimed the unbreakable connection between the movement's progenitor, Martin Luther, and the place with which his church was now indelibly associated, Wittenberg. That would be the enduring achievement of Brand Luther.

Part 3

FRIENDS AND ADVERSARIES

7.

LUTHER'S FRIENDS

T MANY TIMES SINCE the first years of the Reformation Luther had felt the loneliness of command: waiting on Cajetan's decision at Augsburg, facing the assembled Estates of the Empire at Worms, incarcerated at the Wartburg. On such occasions he took comfort in a sense that none of this had come about through his own volition; he was, as he frequently reflected, simply the instrument of God's purpose. This sense of special calling was undoubtedly reinforced by the long months of brooding isolation at the Wartburg, and the swift reassumption of leadership on his return. The self-confident acceptance of the responsibilities of leadership is reflected in a significant change in Luther's bearing. We see this in the style of greeting used in Luther's correspondence, which he now increasingly begins with the Pauline "grace and peace." This assumption of apostolic mission was already a familiar trope among Luther's followers. To Christoph Scheurl of Nuremberg Luther was a preacher "through who alone Paul speaks"; to Ulrich von Hutten "a man of God and apostle of Christ."[1] Other early writers evoked the Old Testament prophet Elijah and heralded Luther as a new Daniel or the good shepherd who Ezekiel had prophesied would tend the flock of Christ.[2]

All of this contributed to the idea of a man alone, singled out by

God to perform great things: the simple monk whose bold challenge had shaken the kingdom of Antichrist to its core. This intense focus on the person of Martin Luther was encouraged in the public mind by the wide circulation of woodcut images of the reformer, always in the first years presented as a solitary figure, in monk's cowl, with the gaze of the visionary and the humble bearing of a true servant of Christ.[3] In the years before and after the dramatic confrontation with the emperor at Worms in 1521, public interest in Luther as the symbol of national resistance to an alien authority far outstripped any public understanding of his theology. This, as the perplexed and angry papal nuncio Aleander had recognized, was the key to his potency—and danger.

Of course, as Luther was well aware, this perception vastly oversimplified the motive power of his movement. Indeed, had Luther been such a solitary figure, the man alone, the voice crying in the wilderness, his Reformation would quickly have died. Certainly the movement could not have been sustained once the drama of Worms faded from memory. Luther would not have survived to face his critics at the Diet without the steady support of influential friends who had stuck with him through all the twists and turns of the previous four years. These crucial early supporters included, as we have seen, ecclesiastical superiors such as Staupitz, university colleagues, Georg Spalatin at the Saxon court, and the Elector Frederick, his enigmatic and to Luther largely silent patron. Pondering the increasingly worrying developments in Wittenberg during his enforced absence in 1521, Luther looked to Melanchthon to take on the burdens of leadership, and to his friends on the city council, Cranach and Döring, to hold the line for the necessary measures to restore order.[4] Luther, as politically literate as he was theologically inspired, was well aware of the need for friends.

The next five years would test the solidarity of these early companions to the limit. The years between 1522, when Luther returned to assert his authority over the Wittenberg movement, and 1526 were a time of decision for both individuals and communities. Many admired Luther, but would they follow him out of the church? Princes and city councils also had to weigh the attractions of reform on the Wittenberg model against the dangers of defying imperial law and putting themselves at the mercy of ambitious neighbors. Thus far the cities had been the center of evangelical agitation. But it was one thing to thrill to the excitement caused by Luther's defiance of the pope, or to crowd the churches to hear their own ministers lambast the corruptions of the clerical order; quite another to contemplate the creation of an institutional framework of an entirely new church adhering to Luther's Gospel teaching. Inevitably this was a process stretching over several years, with halting steps and many misgivings. But by the end of the 1520s many German cities, including powerful regional centers such as Hamburg, Strasbourg, and Nuremberg, had taken the essential measures to institute a state-led Reformation.[5] Sometimes (as in Hamburg) they looked to Wittenberg for help; elsewhere the Reformation depended on powerful local figures.

This stage in the development of an institutionalized church in turn inspired a significant backlash: from those who had always viewed with horror Luther's assault on familiar institutions and authority, and from others who had initially followed his leadership, sometimes passionately, but now fell by the wayside. This trauma of separation from once-faithful friends and supporters was particularly acute in the middle years of this difficult decade, when a revolt among the peasantry (1524–1525) faced the movement with its first existential crisis: the more so because many of its leaders, to Wittenberg's great embarrassment, claimed to be inspired to their gospel of social justice by Luther's teaching. This was the decade when the Reformation took institutional root, but also a time of a painful and damaging parting of ways with valued former friends.[6]

These were testing times, but crucial if Luther's movement was to develop beyond the initial cry for reform and fervent denunciation of the papacy to present its own positive vision of a reformed Christian life. In these moments of decision, often the occasion for lonely and stark choices, Luther's movement relied very heavily on the gifts of those who pledged their eloquence and authority to his cause. The making of the Reformation depended during these years on radiating circles of adher-

ents, often considerable figures in their own right, who lent their expertise and reputation to making tangible the fruits of Luther's teaching
in their own locality. Luther understood this clearly. He placed himself at
the heart of this movement, nurturing and cajoling, offering encouragement and advice. This was simultaneously a collective and a very personal achievement.

THE FOUR EVANGELISTS

Among the Catholic theologians who entered the lists against Luther, none was more doggedly persistent than Johannes Cochlaeus. A
Catholic priest well connected in humanist circles, Cochlaeus had initially been attracted to Luther. He witnessed Luther's defiance at the
Diet of Worms, and subsequently sought him out for a personal audience. But Cochlaeus became convinced that Luther's teachings, and in
particular his promotion of a vernacular Bible, would break the sacred
bond that preserved the special status of the priesthood. He became an
implacable opponent: the two hundred or more writings that flowed
from his pen included a cascade of anti-Lutheran polemics. Among them
was the exotically titled *Fascicule of Calumnies, Ravings and Illusions of
Martin Luther,* carefully classifying dozens of Luther's statements into
these three categories. Cochlaeus was also the inventor of the famous
seven-headed Luther, the seven personalities that in Cochlaeus's ingenious representation Luther exhibited in his work: doctor, fanatic, fool,
church visitor, churchman, criminal, and Barabbas. Cochlaeus, who out-
lived his antagonist by the best part of a decade, was also the first to
attempt a full biography of Luther. This painstaking chronological reconstruction of Luther's career was often bitterly personal in tone. But
Cochlaeus was also very shrewd. He recognized that Luther did not
stand alone. Increasingly, especially in his treatment of Luther's mature
career, he recognized the contribution of those who worked with Luther

to build his church, singling out for special opprobrium those whom he characterized as "the four evangelists of Wittenberg": Luther, Philip Melanchthon, Johannes Bugenhagen, and Justus Jonas.[7] Though intending no compliments, Cochlaeus thus provides a useful point of entry to the community that sustained Luther in Wittenberg from 1518 to the end of his life. These companions were all in their different ways essential to the success of the Reformation.

Of all Luther's Wittenberg colleagues none was more important or forged such a close emotional bond with Luther than Philip Melanchthon, the towering intellectual force of Wittenberg's Reformation. Melanchthon had been recognized as a scholarly prodigy from an early age. In this he was undoubtedly helped by his family connection to Johann Reuchlin, his great uncle, whose defense of Hebrew scholarship had been such a fashionable cause in the mid-1510s.[8] As a result young Philip's early career was followed with approval by leading humanist scholars across Europe, many of whom had also rallied to Reuchlin's defense. Philip obtained his BA from Heidelberg at the age of thirteen, and an MA from Tübingen three years later. By the time he was summoned to the new chair in Greek at Wittenberg University in 1518, at the age of twenty-one, he was already a published author. He had also gained valuable experience of the printing press working as a proofreader in the Tübingen print shop of Thomas Anselm. Even as he made his way from Tübingen to take up his new responsibilities, universities in two of the cities along his route, Ingolstadt and Leipzig, attempted to poach him. On this occasion his escort, the reliable Spalatin, was able to steer him past these temptations, but it remained a constant fear for Luther that Melanchthon might flee to a more prestigious university or be lured away by a higher salary.

That said, Luther's first impressions of his new colleague were not particularly favorable. On first acquaintance he found it hard to match the towering reputation to the shy, stammering, and frankly puny youth who stood before him. He was diminutive and frail, and even Lucas Cra-

PHILIP MELANCHTHON

A delicate rendering of Luther's chief lieutenant by Cranach. In real life Melanchthon was slightly built and intense, and never an imposing physical presence.

nach's artistry could do little to make Philip handsome. Luther's misgivings lasted only until his inaugural lecture four days later. This was universally recognized as a tour de force, a rousing defense of curriculum reform in Wittenberg shaped around a call for the study of the ancient languages as the necessary basis for theological study. Here, along with his own discipline of Greek, Melanchthon offered a robust recommendation of the study of Hebrew, a deft acknowledgment of his famous relative, his great-uncle Reuchlin. This lecture, published by Rhau-Grunenberg under the title *De Corrigensis Adolescentium Studiis* (*On Improving the Studies of Youth*), was immediately reprinted in the citadel of humanist scholarship, Basel, by Johann Froben, Erasmus's own printer.[9] There could be no higher accolade for what would normally have been a routine academic exercise.

Luther was ecstatic.[10] From this point on he regarded Melanchthon as the principal, essential collaborator of his life's work. Melanchthon, in his turn, would offer Luther a patient loyalty, even when Luther's tempestuous outbursts clearly went against the grain of his more cautious and temperate personality. The partnership would remain intact, through all the strains and stresses of the coming years, until Luther's death in 1546, at which point Melanchthon reluctantly assumed the mantle of leadership as his anointed heir. There remained, however, a curious dualism about Luther's attitude to his younger colleague. On the one side he loved him dearly, fretting about his welfare and offering him solicitous advice on such matters as marriage and diet. For a proud and increasingly imperious patriarch, Luther was also always endearingly frank about the fact that with Philip he knew himself to be in the presence of a superior intellect; he relied upon him to correct and improve his own work, just as he was always eager to see Philip's writings in proof sheets before publication. In later life Luther would always name Melanchthon's systematic statement of the new Reformation theology, the *Loci Communes,* as the one indispensable text alongside the German Bible, ahead of any of his own works. His letters from the Wartburg ask continuously when it might be published. On the other hand he could easily become impatient at what he saw as Philip's timidity and reluctance to assert himself. This was particularly acute when Luther was cooped up at the Wartburg, fretting that Melanchthon could not deal with Karlstadt and the Zwickau prophets, three self-taught laymen who arrived in Wittenberg claiming divine inspiration for their advocacy of radical reform. In this he was not incorrect. At the height of the crisis Melanchthon came close to panic, asking Spalatin if it would not be possible to send the prophets to Luther so he could put them straight.

The relationship worked as it did partly because both men recognized their own limitations, and the corresponding strengths of the other. The difference was encapsulated rather charmingly in a dedicatory preface Luther provided for one of Philip's works in 1529:

> I was born for this purpose: to fight with the rebels and the devils and to lead the charge. Therefore my books are very stormy and warlike. I have to uproot trunks and stumps, hack at thorns and hedges, and fill in the potholes. So I am the crude woodsman, who has to clear and make the path. But Master Philip comes after me meticulously and quietly, builds and plants, sows and waters happily, according to the talents God has richly given him.[11]

Of course, Luther was here playing up the contrast for effect. He was no crude woodsman, and Melanchthon was not always sweet tempered. Philip could be sharp and impatient, particularly with students, more so indeed than Luther. But this elegant, generous tribute does capture something of why this partnership of opposites worked so well. It was sustained, also, because Melanchthon was from the beginning utterly, unflinchingly committed to Luther's Reformation, a consideration that came before all others in his relationship with other scholars. When Erasmus broke definitively with Luther, it was to Melanchthon that he sent a copy of his challenge to Luther's teachings on justification, *On Free Will*, hoping, quite correctly, for a more friendly reception than had he sent it to Luther. Philip wrote back encouragingly, and he never ceased to hope that the two great lodestars of his life could remain in civil communication. But when that hope was blighted, his first loyalty was always to Luther and Wittenberg. Without Melanchthon, his forensic intelligence and powerful capacity for methodological theological thought, his lifelong commitment to the reform of the university curriculum and the education of the young, and his calm, restraining presence at Luther's side, the Reformation would have been immeasurably diminished.

None of Luther's other Wittenberg colleagues, protégés, and disciples ever came close to matching Melanchthon in importance, but many played an important role in building his movement and defending his teachings in public and in print. This was especially true of the other two who made up Cochlaeus's four evangelists, Johannes Bugenhagen and Justus Jonas. Justus Jonas was part of the Erfurt humanist connection.[12] Although he was a student at Wittenberg, and must have made Luther's acquaintance there, it was at Erfurt, the senior university, that he chose to make his career. By 1518 he was a professor in the Faculty of Arts and a leading light in the university's modernizing faction. In 1519 Jonas made the ultimate humanist pilgrimage, a visit to Erasmus in Louvain. He carried with him letters from both Frederick the Wise and Luther: this was, in fact, the first time that Luther had addressed himself directly to the great humanist. Jonas returned to find that he had been elected rector of Erfurt University, a post that he held throughout the period of the Leipzig Disputation. At this point Jonas saw the Reformation very much through a humanist perspective. He condemned Johann Eck's performance at the Leipzig Disputation, not so much for his attack on Luther but for his criticism of Erasmus. When he published his preface to a course of lectures on Corinthians in 1520, it was accompanied by a letter from his friend Petrus Mosellanus, another humanist; curiously he chose not to include a similar letter he had received from Martin Luther.

The bond with Luther was forged at the time of the Diet of Worms. When Luther made his triumphant approach to Erfurt on his way to the Diet, Jonas rode as far as Weimar to greet him, and traveled on with his other companions. At Worms he met Cochlaeus, who described him, generously in the light of their later history, as "an excellent young man, of tall stature and very cultivated."[13] Within a month of his return to Erfurt Jonas had been appointed to a position in Wittenberg, where he would remain to the end of his life.

Jonas was quickly integrated into Luther's inner circle. He was promoted to a doctorate in theology in 1521 and served both as dean of the Theology Faculty and rector of the university. He was one of the first of Luther's intimates to marry. But he was no Philip Melanchthon; though he engaged gamely in the polemical controversies, and thus earned the

Auslegung
D. Mart. Luthers/
vber das Lied Mose
am Zwey vnd Dreissigsten
Cap. Deutero. Vordeut-
schet aus dem La-
tin / durch

Justum Jonam.

Gedruckt zu Wittemberg
im M. D. XXXII.

JUSTUS JONAS TRANSLATING LUTHER

Although Jonas was a dutiful participant in the Reformation's polemical debates, his main service to the Reformation was as an editor and translator. This translation of Luther was published with a superb Cranach title page (Samson and the lion).

ire of Cochlaeus, his principal service was as the editor and translator of the works of others. He was responsible for a fine, free translation of Luther's *De Servo Arbitrio,* and also translated both Melanchthon's *Loci Communes* and his *Apologia* for the Augsburg Confession. But Jonas was also his own man. His transfer to Wittenberg from Erfurt was delayed by his reluctance to take on his originally prescribed duties (Jonas was intended to teach Canon Law) and he retained a loyal affection for Erasmus long after it was politic to do so. This was sufficiently public that Luther chose to refer to this rather pointedly in print: "My dear Dr. Justus Jonas would not leave me in peace and kept urging me to deal sincerely with Erasmus and to write against him with due reverence. 'Doctor, sir,' he said to me, 'you have no idea what a noble and reverend old man he is.'" This very public prompt clearly had the desired effect. Later that same year Luther could write to Jonas, "I congratulate you on your recantation. Finally you depict Erasmus in his proper colors, as a deadly viper full of stings. Before that, you honored him with many complimentary epithets, but now you recognize his true nature."[14] In Luther's Wittenberg it was ultimately not possible to serve two masters.

Johannes Bugenhagen came to Luther's circle by a rather different route. Born in Wolin, a Baltic island off the Pomeranian coast, and educated at the University of Greifswald, Bugenhagen first became acquainted with Luther's teachings when the reformer's works began to circulate locally. In 1520 Bugenhagen came across a copy of Luther's *Babylonian Captivity* in the house of a friend, who asked Bugenhagen his opinion. Like many, Bugenhagen was first repelled by its radicalism. According to a later authority his first reaction was uncompromisingly negative: "There have been many heretics since Christ's death, but no greater heretic has ever lived than the one who has written this book." But he was also fascinated, and asked his friend for the loan of the book to peruse it more carefully. This study made him a disciple. "What shall I say to you?" he told his friend a few days later. "The whole world lies in complete blindness, but this man alone sees the truth."[15] Bugenhagen now contacted Luther directly and asked for guidance. Luther sent an encouraging letter along with a copy of his *Freedom of a Christian Man.* That was enough. In the spring of 1521 Bugenhagen left Treptow for Wittenberg.

Bugenhagen's initial intention was to study, so he enrolled as a student in the university (a rather mature one, since he was now thirty-two). But he was soon in demand as a teacher, initially to younger students from his native Pomerania, to whom he offered a lecture course on the Psalms. One of the first to recognize Bugenhagen as a special talent was Philip Melanchthon, who had dropped in to sample these private lectures and encouraged Bugenhagen to continue the course in public. Bugenhagen thus became an unofficial member of the university faculty, though this status was only officially recognized in 1533 once he had received his doctorate.

Luther was also quick to recognize Bugenhagen's qualities. He earned Luther's respect by his firm support of restraint and order during the turmoil unleashed by Karlstadt and the Zwickau prophets while Luther was absent in the Wartburg. In 1522 he took a further decisive step by taking a wife. This was not without a certain degree of emotional trauma, since his first choice of spouse got cold feet and called off the engagement: in 1522 to enter into marriage with an evangelical minister was still a difficult choice for a young woman of respectable family. But in October Bugenhagen married the excellent Walpurga, a spirited and practical-minded life partner who would be a constant support for Johannes in all of his future endeavors. With these extra responsibilities Bugenhagen was now urgently in need of a settled income; the problem was simply solved with his appointment as minister to the local parish church.

Here he would be both Luther's colleague and his pastor, responsible for ministering to the reformer's spiritual needs. This would be the basis of a lifelong and trusting friendship. When Bugenhagen's *Commentary on the Psalms*, the fruits of his early Wittenberg lectures, was published in 1524, it included commendatory recommendations from both Luther and Melanchthon. Luther's preface spoke eloquently of both their friendship and his regard for his colleague's talent. Instead of waiting on Luther's own long-delayed Psalm commentary, the reader should rejoice in Bugenhagen's work: "I make bold to say that no one (of those whose books survive) has ever expounded David's Psalter in such a way as to be called an interpreter of the Psalter, and that [Bugenhagen] is the first man in the world to deserve that title."[16] Praise indeed.

This Psalm commentary, published in a fine edition in Basel, was the first of a considerable sequence, which took in expository works on Deuteronomy, the historical books of the Old Testament, and the Pauline Epistles. Fine theologian though Bugenhagen was, however, his principal service to the Reformation would be as a church organizer. In 1524 the congregation of the Church of St. Nicholas in Hamburg wrote to invite Bugenhagen to be their pastor.[17] This was obstructed by the Hamburg City Council, and a similar call from Danzig (Gdansk) in 1525 was declined because the Wittenberg congregation refused to release him. But the requests for Bugenhagen's services continued: he was especially in demand when cities and princely territories wished to make the decisive step and adopt an evangelical church settlement. For this important purpose his Wittenberg colleagues were prepared to release him, even if this meant Luther had to shoulder many of Bugenhagen's preaching duties in the Wittenberg parish church. In 1528 Bugenhagen was allowed to make an extended trip to assist the city of Braunschweig in organizing the local church. This resulted in the drafting of the first of a series of highly influential church orders, for Hamburg and Lübeck, later for his own native Pomerania (1534) and Schleswig-Holstein (1542). Bugenhagen also led the way in his emphasis on the importance of well-organized and regulated schools; he was also one of the few in Luther's inner circle who spoke and wrote the language of the north, Low German. He translated Luther's *Catechism* into Low German, and also played a leading role in the preparation of the first Low German edition of the Luther Bible.

Luther could be a difficult and demanding friend. But to those in his inner circle he was loyal and supportive, in public and private. Cochlaeus's identification of the four evangelists as the core of the Wittenberg movement thus struck at an essential truth: that as the Luther controversy moved from protest to movement, Luther could not be a man alone. This applied not only to his closest workmates, and to the younger men who flocked to hear him and hung on his every word at the family supper table. Luther also grasped the role that the medium of print could play in building and publicly proclaiming this new community of evangelical truth.

A HELPING HAND

We have seen how shrewdly Luther intervened to build the printing industry in Wittenberg, drawing to the city an experienced printer to assist the overburdened and unimaginative Rhau-Grunenberg keep up with demand for his works. He was impatient with what he regarded as shoddy work, as the angry stream of letters from the Wartburg bears witness.[18] Wittenberg printers must have found him a demanding presence as he scrutinized their workmanship. But there was also a very positive side to Luther's mastery of the technical demands of the trade. He was sufficiently well versed in these practical considerations to be able to accommodate his own work to its rhythms and timetables, and he took a close interest in the process by which his manuscripts made their way into printed form.

Luther also understood his own importance to the Reformation's extraordinary success. However he might muse in his letters and sermons on his role as the humble instrument of God's purpose, he was fully aware that his own personality and the drama of his struggle with the church authorities was what had piqued public interest and furnished the movement with its most powerful shield against those who would destroy it. There is a fascinating little vignette in an otherwise routine letter to Spalatin in early March 1521, while Luther was awaiting his summons to the Diet of Worms. With this letter he enclosed some copies of Cranach's early engraved portrait of himself, which at Cranach's request he had also autographed.[19] The signed portrait as gift is something we associate with modern celebrity culture, to be displayed by the honored recipient as a token of acquaintance with leading statesmen, actors, or musical artists. It is curious to find Luther already engaged in something similar.

This is not the only way in which Luther exploited his fame to build the movement. In the published works of the Reformation, Luther also lent his prestige to works written by others by furnishing a brief preface or recommendation. These celebrity endorsements offered a seal of approval for a writing campaign that was self-evidently increasingly a team effort.

As with so much in the dramas of the Reformation, this program of prefatory endorsements began somewhat accidentally. Already in 1521 Luther was concerned at the increasing burden of answering his Catholic critics. Particularly irksome was the indefatigable secretary of Duke George of Saxony, Jerome Emser, who had kept up a fairly constant barrage since the Leipzig Disputation. When Emser published his *Quadruplica*, a further riposte to Luther's *Answer to the Book of the Goat Emser*, Luther had had enough. "I shall not answer Emser," he wrote to Melanchthon. "Anyone who seems fitting to you may answer, perhaps Amsdorf, if he is not too good for dealing with this dung."[20] To Amsdorf he apologized for shuffling off this unwelcome burden, though he was already beginning to have second thoughts.

> Philip wrote that you intend to answer Emser, if it seems wise to me. But I am afraid that he is not worthy of having you as a respondent. On the other hand he may laugh and mock if one of the young people should answer him, since he is full of Satan.[21]

Here lay the dilemma. Luther did not want to dignify his opponent's efforts with a response. On the other hand a reply by an inexperienced or callow disputant might hand the Romanists a propaganda victory, a lesson Luther had learned from Andreas von Karlstadt's enthusiastic but not always well-judged interventions in his cause. In the event, on this occasion Luther bit the bullet and replied himself, but from this point he was always happy when one of his more experienced colleagues would share the burdens of the print exchanges.

In 1522 Luther's *Judgment on Monastic Vows* unleashed a storm of protest from conservatives, particularly those themselves in holy orders. Among those who wrote against him was the Bavarian Franciscan Caspar Schatzgeyer. On this occasion Luther felt that Schatzgeyer, a relatively obscure figure, could be left to a friend, and he commissioned Johann Briesmann to undertake the task. This was a shrewd choice. Briesmann was well-known to the Wittenbergers, having served briefly on the university faculty before returning to his native Cottbus to pursue the task of reform in Brandenburg. As a former Franciscan, Briesmann was also able to take on Schatzgeyer on his own ground. In this instance Luther's preface was clearly written before the main text, since Luther laid out the agenda he hoped Briesmann would follow fairly fully.[22] This was one of the longer prefaces; on other occasions Luther would write no more than a few paragraphs, praising the author and signaling his approval of the contents.

Luther's fellow "evangelists" were among the first to benefit from his imprimatur. In the case of Melanchthon, Luther's first intervention did not entirely redound to the reformer's credit, since he had sent Philip's lectures on Romans and Corinthians to the press without the author's permission. Melanchthon had been reluctant to publish this work despite Luther's frequent urgings, so Luther dispatched his own copy to a friendly Nuremberg printer, along with his own slightly shamefaced letter of dedication to the reluctant author.[23] Presumably it had not been given to a Wittenberg printer in case Philip stumbled upon it: Melanchthon, like Luther, would have been a frequent visitor to the printers' workshops. Given he was also a steady source of work for the Wittenberg printers, none of them would have been entirely comfortable printing one of his works without his permission. In the event, this devious stratagem backfired badly as the Nuremberg printer made rather a mess of the task, publishing an edition so full of errors that these could only partially be corrected in subsequent editions. Had this happened to Luther's own work he would have been furious. In this case he decided to brazen it out, dispatching a further set of Philip's lectures (on John's

Gospel) for printing in Hagenau, complete with a letter of dedication to his friend Nikolaus Gerbel:

> I have already purloined our Philip's Annotations on three Epistles of Paul. And though he was not at liberty to rage against that thief Luther for it, he nevertheless thought he had been most satisfactorily avenged against me in that the little volume had come out so full of errors due to the negligence of the printers that I was nearly ashamed and regretted having invested my stolen property so poorly. Meanwhile, he has been making fun of me, hoping that henceforth I would abstain from such theft, having been taught a lesson by my predicament. But I, not troubled at all by this derision, have grown even more audacious, and now I take his Annotations on John the Evangelist not by stealth but by force, while the author resists in vain.[24]

All of this was rather tongue in cheek, but whether Philip saw the joke we do not know. The choice of Hagenau was an olive branch of sorts, since the text was consigned to Johann Setzer, the son-in-law of Thomas Anselm for whom Melanchthon had worked in his youth in Tübingen. Young Setzer rose to the occasion, as the title page proudly proclaims:

> The Annotations on John of Philip Melanchthon, more correct than those previously published, inasmuch as in this edition are contained many things missing from the others, along with a letter of commendation by M. Luther and an index.[25]

This rather extended history of Luther's imperious commandeering of his colleague's work is worth recounting, because these volumes introduce several features that would be quite characteristic of the works published with Luther's endorsement. First, they were frequently put to the press outside Wittenberg. Just as Melanchthon's works were sent to Nuremberg and Hagenau (and immediately reprinted elsewhere), so Bugenhagen's lectures on the Psalms were published in Basel. Second, Luther's letters of dedication were frequently addressed not to the author himself but to a third party, as here to Nikolaus Gerbel. Both features advertised to the reading public the expanding circles of those committed to the Wittenberg cause, in the German print world and among its leading intellectuals. Finally, we see Setzer's astute reference to Luther's involvement on the title page. Whatever the author's own reputation (high in Melanchthon's case) the advertisement of Luther's participation could only increase the book's salability.

In the course of the next twenty-three years Luther would provide a preface for over ninety works: the last, in 1545, adorned a posthumous edition of the English reformer Robert Barnes, whose *Lives of the Roman Pontiffs* Luther had enthusiastically endorsed in 1536.[26] Sometimes he clearly found it rather burdensome: as he wearily remarked in 1537, "I must now be a professional writer of prefaces."[27] Some were dashed off rather hurriedly, and amounted to no more than a couple of rather bland paragraphs. This was not his most considered work. But Luther was probably well aware that it was not the substance of his remarks but the mere fact that he offered his endorsement that elevated the book in the eyes of purchasers and book-trade professionals.

These prefatory remarks do, however, offer an interesting barometer of Luther's preoccupations as the movement shifts from the early direct engagement with the papacy to a period of consolidation and church building. Some preoccupations are enduring: the Turkish threat, the defense of matrimony, and particularly clerical marriage. Luther also sometimes uses a preface to signal an adjustment to previous literary missteps. The sea change in his attitude to Jan Hus and the Czech Unity of Brethren is reflected in several prefaces from the 1530s in which he wrote candidly of his earlier blindness to the virtues of the Czech reformer. A preface to twenty-two trenchant sermons by Johann Brenz published in 1532 also allowed him to distance himself from earlier remarks that seemed to advocate nonresistance against the Turkish invaders.[28] Throughout his career Luther was restlessly preoccupied by the Turkish threat to European Christendom, but aware also of his own ignorance of the Muslim faith. In 1530, introducing George of Hungary's description of Turkish ceremonies, he confessed that he had not yet been able to procure a translation of the Koran. When in 1542 this was finally furnished by the publication in Basel of Theodor Bibliander's translation, Luther intervened directly to ensure the success of this controversial project, writing to the Basel Council to secure the freedom of the incarcerated printer Johannes Oporinus, and providing a preface for publication.[29]

Luther was deeply obliged to the radiating circle of clergy and laypeople who committed themselves to his cause; he realized that their wholehearted commitment, their theological expertise and literary virtuosity, was vital to his survival. These prefaces show how he nurtured and tended this community to ensure that the Reformation would not stand or fall "by Luther alone." It is one of the most fascinating and understated aspects of his lifelong engagement with the printing industry.

THE WORD OF GOD

One collective effort towered above all others in the Wittenberg pantheon: the translation of the Bible. When Luther embarked on the work of translating the New Testament during his last weeks in the Wartburg, he was always clear that this enterprise would be shared with others. Even in beginning the task, he frankly acknowledged to Amsdorf, "I have here shouldered a burden beyond my powers."[30] Luther had no sense of proprietorship for this work. When he heard that his friend Lang was engaged on a Bible translation at Erfurt, he urged him to continue: "I wish every town would have its interpreter." Although he completed his first translation of the New Testament in eleven weeks, he knew he could go no further without help; a large part of his reason for bringing forward his return to Wittenberg was to engage his friends in this task.

So urgent was this in his mind that at one point he contemplated returning secretly and taking a room somewhere in Wittenberg, where he could remain closeted with the translation work and have his friends make clandestine visits to offer their help.

This, of course, was a pipe dream. In the event, Luther would make a very public return to his pulpit and place of authority within the church. But the work with the Bible was soon resumed. It would engage Luther, his colleagues, and his friends in the Wittenberg publishing industry for the best part of a further twelve years.

First there was the publication of Luther's New Testament to be supervised. Notwithstanding Luther's modest words of self-deprecation to Amsdorf, there was little time for fundamental revision of his work before the text was passed to the printer. Between Luther's dramatic return from the Wartburg on March 6 and the setting of the first sheets was only two months, time enough only for a final review of the text in the company of Philip Melanchthon. The timetable Luther set his printers was equally hectic. The completed work was to be ready by September, in time for sale at the Frankfurt Fair (it has become known, in consequence, as the September Testament).

The Frankfurt Fair was by this time Europe's principal emporium for the wholesale trade in books, dwarfing the other major seasonal fairs established over the course of the previous centuries. It took place twice a year, at Easter and in September, and was attended by publishers and booksellers from all of Europe's major book markets.[31] It was a mark of the growing maturity of Wittenberg's book industry that it was now organizing its production timetable around the established biannual fairs; notable, too, that by dealing with Frankfurt, Wittenberg's printers were able to bypass the previously dominant regional market at Leipzig, the now ailing local rival.

A good sale at Frankfurt was considered critical, since it had been decided that the September Testament should be published in a huge edition of some three thousand copies. This was an extremely tall order. The Wittenberg printing industry had grown very substantially in the last five years, particularly when measured in terms of output. But its printers had never taken on a task of this size and complexity. Most of Luther's writings were short and relatively simple tasks for a printer. This on Luther's part was quite deliberate. He was spreading the word to an audience with many inexperienced readers. He also knew Rhau-Grunenberg's limitations: when the printer had attempted something more demanding, like the Psalm commentaries, he had quickly got into trouble.

Melchior Lotter had brought greater professionalism, but the industry's capacity was still limited, and fairly stretched just keeping up with the steady stream of new works emanating from Luther's own pen. In the summer of 1521, according to Luther, there were six presses operating in Wittenberg. This probably equates to four in Lotter's shop and two in that of Rhau-Grunenberg. But as Luther only half flippantly remarked, these were kept pretty busy, four publishing his own works, and one each for Melanchthon and Karlstadt.[32] Now space had to be found for the Bible project, a book of serious size, heavily illustrated in significant portions of the text. For Lucas Cranach had prepared for this milestone text one of his masterpieces: a series of full-page woodcuts with which to dramatize the vivid prophecies of the apocalypse.[33] Custom and use also demanded that the New Testament be published in the large, folio format, almost the first book that the Wittenberg presses had taken on in this larger size.

For all these reasons the publication of the New Testament needed to engage the best talents available in the Wittenberg printing industry. Inevitably Rhau-Grunenberg was bypassed for a task of this complexity. The Bible project was consigned to Luther's reliable partners Christian Döring and Lucas Cranach, using Melchior Lotter's presses. Only this combination, working together, offered the prospect of bringing it to a successful conclusion. Döring could provide the necessary investment capital. Cranach's paper mill could furnish the raw materials, his workshop the woodcuts. Melchior Lotter would manage the work through the press. Then Döring's transportation firm could deliver the stock to Frankfurt.

Somehow Lotter managed to clear three presses of other tasks and the work began. The schedule was almost impossibly daunting, but Cranach and Lotter were both hard, driven men. The presses were cajoled into producing the required number of printed sheets; at least in Cranach's vast factory workshop there would have been no problem with storage space or with recruiting extra hands to stack and collate the finished sheets. On May 10 the first fascicule was completed.[34] Work progressed steadily through the Gospels and Epistles, at first in some secrecy, since the publishers had no wish to be preempted by another printer getting hold of the parts and creating his own competing edition. By September 21, miraculously, the whole edition was finished and Luther could send the last parts to Spalatin, which gave him three complete copies: one for himself, one for the elector, and one for Duke John.[35] The rest of the edition was now released for local sale and shipping to Frankfurt; and just as swiftly it was gone, sold out. Lotter began immediately with a new edition, to be published in December with Luther's hurried corrections and improvements. But the market was insatiable, sufficiently robust for Adam Petri to publish his own folio edition by year's end at Basel.

Lotter's September Testament was the first of more than 443 whole or partial editions of the Bible that would appear between 1522 and Luther's death in 1546.[36] It swiftly became a mainstay of the printing industry in Germany, a text so popular that it would justify repeated reprints in all of the major places publishing Luther's works and others besides. This was, above all, a very versatile text. While Lotter concentrated initially on large-format folio editions, other printers experimented· with editions of the New Testament text in the smaller, portable octavo format, with small editions of individual books of the Bible often no longer than one of the pamphlet *Flugschriften*. The year 1523 witnessed the first edition in Low German, the language of Hamburg and the north. Naturally the larger print centers took the lion's share, with major production in Basel, Nuremberg, and Strasbourg, as well as Wittenberg. Magdeburg swiftly established itself as the center of production for editions in Low

LUTHER'S NEW TESTAMENT

This elegant edition was a reprint by Adam Petri in Basel. It is an extraordinary testimony of the demand for Luther's translation that it went through three large editions (probably 9,000 copies) in under four months.

German. But there was still room for other, more ephemeral presses to enter this lucrative trade, such as the tiny shop established in 1522 by Nikolaus Widemar in Grimma. Grimma was a small habitation around twenty miles southeast of Leipzig, and there was more to the establishment of this printing press than meets the eye, as we will see in the next chapter. Widemar published only twelve books before moving on, but these included a copy of the Luther New Testament and two pamphlet versions of individual books, the Epistles to the Romans and Galatians.[37]

Through all of this sound and fury Luther and his brain trust worked steadily on with the translation of the Old Testament. At first this progressed well enough. Luther and Melanchthon moved smoothly through the Pentateuch, which was ready for Lotter by the end of 1522, and could thus conveniently occupy the presses once the second edition of the New Testament was finished. Luther, ever mindful of the pockets of potential purchasers, had always intended that the Old Testament would be published in three parts. This was also helpful to publishers; it gave them three manageable projects with separate sales, and purchasers could then bind together the whole work when it was finished. In the event, this would take much longer than expected.[38] Joshua to Esther was ready by the end of 1523, to be published in the following year. But then progress slowed dramatically. Because Job had occupied more time than Luther had expected, the poetic books (Job to the Song of Songs) were issued as a separate fascicule in the autumn of 1524.

Then other responsibilities intervened. In 1525 and 1526 Luther's attention was entirely taken up by the fallout from the Peasants' War and the dispute with Erasmus; then in 1527 the university moved to Jena because of an outbreak of plague. Although Luther and Bugenhagen both remained in Wittenberg, the work on the Prophets could not be continued in the absence of Melanchthon; this was doubly frustrating because Luther had, in fact, prepared a translation of the Prophets for his lectures in 1524. Because it was now obvious that this section of the Bible would not be finished imminently, Isaiah was released for separate publication in 1528.

The years 1529 and 1530 brought new difficulties, thanks to Melanchthon's renewed absence at the Diet of Speyer and then at the Diet of Augsburg. Luther poured out his frustrations by translating the Book of Daniel: in apocalyptic mood after his work with Daniel's prophecies, he now wondered if the end of the world would come before the Bible translation was finished. Only in 1532 had he and Melanchthon managed to find time to sign off on the Prophets, now published once again as a separate volume. That left only the Apocrypha, never Luther's favorite: this he was prepared to delegate largely to Melanchthon and Justus Jonas. Their task was completed finally in 1534, clearing the way for the much-delayed complete Wittenberg Bible.

Luther's relief at the dispatch of the final stages of this mammoth project vied with his frustration after the endless delays. As usual he was of a mind to blame the printers, though they had faithfully executed any work that was put their way. In fact, the long period of gestation of the Luther Bible was something for which the industry could be grateful. The steady sequence of partial editions, though messy, made for very good business, keeping the presses rolling without exposing the printers to substantial risk. These successive partial editions also had the welcome by-product of directing attention to some of the usually less-studied parts of the biblical canon: when Jonah and Habakkuk were the only new books available in 1526, for instance, they went through multiple editions.[39] Interestingly, the practice of publishing small, partial editions continued even after the whole Bible was finally available.

During the twelve years between the publication of the September Testament and the full Bible in 1534 the Wittenberg print industry had matured significantly. The complete Bible of 1534 and other subsequent editions were all published by men new on the scene since the time that printing in Wittenberg had relied on the old duopoly of Rhau-Grunenberg and Lotter: Hans Lufft, Georg Rhau, and Nickel Schirlentz. Hans Lufft's Bible of 1534 was itself a monument to how far the industry had come, a magnificent folio of over eight hundred leaves, a very substantial publishing project on its own. Even here, old habits died hard. The Bible was not paginated continuously through, but in six sections. It would still have occupied four presses in Lufft's shop for the best part of six months. This was a reminder that the capacity to publish such a project was not easily created—it had been a work of two decades to build such an industry in Wittenberg, fueled and underwritten by the enormous demand for Luther's writings.

This was a project at the heart of the Wittenberg Reformation. From the first days that Luther's name was known outside Saxony, those who joined their voices to the call for reform had a ready-made slogan: they demanded that their councils allow their priests to preach the pure Gospel, *"reines Evangelium."* But for this to be possible, the Word of God had also to be accessible: this is why the production of a new vernacular translation to replace the Latin Vulgate was for Luther such an urgent priority. And it had been, at every stage of the creative process, a team effort, from those who assisted in the process of translation, to the men who toiled in Hans Lufft's workshop and the carters who transported the copies to distant bookshops. These men, too, played their part in creating the Wittenberg Reformation.

BLACK SHEEP

In all movements propelled by charismatic personalities there will be bruising encounters along the way. A core of disciples will pledge total loyalty; others initially drawn to the movement will quietly go their separate ways. Most difficult of all are the cases of the early enthusiasts who burn brightly but are ultimately cast out. Such would be the case with one of Luther's most passionate supporters, his Wittenberg colleague Andreas von Karlstadt.

Karlstadt had been an important early convert to Luther's cause. In the years before the indulgence controversy he had been Luther's senior colleague in the university (a fact that inevitably colored their relationship in subsequent years). A firm adherent of Scholasticism, his initial inclination to take umbrage at Luther's criticisms was transformed by his own reading of Augustine. From that point on he was Luther's most fervent supporter, always prepared to dive into print in defense of Wittenberg teachings. He was brave, passionate, and learned. Indeed, Karlstadt was possessed of every necessary talent except good judgment.

Here lay the root of the problem. When Karlstadt published his excessive 380 theses in defense of Luther's doctrines in 1518, it did not require an adversary as shrewd as Johann Eck to discern a possible weak link in Wittenberg's armor. Eck's challenge to Karlstadt posed Luther a considerable problem, and it was only with some difficulty that he managed to insinuate himself into the Leipzig Disputation and make himself the defender in his own cause. Then came the Wartburg, and a chance for Karlstadt to exercise the leadership he may well have felt was his due. The result was very nearly catastrophic. Karlstadt advocated a series of radical changes to the worship service in Wittenberg, including a German liturgy. He invited the laity to receive both the bread and wine; he abandoned the traditional priestly vestments. Eyebrows were raised when he took a wife; for the reformers this would ultimately become routine, but Karlstadt's new bride was only fifteen.[40] All of Karlstadt's changes would later become part of the new Protestant order. But this was too much too fast. The elector, Frederick the Wise, was nervous, and in the Wartburg Luther was increasingly concerned.

Karlstadt's energetic reconstruction of the Wittenberg church order put Luther in a bind. Earlier in the summer, Karlstadt had denounced the legitimacy of monastic vows. This, too, was embarrassing to Luther, but he was reluctant to intervene. Karlstadt could easily be refuted, he confided to Amsdorf, but were he to speak against him "an occasion would be given to our enemies to boast over our internal disagreement; this would be a great stumbling block for the weak."[41]

In this Luther was absolutely correct, and in years to come Catholic critics would make hay with the emerging differences among the reformers. But as the situation in Wittenberg deteriorated further, Luther's reticence risked allowing the Reformation to drift toward anarchy. First Karlstadt's preaching induced a disorderly flight of monks from the Augustinian house in Wittenberg. Worse, news of the events in Wittenberg then attracted to the city others who shared Karlstadt's vision of radical reform, including the so-called Zwickau prophets, laymen whose confident exposition of the Bible belied their lack of formal theological training. With Karlstadt also pursuing his plans for root-and-branch reform the city was soon in uproar, and Luther's trusted lieutenants were close to despair.

It required Luther's unexpected return and stern sermons against fanaticism to restore control. The Zwickau prophets were sent packing. Karlstadt was crushed; humiliated and ostracized, he insisted on continuing to wear lay garb and renounced his responsibilities in the university. It was a relief to all when in 1523 he accepted an invitation to leave Wittenberg and take up a position as minister in Orlamünde, a small town some 125 miles distant. Karlstadt renounced none of his radical views and reformed worship in Orlamünde according to his lights; he also continued to write. He retained a following and an audience; his works were still widely published and purchased although Luther made sure that the Wittenberg presses were now closed to him. In 1524 his continued advocacy of iconoclasm called forth a furious rebuttal from Luther, *Against the Heavenly Prophets,* Luther's most trenchant denunciation of radicalism. Karlstadt replied in kind, and the breach between the two old colleagues was complete.

The outbreak of the Peasants' War, which we will discuss in chapter 9, brought new dangers. Karlstadt feared, with some justice, that his views would single him out for retribution when the revolt collapsed, and fled back to Wittenberg, where Luther offered him sanctuary. A condition was that Karlstadt should publicly disassociate himself from the revolt and his wilder teaching on the Lord's Supper; these two writings were duly published in Wittenberg with a hostile introductory essay by Luther in each case.[42] But the two men were never truly reconciled, as Luther's excoriating introduction to the *Defense Against the False Charge of Rebellion* makes clear: "Now Dr. Karlstadt is my greatest enemy with respect to doctrine, and concerning it we have attacked each other so vehemently that there is no hope of any reconciliation or further fellowship."[43]

Clearly a preface was not always used for team building and compliments. This amounted to a public shaming, through the instrument of print; a brutal humiliation for a man who had once been one of the major spokesmen of the Reformation, his works published in all the key centers of evangelical publishing. Karlstadt had now hit rock bottom. For three years he supported his family as a peasant farmer, but a new confrontation with Luther in 1529 forced him to leave Saxony for good. He found his way to Switzerland, and a refuge with churches that had their own problems with Luther's autocratic leadership. In 1541 he died of the plague in Basel.

A falling out among friends is never pretty, but for Luther a repudiation of this formerly valued colleague was the necessary price for the preservation of the integrity of the Wittenberg Reformation. The other notable casualty of these years was also an intimate colleague, this time in the printing industry. But whereas Karlstadt had given signs of his waywardness from the earliest years, the downfall of the dependable Melchior Lotter Junior was swift and precipitate.

Lotter had ended 1522 in triumph with the publication of the December Testament. Work began with the Old Testament, and with the prospect of an enhanced flow of work, Melchior Senior dispatched his third son, Michael, from Leipzig to join the Wittenberg firm. But 1523 brought a falling out with Cranach and Döring. The two entrepreneurs were eager to publish further parts of the Luther Bible under their own imprint, and so installed a new printer, Joseph Klug, in their capacious factory. A furious Lotter protested to the elector, but in vain; sympathy for his predicament vanished when he took out his frustration on a young print worker, beating him very severely. In normal circumstances the right of a master craftsman to impose physical discipline on a lazy or negligent youngster in his employment would not have been challenged, but this was something of a different order, and Lotter found himself up before the local magistrates and heavily fined. Worse, Cranach now took the opportunity to expel him from the Schloßstrasse premises. Melchior and Michael found a refuge on the Juristenstrasse and then in the Franciscan monastery. But without access to the resources of the Cranach workshop their firm was badly disadvantaged; Luther, too, distanced himself from his former protégé. By 1525 the firm was in financial difficulties, and Melchior retreated back to Leipzig; there is no evidence that he ever ran his own independent enterprise again, though he lived for another twenty years. Michael continued to publish on his own account until 1528, when he transferred his business to Magdeburg, with great success.

The breach with Lotter was hard for Luther but final. In his later table conversation he chose to remember not Melchior's early transformation of the Wittenberg printing industry, but how much money Lotter had made from publishing his works, "a Godless and disagreeable profit." Significantly Lotter is unfavorably compared in this reminiscence with Rhau-Grunenberg, who expressed conscientious scruples at the unprecedented profit to be made from printing Luther: "Dear Doctor, the yield is too great; I don't like to have such books."[44] To focus on this, rather than Lotter's enormous contribution to the Wittenberg industry, was graceless, but the dispute with Cranach and Döring, to whom Luther was very close, put the reformer in an invidious position. He conspicuously continued to support the younger brother's enterprise after Melchior's departure. Melanchthon seems also to have had some sympathy with Melchior's predicament, and in an unusual demonstration of defiant independence continued to put work his way after the breach with Cranach.[45]

Printing was a rough, tough business, and it would be naive to think it could be any less so because the profits to be won came from editions of Scripture and Luther's own work. The competition for Luther's patronage was intense, and would be more so still when the success of the industry attracted other ambitious and capable practitioners to try their hand in Wittenberg. On the whole Luther handled the distribution of work among the competing houses well. It is sad that the most significant casualty should be a man who had made so fundamental a contribution to Wittenberg's print revolution.

8.

THE REFORMATION
IN THE CITIES

I T IS TIME TO leave Wittenberg for a while, and to follow Luther (and his books) beyond the safe haven created by Elector Frederick in Electoral Saxony. This is where it would be tested how far Luther's call for reform would fare in the wider world: the teeming, gossipy public arenas of Germany's bustling cities; the political maelstrom of its patchwork of princely states. The first indications of interest, indeed enthusiasm for Luther, had been extremely promising. But it was one thing to shout "death to the Romanists" in the excitement of an Imperial Diet; quite another to follow Wittenberg into effective schism, and undertake a root-and-branch renovation of the familiar practice of religion.

In this respect 1521, and the promulgation of the Edict of Worms, was a critical juncture. Up until 1521 it had been relatively safe to show an interest in Luther. Most would agree that whereas they might not accept his wilder pronouncements, there was plenty in the reform agenda with which they might feel sympathy. But after the imperial edict was published the issue was very different. To express support for Luther was to give comfort to a condemned heretic and outlaw.

This was especially tricky for those who had previously shown the most interest in Luther's criticisms of the established order, the urban patriciate of the imperial free cities. These were circles in which Luther's challenge to the pope had been widely discussed. But to pursue this agenda any further might prove extremely perilous. The cities cherished their political independence, but equally their governments were conscious that this could not be guaranteed. They were well aware that their neighbors among the territorial princes were always anxious to extend their power. In some places questions of authority and the rights of competing jurisdictions were still partially unresolved. Traditionally the cities looked to the emperor to uphold their cause in any attempts to impugn their rights. But the emperor had now spoken out against Luther; to defy him in this was to risk a terrible retribution.

So the city fathers were inclined to tread carefully. The choices they faced were difficult and dangerous, the prospects for the future uncertain. They could see the strength of the agitation raised by Luther's cause. They could sense it as they walked the streets of the city (for this was an era when the rulers were not physically separated from the ruled, who had many opportunities to signal their discontent on the city's crowded thoroughfares). They reacted with extreme nervousness when the public excitements threatened to get out of hand. They could see the evidence of the Reformation's success in attracting public interest in the pamphlets piled up on the booksellers' stalls. But the dangers of precipitate action on their part often outweighed the dangers of public agitation. Did the public excitement really represent the developing view of the community, or just a noisy minority? And what of the political dangers? The emperor had made his opinion of Luther all too clear. Could they risk defiance?

So the city councils, often a self-contained oligarchy of powerful families, generally took a cautious approach, even if some of their members personally sympathized with the new teachings. Timid in the face of the emperor's wrath, but also discerning in the evangelical agitation the potential for unwelcome disruption to the social order, they often moved to stifle the first signs of enthusiasm for Luther's movement, whether this was the local printing of evangelical pamphlets or a preacher speaking in Luther's favor. They were particularly alert for any sign that sympathizers for Luther's cause might be attempting to institute their own local Reformation. So it required some courage for those who did continue to speak out, particularly members of the clergy who used their own pulpits to proclaim their fealty to Luther's movement.

Yet the Reformation could not have succeeded—would not indeed have survived—without men of this stamp. However eagerly Luther's books were circulated and read, this in itself would not have been sufficient. It required the emergence of leaders, of trusted and respected local figures, prepared to commit themselves openly to the cause. This required great courage. Most knew there would be no protector like the Elector Frederick to ensure their safety. Many put their lives, and certainly their livelihoods, at risk by speaking up for Luther and the Gospel teaching. In the first years some would be hounded out of their pulpits and into an ignominious exile. It required the emergence of a genuine popular movement to ensure their return.

GOD'S WORD TRULY PREACHED

The early Reformation was in many respects profoundly anticlerical in tone. Luther led the way in his criticism of the church hierarchy, his denunciation of clerical greed, and his articulation of a new role for a theologically literate laity. Much of this found a resonance in the German cities. Many in the city governments were all too eager to cut the local church down to size: to challenge church immunities from local taxes, to repossess valuable urban property willed to church institutions, to wrest control over schools from the local cathedral chapter.[1] So while bearing all this in mind, it is important to reflect that in the first years at least, the revolt against the church came largely from within the church. Most of Luther's first and most influential supporters were, like him, churchmen. The Reformation in the cities would be driven very largely by the clergy. These clerical supporters would play a crucial role in preaching Luther's message to new audiences.

Those who associated themselves with Luther's teaching in these first years came to his movement in one of three ways. They might be members of one of the existing intellectual circles of which Luther or one of his Wittenberg colleagues was part. They might have met Luther in person; here his three long journeys across Germany between 1518 and 1521 played a crucial role in gathering a following. Or they might have been drawn to the Reformation from reading his books, sometimes reinforced by correspondence with friends already turning toward reform.

The direct influence of Luther and his circle was most obvious in northern Germany, within the geographical orbit of Wittenberg. In Erfurt, the first to advocate the reform agenda were two close allies, Johann Lang, a longtime friend, and Justus Jonas. Both were preaching in the city churches from 1520. The Reformation in Erfurt found its strongest support from within the university community. The extraordinary demonstration of enthusiasm for Luther as he passed through on his way to Worms was critical to the development of a local Reformation movement, which from this point would progress in close communication with Wittenberg.[2] Wittenberg's influence also reverberated strongly in Leipzig (though here the Reformation would be held back by the determined hostility of Duke George) and in Nuremberg. The first to preach in Luther's support in Nuremberg was Wenzeslaus Linck, a graduate of Wittenberg University and a former colleague of Luther on the teaching faculty. Linck made his first visit to Nuremberg in 1516, and became a popular preacher; he also became deeply embedded in the intellectual circle that gathered around Staupitz.[3]

Nuremberg had been deeply engaged in Luther's cause since he had passed through the city on his way to his Augsburg meeting with Cajetan in 1518. Two members of the humanist group who greeted him warmly on this occasion would later be included, to the city's embarrassment, on the list of those who shared Luther's excommunication in *Exsurge Domine*. In Nuremberg, more than anywhere, patrician intellectuals were drawn to Luther because they saw him as sharing their reform preoccupations; they were less sympathetic with the implicit radicalism of his developing theology or the explicit and violent repudiation of papal authority. Of his early Nuremberg admirers, a number, most prominently Pirckheimer and Scheurl, would eventually disassociate themselves from Luther. It was left to the preachers to push the matter forward: first Wenzeslaus Linck, and from 1521 Andreas Osiander. Osiander was well acquainted with all the leading players in Nuremberg politics, a member of the *Sodalitas Staupitziana,* a teacher of Hebrew, and a former Wittenberg student.[4] So when Osiander began to preach more aggressively against papal authority, the council reacted with much less alarm than had the preacher been a lowborn incomer.

The Nuremberg Council's management of the reform process during these years provides a vivid illustration of the conflicting pressures under which the imperial cities were forced to operate. The Edict of Worms was obediently posted at the town hall, and the city's publishers, no doubt to their great frustration, were ordered not to publish Luther's books. As a result, from 1521 Nuremberg contributed much less to the total volume of Luther imprints than one would expect. But the booksellers' stalls were still crammed with Luther's works, and eagerly purchased, as the papal nuncio Francesco Chieregati rather sourly noted.[5] When a vacancy arose for a preaching position at the church of St. Sebald in 1521, the council invited Luther to advise on a suitable candidate and appointed the man he proposed. So in the same years when Luther's initial enthusiasts among Nuremberg's intellectual elite were beginning to have second thoughts, the Nuremberg Council was carefully, watchfully, moving toward a more decisive alignment of the city with the evangelical cause.

Wittenberg would continue to act as an important center for the diffusion of the Reformation in northern and eastern Germany for years to come. It was to Wittenberg in 1524 that the beleaguered evangelicals of Hamburg appealed for a preacher, one of many such requests.[6] Wittenberg also functioned as a place of refuge for many among the first generation of evangelical preachers whose untimely adherence to the Reformation had put them in danger. The former Dominican Jacob Strauss first preached in the evangelical cause at Hall in the Austrian Tyrol. Expelled on the order of the local bishop in 1522, Strauss came to Wittenberg and enrolled as a student. In 1523 he was reassigned to the Church of St. George in Eisenach.[7] Paul Speratus was one of the first to declare for the cause of reform, preaching at Würzburg in 1519. Summarily expelled, again on the order of the bishop, by 1522 he had come to Wittenberg, where he made himself useful translating some of Luther's Latin works into German.[8] In 1525 he was dispatched to Königsberg, to orchestrate reform in the Prussian lands of the Teutonic Knights. In this way Wittenberg contrived to place well trained and passionately committed agents of its reform in key centers across the region; this would be the stronghold of Lutheranism for centuries to come.

The situation was rather different in the larger, sophisticated urban centers of the German south and west, where direct connections with Wittenberg were far more attenuated. Even here though, a number of those who played a critical role in the preaching of the Gospel message could date their adherence to the Reformation to a personal meeting with Luther. The most famous example was that of Martin Bucer, who first encountered Luther as a Dominican interloper present to hear Luther defend his teachings at the meeting of the Augustinian chapter in Heidelberg. This experience in March 1518 made Bucer an instant disciple; he would go on to play a leading role in the Strasbourg Reformation and would become a significant figure in the European Reformation in his own right.[9] Johann Brenz was another who heard Luther at Heidelberg. Then still a student, by 1522 he would be preaching the Gospel in Schwäbisch Hall, the beginning of a long and distinguished career at the heart of Lutheran churches in southern Germany.[10]

Among those who met Luther on his second major trip across Germany, the confrontation with Cajetan at Augsburg, was Johann Oecolampadius, then preacher and confessor at the local cathedral. Powerfully

THE REFORMATION DIALOG

The Reformation relied as much on public discourse and conversation as on the printed word. Here a priest is worsted by a worthy citizen.

moved by the experience, Oecolampadius withdrew to the monastery at Altomünster to resolve his own position in the Reformation debate, emerging a convinced supporter of Luther's doctrines. By 1522 he had graduated to Basel where, after a period working for the printer Andreas Cratander, he took on a leading role in the city's Reformation.[11] Johann Briesmann, who met Luther at the Leipzig Disputation, would go on to preach in Cottbus and Königsberg. Perhaps the most interesting figure in this category was Wolfgang Capito, a distinguished and respected figure in the world of south German humanism. In 1515 he was appointed professor of theology in the University of Basel, where he also established a close working relationship with the printer Johann Froben. He also became close to Erasmus. For Capito, Luther's teaching seemed at first to be a natural continuation of the church reform discussed in Erasmus's circle. It was Capito who first suggested to Froben the collected edition of Luther's early works that brought the printer such commercial success.[12] But the growing chill between Luther and Erasmus left Capito seriously embarrassed. In 1520 he moved to Mainz, where he became an intimate adviser of Albrecht of Brandenburg, archbishop of Mainz. Although advising moderation on both sides, Capito was increasingly troubled by the capacity of the Reformation to stir social unrest. He and Luther corresponded, on Luther's side with characteristic bluntness.[13] An agitated Capito then made two visits to Wittenberg, one while Luther was still in the Wartburg, then again immediately on his return. This second meeting was decisive; within a year Capito would sever his connection with Albrecht and move to Strasbourg to assist Bucer in preaching the Reformation.

With Bucer and Capito the Strasbourg Reformation had two heavyweight local advocates, but the first to preach the evangelical cause in the city was a far less celebrated figure, Matthias Zell. Zell seems to have had no personal connection with Luther. He had moved to Strasbourg from Freiburg im Breisgau (where he had been rector of the university) to take up a position in the cathedral parish church of St. Laurence in 1518. There, from his own pulpit, he was in 1521 moved to a defense of Martin Luther. He then began to preach in a Lutheran manner, and later, as conservative forces attempted to have him removed, he started to publish in his own defense.[14]

The process by which such men adopted the Reformation remains opaque. Not all record the blinding flash of revelation with which Johannes Bugenhagen perused the *Babylonian Captivity*. In many cases adherence to the evangelical cause followed a period of cautious deliberation. In the early years members of Germany's humanist circles would sometimes share their reflections on reading Luther's works in correspondence with friends. Michael Hummelberg and Joachim Vadian were obviously already in agreement. "Your opinion of Luther greatly pleased me. I think him a man of eminent genius and erudition and of singular judgment. His writings for the most part breathe out Christ himself."[15] Thomas Blaurer's friend John von Botzheim needed more persuading. "Please change your opinion about Luther writing more bitterly than need be. He does it for the good of the Christian flock, nor can he do it without bitterness."[16] Clearly all of these men had Luther's works in their hands and were eager for more. "I have seen the bull against Luther printed at Paris," wrote Boniface Amerbach to his brother Basil. "Beatus has written that the bull is published with notes by Hutten. Please send me this and any other new and agreeable German publications when you can. I mean little pamphlets, for it is sufficient to give me the titles of large books."[17] Luther did what he could to help, sending letters and copies of his published works, exhorting and offering comfortable words. It is worth making the point that despite this, many followed the same course of inquiry and took the opposite view. They read Luther and were repelled; they talked to friends and were persuaded to stay with established allegiances. But enough were persuaded to throw in their lot with Luther to furnish the leadership for movements of reform in cities across Germany.

Many of Luther's advocates left no record at all of how they arrived at their beliefs. For many the decision to preach Luther's Gospel was solitary and intensely personal. These, in many ways, were the boldest of the Reformation's pioneers, acting without the support of an extended circle of fellow enthusiasts, moved solely by their sense of the rightness of the new evangelical doctrines. This could be a lonely and dangerous road, speaking in defiance of the still prevailing orthodoxy, risking livelihoods or more. Such was the case with Paul Speratus, Jacob Strauss, and Stephan Agricola, all of whom had suffered deprivation and hardship after preaching the Reformation. None of them had any known previous association with Luther; they must have been converted through reading his books. In the case of Agricola this inspired a brave but foolhardy attempt to preach the Gospel in Vienna, the center of Habsburg authority. Agricola was arrested and imprisoned, escaping only in 1524 during the turbulence of the Peasants' War. He made his way to Augsburg, where he was swiftly engaged in the local Reformation.[18]

Agricola was one of a number of preachers now gathered around Urbanus Rhegius, the leading spirit of Augsburg's Reformation. Rhegius had come to Augsburg in 1520 on his appointment as preacher in the city's cathedral. In this prestigious role one of his first duties was to read from the pulpit the papal bull of excommunication against Luther. Within a few months, however, Rhegius had decided that the bull, rather than the condemned writings of Luther, posed the real danger to the church. Rhegius expressed this view in a published pamphlet and from the pulpit. This sensational apostasy led to his rapid deposition. Rhegius left the city but continued to publish: he would, in fact, be the most published clerical author to emerge from outside the Wittenberg circle in the first decade of the Reformation.[19] The huge popularity of these writings no doubt contributed to the public agitation for Rhegius's return; reappointed by the city council in 1523, he would play a directing role in Augsburg's Reformation for the next seven years.

THE WISDOM OF CROWDS

Those who preached the Gospel around Germany in these tumultuous years played a vitally important role in spreading Luther's teachings. This was an age, we must remember, in which a large proportion of the population could not read, even in relatively sophisticated urban societies such as the German imperial cities. At a time when the overwhelming majority of a population would attend church at least once a week, the pulpit represented one of the most important instruments of public communication. What was said in the church could play a crucial role in shaping public opinion and for that reason was closely monitored. When preachers, often respected local figures like Urbanus Rhegius, spoke out against the established order, they were heeded; but they also caused disquiet. Those who preached without proper authorization caused a public scandal. Parties were formed, civic society was divided. In such cases the first instinct of the local authorities was to close down debate, to silence the dissident preacher, and to restore authority.

This might have been the end of the matter, but for the most extraordinary aspect of the movement stirred by Luther: the determination of the laity to be heard. In the years after 1521 in cities around Germany citizen groups made it clear that they were not prepared to accept the removal of a favored preacher spreading the Gospel message. They agitated for his return, even for the right of a congregation to appoint its own minister. In many places this tussle, which was often extended over a number of years, was crucial to the final triumph of the Reformation.

What animated this resistance? No doubt in many cases it was what the city's inhabitants had heard from the pulpit or discussed with friends. But a major role can be attributed to the tumultuous maelstrom of pamphlets cascading from the German presses. For it was in precisely these years, 1520 to 1525, that the print onslaught reached its peak: a torrent of urgent, biting satire, excoriating denunciations of traditional authority, and pious reflections on the Christian life.

The sheer scale of this publishing effort is quite astonishing. Between 1520 and 1525 the presses of Germany turned out over seven thousand editions, more than doubling output since the previous decade. Almost all of this extra capacity can be accounted for by the controversies of the Reformation. It says a great deal for the flexibility of the industry that this increased level of production could be accommodated; it is equally extraordinary that this vastly increased number of books found so ready a market. That they did so is clear not least from the number of Reformation pamphlets that went through multiple editions, the most reliable indication we have of contemporary popularity.

The obvious enthusiasm for Luther's writings among the book-buying public also encouraged printers to risk larger editions, sometimes up to three thousand copies, against an industry norm of three hundred to seven hundred for small pamphlets. All told, the German market may during these years have absorbed something close to four million copies of the various works of the controversy and instruction generated by the Reformation.[20] This was an enormous volume of work, and it posed a significant challenge to the German book industry simply to keep up with this demand.

It helped that evangelical authors could find willing publishers in almost all of Germany's print centers. Of Germany's major pre-Reformation centers of the publishing industry only Cologne was wholly closed to the evangelical cause. The other five (Augsburg, Nuremberg, Strasbourg, Leipzig, and Basel), together with Wittenberg and Erfurt, accounted for over 85 percent of the published writings of Luther and his colleagues. They also began during these years to publish the works of local Reformation preachers, a crucial enhancement of the message emanating from Wittenberg.

The pattern of production varied from place to place. In Strasbourg all five of the major publishing firms engaged themselves to some extent with printing for the Reformation, though less so in the case of the determinedly Catholic Johann Grüninger.[21] In Augsburg, which had long specialized in the production of cheap books in the vernacular, the publication of Luther's works was spread among at least ten different printers.[22] In contrast, Basel had to this point been largely a center of scholarly Latin publishing. This created a clear opportunity for Adam Petri, who was able to corner the local market in evangelical works.

Why did this print onslaught matter? Partly, of course, for what these works contained. Although many of Germany's citizens did not read, the highest proportion of readers was definitely concentrated in the cities, precisely where the Reformation was most hotly debated. In the first years, 1517 to 1520, the most important readers were to be found among the clergy and local intelligentsia, men who would then go on to be leaders in their own right. This was the period when a relatively high proportion of the literature of the Reformation was still in Latin,

PRINTING LUTHER IN AUGSBURG

Although this claims to be a Wittenberg publication, this work was in fact printed in Augsburg using a copy of Cranach's woodcut. Shameless, but a tribute to the potency of "Brand Luther."

the language of clerical conversation. But in the five years after Luther's condemnation at Worms in 1521, 85 percent of the published editions of his works were in German; this applied also in the case of works written by Luther's followers and allies.[23]

These vernacular works played a crucial role in building support for the Reformation. They might serve as a surrogate preacher when an evangelical minister had been dismissed. They helped maintain the solidarity of the movement's supporters in difficult times and won new adherents to the cause. But the pamphlets were important in more ways than just for their content. Merely the fact that they could still be published and circulated when evangelical preaching was banned was a tangible symbol of defiance. As we have seen, Reformation *Flugschriften* were often instantly recognizable, with their strong visual appeal. The reluctance or inability of the city authorities to inhibit their sale was in itself an important victory for the evangelical cause. The city of Nuremberg, for instance, cautioned its printers against publishing Luther, but took no action against booksellers who continued to stock Reformation pamphlets. Here, and elsewhere, the sheer abundance of these pamphlets gave an irresistible impression of strength.

In the years between 1521 and 1525, when the pamphlet war was at its height, Luther and his supporters outpublished their opponents by a margin of nine to one. The impact of this was not lost on those in the city council chambers who had until this point held the line against the Reformation, if necessary expelling evangelical preachers from their cities. In this age, communities functioned largely by consensus. The city might be ruled by a relatively narrow oligarchy, but these councillors walked the same streets as their fellow citizens, they heard the catcalls and muttering in the market square, the tavern gossip. Townspeople might not have the vote, but they had many ways of making their views known. The overwhelming plurality of published literature on the evangelical side provided a sort of surrogate for a popular vote. It gave the clear impression of an emerging consensus, a new public mood for reform, particularly when it was backed, as it often was, by noisy demonstrations of disapprobation at attempts to preach conservative doctrine or circulate anti Lutheran tracts. With the passage of time the city oligarchs found this increasingly hard to resist.

Much of this had been clear to the papal legate Aleander when he arrived in Worms to prepare for the Imperial Diet. He immediately sensed that these were unusual times. His arrival had been greeted by a flurry of hostile and scabrous pamphlets; the fact that this went unpunished emboldened the citizens to new indignities. Aleander was denied access to his lodgings; men touched their swords significantly as he passed on the streets. Pictures of Luther were treated like holy relics. Men gathered in the square to debate Luther's teaching, and nobles carried his books into meetings of the Diet. Here was the Reformation in a single, well-observed vignette.[24] Worst of all:

> A shower of Lutheran writings in German and Latin comes out daily. There is even a press maintained here, where hitherto this art has been unknown. Nothing else is bought here except Luther's books even in the imperial court, for the people stick together remarkably and have lots of money.[25]

With respect to the press, this was only half right. There was a press newly established in Worms, largely because the emperor required one to print the official proceedings of the Diet, but it played little role in the publication of evangelical works.[26] These were all brought to Worms from elsewhere. This, of course, made retribution against the publishers well-nigh impossible, and the city authorities clearly did not feel secure enough to go after the local booksellers.

This was a trial of strength, as everyone knew, and pamphlets were major weapons of this struggle to determine the future direction of Germany's religion. Often this was quite literally the case, as books, and their public circulation, became flashpoints in the battle for local supremacy. In Magdeburg an early polemical writing of Jerome Emser was pinned up in what Luther described decorously as "a shameful place," probably the town's privy or place of public execution. A rod was also attached to hint at the chastisement that would befall the author if he ever showed his face.[27] Official writings condemning Luther were torn down and evangelical writings pinned up in their place. In Erfurt in 1520 an anonymous pamphlet was affixed to the doors of the university's Great College defending Luther and attacking Eck. The pamphlet sought to rally the university community in defense of Luther, but the language was far from academic.

We exhort in the Lord Jesus Christ, rise up and act courageously in the word of Christ. Resist by warding off the brutes; protest even with hands and feet against the most rabid detractors of that aforesaid Martin. Lest the ideas manifestly raised up by him from the dust into the light be somehow suppressed, fight back![28]

This was not exactly the spirit of Erasmus, and the fact that official academic space had been appropriated in this way was a serious offense. An official investigation was set in train but no culprits could be identified. Even the printer could not be brought to book, since the work had been commissioned from a printer outside the city, and bore no identifying marks (it was, in fact, the work of Melchior Ramminger of Augsburg).[29] This demonstration was clearly carefully planned, and represented a deliberate escalation of the confrontation with authority. Even in these academic circles there was a clear sense that the old ways of doing business, the language and formal procedures of disputation, no longer met the needs of the present situation. This sentiment had been building since the Leipzig Disputation of 1519. Johann Lang was responsible for publishing the proceedings of the disputation in Erfurt, but realized that the academic to and fro was not really comprehensible to anyone but a clerical insider. The printer, Matthes Maler, warned the unwary reader that he might find it a "chaotic sea of words."[30] Many thought the Leipzig Disputation did not live up to the importance of the issues at stake, but it may have been simply that the medieval type of oral disputation, formal and extraordinarily long, did not lend itself to the medium of the printed pamphlet.[31]

By 1521 the dam had burst; Germany's cities had to choose between enforcing the Worms Edict or proceeding down the path of reform. The deluge of printed works, addressing the reform agenda in all its aspects, showed how the habit of obedience had now been overtaken by a clear desire to continue along the road indicated by Luther's defiance. Surveying this great mass of literature, several things become clear. We can see the overwhelming, commanding presence of Luther as spiritual leader of the movement. Luther's works outstrip those of any other author by a factor of ten; he outpublished the most successful of his Catholic opponents by a factor of thirty. Even this bald statistic understates the dominant role of Wittenberg in the printed works of the Reformation. After Luther, three of the next four most published authors were Melanchthon, Bugenhagen, and Justus Jonas; the only author to break into this Wittenberg cartel was Urbanus Rhegius of Augsburg.[32] Melanchthon played a particularly important role as a Latin author. Even if we cast our eye over the less celebrated authors of the Reformation, the continuing role of Wittenberg as a guiding force is clear. The debate that followed the publication in 1523 of Luther's *Judgment on Monastic Vows* drew forth supportive contributions from a number of authors on the evangelical side: Johann Schwan, Francis Lambert, Johann Briesmann, and Johann Eberlin von Günzburg. In 1523 all four were resident in Wittenberg.[33] The clear sense of direction provided by Wittenberg to the printing campaign of the early evangelical movement helps explain the relative doctrinal coherence of the Reformation in these early years.[34]

There was one very important exception to this Wittenberg domination, for these years also witnessed the first significant interventions in the debate by local leaders. In addition to numerous reprints of the works of Luther and his Wittenberg colleagues, the Strasbourg presses published works by Zell, Bucer, and Capito; Augsburg had a prominent spokesman in Urbanus Rhegius; and Ulrich Zwingli emerged as a dominant force in Zurich. These men could speak with authority to their own congregations; as Zell put it in his *Christian Apology* of 1523, he was now putting into writing what he had already taught orally to over three thousand people. The preachers would bear witness, as they had in their sermons, that Luther's teachings were not just the doctrine of denunciation, but the template for a new Christian art of living in their own communities. They insisted that Luther was pious and right, that his writings were "just and Christian," that he was an "innocent revealer of truth."[35]

This sort of character reference was every bit as important as the trenchant controversy in which the Wittenbergers perforce engaged.

The local pastors also echoed Luther's denunciations of the papacy and his criticism of the venality of the clergy. This to some extent vitiated the charge of rebellion and disobedience, one of the most telling weapons in the armory of Luther's opponents. Such issues also spoke more directly to the concerns of their congregations than the more abstruse theological propositions developed by Luther in response to his Catholic critics. This was important, because it was precisely in these years that members of the lay community were themselves taking to print to express their own support for Luther's teachings.[36] Here, too, the concentration was rather more on attesting to Luther's credentials as a teacher and pastor than in articulating a particularly sophisticated view of his main theological precepts. They all recognized that Luther was a learned doctor whose dedication to the Christian faith had put him at odds with the institutional church. They accepted Luther's precept that this truth could be established only on the basis of Scripture. Beyond this they were prepared to put a great deal of faith in Luther's credentials as a man of God and truthful interpreter. As Lazarus Spengler, secretary of the Nuremberg City Council, put it in an influential tract, "No teaching or preaching has seemed more straightforwardly reasonable, and I also cannot conceive of anything that would more closely match my understanding of Christian order as Luther's and his followers' teaching and instruction." Spengler then went on to make a highly significant remark. "Up to this point I have also often heard from many excellent highly learned people of the spiritual and worldly estates that they were thankful to God that they lived to see the day when they could hear Doctor Luther and his teaching."[37] This was the wisdom of crowds: a growing consensus that in the battle with his shrill, intemperate opponents, Luther was the better man.

OPPOSING LUTHER

If Luther and his allies enjoyed an overwhelming supremacy in the field of print, this was not for any lack of effort on the part of defenders

VIVA IMAGO · MAGNI · ILLIVS · THEOLOGI · IOHANNIS · ECKII. CATHOLICÆ · RELIGIONIS · PROPVGNATORIS · INVICTI ÆTATIS · SVÆ XLIII ECKIVS · INSIGNIS · MYSTES · DIVVMQVE · SACERDOS · DETEXIT · FRAVDES · HÆRESIVMQVE · DOLOS · ANNO · M · D · L · X · X · II

JOHANN ECK

One of the small group of Catholic theologians who pursued Luther doggedly in print, despite the decided lack of enthusiasm for their works in the printing fraternity.

of the traditional order. They recognized the danger, and the need that the Lutheran threat should be combatted. Luther had many and capable foes, and we have met several of them in preceding chapters: Tetzel, Eck, Cochlaeus, Emser. All these men showed courage, resolution, and persistence. But there is no doubt that, in publishing terms at least, they were swimming against the tide.

Why was the Catholic counterattack ultimately so ineffective? Several reasons have been advanced for the failure to dent Luther's overwhelming supremacy in the battle of the books. It has, for instance, often been suggested that in engaging Luther the Catholic theologians fought with one hand tied behind their back, inhibited by their reluctance to engage in controversy in the vernacular.[38] Part of the scandal of Luther was that he had appealed over the heads of his clerical brethren to a wider popular audience. Many of his opponents deplored that a theological quarrel should, in this way, be brought into the glare of public controversy; such a discussion should be conducted in Latin, the language of academic debate.

This certainly has the ring of truth. The Latin exchanges of the years after 1517 were intended largely to engage a clerical audience; on the conservative side it was crucial to address this group and stem the hemorrhaging of support among the clergy to Luther's side. This is all the more obvious when, as we have seen, we consider the vital role that such early clerical converts would play in building the Reformation in the cities across Germany. But there was also a genuine belief, as the Franciscan Thomas Murner put it, that "matters of faith should not be disputed before the ignorant common folk." This was true irrespective of the truth or otherwise of Luther's teachings; merely the appearance of discord among the clergy "caused great scandal and disobedience among ignorant Christians." "As we unfortunately now can clearly see, not many Christians have been moved to reverence by doctor Martin's teaching but only to rebellion."[39]

The irony is that these trenchant reflections included in Murner's *Concerning Doctor Martin Luther's Teaching and Preaching* were written and published in German, one of five such vernacular writings published by Murner in a barrage against Luther in Strasbourg in the years 1520 and 1521. In this Murner was not alone. Johann Tetzel, as we have seen, recognized the need to confute Luther's German writings very early, and the indefatigable Jerome Emser would publish more in German than in Latin.

The problem was not that Catholic authors could not, or would not, write in German, but that these works were not particularly successful. Few of those works that were published had much resonance, and hardly any went through more than one or two editions; many could not be published at all. For this failure to find publishers for their works Catholic authors were often inclined to blame the malign partisanship of the printing industry. Already in 1521 Aleander at Worms was remarking on the difficulty of finding printers for Catholic works, and two years later Cochlaeus would attribute the delay in publishing Schatzgeyer's reply to Johann Briesmann's attack on his work on monastic vows to the influence of Lutheran sympathizers in southern Germany.[40] This mattered, particularly if in the rapid fire of controversy Catholics could not get their replies into print, and it appeared as if they were ceding the field to their evangelical opponents. But it was easy, and not likely true, to imply these difficulties occurred because printers were committed to the evangelical cause. As we have seen, most printers would cheerfully publish for both sides, or move from one to the other, if it was worth their while. The real answer was that printers could see which way the wind was blowing. Reading the market was an essential skill in the publishing industry, which depended on assessing risk and seizing opportunity. And here the evidence flowed all one way. The enthusiasm for the writings of Luther and his followers was palpable and obvious. Printers could see this in the speed with which editions sold out and the demand for reprints and new titles. The real disincentive to publishing Catholic works was the irrefutable evidence that those of Luther's supporters sold much better.

It was also the case that printers who took on the works of Luther and his colleagues faced little danger of retribution for doing so. This was not the case everywhere. In France, England, and the Low Countries, printers faced serious consequences if they published evangelical works. They were arrested and occasionally executed when their responsibility for heretical publications could be proved. With few exceptions this was not the case in Germany, especially in these early years. In Germany most authorities instituted a form of censorship, but this did little to inhibit the flow of books since jurisdictions were so very local: here the fact that Germany was a patchwork of hundreds of small city and princely states militated against effective control.[41] Production was also very decentralized. In England, books for sale in St. Paul's Churchyard, if they were in English, would have been printed in one of a limited number of shops all less than a mile away. This was an industry that was very easily controlled. In Frankfurt, Augsburg, or a host of other places, the pamphlets on a bookseller's stall might have come from two dozen different places. Most were printed without the printer's name on the title page, and so even if the authorities were inclined to investigate it was difficult to know where to start. Anything that might put a local printer at risk could be sent to another print shop a day's ride away, and the pamphlet or broadsheet could be back for local sale within a couple of days.[42] So even in a loyally Catholic jurisdiction the risk of such sales fell on the bookseller rather than the printer.

All of these factors conspired to ensure that in Germany, and uniquely in Germany, the printing industry felt a strong if pragmatic affinity with the evangelical cause. Even the most distinguished defenders of the Roman obedience might experience cool responses when they took their manuscripts to a print shop, an experience that left them bruised and resentful. In 1520 Johannes Cochlaeus finished a rebuttal of Luther's *To the Christian Nobility;* this was clearly an exceptionally important work, but he could not raise the funds to have it printed. His *Assertio pro Emsero,* written in 1521 to support Jerome Emser, was not published until 1545. The dogged determination of Cochlaeus to see his works into print was a continuous drain on his resources throughout his career, and it was only in 1535, when Cochlaeus became a canon of Meissen, that he found an effective solution by underwriting the establishment of a new press in Leipzig. Cochlaeus provided one thousand gulden of start-up capital to pay for three presses and meet the costs of the first publications. The press was run by his nephew Nikolaus Wolrab.[43] Emser and Murner also found themselves having to bear their own production costs.[44]

This was not unusual in the Renaissance book world: authors were often forced to make a significant contribution to underwriting the cost of seeing their works into print. It was taken as a given that Catholics writing against Luther would have to contribute in this way. In a scathing review of the Catholic propaganda effort, the bishop of Vienna, Johann Fabri, thought the Catholic cause had suffered because they had paid so little attention to the needs of their scholars. "The capable and steadfast are for the most part dead. Only a very few remain who are able and dare to resist; and those who are able to contradict [the Lutherans] or rather to prevail over them scarcely have the means to feed themselves not to mention the means to pay the printers."[45] But this was certainly not a problem faced by Luther or his fellow evangelicals, since publishers could be confident that their books would sell, and provide them with a lucrative harvest of reprints. Here, in the reach of their writings and the sheer quantities of copies in the public domain, was where reformers enjoyed an absolutely critical advantage. For Catholic authors, even if they were prepared to subsidize their own writings, there was seldom any benefit in terms of reprints or further editions published elsewhere. And even if they could cajole a printer into taking their works, the indignities faced by conservative authors were not necessarily at an end. Conservative publications were not infrequently subjected to boisterous acts of ritual humiliation, their books standing as surrogates for their invisible authors. We have seen how Emser's works were publicly mocked in Magdeburg; in other instances Catholic works were forcibly removed from booksellers' stalls.

This sort of direct action was extremely effective, as printers were highly sensitive to these sorts of cues. The Erfurt printer Johann Knappe was well connected in humanist circles and happy to publish Luther when the opportunity arose. He was less happy when Johann Eck asked him to publish a local edition of the papal bull condemning Luther. The commission was hard to refuse, so Knappe tried to hedge his bets. He printed *Exsurge Domine,* but in a quasi-facsimile of the Rome original, with "Rome" and the name of the original printer given in place of his own imprint.[46] We have seen how Augsburg printers used "Wittenberg" on their title pages to increase their sales; in Knappe's case the deception was a purely defensive strategy. Even so, it did not work: most of the edition was lost when students from the university stormed his shop and hurled the copies into the river.

Those who wrote against Luther plowed a lonely furrow, with little help from the printing industry. Printers would often only take on their works if paid, or if obliged to do so, and with good reason, for these works simply could not match the sales of evangelical authors. The evangelical *Flugschriften* were the lifeblood of the industry in these years, the motor of rapid growth and huge potential profits. Any printers cut out of this market faced hard times. If any of Germany's publishers doubted this they had only to consider the cautionary tale of Leipzig.

LEIPZIG

Where Germany's local authorities did make determined efforts to forbid the publication of evangelical works this could usually be done. We have seen that this was the case in Nuremberg, which in consequence played a much more modest part in the publication of Luther's books than might have been expected. This did not necessarily inhibit access to Lutheran texts, which in Nuremberg were fairly freely available, since the council turned a blind eye to their sale so long as the local printers were not responsible. In this case, too, the absence of Luther's works from the local presses encouraged the growth of alternative markets, such as dramas and the poems of Hans Sachs, a hugely successful author and a firm supporter of the Wittenberg reformer [47]

It required real commitment on the part of the local power to prevent the publication and sale of Lutheran books altogether. This could be achieved, but the effect on the local book industry could be devastating.

In 1515 Leipzig was Germany's principal printing center, nudging ahead of other major centers of production such as Basel, Augsburg, and Strasbourg. This was a remarkable achievement, since Leipzig was some way distant from the major nodes of commerce and communications in the Rhineland and Danube basin, which gave access to Europe's most important markets. But Leipzig had its own markets to the north and east, and profited from its dominant role in the supply of books to these regions and the universities and cultural capitals of central Europe.

Not surprisingly, Leipzig's printers took very eagerly to publishing Luther, with an early pirate edition of the ninety-five theses followed by forty-three editions of his works in 1518 spread among four different printers: Landsberg, Lotter, Stöckel, and Schumann.[48] The summer of 1519 was golden, as the city briefly became the center of the drama with the Leipzig Disputation. Printers cheerfully turned out editions of the disputation proceedings and multiple copies of the furious polemical exchanges that followed, along with numerous of Luther's other works. But the Leipzig Disputation, which he attended in person, also turned Duke George decisively against the Reformation. When the Emperor Charles pronounced Luther's final condemnation at the Diet of Worms, Duke George moved firmly to enact the edict's full terms, including the prohibition of printing, buying, and selling Lutheran books. So meticulous was he in the performance of these obligations that when the Luther New Testament was published in 1522, Duke George ordered that all purchasers should surrender their copies (they would be refunded the purchase price).[49]

This prohibition on the publication of evangelical books, so strictly enforced, was an absolute disaster for Leipzig's previously buoyant book trade. Printers protested, but in vain. Production plummeted. In 1519 and 1520 the Leipzig presses had turned out respectively 190 and 188 editions, a higher level of production than they would reach at any subsequent time in the sixteenth century. But production halved in 1521 and 1522, and in 1523 and 1524 collapsed altogether. In 1524 Leipzig's mighty printing houses turned out only 25 editions between them.

In desperation the printers approached the town council to petition Duke George on their behalf. This remarkable document sums up with admirable economy the difficulties faced by those committed, by force of necessity, to uphold traditional religion in these years. The printers were in danger of losing "house, home and all their livelihood," because they were not allowed

> To print or sell anything new that is made in Wittenberg or else-where. For that which one would gladly sell and for which there is demand they are not allowed to have or sell. But what they have in over abundance [Catholic treatises] are desired by no one and can-not even be given away.[50]

Duke George was, of course, unmoved. In fact, he had added to the difficulties of his Leipzig printers by setting up a press in his capital, Dresden. This was to provide an outlet, under the close supervision of his court, for the works of his secretary and loyal propagandist, Jerome Emser.[51] This press was not particularly active, but sucked further life out of the Leipzig industry at an especially difficult time. The real bene-ficiary of Leipzig's decline was its local rival Erfurt. Until these years the production of the Erfurt press had been negligible, averaging fewer than 20 editions a year before 1520. But Leipzig's misfortune was Erfurt's op-portunity. In 1523 Erfurt printers published an astonishing 179 editions, almost all of them works of Luther and other evangelical authors.[52]

Often one needs to take protestations of poverty on the part of six-teenth-century craftsmen with a pinch of salt; but on this occasion the Leipzig printing industry really was in desperate straits. Wolfgang Stöckel, a printer in Leipzig since 1493 and a true giant of the industry, had in 1508 bought a large house in the Grimmaische Strasse. In 1525 he was forced to sell it because of his mounting debts.[53] Two printers, Jakob Thanner (the printer of the ninety-five theses) and Michael Blum, tried printing forbidden evangelical literature, but were apprehended and pun-ished. Both Nickel Schmidt and Valentin Schumann attempted to trans-fer to Wittenberg, and Schmidt worked there briefly as a bookbinder before returning disconsolate to Leipzig.[54] Even before he was rebuffed by Wittenberg, Schumann had something altogether more audacious in

DUKE GEORGE OF SAXONY BY LUCAS CRANACH

High principled, moral, and chivalrous, George was Luther's most formidable opponent.
Cranach was always content to take commissions from Catholic patrons; if Luther
disapproved he was wise enough to keep his thoughts to himself.

mind. In 1522 he set up a branch office in Grimma, some fifteen miles
south of Leipzig. Here his factor, Nikolaus Widemar, turned out a range
of small evangelical books, works by Luther and others, including
the partial editions of the New Testament already spoken of.[55] In 1523
the shop was moved to Eilenburg, again under the management of
Widemar but now in partnership with Wolfgang Stöckel.[56] There was
nothing ideological in this for Schumann (or indeed Stöckel); Schumann
had also provided the types for the Emser press in Dresden.[57] It represented simply a desperate attempt to put bread on the table. In 1526,

to stave off financial ruin, Stöckel abandoned Leipzig and moved his operation to Dresden. A residual press he left behind in Leipzig in the hands of his son Jakob published no more than a handful of works.[58]

The Grimma and Eilenburg experiments were the first example of a practice that would find several imitators in the century of the Reformation: the establishment of a surreptitious branch office in neutral territory to take advantage of a lucrative but forbidden trade. The great Antwerp publishing magnate Christophe Plantin would attempt something similar to print Protestant books during the Dutch Revolt.[59] Wenzeslaus Linck was behind the establishment of a press in Altenburg, at a time when evangelical printing was banned in Nuremberg.[60] But for Leipzig's printers it was a sign of desperation, a Band-Aid for an amputated limb. Without the trade in Reformation books, which accounted for almost half the German book trade in these years, the presses were doomed to decline.

Leipzig's main publishers were experienced and highly capable; they were also, as these examples show, inventive and resourceful. But they were washed away by an economic tide so fierce that they were unable to stand in its path. Demand for evangelical books was so strong in these years that it sucked up most of the spending power available for books, making it virtually impossible for Leipzig's printers to develop alternative markets. Their attempts to do so were thwarted by Duke George's iron determination, the weak demand for conservative theology, and the buoyancy of local rivals Erfurt and Wittenberg. Like handloom weavers confronting their first spinning jenny, the Leipzig printers could do little except gaze upon their doom, their hands tied from taking any of the actions that could have rescued their business. Duke George lived on until 1539, firmly upholding his Catholic faith. Only then would his successor move Ducal Saxony into the evangelical camp, twenty years too late for Leipzig's printers.

9.

PARTINGS

O N JUNE 13, 1525, a small private ceremony took place in the Augustinian house at Wittenberg, now Luther's home. Present were Justus Jonas, Bugenhagen, and Johann Apel, professor of law at the university, along with Lucas Cranach and his wife. They were there to witness an extraordinary event, the betrothal of a forty-two-year-old former monk to a twenty-six-year-old former nun, Katharina von Bora. Bugenhagen presided and the Cranachs acted as sponsors and witnesses. Unusually, and in the same limited company, the wedding proceeded the very same evening. Only two weeks later was there any public festivity to celebrate Martin Luther's transition to married life.

This was in many respects a strangely subdued, almost furtive way for Luther to mark this important, and ultimately joyous, milestone in his life. The reformer was a hugely popular figure in Wittenberg, and one would have thought that he would want to take this momentous step in the company of his friends and congregation. Yet not even his loyal friend Philip Melanchthon was invited (Philip was deeply hurt, and found it hard to disguise his sense of outrage in his letters recording the event).[1] It was not as if Luther was blazing a trail in taking a wife. Most of his Wittenberg colleagues were already married, and with his full approval. He had been a consistent advocate of clerical marriage in his writings since at least 1520. But Luther knew his was a special case. Not only was he a former monk, and his wife a runaway nun; he was also a condemned outlaw and heretic. What sort of life was Katharina taking on? And Luther knew he was handing a huge propaganda opportunity to his enemies. In the deeply personal pamphlet exchanges of the early Reformation, every aspect of Luther's conduct was exposed to opprobrium: his vanity, his arrogance in his own judgment, his ungovernable temper. Now all was clear: the church had been turned upside down, monasteries cleared and convents emptied, so that Father Luther could satisfy his sexual appetites.[2]

Luther knew all this would be said; he also knew that this would add fuel to the fire at a time when the Reformation faced a barrage of criticism from many separate quarters. Luther's marriage came, most unhappily, at the juncture of the most serious crisis that had faced Luther's movement since its first turbulent months. In 1524 the great humanist Desiderius Erasmus published the long-awaited attack on Luther's theology, precipitating a complete break between the two men. Luther recognized the importance of this, but the need to craft a suitable reply had, most unusually for Luther, been repeatedly delayed, overcome by the still more serious calamity of the Peasants' War.

His duties as witness performed, Lucas Cranach was in the position to offer a further gift, a wedding portrait of the happy couple. This double portrait was, as was the usual custom, composed as two separate panels, which could be hung side by side with man and wife facing toward each other. The portrait of Luther is one of Cranach's greatest works, a psychological study of great honesty. Here Luther is stripped of the polemical armor of Cranach's first depictions of the young reformer. It shows a lean, tense figure, staring with a distracted absence into the middle distance. Gone is the confident optimism of the first years of the Reformation, the iron-willed zeal of the young monk; this is a man close to the edge of his endurance. And with good reason. For in June 1525, when Luther first took on the obligations of a family, he was confronting a challenge that might well have consumed his Reformation. Germany

MARTIN AND KATHARINA: THE MARRIAGE PORTRAIT

Cranach's powerful psychological portrait does not disguise the tension of this momentous year. Katharina looks ready for the challenges ahead.

was in revolt, and Luther, for once, struggled to find the words to give his movement direction.

ERASMUS

When Luther first loomed on his consciousness, Erasmus had just enjoyed the most successful years of his career. In the twelve months from August 1515 Erasmus sent to the press three works of huge significance: his editions of Seneca, Jerome, and the first recension of the Greek New Testament. These resonated throughout the European scholarly community. In 1516 friends began preparing the first collective catalog of his work; during the four years between 1514 and 1517 Erasmus would be Europe's most published living author (a title he relinquished in 1518 to Martin Luther).[3] Not surprisingly, Europe's printers competed for his attention and his patronage. He had become that rare phenomenon: a scholar who could make money from writing.

Erasmus now enjoyed a towering reputation among humanist scholars across all of Europe. Especially among the humanist sodalities of Germany, Erasmus was lionized. Among those from central Europe who vied for his attention were some of those who would later be Luther's closest supporters, among them Melanchthon, Capito, and Spalatin. Spalatin wrote to inform Erasmus that Frederick the Wise had purchased all of his published works that he could find for the library in Wittenberg. The youthful Melanchthon sent a verse composition.[4] This adulation was not, at the time, in any way reciprocal. As Erasmus shuttled back and forth between Paris, Louvain, and Basel, Wittenberg scarcely figured on his consciousness. In a revealing aside in a letter to Frederick the Wise, as late as April 1519, Erasmus apologized that he had not responded to Frederick's respectful greeting by sending him a book, but he had, he said, no one he knew in Wittenberg to send it to.[5]

The first mention of Luther in the great humanist's correspondence is strangely oblique. In December 1516 Spalatin had written to Erasmus to ask his view on some of the intellectual currents then circulating in Germany. "My friend," he wrote, not mentioning Luther by name, "writes to me that in interpreting St. Paul you understand justification by works . . . ; and secondly that you would not have the Apostle in his epistle to the Romans to be speaking at all about original sin. He thinks therefore that you should read Augustine."[6] Erasmus did not engage. At this time he was embroiled with controversies closer to home: the long and complex arm wrestling with the French theologian (and rival biblical scholar) Jacques Lefèvre d'Étaples, and his mounting irritation with the young English scholar Edward Lee, a former protégé whose criticism of his New Testament would become a dangerous obsession for Erasmus over the next few years. When Erasmus received a copy of the ninety-five theses in March 1518 he was interested enough to send the copy on to his friend Thomas More in London, but his covering letter does not name Luther as the author.[7]

Yet it was Erasmus's fate that at this point his admirers, and those of the Wittenberg reformer, largely converged. When a friend sent Erasmus two of Luther's early works in December 1518, he assumed that Erasmus would approve of what he read.[8] In March 1519 Erasmus received a delegation of German admirers who had traveled from Erfurt and Wittenberg to meet him. They brought with them a letter from Martin Luther, the first indeed that passed between the two men. Erasmus replied with cautious courtesy, but the exchange of compliments masked a growing sense of unease.[9] Erasmus was happy, as were his followers, to concur with many of Luther's criticisms of church practice and ceremonies. The critics of indulgences included many humanist scholars. But the escalation of Luther's defiance, his growing alienation from the church hierarchy, and the increasingly strident language of his denunciation of the papacy all filled Erasmus with alarm. He could see that they were men of very different temper. Furthermore he feared that his own more measured reforming agenda, characterized as so often in the humanist community by wit and irony rather than a direct challenge, might be tarnished by association. The Luther affair became an increasing preoccupation: on the part of those friends urging Erasmus to speak out for Luther and those warning that Erasmus's enemies were seeking to tar him with the same brush. Wolfgang Capito was among those pleading with Erasmus for restraint: "There is nothing [Luther's] enemies wish more than to see you indignant with him."[10]

Erasmus attempted to find a middle way: to signal sympathy for Luther while withholding support. In a careful letter to Frederick the Wise, Erasmus refused to be drawn into a theological discussion. Instead he took aim against the immoderation of those who condemned the Wittenberger. "One would think they thirsted for human blood rather than the salvation of souls."[11] This formula, that Luther deserved to be heard rather than condemned, was one that Erasmus would hold to through the critical years when Luther's cause was debated in Germany and Rome, and one that earned him considerable opprobrium from the papal party.[12]

Luther, for his part, reckoned that he had got Erasmus's measure. He was an early reader of Erasmus's New Testament, and had a copy of the Basel edition in his hands soon after its publication in March 1516. He rejoiced in Erasmus's denunciation of clerical hypocrisy: "he trounced the religious and the clergy so manfully and learnedly, and had torn the veil off their out-of-date rubbish." But he also recognized that the two men came to their views of contemporary church questions in very different ways: "How different is the judgment of the man who yields something to free will than one who knows something of grace." His conclusion was harsh: "I see that not everyone is a truly wise Christian just because he knows Greek and Hebrew."[13]

Nevertheless Luther reached out, because he realized that the movement would be stronger if the two were not seen to be at odds. And for a time this was certainly the case. In the first difficult years Erasmus's interventions were more helpful to Luther's cause than the opposite, as Luther would grudgingly acknowledge. "Some people had in hand a magnificent letter of Erasmus to the Cardinal of Mainz. [Erasmus] protects me quite nobly, yet in his usual skillful way, which is to defend me strongly while seeming not to defend me at all."[14] In particular Erasmus made one crucial intervention when Frederick the Wise consulted him for his opinion when their paths crossed in Cologne in November 1520. This was Erasmus's chance to damage Luther had he so wished, in a private conversation with Luther's indispensible protector. But whatever his irritation at the difficulties Luther might be causing him, Erasmus was surprisingly supportive. Even at this relatively late stage in Luther's process (the bull *Exsurge Domine* had already been published), Erasmus was prepared to aver that good men and lovers of the Gospel were those who had taken the least offense at Luther. "[T]he whole fight against Luther sprang from hatred of the classics and from tyrannical ignorance."[15]

All of this changed with Luther's condemnation at the Diet of

Worms. However much he regretted the virulence with which Luther had been pursued, Erasmus knew he could not follow him into schism. Already he was extremely concerned that his own reputation would be dragged down with Luther. In a letter of August 1520 he frankly asked Luther not to involve him in his business. Luther agreed to respect his wish, though not without a certain bitterness. Erasmus, he had concluded, "was not concerned for the cross but for peace. He thinks that everything should be discussed and handled in a civil manner and with a certain benevolent kindliness."[16] This appraisal was one with which the great humanist would probably concur. He understood his own temper all too well. In an unusually frank and revealing letter to an English friend, Richard Pace, he confessed as much.

> Even had all [Luther] wrote been religious, mine was never the spirit to risk my life for the truth. Everyone has not the strength needed for martyrdom. . . . Popes and emperors when they make the right decisions I follow, which is godly; if they decide wrongly I tolerate them, which is safe.[17]

Erasmus now came under increasing pressure to denounce Luther publicly. For some years he resisted, with charm, evasion, and sophistry; but in the end the pressure would tell. By 1524 it had become clear that he would write against Luther; rumors that something was in the wind reached Wittenberg, prompting the reformer to write directly to ask Erasmus to hold back.[18] Luther was to be disappointed: the pressure on Erasmus to act was by this point irresistible. But if the breach between the two men was to become public, Luther heartily approved the choice of a battleground. Erasmus chose to address the issue that defined the difference between the two men, theologically and temperamentally, as Luther had recognized since 1516: Luther's denial of human agency in the act of salvation, the doctrine of justification by faith.

De Libero Arbitrio, Erasmus's *Diatribe or Discourse Concerning Free Choice,* was published in September 1524. It is a careful, thoughtfully

LUTHER, ERASMUS, AND THE COMMON MAN

In this famous image, Luther and Erasmus are depicted as allies in the cause of reform, harvesting the word of God from the "host mill." Note the peasant with his flail, preparing to chastise the churchmen who reject the word.

constructed, and in many ways humane consideration of the central problem of Reformation theology. Erasmus recognized that without grace there was no hope of salvation; but here lay the paradox, for without freedom surely man could not be held responsible for sin. Luther's theology, to Erasmus (and many Christians since), required one to discount all good works, merit, and obedience. Surely a righteous God would reward good deeds? Although grace initiated salvation, if it did not require man's free cooperation, then God was responsible for evil—a bleak prognosis indeed.

De Libero Arbitrio achieved considerable success. Especially among the scholarly theological community of Germany it was widely read, with editions in all the main centers of printing in the Empire, with the exception of Wittenberg.[19] Erasmus observed the necessary courtesies, ensuring that it would be known in Wittenberg by sending a copy to Melanchthon. It was immediately obvious that Luther should reply. He read the book almost immediately, though with characteristic disdain ("an unlearned book from such a learned man"). Yet it would be another eleven months before Luther settled to the task, and a further five before the work was finished: his response, *De Servo Arbitrio, On the Bondage of the Will,* appeared from the press of Hans Lufft only on December 31, 1525.[20]

This was distinctly odd for such an experienced and accomplished disputant. When one considers that Luther was here defending the theological core of his movement, the issue that had divided evangelical and humanist approaches to reform since the beginning of the Reformation, it becomes even more so. One must acknowledge that Luther had other pressing preoccupations, particularly in the urgent need to contain the fallout of the Peasants' War. But there was more to it than this. Some part of Luther seems to have felt that Erasmus was not worth the trouble: as he rather rudely expressed it in his reply, if such a great intellectual could do no better than this, it only confirmed his view that free will was a fiction. It was only his friends' insistence that Erasmus's work was achieving traction among supporters of the Reformation that forced Luther to engage.

The result was a crushing, comprehensive restatement of Reformation doctrine. At four times the length of Erasmus's original, it ranged widely and was severe on what he perceived to be his opponent's naive and superficial (if plausibly attractive) restatement of human agency. Luther set out his position with brutal clarity. It was not possible for a person to turn to God. Conversion was God's promise and gracious act, and from this there could be no stepping back. Only the elect fulfilled God's will; as far as salvation and reprobation are concerned, human will could determine nothing. Luther is here the master theologian, rebuking a well-meaning but lazy amateur for a lack of serious engagement with theological truths. The engaging brevity of Erasmus's work is here turned against him.

Erasmus, as was so often the case, took great offense at this personal criticism. His first reaction (also characteristic) was to try to shut Luther down with a behind-the-scenes maneuver, in this case appealing to the new Elector John to reprimand Luther for this insolence. The elector forwarded the letter to Luther, and followed his advice to stay out of the quarrel. Erasmus also took it into his head that Luther had attempted in some way to pull a fast one, and that the publication was timed to prevent him from being able to reply before the spring Frankfurt Fair. This is surely fantastical: had this been the case Luther would have delayed two more months; in any case Luther hardly needed to play this sort of game. One way or another Erasmus was determined that Luther should be answered at the March fair. In contrast to the painful deliberation of Luther's *Bondage,* Erasmus tossed off the first part of his reply, *Hyperaspistes* (the "protector" of the *Diatribe*), in ten days. Froben was persuaded to clear most of his presses to have the work printed, and the task was duly accomplished in time for the fair.[21]

Although this makes a good story, and a fine demonstration of Erasmus's command of the printing process, this seems to have been a private competition with only one participant. Luther had little further interest in sparring with the great humanist; he was sent a copy of the *Hyperaspistes* by Philip of Hesse but was in no hurry to read it. By September it was clear that he would not reply. Erasmus had raised the temperature by responding in kind to Luther's personal abuse, but had not advanced the theological debate in any meaningful way. Although the *Hyperaspistes* was a publishing success, it was probably more for the spectacle of Luther and Erasmus at each other's throats than for its contents.[22] Erasmus published a second part of the *Hyperaspistes* in September

1527, generally agreed to be dull and rather listless. By this point Luther had moved on. He would, interestingly, continue to read Erasmus in later life. He was keen to obtain the revised 1527 edition of Erasmus's New Testament, and his copy is heavily (if critically) annotated. Though Luther had been alarmed at the prospect that Erasmus would speak against him, the controversy when it came did surprisingly little damage. Those humanists who had been attracted to Luther's cause in the early years had already made their choice. Erasmus's work gave comfort to some of Luther's Catholic opponents, but it did little to shift opinion elsewhere. Ultimately it was a much more significant milestone in the life of Erasmus than in the Reformation movement as a whole.

THE PEASANTS' WAR

If the conflict with Erasmus did little to damage Luther, that could not be said of the second great challenge of this crowded year, the Peasants' War. This was a truly existential event for Luther's thriving yet still vulnerable movement: the greatest threat to the new church's survival since the first years of his protest.

The Peasants' War began in the autumn of 1524 as a series of disturbances in the southwest of Germany, in the Black Forest, around Lake Constance, and in Alsace. In itself, this sort of rural uprising was nothing new. The German peasantry was suffering considerably from worsening economic conditions, exacerbated by a sustained effort to restore onerous conditions of labor service (even serfdom) that had been relaxed as a result of the chronic labor shortage in the period following the Black Death. These grievances had provoked a series of local disturbances in the half century before the Reformation, known collectively as the *Bundschuh*, after the heavy peasant boot chosen as a banner of solidarity. In 1514 there was a further serious rebellion, the "Poor Conrad," against the oppressive rule of Duke Ulrich of Württemberg, and a rising in the Rhine Valley in 1517.[23] In this context it was not immediately clear that

Handlung/Articfel/vnnd Jnstruction/so fürgenommen worden sein vonn allen Rottenn vnnd hauffen der Pauren/so sichzesamen verpflicht haben:M:D:XXV:

BAND OF BROTHERS

One of numerous editions of the peasant manifestos, this woodcut plays up the potency of the rebels' military threat.

the events of 1524 would be significantly different. But the peasant musters proved more numerous and more persistent than heretofore. By the early months of 1525 they had spread beyond the usual heartland of the *Bundschuh,* through Bavaria to Franconia, Thuringia, and Saxony.

By this time it was clear that this was not simply a further spasm of pain and distress at declining living standards, but something of an entirely different order. The rebels were better organized, better coordinated, and better led. More dangerously, from Luther's point of view, they had also begun to clothe themselves in the language of the new evangelical movement. In March 1525 members of the various peasant bands met in Memmingen to agree on a common program. The result, the *Twelve Articles,* was in the main conventional enough, with complaints about labor service obligations, denial of the rights to cut wood in forests or trap game, high rents, and the seizure of common land. But it also included a demand that pastors should be elected by their own congregations, a common thread in many of the urban Reformation conflicts unfolding in precisely these years. Most incendiary of all was the fact that the whole document was clothed in evangelical theological language, with copious marginal scriptural citations.

> Third, it has until now been the custom for the lords to own us as their property. This is deplorable, for Christ redeemed and bought us all with his precious blood, the lowliest shepherd as well as the greatest lord, with no exceptions. Thus the Bible proves that we are free and want to be free. . . .
>
> Twelfth, we believe and have decided that if any one or more of these articles is not in agreement with God's word (which we doubt), then this should be proved to us from Holy Writ. We will abandon it, when this is proved by the Bible.[24]

This added fuel to the flames, and certainly seemed to vindicate those who claimed that the insurrection was the inevitable consequence of the challenge to existing authority raised by the evangelical conflicts. The assumed author of the *Twelve Articles,* the furrier Sebastian Lotzer, had no direct connection to Luther, but two of the black sheep of the Wittenberg movement, Andreas von Karlstadt and Thomas Müntzer, were soon deeply embroiled. Karlstadt we have met; his entanglement with the revolt seems to have been a largely unintended consequence of his preaching of the radical gospel in Orlamünde. Müntzer was a problem of an altogether different order. In 1519 he had been an early and aggressive advocate of Luther's movement; in 1520 he preached in Zwickau, on Luther's recommendation. But by 1522 the two men had fallen out. Müntzer was a man of great talent, as was revealed by his German Evangelical Mass of 1524, an imaginative prototype for a vernacular evangelical service.[25] But he was also willful and undisciplined. His incendiary sermons and increasingly direct attacks on the Wittenberg leadership led in 1524 to his deposition from the church at Allstedt. When Müntzer resurfaced at Mühlhausen, he was again expelled; but returning at a critical juncture when the town had effectively thrown in its lot with the rebellious peasants, Müntzer soon emerged as one of the most powerful spokesmen of the insurgency.

This uncomfortable turn of events exposed one of the other salient aspects of the Peasants' War: that it was by no means confined to the countryside. The earlier *Bundschuh* revolts had exposed significant tensions between city dwellers and the inhabitants of the rural hinterland; the roving peasant bands were for the most part feared and despised.[26] But the Peasants' War came at a moment when many towns were already experiencing significant social tension as a result of the Reformation—debates and disputes that set portions of the citizenry against the civil leadership. Here the appointment of clergy, either favorable to the evangelical message or more conservative, was a significant flash point. The new stirs appeared to many in the towns an opportunity to press home their advantage. Alongside the *Twelve Articles* a number of the most important manifestos issued during the revolt were drafted by urban rebels.[27]

These, like the *Twelve Articles,* were widely circulated in print. This use of print represented the final, decisive shift in the nature of the revolt: print became the instrument for molding a national movement, and, in the process, exposing the radicalism of the peasant demands to friend and foe alike. For Luther there was a certain rough justice that the same medium that had brought him to national prominence was now used to broadcast and amplify what he could only see as a frightening perversion of his evangelical message. The key writings that accompanied the Peasants' War were published widely throughout Germany. The *Twelve Articles* of Memmingen went through multiple printings, from Strasbourg and Worms in the west, to Augsburg, Regensburg, and Constance in the south. In the northeast they were printed at Zwickau and Leipzig, Erfurt and Magdeburg; this, for Luther, was dangerously close

North
Sea

Oder

Elbe

Silesia

Antwerp

Rhine

Magdeburg
Wittenberg
Leipzig
Allstedt
Altenburg Saxony
Erfurt Dresden
Jagdeburg
Zwickau
Prague
Breslau

Mainz Würzburg Bamberg
Worms Forchheim
Speyer Nuremberg

KING-
DOM
OF
FRANCE

Strasbourg Reutlingen Regensburg Danube
Augsburg Vienna
Constance

Swiss
Conf.

Savoy Milan Venice

N

● Place of Publication
---- Holy Roman Empire
░ Habsburg Lands, 1525

50 miles

LK

THE BITER BIT

Printing locations of manifestos of the Peasants' War and other associated publications.

to home. Müntzer briefly ran his own press in Allstedt; the *Frankfurt Articles* of April 1525 were also widely circulated.[28] All in all around eighty-five editions of the peasant manifestos and Müntzer's writings proclaimed the case for reform; and their allegiance to a social gospel inspired by Martin Luther.

This was potentially enormously damaging, particularly when the peasant bands turned on their persecutors and began to sack noble castles and fortified houses. Religious houses also felt the force of their antipathy (many peasants paid their rents to clerical landlords). Luther had been initially slow to react to the stirs in the distant Danube basin. With the publication of the *Twelve Articles* he recognized the need to respond, but he did so with a measured evenhandedness that satisfied no one. In his *Admonition to Peace* he naturally condemned the disorder and violence. But equally he warned the princes: in a dangerous sentence he lectured them that the rebellion was also a just punishment for their sins. Their resistance to the Gospel and exploitation of the common man was the cause of the revolt. Only repentance could divert God's wrath.[29] Conventional perhaps, but incendiary; the result was that Luther's first comment on events disappointed both sides, while giving some encouragement to the sentiment that the peasant grievances were justified.

This was, it must be said, an exceptionally difficult period for Luther. Events seemed to be crowding in a torrent of negative headlines: Erasmus, Karlstadt, and Müntzer, the Peasants' War, the abusive reactions to his own marriage. While we can separate these different issues into neat compartments, in the day to day of spring and summer 1525 this must have seemed to Luther like a perfect storm of ceaseless bad news. Luther was perfectly aware that his enemies interpreted this as the wholly predictable denouement of the crisis induced by his own disobedience. It did not help that in precisely these months Luther was having to deal with the transition of authority in Electoral Saxony following the death of Frederick the Wise in May. The relationship between Luther and his first and most crucial patron had been a strange one, but his passing at such a difficult moment left little time for reflection and mourning. In the event, Frederick's successor, his brother John, was even more resolute in his support for the Reformation. But this fact (which would have been clear from Duke John's earlier support for Luther) did not stop speculation that Luther's writings against the peasants were inspired by a wish to cozy up to the Catholic Duke George now that his great protec-

Ermanunge zum
frid / auff die zwölff artickel der
Bawrschafft in Schwaben.

Mart. Luther.
M.D.XXV.

ADMONITION TO PEACE

Too little, too late. In 1525, unusually, Luther failed to find the words to articulate a coherent response to the uprising.

tor was gone. "They say publicly in Leipzig that since the Elector had died, you fear for your skin and play the hypocrite to Duke George by approving of what he is doing."[30]

Luther's enemies were circling, and his friends were nervous. As had now become characteristic of Luther, his reaction was both belligerent and deeply personal. In April and May he visited relatives in Eisleben. Naturally he received invitations to preach, but his reception was very different to what he had come to expect. The atmosphere was aggressive; the congregation rang bells to signal their dissent. Luther had experienced a similar defiance when he tried to bring order to Karlstadt's former congregation in Orlamünde. Here members of the congregation had openly contested his teaching. Later he was helpfully informed that members of the Orlamünde congregation were using his tract *Against the Heavenly Prophets* as toilet paper.[31] When Luther had elaborated his concept of the priesthood of all believers, this was not at all what he had in mind: this was anarchy, the dissolution of social order. Returning to Wittenberg through Weimar Luther was left in no doubt by Duke John of the gravity of the situation: the princes now demanded his allegiance.

This was the background for the most notorious of Luther's works, *Against the Robbing and Murdering Hordes of Peasants.* This had been intended initially as a new third section for the third Wittenberg edition of the *Admonition to Peace,* a context that would have diluted significantly its stark message of retribution. But for the printers, this grim, sustained, remorseless denunciation of the violence was irresistible: it was published as a separate pamphlet and massively printed around Germany. Here, an audience who had perhaps never met this side of Luther could read his bleak verdict on the consequences of rebellion: "Therefore let everyone who can smite, slay, and stab, secretly or openly, remembering that nothing can be more poisonous, hurtful, or devilish than a rebel. It is just as when one must kill a mad dog; if you do not strike him, he will strike you, and a whole land with you."[32]

Against the Robbing and Murdering Hordes was reprinted over twenty times during the course of 1525. Significantly it was also published in Catholic cities where Luther's works seldom found a printer, in Cologne and Ingolstadt, on the Emser press in Dresden.[33] Luther's Catholic opponents could no doubt sense that this was a work that damned Luther and the peasants equally: the Cologne edition was published with a scathing commentary from his old foe and future biographer, Johannes Cochlaeus.[34] For once, Luther's command of the press had let him down. As happens when events turn against you, during 1525 Luther was consistently unlucky with his timing. Earlier in the year the *Admonition to Peace* was already out of date as the movement turned to violence.

Against the Robbing and Murdering Hordes was written before, but published after, the awful butchery of Frankenhausen, where the princes' armies finally caught up with the main peasant host and wreaked a terrible vengeance. Thousands of the peasants were murdered on the field of battle; Thomas Müntzer, who had fled the field, was discovered in hiding nearby, tortured into a humiliating recantation, and executed at Mühlhausen on May 27.

Read alongside reports of the bloodshed at Frankenhausen, *Against the Robbing and Murdering Hordes* caused widespread revulsion. Even Luther's closest associates expressed disquiet; others wrote to tell him that their congregations found it difficult to reconcile the savage tone of this tract with Christian love and mercy. Luther was characteristically defiant. It was only with the greatest difficulty that he was persuaded to return to the subject again, with *An Open Letter on the Harsh Book Against the Peasants,* which gave little ground to his critics.[35] Luther seems to have had no conception of the damage done to his movement. In September the new Erfurt Council asked Luther and Melanchthon to advise them about articles that been presented to them in April, drafted by a committee drawn from members of the urban opposition and members of the local peasantry. A copy exists with Luther's annotations, flippant and contemptuous. "If one does not trust the town council, why set one up? Why have one at all?" "Indeed, that the council should not be a council, but that the mob should rule everything." Best of all is the sarcastic peroration:

> But one article has been left out, that the council may do nothing, have no power entrusted to it, but must sit there like a ninny and kowtow to the commune like a child, govern with hands and feet tied, and pull the wagon like a horse while the driver reins in and pulls the horses back. Thus it would be according to the illustrious model of these articles.[36]

One senses a man driven to the limits of his endurance and understanding, exasperated and petulant, utterly unwilling to acknowledge any link between his evangelical teaching and the hopes that fueled the tragic mobilization of the revolt of 1525. As he put it in a belligerent letter to his friend Wenzeslaus Linck, "[H]e that will not understand, let him not understand; he that will not know, let him be ignorant; it is enough that my conscience pleases Christ."[37]

The impact of the events of this year on Luther's movement would be profound. Luther had been forced to choose sides, and he had done so decisively. He had reassured the princes that the Reformation posed no threat to the social order. In the short term the movement would reap the benefit; the next ten years would witness a sequence of princely states and territories adhering to the movement and proclaiming a new evangelical church order on the Saxon model. In the longer term, the reformed evangelical clergy would become in effect servants of the state, drawing their salaries from state funds and cooperating with state-appointed supervisors and visitors in the management of the church and the lives of their congregations. This was a long way from the evangelical freedom envisaged in the first buoyant years of protest and discovery, but it was an essential step in the process of church building.[38]

For the poor and the dispossessed, Luther's writings of 1525 represented a cruel awakening. This was the year when the movement finally lost its innocence; the soaring hopes inspired by Luther's leadership of a national movement of regeneration and renewal were dashed. The awful denouement at Frankenhausen provided the most graphic demonstration that the hope that Luther articulated was for salvation in the hereafter: the promise of a social gospel was for Luther an irrelevant and ultimately cruel delusion.

ZURICH

The Peasants' War was the first occasion wherein Luther was truly mastered by events. He finally found the words to steady the ship and the Reformation survived, though at a terrible cost to the wider appeal of the evangelical movement and his own reputation.

The breach with Zwingli, on the other hand, was an entirely self-inflicted wound. It is hard not to admire the courage and fortitude with which Luther had faced the conflict with his church in the years after 1518. It required a rare combination of skills and personal qualities: this was what made Luther such an attractive figure to the German people in these years. Perhaps it was inevitable that this resolution and extraordinary clarity of purpose would harden into something less attractive: a stubborn refusal to listen to the opinions of others who, examining Scripture anew, drew different conclusions.

In the tussles with Karlstadt and Müntzer, Luther refined his understanding of the existential struggle between good and evil. In the first days Antichrist had been identified with the corrupted papal hierarchy, the pope and his agents. But having been vanquished in this first assault, Satan adopted a more subtle approach, attempting to undermine the citadel of evangelical truth from within. His new instruments were the "false brethren," men who espoused evangelical principles but distorted and corrupted them.[39]

By 1526 Luther had seen off the first generation of those he clumped together as "fanatics," the Zwickau prophets, Karlstadt, and Müntzer, whose horrendous tortured death after Frankenhausen Luther viewed with dry-eyed detachment. But in his continuing literary exchanges with Karlstadt, for the first time in 1524 Luther began to associate new names with these local challenges to his authorities, specifically the leaders of the Swiss Reformation, Zwingli and Oecolampadius.

In the years after 1520 the Swiss city of Zurich had emerged very rapidly as the Reformation's southern pole. This, in itself, might have been somewhat unexpected. The city was much smaller than many of the southern cities of the Empire. In its immediate vicinity it stood in the intellectual shadow of Basel, the great university city and center of humanist scholarship (a neat mirror of the relationship between Leipzig and Wittenberg in the northeast). Here, in the south, Basel was a major printing emporium, strategically placed on the trade routes of the Rhine, simultaneously facing north to the Netherlands and France, and south across the Alps to Italy. Zurich had no university and very little printing; indeed, there was no printing press active in the city between 1514 and 1519. Nevertheless Zurich was an important regional power, geographically the largest of the German-speaking cantons. And in 1519 it had a religious leader of remarkable charisma and drive.

Ulrich Zwingli was the son of a farmer, a father sufficiently wealthy to sponsor his son through studies in the universities of Vienna and Basel.[40] In 1518, after service in Glarus and Einsiedeln, he was chosen for the important position of *Leutpriester* at the Zurich Grossmünster, essentially the city's preacher. Zwingli used his pulpit to criticize the failings of the clergy and to question traditional teachings of popular devotions such as the veneration of saints. In January 1519 he denounced the local preaching of the St. Peter's indulgence. Although there was clearly a strong convergence of themes here, Zwingli was always touchy on the issue of how far his thinking was shaped by Luther. In later times it suited him to claim that his intellectual development was entirely independent of the Wittenberg reformer, though Luther's works would certainly have been freely available in Zurich through their numerous Basel reprints. In 1520 the newly established Zurich print shop of Christopher Froschauer also began printing Luther locally.[41]

Froschauer was a close friend of Zwingli, and it was in the printer's workshop that the next major step in the Zurich Reformation was plotted. During Lent 1522, with Zwingli in attendance, Froschauer and a few other close associates consumed two smoked sausages. Zwingli did not partake in the sausage, but he did defend (and publicize) this deliberate transgression of church discipline in a sermon shortly after, then duly published by Froschauer.[42] The pace of events now quickened. Zwingli preached against clerical celibacy and took a wife. When the bishop of Constance attempted to restore discipline, reformers on the city council ensured that Zwingli was protected, a decision ratified by the first of two public disputations over which the local authorities would preside. In the second disputation the question of images came to the fore, identifying what would be a critical issue of division between Wittenberg and Zurich; in 1524 the council prescribed the orderly removal of images from Zurich's churches. In 1525 Zwingli (like Müntzer the year before) celebrated his new vernacular Communion liturgy.

Thus far the process of reform had been remarkably smooth and clinical. Zwingli's success in transforming the church in Zurich lit a beacon for others in the Swiss Confederation; it also established another dynamic pole for the Reformation movement substantially independent from the intellectual influence of Wittenberg. In a debate between the contending parties within the Confederation at Baden in 1526, the lead was taken by Johann Oecolampadius of Basel; Basel and Bern were increasingly drawn into the orbit of Zurich, and Zwingli's clinically austere view of the worship service would also prove attractive to many in Germany.[43] The public disputations that had sealed the evangelical victory in Zurich offered a prototype of orderly transition that would later be adopted by many German cities.

Zwingli's confident pursuit of his own reforming agenda was not altogether welcome in Wittenberg. Though his radical purging of images was disapproved, raising uncomfortable memories of Karlstadt's assault on the Wittenberg churches in 1521, it was Zwingli's developing teaching on the Lord's Supper that caused most alarm. By 1523 it was clear that Zwingli was increasingly drawn to a symbolic understanding of the words of institution in the Communion service; over the following years Luther received worrying reports that these views were gaining traction among supporters of the Reformation elsewhere.[44] In 1525 Johannes Bugenhagen wrote a trenchant *Open Letter Against the New Error Concerning the Sacrament*.[45] Luther made clear his views mostly in sermons; it did not help the attempts at mediation now initiated by various parties that some of these sermons were printed in October 1526 under the provocative title *The Sacrament of the Body and Blood of Christ Against the Fanatics*.[46] Zwingli was obliged to respond. His *Friendly Exposition* was expounded in a tone of patient civility, though not necessarily calculated to conciliate. He excused Luther his solecisms and theological missteps: "Sometimes even Homer sleeps." This touched a nerve. Luther could shrug off the insults of his Romanist opponents, but he would not tolerate being patronized. Zwingli's work was "full of pride, accusations, stubbornness, hate, and almost every wickedness, even though couched in the best words." Luther fired back. The title, *That These Words of Christ "This Is My Body," etc., Still Stand Firm Against the Fanatics,* offers a clear view of the contents.[47]

This exchange, and subsequent volleys through 1527 and 1528, was immensely destabilizing to the evangelical movement. Some form of reconciliation was urgently required. By 1528 the towns and princely states that had adhered to the Reformation had begun to consider an active policy of collective defense to protect their churches and territories. They could hardly do this if two increasingly alienated wings of the movement were constantly at each other's throats. In 1529, following the renewed condemnation of the evangelicals at the Imperial Diet, Philip of Hesse sought to bring the quarreling parties together to settle their differences. Since Duke John had given his blessing, Luther could hardly refuse to attend, though he made clear enough he expected nothing good to come of it.

The colloquy was set for October in Marburg. Luther and Melanchthon led for Wittenberg, and Zwingli and Oecolampadius for the Swiss. An impressive supporting cast included Bucer from Strasbourg and Brenz from Württemberg. Luther made clear from the start that there would be no change in his views; he hoped, without expectation, that his opponents would allow themselves to be instructed.[48] Luther told his wife that progress was impeded by the fact that Zwingli and Oecolampadius were "simple-minded and inexperienced debaters." Zwingli, for his part, believed that he had had the better of the exchanges. Both parties present were able to put their names to an agreement, reflecting considerable areas of common ground.[49] But the central issue of the Lord's Supper remained unresolved.

THE COLLOQUY OF MARBURG

Philip of Hesse is flanked by Zwingli and Luther in a near contemporary representation of a meeting that could have healed the breach between Wittenberg and Zurich, but ended up highlighting fatal divisions.

Many of the signatories of this document left Marburg with the profound sense of an opportunity lost. The two wings of the Reformation would go their separate ways, and the cities of southern Germany would be forced to choose, often with difficulty and acrimony, which route to follow. Zwingli met a tragically early death, accompanying the Zurich army in the confessionally charged Kappel War of 1531. Luther regarded this as God's judgment for his blasphemy of the Lord's Supper, an opinion confirmed in his mind by the death of Oecolampadius only seven weeks later. This double decapitation substantially weakened Swiss influence over the Reformation. Zwingli's successor, the capable Heinrich Bullinger, had to bend every sinew to preserve the Zurich Reformation and conciliate a chastened and humiliated city council. The scars of the conflict ran deep, as another Swiss church leader, John Calvin, would discover when two decades later he attempted to reach out to Luther's heirs and was sharply rebuffed. Reconciliation between Luther and the Reformed would wait another four centuries, arriving only in the very different confessional context of the late twentieth century.

The denouement of Marburg was a tragedy for the Reformation every bit as profound as the slaughter of the Peasants' War. The prolonged efforts to bring the two parties to agreement, and profound depression that these efforts had failed, reflected a clear perception that the Reformation had reached a decisive moment. From a modern perspective it is hard to reconcile Luther's certainty in his unique power to interpret true belief with his furious denunciation of "fanatics" who exercised the same freedom of scriptural interpretation. Zwingli expressed the sentiment with succinct anguish with his frustrated cry at the end of the first day's deliberations at Marburg: "Should, then, everything go according to your will?"[50] By 1529 Luther's worldview had hardened into a reflex of didactic certainties, friend or foe, God or the Devil. God had chosen him as his instrument; he would not be moved by worldly considerations to compromise truth. In the last two decades of his life he would set about the building of a church on these principles. Those who were with him would follow; others would await God's judgment. The church he built would be a reflection of both these adamantine strengths and Luther's very human weaknesses.

Part 4

BUILDING THE CHURCH

10.

THE NATION'S PASTOR

I N THE YEARS FOLLOWING the Colloquy of Marburg the Reformation moved into a new phase. Gone were the apparently limitless horizons of the first years, the endless astonishing triumphs in adversity, the perplexity of old institutions baffled and dismayed by the phenomenon that was Martin Luther. The years of adversity of the mid-1520s had changed all that: the limitations of Luther's movement, theological, social, and emotional, had been cruelly exposed. Luther's enemies in the old church were now irreconcilable, and had been joined by an increasing number whose hopes of sharing the new evangelical freedoms had been cruelly dashed. It was time to tend the needs of those who, for better or ill, had thrown in their lot with Luther.

These, it turned out, were still very numerous. Since 1521 and the condemnation of Luther at the Diet of Worms, representatives of territories sympathetic to the evangelical cause had fought an increasingly dogged battle to ameliorate the edict's conditions and prevent its enforcement. In 1526, when the Diet convened at Speyer, they were able to extract a significant concession. The emperor and his brother Ferdinand were in a weak position, since they desperately needed help from the German Estates to combat the imminent Turkish threat to Hungary. In return for the necessary funds they were obliged to concede that until final resolution of the matter at a general council of the church the German territories should make what arrangements they thought proper for the regulation of religion. This effectively suspended the Edict of Worms in evangelical territories; Charles, who had not been present at Speyer, was appalled, and when the Estates reconvened in 1529, again in Speyer, he insisted this compromise be repudiated. The majority of the German Estates accepted this verdict, but six of the Protestant princes and fourteen of the imperial cities would not. These dissidents, led by John of Saxony and Philip of Hesse, made a formal written protest against this decision; the Protestation of Speyer was the prelude to the creation of a formal association of territories adhering to the Reformation (and, incidentally, the origin of the name Protestant). In 1530 they adopted a common statement of faith, the Confession of Augsburg. In 1531 their leading figures entered into a mutual defensive alliance, the Schmalkaldic League.

Luther and Wittenberg were central to all of these endeavors. Much of Luther's energy in these years was expended as an adviser to princes, a strategist in the high stakes game of ecclesiastical politics.[1] But the reformer was always clear that this was only a means to an end. His central role, doggedly pursued in the middle of all other preoccupations, was preaching the Gospel, teaching and exhorting: the nation's pastor. Wittenberg was the fulcrum, its congregation always the immediate focus of his pastoral care and the experimental laboratory for the creation of a new Christian community. Luther and his colleagues also devoted a great deal of attention to building the institutional structures of a new church, a fitting Christian home for the people he had drawn out of Babylon.

These multiple obligations could not have been undertaken by one man. Luther was fully aware that many of these time-consuming tasks required skills that others possessed more abundantly than he. The creation of a systematic theology for the new church required the forensic clarity of a Melanchthon; the drafting of numerous church orders was the particular vocation of Johannes Bugenhagen. These fellow laborers in the vineyard included a new generation of Wittenberg printers who now replaced the early pioneers, Rhau-Grunenberg and Lotter. Well-organized and highly professional, these new men now smoothly expanded production to meet the very considerable demand for Wittenberg Bibles, prayer books, and pastoral theology.

Luther was harassed, busy, and always in demand. But he was also very rooted in Wittenberg, among a circle of loyal and devoted colleagues, and in his growing family. The Augustinian cloister was no longer an empty shell, but a house full of noise: the noise of children, students, and lodgers. This, too, was the domain of the remarkable Katharina von Bora, mistress of the household and an indispensable helpmate to Luther in all his work. This was Luther's new world, the place where much of the work of the Reformation was conducted and the model of the new Protestant family was built. It provided an important lodestar for the new church he was creating, and the home comforts to sustain him in adversity.

THE FIRST FAMILY

Through all the trials of the years after 1525, Luther's greatest consolation was that he found himself at the center of a growing, happy family. This was for Martin as surprising as it was unexpected. Although he made clear very early his opposition to clerical celibacy, he had no desire or intention to take advantage of the new freedoms himself. He supported and approved the marriage of his colleagues and others among the evangelical leadership, but gently parried well-meaning attempts to find him a suitable life partner.[2] The alliance with Katharina von Bora was not, as he freely admitted, a love match. He allowed himself to be proposed as suitor only when other possibilities had fallen through: had he had his choice, he rather ungallantly confessed, it would have been another of the fugitive nuns.

Katharina, for her part, was in love—but with someone else. Shortly after arriving in Wittenberg she had met Jerome Baumgärtner, a young scholar in the Melanchthon circle.[3] The two swiftly came to an understanding. The young lovers had not, however, reckoned with Jerome's father, a prominent member of the Nuremberg patriciate, who had no intention of marrying his son to a runaway nun. Jerome, who had hastened home to secure his father's blessing, was not permitted to return. Katharina took this hard and showed little enthusiasm for the proposed substitute, Dr. Kaspar Glatz, pastor at Orlamünde. Only to avoid this fate did Katharina suggest, with a levity perhaps concealing a serious purpose, that she might marry Luther.

Despite these unpromising beginnings the union soon blossomed into a partnership of real depth and touching devotion. Katharina set about bringing order to Luther's rather chaotic bachelor home: refreshing fetid bedding that Luther had allowed to rot unchanged for far too long; tidying and creating a home in the cavernous Augustinian house, where Luther had to this point presided over a fluid and changing household of guests, visitors, and boarding scholars. Katharina now took this in hand, discovering a flair for business and administration that created, finally, a solid foundation for Luther's home life. Until this point Luther had lived rather a hand-to-mouth existence. He should, in principle, have had no money worries. The Augustinian cloister was now his own, and gifts of money and produce augmented a relatively generous salary. But the outgoings of the household were also considerable, and Luther was a generous and imprudent giver. He also made nothing from his most marketable resource, his writings, refusing offers of payment from his publishers out of a scrupulous desire to retain his intellectual independence. In consequence he frequently felt short of money and put upon, as the complaints in his letters about money matters attest.

Happily for Luther, Katharina proved equal to the task. Bringing order to the household finances became her vocation, pursued with energy and considerable flair.[4] While Luther held forth at the dinner table, Katharina ensured that it was well stocked from her substantial market garden. While students and disciples hung on the great man's every word, Katharina was on hand to ensure that they kept up to the mark with their boarding fees. The result was that the family could soon boast a modest prosperity. When in 1540 Katharina's brother looked likely to default on a mortgage and lose the family farm, Luther was able to step in and purchase the property. Improvements were also undertaken to ensure that the Augustinian cloister was suitable for the expanding household.

This soon included the couple's own children. As was usually the case in the sixteenth century, children followed very quickly after marriage. Hans (named for Bugenhagen) arrived in 1526; Lucas Cranach was the godfather. A first daughter, Elizabeth, followed in 1527, with four further children born between 1529 and 1534: Magdalena, Martin, Paul, and Margarethe. Like many men who experience fatherhood relatively late in life, Luther was a devoted parent. He involved himself very directly in the children's upbringing. When Elizabeth died in infancy, an all too common event for parents in those days, Luther was distraught. It used to be claimed that parents in this period prepared for the savage frequency of losing their young by keeping an emotional detachment from their children. Luther's utter wretchedness suggests otherwise.[5]

When away from home, Luther wrote his children letters of touching intensity, patiently converting the joys of the Christian life into a language of storytelling fit for the very young.[6] The same correspondence demonstrates how much Luther had come to respect and love his wife. Katharina was, within a very few years, his trusted soul mate, with whom he shared his hopes and fears, as well as instructions for managing affairs in his absence.

Luther's experience of marriage and fatherhood was important for his movement in a number of ways. His new family circumstances helped turn his very practical mind to a future that involved building a community. In recent years there had been much comment on the very strong strand of apocalyptic expectation in Luther's approach to the trials of the Reformation. He believed that he was living through the last days, the climactic struggle between God and Antichrist that would

THE LUTHER FAMILY MAKING MUSIC

Luther was a passionate musician and a devoted father; this sentimental nineteenth-century portrayal distills the importance of Martin and Katharina for the creation of a new model of the Protestant family. Philip Melanchthon looks as if he would rather be elsewhere.

precede the coming of the Kingdom. This was undoubtedly a source of great strength to him as Luther contemplated his expulsion from the church and the likelihood that his defiance would end in his own death.[7] But it is impossible to be a father without also focusing on the future of children on this earth—contemplating that there may indeed be a future. This mental reorientation undoubtedly helped Luther focus his mind on the task of church building, and particularly on the task of Christian education.

The joyous success of Luther's family life also provided a welcome refuge against the constant barrage of events, the turmoil of crisis and decision making that scarcely receded in his later years. A home full of children was hardly restful, but it certainly provided distraction from complex events in the Empire and crises in the church. It brought out the best in Luther, in a way that theological disputation patently did not. But most of all, Luther's home life, lived in a very public way, provided the new church with a powerful archetype of the new Protestant family. In the Catholic Church such family comforts as priests had enjoyed had been furtive and semiclandestine. The priest's woman was often the subject of public mockery and faced a dismal prospect of dispossession and penury in the event that the priest died. Children were always illegitimate.[8] Now the Protestant churches not only regularized these unions; they provided the potential for a stable family at the heart of each local community, the children educated in the new faith and suited for a profession of their own. Often they followed their fathers into the church. The power of Luther and Katharina as a model and exemplar is demonstrated in the proliferation of copies of Cranach's double marriage portrait.[9] Quite quickly in these portrait pairs the haunted psychological study of Luther taken for his marriage was replaced by a dignified picture of the mature patriarch. Copies of this paired portrait hung in many sober Protestant homes, presiding over households where the Christian life was both lived and taught: the holy household as church.

FOR THE CHILDREN

Luther's preoccupation with Christian education long preceded the arrival of his own family. As we have seen, even in the most turbulent days of the first Reformation controversies he still found time to instruct the youth of Wittenberg in the essentials of the faith, a patient task that perhaps provided welcome respite from the turmoil of events that swirled around him.[10] This task of Christian education became for Luther a lifelong vocation, extending out from Wittenberg and Electoral Saxony to the whole family of cities and territories that had adhered to the new evangelical way.

This task consisted of two closely related elements: the design of a catechism, or catechisms, that would make the essentials of the new faith evident to new generations entering the church, and the provision of schools. In the matter of the catechism Luther was not in any way minded to be prescriptive. There was to be no single text or formula required for use: in this, as in other tasks of preaching the Gospel, he valued individual initiatives from others of the talented band of scholars gathered around him.

The impetus for the drafting of new handbooks of catechismal instruction came from the obvious need for a general survey of the new church emerging in Saxony by the middle of the 1520s. It was clear that the church had become separated from the Church of Rome, but what had taken its place? Were the new churches adequately supplied with Christian preachers? And what of the congregations? What did they know of their faith? What indeed should they be taught? The first road map to a new standard of Christian knowledge was provided by Luther in two early works: the short manual of prayers known as the *Betbuchlein,* and the preface to his *Deutsche Messe,* the new vernacular worship service (1525).[11] Here he sketched out the need for simple, straightforward works of instruction, set out in question and answer form, on the Ten Commandments, the Creed, and the Lord's Prayer. His subsequent description of the educational regime envisaged for Wittenberg, with German instruction on Mondays and Tuesdays, added two further themes, baptism and the sacraments. Thus was established the catechismal agenda that would shape all subsequent efforts at Christian education in Wittenberg and beyond.

Luther's ministerial colleagues rose to the task. Between 1522 and 1529 some sixty different editions of thirteen different instructional works were published in Wittenberg. These texts took many forms. Among the most successful was a work of the Augsburg reformer Urbanus Rhegius, *A Comforting Disputation in Question and Answer Form Between Two Craftsmen.* This pamphlet would not normally be thought of as a catechism, though it followed exactly the agenda set out by Luther in his preface to the *German Mass.* It is also a reminder that at this point the work of Christian instruction was by no means confined to small children, but extended to adults drawn into the new movement, by choice or accident of geography. Rhegius's work enjoyed a huge success, with eighteen editions in three years, including eight in Wittenberg and four in Nuremberg.[12] The publication of catechismal works engaged all of Wittenberg's printers: these works, after all, stood in the first rank of the task of building the new church. It was only in 1529, after a full decade of widely disseminated publications of this sort, that Luther himself took the task in hand with the two works that would come to dominate this field, his *Small Catechism* and *Large Catechism*.

The *Large Catechism* was intended specifically as a manual for those teaching the faith, clergymen instructing their congregations, and (in an ideal world) parents their children. It offered a fairly full exposition of the five crucial elements of faith as defined in Luther's agenda-setting exposition of 1525. The *Small Catechism* served the needs of those of meaner understanding. The highly emotional tone of the preface to this work laid out the urgency of the task.

> The deplorable, miserable condition which I discovered lately when I, too, was a visitor, has forced and urged me to prepare [publish] this Catechism, or Christian doctrine, in this small, plain, simple form. Mercy! Good God! What manifold misery I beheld! The common people, especially in the villages, have no knowledge whatever of Christian doctrine, and, alas! many pastors are altogether incapable and incompetent to teach. . . .
>
> Therefore I entreat [and adjure] you all for God's sake, my dear sirs and brethren, who are pastors or preachers, to devote yourselves heartily to your office, to have pity on the people who are entrusted to you, and to help us inculcate the Catechism upon the people, and especially upon the young.[13]

These two works were immediately disbursed in multiple editions in Wittenberg and beyond, published and republished in a steady sequence. The *Small Catechism*, in particular, proved to be an infinitely malleable text, published as a wall chart and in a school text, in Latin and German, to combine both language training and religious instruction; all this in addition to numerous editions of the German original (assigned to the grateful Nickel Schirlentz) and translations into French, Dutch, and Danish, as well as Low German.[14] Yet this publishing success, if anything, understated the importance of Luther's works. Luther's models would be enormously influential on the future development of the catechismal form in several respects, such as the establishment of the main subject categories and his pioneering of a hierarchy of texts for different levels of instruction. Equally important was his encouragement of a vivid variety of texts rather than insisting that the church use exclusively his own works. This was especially so of the church in England, where numerous catechisms were in use after the establishment of a Protestant church, and new ones written and sold throughout the reign of Elizabeth.[15] The catechism would continue to be one of the most popular and characteristic forms of instructional writing of the Protestant tradition and a steady source of work for its printers in many parts of Europe.

By 1529 Luther had also refined his understanding of how Christian education should be accomplished. In particular he no longer believed that this crucial task could be left in the hands of parents or even pastors. Ministers could exhort, reprove, and extol, but if parents did not value education then their children would not be sent to school. Reluctantly Luther now conceded that this was the case. Parents, particularly those engaged in agriculture, would not sacrifice their children from necessary tasks in the home or fields for the doubtful benefits of learning their ABCs. The only solution was to place responsibility for ensuring attendance in the hands of the local government. The state, as Luther bluntly told Duke John in 1526, must be the "guardian-general of the young," taking on the obligations of negligent parents. In Melanchthon's more melodious phrase, government should serve "as a common father."[16]

The duty of compulsory school provision was later routinely encapsulated in the church orders and ecclesiastical constitutions provided for Lutheran cities and territories. This ambitious program called for a vast increase in school places, the establishment of new schools, as well as the expansion of existing provision. School ordinances, enabling charters for these new schools, were often appended to the new church orders.[17] This represented a potentially revolutionary consequence of the new evangelical regimes, particularly as all of these new schools would be placed under the control of the local authorities.

In medieval Europe schooling had largely been a prerogative of the church, not least because literacy was an essential entry requirement for the priestly office. This monopoly on literacy was increasingly challenged in the late Middle Ages, as cities set up new schools in competition with church institutions to provide an education for the children of their own civic elite. In this respect the new Lutheran educational agenda only confirmed an existing trend and meshed well with the clear desire of civic authorities to take control of local educational institutions. But the aspiration toward universal provision articulated by Luther and Melanchthon was essentially new.

The state would be the guardian of the new educational institutions, but they would still serve the purposes of the church. This was made clear in Luther's influential and widely disseminated *Sermon on Keeping Children in School*.[18] For Luther, as he here made plain, the chief purpose of schooling was to train up a new generation of ministers. The church could no longer subsist on the largely ad hoc process by which priests had committed themselves to the new evangelical teachings, with a greater or lesser degree of sincerity. Saxony alone had eighteen hundred parishes; who was to man them when the first generation had passed on? So Luther addressed himself to parents to urge them to regard the church as a proper vocation for their children. It was only should this plea fail that he resorted to an argument of self-interest: education, he admitted, could also fit their children for a career in commerce or business that could make them a good living, or prepare them for a career in local administration. Luther's priorities were echoed in Melanchthon's commentary for the Saxon school ordinance of 1528. Schools, he wrote, were "for raising up people who are skilled to teach in the church and govern in the world."[19]

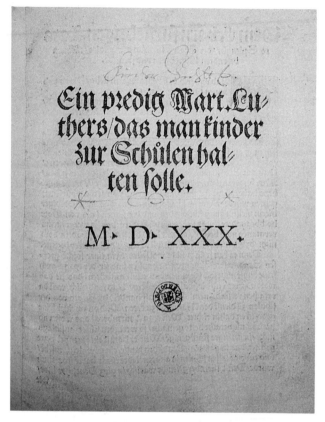

LUTHER'S *SERMON ON KEEPING CHILDREN IN SCHOOL*

Wittenberg was at the heart of an agricultural region, and Luther understood why parents were reluctant to send their children to school. It required the concerted efforts of church and magistrate to promote the virtues of literacy, but the rapid growth in educational provision was impressive.

Luther's writing provides the essential context for understanding the enormous, and at first sight impressive, growth in educational provision in Lutheran Germany. New schools proliferated in the second quarter of the sixteenth century, first in the towns then rapidly advancing into smaller communities. But with Luther and Melanchthon the emphasis remained primarily on equipping the city elite for their tasks in church and state.[20] For the most part the clientele for such schools was confined to the upper ranks of the urban citizenry, the patriciate and aspirant merchant class, the sort indeed likely to provide candidates for the new ministry and expanding state bureaucracies.

Such indeed were the social backgrounds of the young people flocking to the University of Wittenberg in ever-increasing numbers. The vast number of students now in Wittenberg brought its own challenges: an acute shortage of lodging and rampant inflation in the cost of basic foodstuffs.[21] The students were not always popular with the townsfolk, and frequently reciprocated this dislike. Nor was the booming matriculation register in Wittenberg necessarily reflected in enrollments of other universities in the German northeast, Erfurt and Leipzig. But demand was on a generally upward curve. With Luther's prompting, a new university was founded in Königsberg in the recently Protestantized Brandenburg. The evangelical church would get its new educated clergy.

It took time to understand that this ideal of a Latin education could not be realized outside the main urban centers, but this lesson was gradually learned. This prompted the foundation of so-called German schools, teaching a more practical curriculum. By 1600 Württemberg had 401 schools spread among the duchy's 512 communities, or one for every thousand in the population. Luther's goal of universal provision, if not universal attendance, was now close to being realized.

Luther was also a notable pioneer in the field of female education. If the goal of an informed Christian people was to be realized, then this applied equally to girls as to boys. As early as 1520 Luther committed himself firmly to this cause. In his address *To the Christian Nobility of the German Nation* Luther lamented that convents had abandoned their educational vocation. He called for the establishment of new schools for women: "And would to God that every city also had a girls' school where the girls could hear the Gospel for an hour every day, whether in German or Latin." Four years later it was the turn of the civic fathers of the German cities, whom Luther now exhorted to create "the best possible schools both for boys and girls in every locality."[22] This pamphlet, *An die*

Ratsherren Aller Städte Deutschen Landes, was one of the most widely circulated of Luther's works in this period, with eleven editions published in a single year in eight different cities.[23]

The cause of female education was pursued in all of the subsequent Lutheran church orders. In his church order for Braunschweig, Bugenhagen made provision for the regulation of the curriculum in the two existing Latin schools and the establishment of two new German schools for boys. In addition there were to be four schools for girls. Similar measures were adopted in the church orders of Lübeck, Hamburg, and other north German territories, as well as Wittenberg itself. The Wittenberg agenda was followed in Strasbourg, where Bucer made provision for the establishment of six girls' schools, as well as the German southwest, where Brenz led the way.

The new girls' schools generally followed a curriculum similar to that of the German boys' schools; the Latin curriculum was reserved for the elite urban institutions. The establishment, so rapidly, of so many new schools was a tall order, both in terms of resources and provision of the necessary buildings; suitable teachers were also in short supply. Yet by the end of the century enormous strides had been made. The full measure of this achievement can best be gauged if we contrast Lutheran Germany with a survey taken of the schools of Venice in 1587. Venice had many schools with several thousand pupils, but of these girls made up a meager 0.2 percent. In Germany, in many rural areas, later surveys show that girls made up close to half the enrolled pupils,[24] Luther's achievement as a pioneer in this field is seldom recognized; recent scholarship has preferred to focus more on the reformer's rumbustious reflections on female frailties in the tipsy obiter dicta of the *Table Talk.* His real, passionate commitment to female education tells a different story. It deserves to be better known.

PRINTING THE REFORMATION

Catechisms and prayer books, Bibles and hymnals, sermons, church orders, and commentaries: the work of church building generated a huge volume of print, both for the use of the churches in Saxony and elsewhere in Germany. For the Wittenberg printing industry this was a golden period, the era in which it reached its full maturity. The pioneers of the first Reformation years, Rhau-Grunenberg and Lotter, were replaced by a new generation, whose work now moved Wittenberg into the first rank of the German print industry. Between 1530 and 1546 Wittenberg's presses turned out over sixteen hundred editions, a total surpassed only by Nuremberg. Moreover, this total included many books of very substantial size; the short, cheap, easily produced pamphlets that had underpinned the first huge growth in the printing industry in Germany now played a diminished role in overall output.

Wittenberg's printing industry took on a new solidity, dominated by four new workshops, all of which proved remarkably long-lived. Hans Lufft, who arrived in Wittenberg in 1523, would manage his workshop until 1584, when he died at the age of eighty-nine. His companions and competitors in this era, Georg Rhau, Nickel Schirlentz, and Joseph Klug, all sustained their enterprises for a generation or more. The manufacture, sale, and distribution of books was now Wittenberg's largest industry, supplying churches and customers throughout Germany. At its heart was Martin Luther, still ceaselessly active in writing, apportioning work among the firms, and seeing books through the press.

The reconstruction of the Wittenberg printing industry entered a new phase with the arrival, between 1520 and 1525, of the four men who would come to dominate it. None, interestingly, had any previous connection to Wittenberg. Joseph Klug, initially employed to run the press established by Cranach and Döring, was the son of a Nuremberg printer.[25] Lufft may have been a printer's apprentice; Rhau, a schoolmaster, and Schirlentz were essentially new to the industry. All were attracted to Wittenberg by the apparently limitless possibilities opened up by Luther's new movement. With the passage of Lotter and Rhau-Grunenberg, their four firms would together guide the Wittenberg industry into a new phase of expansion.[26]

The key role in this transformation was played by Hans Lufft. His was by far the largest shop, and it made by far the most money. In a career of extraordinary length, Lufft, who published over nine hundred editions in Wittenberg, devoted himself entirely to the service of the Reformation. In the process he built both a close working relationship with Luther and a position of wealth and respect as one of Wittenberg's leading citizens.

The critical moment of Lufft's career was the decision of Lucas Cranach to withdraw from direct involvement in the printing industry following the collapse of his working relationship with Christian Döring. For Luther this may have come as something of a relief. Cranach and Döring had played an important role in the printing industry at an important time, providing the investment capital that the industry previously lacked and underwriting the cost of key ventures such as the publication of the first two editions of Luther's New Testament. Cranach brought to his business dealings both real entrepreneurial flair and a certain ruthlessness. It was no secret that he hoped to exploit his friendship with Luther to establish an effective monopoly on the publication of the reformer's new works. Luther, to his credit, resisted. He had sufficient understanding of the workings of the publishing industry to understand that this would spell disaster for other local firms. When in 1526 Cranach turned the printing shop over to its manager, Klug, Cranach could still retain his interest in the industry, since his workshop provided most of the illustrative material that appeared in Wittenberg books; but his withdrawal from direct involvement in printing allowed breathing space for others to grow. The work of publishing successive parts of the Bible now fell to Lufft, who over the next decade turned out a number of elegant folio and quarto editions. This sequence culminated in 1534 with his magnificent edition of the complete Bible.

This was a book that could not be undertaken in a small shop: a folio of some six hundred leaves, lavishly illustrated with Cranach's woodcuts, it would have been enormously expensive and time consuming to print. Lufft simplified the task by dividing the work into self-contained parts; this allowed the printing to proceed on several presses simultaneously. But the project still required enormous investment capital simply to purchase a sufficient quantity of paper and to keep the presses rolling. Happily the Lufft workshop was by this point a very well-established concern. Luther had played a considerable role in helping build its reputation and capacity by providing a steady sequence of lucrative and prestigious projects.

Lufft was, of course, not the only beneficiary of Luther's patronage. While Lufft's workshop was by some distance the largest in Wittenberg, Luther ensured that his competitors also had the chance to build a viable business. Luther's works and other key texts critical to the Reformation were spread around all of Wittenberg's different print shops: indeed, given the level of concentration in the Wittenberg industry on religious texts, none would have been viable without Luther's support. The passing of the years brought no diminution of Luther's fascination for the mechanics of the printing process. He remained closely involved in every aspect of the business—seeing his own texts and others in which he had a personal interest through the press, offering forthright advice to the printers, and reproving them for their derelictions, real and imagined.

As was the case when Luther was holed up in the Wartburg in 1521, we only get a full sense of Luther's day-to-day involvement with the printing industry when he was forced to spend an extended period away from Wittenberg. In such circumstances he was obliged to commit to paper the sort of advice and instructions that would usually be conveyed in person. One such period coincided with the negotiations surrounding the planned evangelical confession of faith at the Imperial Diet of

Augsburg in 1530. Luther, as an outlaw, could not join the other Wittenberg delegates in Augsburg. He accompanied them only as far as Coburg Castle, where he remained for several months, observing events from afar and offering Melanchthon and other colleagues a running commentary on developments and advice on their conduct of negotiations.

This was an anxious and frustrating time for Luther, separated from home yet far from the center of events. As so often, he poured his energies into a fury of creative writing. Interestingly, the eleven new works he completed during this period were distributed among five different Wittenberg printers. Lufft had four, Schirlentz three, and Rhau two; this left one each for Klug and another relative newcomer, Hans Weiss.[27] Weiss's print shop was by far the smallest then operating in Wittenberg, with only ninety-seven known editions published in fifteen years. But he was not for that reason neglected by Luther; indeed, the reformer was disproportionately generous to what was in effect a boutique business. More than half of the modest output of Weiss's shop consisted of works by Luther.

In addition to the careful apportionment of the first editions of Luther's own works, the reformers ensured that all of the Wittenberg printing houses were able to build their own particular specialism. In addition to his grip on the publishing of the Wittenberg Bible, Lufft was responsible for printing Luther's *Betbuchlein* and the postils. Joseph Klug was responsible for the German songbook and a large proportion of the scholarly works of the university community. He was, for instance, Melanchthon's favored printer. Klug was also the first in Wittenberg to print with Hebrew type.

Schirlentz enjoyed the local monopoly on the publication of the *Small Catechism,* a book in fairly constant demand in Wittenberg and elsewhere. Schirlentz was an interesting case, because when he first arrived in 1521 he set up shop in the house of Andreas von Karlstadt. The association with Luther's soon disgraced colleague seems to have done him no harm. Over the years before his death in 1547 he printed 143 of Luther's works, an impressive 40 percent of his total output. Finally, in this division of labor, the workshop of Georg Rhau was allocated the *Large Catechism*, editions of the *Confessio Augustana*, and Melanchthon's *Apologia*. Within the constraints of Luther's relationship with the much larger business of Lufft, Rhau seems to have been something of a favorite. Luther regarded him as especially reliable, and Rhau also held the valuable privilege of publishing official mandates and proclamations for the elector.[28] In 1546 this contract required him to equip a field press to accompany the elector on campaign, where he would be on hand for the printing of orders from the camp or news of the army's military success. Sadly for the Protestant cause such dispatches proved to be in short supply, and Rhau's press was impounded by the victorious Catholic forces after the calamity of Mühlberg.[29]

In the century after the invention of printing it had not taken those active in Europe's new publishing industry long to realize that competition among them could be ruinous. In addition to the protections provided by the state to reward investment, the industry developed its own mechanisms to ensure that different printers operating in the same markets did not cut each other's throats. These informal systems worked differently from place to place. In Paris the industry developed a complex series of alliances between its leading families, which effectively froze out newcomers and prevented them from gaining a foothold. But Wittenberg provides the only example in which the division of labor was effectively decided and enforced by the informal influence of a single powerful arbiter: a man who was simultaneously the leader of the local church and its leading author.

Unusual this may have been, but Luther exercised this role with great gusto, as the letters penned from Coburg make clear. At the end of April 1530 he determined to stiffen the resolve of Wittenberg's negotiators with an *Admonition to the Clergy Assembled at the Reichstag*. The manuscript of this text was dispatched 150 miles north for printing in Wittenberg. On June 2, Luther received copies from a messenger hurrying south to capture the market in Augsburg before a competing pirate edition could be published locally. This was duly achieved: on June 13,

Justus Jonas reported from the Diet that five hundred copies had been sold.[30]

This complex procedure required a 300-mile round trip for the text of Luther's manuscript, and a further 150-mile journey to Augsburg for the printed copies. But Luther knew what he was about. There may have been a printer available more conveniently placed nearer to Augsburg, but Luther trusted Lufft to make a good job of a critical text. Luther also wanted to reserve for Wittenberg the first edition of a book likely to sell well. This proved to be wise. By the end of the year, the *Admonition* had been reproduced in five other cities, and in a Wittenberg reprint by Klug.[31] But not in Augsburg; there the Lufft edition had cornered the market.

Luther was solicitous of his friends in the printing industry, but also demanding. He harbored dark suspicions, particularly when brooding in the enforced seclusion of Coburg, that his wishes were not always respected when he was not there to keep the printers up to the mark. Luther continued to spend a lot of time in and out of the print shops, as did many prudent authors. We catch echoes of this in his prefaces: "I have gladly seen this little book into print, as I have done before with several others."[32] But he knew also that the printers were first and foremost businessmen bent on profit. It did not need much to incite suspicions that without his commanding presence in Wittenberg the printers would consult their own best interest rather than his. First Lufft attracted Luther's ire by delaying publication of a book in which the reformer was involved, apparently so that publication would coincide with the autumn fair in Frankfurt.[33] Now it seemed that Schirlentz, offered Luther's *Sermon on Keeping Children in School,* planned to shelve it for the winter to catch the spring fair. Luther was beside himself. Katharina was ordered to march into the shop, remove the manuscript, and reassign it to Rhau.[34]

In September it was Weiss in the firing line, this time for refusing to publish Luther's *Exposition of Psalm 117.* Why had he not wanted to do it?[35] Actually the reason was clear enough, since Luther had already had this work printed in Coburg (a goodwill gift to a very small local shop).[36]

Weiss felt he could not take the risk that the market was sufficiently large for a reprint. Luther ordered this work also to be reassigned to Rhau. Luther's correspondents knew to take these outbursts with a pinch of salt. The impatient reformer had judged Schirlentz too harshly: a copy of the *Sermon* was already on its way and crossed Luther's angry letter on the road. And there were no hard feelings for Weiss, who published original Luther works every year between 1525 and 1532.

Luther's attitude to the printing of his works had undergone a substantial change over the course of the years since 1517. In the first years his only priority was to see his works in the public domain; he welcomed the widest possible distribution through frequent reprints around Germany. From 1519 he recognized the need to recruit capable printers to Wittenberg, partly to improve the speed of production, but also so that the appearance and quality of Wittenberg editions did justice to his developing theology and movement. Now, in the 1530s, with the Reformation an established fact, Luther was increasingly concerned to retain for his own city as substantial a portion of his printed output as possible.

This was not solely for commercial reasons, although the publishing industry was now a cornerstone of the Wittenberg economy. Luther was also concerned that the canonical texts of the movement should be published accurately and without error or amendment. Luther had been sensitized to this issue during the early stages of the dispute with Zurich, when a well-meaning intervention of the Strasbourg reformer Martin Bucer caused great offense. In 1526 Bucer had sought and obtained permission from Johannes Bugenhagen to translate his Psalter into German. Bucer's translated text, however, incorporated a spiritual interpretation of the Lord's Supper far closer to the position of Zurich. The accompanying translation into Latin of Luther's fourth postil included a commentary criticizing the Wittenberg position on the Eucharist. Luther was furious, particularly as the Bugenhagen work included separate prefaces by both Luther and Melanchthon: it might, therefore, seem that this shift in meaning had their endorsement.[37]

Luther had a long memory for sharp practice of this sort. When in

Vom kriege
widder die
Türcken.
Mar. Luther.
M.D.XXVIII.
Wittemberg.

CONCERNING WAR AGAINST THE TURKS

The publisher Hans Weiss ran one of Wittenberg's smaller print shops. Nevertheless Luther was still generous in the allocation of his compositions, as in the case of this exhortation to solidarity against the Turk.

1536 Wolfgang Capito approached Luther to see if the reformer would authorize a Strasbourg edition of his collected Latin works that Capito and Bucer wished to publish, Luther indicated that he would not grant his consent.[38] When the long-planned collective edition was eventually put in hand, the task was reserved for Wittenberg and the reliable Hans Lufft.

The degree of control that Luther exercised over the publication of his works was by this point very striking. We remember that when Johann Froben of Basel was moved to exploit the sudden interest in the

Luther controversies in 1518, he did not think to ask Luther's permission before publishing a miscellany of his writings on indulgences. Indeed, it was only some months later that he thought to send Luther a copy.[39] A decade later such a casual appropriation of Luther's intellectual property would have been rash for any established publisher in one of Germany's evangelical cities.

THE POWER OF PATRONAGE

In the last fifteen years of his life Luther exercised an extraordinary influence over the output of the German press. Wittenberg's printers revered him for the amount of work he could put their way, and not just his own writings. In 1531 the town council of Göttingen dispatched their new church order to Luther, along with an honorarium, asking him to review and if necessary correct it. This work done, Luther passed it to Hans Lufft with his own approving preface, but without apparently passing it back to Göttingen for final copy approval.[40] The same procedure was followed for Brenz's commentary on Amos. Luther received this work while in residence at the Coburg, before sending it north for printing in Wittenberg. Presumably from there a large part of the edition would have been sent back to Brenz for distribution in southern Germany. Brenz was a substantial figure in the movement, and Luther's preface contained a gracious acknowledgment that such a fine theologian scarcely required Luther's imprimatur; but Wittenberg still got the work.

Many other lesser lights also sent writings to Luther in the hope that he would read and approve of them. Luther recognized the danger that he would become, in effect, his movement's chief censor. "One of your [Erfurt] preachers, Herr Justus Menius, has sent me a little book that he composed against the Franciscan monastery in your city, so that I should judge whether it might be sufficiently deserving of publication. Now, I have no intention—and may God guard me against it—of taking upon myself to be judge or ruler over other preachers, lest I start my own papacy." But, he continued, "I am obligated—and indeed, am glad to do so—to serve everyone, by bearing witness to his doctrine where it is correct. . . . Accordingly I give this little book my attestation."[41]

By this point most of the cities and territories of Germany had introduced some form of control of the contents of books printed locally, mostly by establishing, in theory at least, the requirement for prior inspection of any texts likely to prove controversial.[42] In Wittenberg it was expected that the members of the university would submit their texts for approval by the faculty; most indeed voluntarily sought the opinion of colleagues, as did aspiring authors from outside the city. In 1525 Johann Toltz, a schoolmaster from Plauen, some 125 miles south of Wittenberg, sent his small catechismal handbook to the university for approval. The task was assigned to Bugenhagen, who on December 18 was able to testify that "according to my understanding I know nothing else than that this booklet is godly and useful."[43] The text was then passed to Georg Rhau for publication.

Plauen had no press, so this apparently voluntary act was probably a necessary preliminary for an aspiring author like Toltz if he was to find a printer. The Wittenberg printers in any case would by this stage not have printed anything from an unknown author without assuring themselves that the work was doctrinally sound. They simply would not print anything that they thought Luther would disapprove of, for fear that the reformer would withdraw his patronage. The awful example of Melchior Lotter hung heavy on the memory.[44] In this respect by far the most important control of the press in Wittenberg was self-censorship by the printers.

A revealing indication of the strength of this sentiment comes from letters exchanged between the printer Georg Rhau and his brother-in-law in 1527. Rhau wished to put to the press an edition of the popular catechismal text the *Buchlin,* edited by the Zwickau town secretary (*Stadtschreiber*) Stephan Roth. Roth was a man of high reputation, but Rhau was taking no chances. He waited three months before he could report the happy news that "Doctor Martin has permitted me to publish my prayer booklet, which you organized, and as soon as I have nothing else to print, I will typeset it and get someone to make woodcuts for it right away.[45]

Luther's influence was also increasingly felt beyond the borders of Electoral Saxony. His friendly relationship with neighboring princes could be called upon to prevent the publication of editions that breached a Wittenberg monopoly. In 1539 the death of his old antagonist, Duke George, and the accession of his brother Henry brought about a rapid conversion of Ducal Saxony to the evangelical cause. This was undoubtedly welcome, but not without danger to Wittenberg's printers, particularly if it sparked a revival of Leipzig's moribund printing industry. Leipzig's printers, who had lived off the thin gruel of Catholic polemic for twenty years, were naturally eager to share in the much more robust Protestant market. This applied even to Nikolaus Wolrab, whose press had been established specifically to publish the works of his uncle Johannes Cochlaeus. Now to his patron's horror he proposed to revive his fortunes by publishing an Edition of the Wittenberg Bible. Luther was equally scandalized, and he appealed to Elector John Frederick (who had succeeded his father in 1532) to make representations to his cousin. "How unfair it is that this scoundrel should be able to use the labor and expense of our printers for his own profit and their damage."[46]

Here Luther articulated the classic printing industry argument for market regulation, that the prior investment of the first printer, on editorial work, translation costs, new types, or woodcuts, should be protected against competition. He then added a further very interesting remark. "It can easily be figured out that the printers at Leipzig can more easily sell a thousand copies, because all the markets [fairs] are in Leipzig, than our printers can sell a hundred copies."

This certainly expressed the historic relationship between Leipzig and Wittenberg, but it is very doubtful that this was any longer the case. Wittenberg's powerful publishing consortia, who now undertook much of the work of wholesaling and distribution on the printers' behalf, had

CAVSAE QVARE
SYNODVM INDICTAM
a Romano Pontifice Paulo . III.
recusarint, Principes, Status & Ci=
uitates Imperij, profitentes pu=
ram & Catholicam Euan=
gelij Doctrinam.

VITEBERGAE.
M.D. XXXVII.

THE LAW AND THE GOSPEL

*Cranach's most original
iconographical creation, here
adapted for book-title pages in
two subtly different versions.*

Die drey
Symbola oder Be
kentnis des glau=
bens Christi jnn der
kirchen eintrechtig
lich gebraucht.
Mart. Luther D.

Wittemberg M.
D.XXXVIII.

developed highly efficient means of bringing their books to the market-place. In the event, Leipzig never did recover fully the ground given up in the two lost decades. Rather, the opening up of its fairs to Protestant literature only further strengthened Wittenberg's access to its markets. Wittenberg would remain the regional capital of print to the end of the century.[47]

This, of course, could not all have been foreseen in 1539, when the new competition from Leipzig seemed all too daunting. This awareness of the fragility of the market, and its utter dependence on Luther, helps explain one remarkable conversation that took place in this same summer. Around the end of June, quite probably when news of the proposed Leipzig edition of the Bible had reached Luther, the printers of Wittenberg approached him with an extraordinary proposition: that in return for a guarantee of first access to any future works they would provide him with a supplementary annual income of four hundred gulden. This was serious money: Luther's salary was never above two hundred gulden; this would have tripled it.

Luther refused: he preferred to make no money from his books, written always in God's cause, and to give no further ammunition to his enemies by profiteering from God's work.[48] Actually he could now well afford this high-mindedness, thanks partly to his businesswoman wife, who kept the household well provided for and brought in considerable extra income from her various business ventures. Although he complained intermittently of money worries, Luther was actually comfortably well-off. That is not the real point. What is remarkable about this story is that the printers were prepared to pay so much, at a time when Luther's productivity was declining steeply, for what in any case he provided them for free. There could be no more graphic demonstration of Luther's personal importance to the industry that made Wittenberg— and indeed made the fortunes of the friends in the industry whose generosity Luther now politely refused.

One can well understand the ties of affection and obligation that bound Wittenberg printers to "Father Martin." Luther's oversight of the industry was all-embracing. Printers relied on access to the valuable first editions of Luther's copious writings, as well as those he sponsored for others. In addition he exercised an effective veto over anything he or his university colleagues deemed to be unsuitable. No printer who wanted to work again would think to challenge this authority. In this way Luther exercised near total control over the flow of texts that publishers needed to obtain to sustain their business. Yet printers were happy to work within these constraints, since the profits to be made were great and the work so reliable. They knew, as did Luther, how much his works were worth in the German marketplace. A preface by Luther could justify a new edition of a work already published elsewhere in Germany;[49] the presence of Luther's name could add value to the first edition of a sermon or catechism by an otherwise obscure author. As Luther rather guilelessly acknowledged in the preface to one of the works contributed to the campaign against Erasmus, "The printer has pried from me this preface that is supposed to be published under my name, so that this little book, marketable enough by itself, might be regarded with all the more favor on account of my endorsement."[50]

From the first days when his writings revolutionized production in Wittenberg, to the end of his life and beyond, Luther was the true patron saint of the Wittenberg printing industry. By the last decade of his life the industry was sustaining several hundred employed directly in the business of books and others in ancillary trades.[51] If one factors in the hundreds of students drawn to Wittenberg to study, and those who lived on servicing their needs, it is clear that Luther was the major motor of the town's revived economy. No wonder he could rely on a cheerful greeting as he plodded through its streets.

II.

ENDINGS

N 1537, WHEN LUTHER entered the last decade of his life, he had lived in Wittenberg for twenty-six years: six in relative tranquillity as a young and comparatively unknown professor, followed by two decades in the maelstrom unleashed by his challenge to the church hierarchy. This had been a turbulent, often frantic time, and Luther's last years would bring no real relief. The calls on his time and expertise were incessant, an endless round of appeals for his judgment, letters to write, advice to princes, all, of course, alongside the day-to-day duties in Wittenberg. There was no letup either in the demands for new works from his pen. The next ten years would see Luther make frequent and influential contributions to several new and ongoing controversies. Readers seeking the familiar truculence and passion would not be disappointed, though the vivid writing of these last battles could also take on a darker, more menacing tone.

All of this made enormous demands on a man who could no longer call upon the boundless reserves of energy that had sustained him through the first Reformation controversies. The self-confidence and charisma were undiminished, but the body was failing. In 1537 Luther was fifty-four years old; not old by today's standards, but in an era when medical treatment could do little to alleviate the pains of illness or chronic conditions—or even provide accurate diagnosis—the wear and tear led to increasingly severe health problems.

Luther had always suffered problems with his digestion. The letters from the Wartburg in 1521 offer an obsessive and at times all too detailed narrative of his battles with constipation. The pleasures of a settled home and Katharina's market garden helped to some extent in this respect, but as Luther lost some of his physical vitality other problems intervened. In 1527 he collapsed in the pulpit while preaching, the first of many dizzy spells that troubled and disorientated him thereafter; these attacks could also leave a residue of ringing in the ears that persisted for months. Luther also began about this time to experience the first symptoms of angina; in December 1536 he would suffer a severe heart attack. From 1533 Luther also had to deal with the dreadful and debilitating pain of kidney stones. This was a common condition in the sixteenth century, particularly among those who ate a richer diet; Luther, who loved the pleasures of the table, was always a likely victim. The result was frequent, incapacitating pain, which only exacerbated Luther's problems with his digestion. In 1537, while at an assembly of the Protestant League in Schmalkalden, Luther suffered a urinary blockage so severe that his friends feared for his life. An operation was considered, but without anesthetic the chances of survival were grim, and Luther was in any case too weak for this to be contemplated. The crisis passed, but recovery was slow. In 1538 his entire family was struck with dysentery; in 1541 he developed a painful abscess in the neck and suffered a perforated eardrum.

Luther was by this point an old man, in almost constant pain, dosed by doctors, tended by an anxious wife, but beset always by constant work, the press of problems humdrum or acute that would inevitably be referred to him so long as he drew breath. So if during these last years his judgment or his temper failed, we must bear in mind that like many in this era he lived his life in a constant state of low-level illness or debility, flaring up into acute episodes in which the agony was unbearable. At such times Luther longed for the death that would free him from these burdens. But it would, in fact, be another decade since his life was first despaired of in 1536 before his release would come. In this extra ten years much would be done to secure his movement, whatever the cost to its indispensable leader.

THE PRINCES' FRIEND

Luther's attitude to authority—not least his own—was complicated and shot through by contradictions. In the first years of the Reformation more pacific spirits had recoiled from the radical implications of his assault on the church hierarchy. But while Luther made no apology for his treatment of the pope and his minions, in other respects he was profoundly conservative. Attempts to introduce precipitate change into the worship service at Wittenberg left him deeply uncomfortable, and he never wavered in his support for the established civil order. How Christian freedom and the restraint of licentiousness should be reconciled was a question to which he first systematically addressed himself in a series of sermons in 1522. These became the important tract *Secular Authority: To What Extent It Should Be Obeyed,* published in the following year.[1] Here Luther laid out for the first time his doctrine of the two kingdoms: the spiritual kingdom, in which man exists purely in relationship with God, and the temporal kingdom, in which man's fleshly needs and sinful nature have necessarily to be restrained by the exercise of civil authority. The events of the Peasants' War in 1525 only confirmed Luther in this sense that society required firm and sometimes cruel regulation, and that the current order of government in Germany was ordained by God for this purpose. To those who charged him with responsibility for the peasant uprisings he would reply with justice, if somewhat defensively, that "the temporal sword and government have never been so clearly described or so highly valued as by me."[2] Any sort of resistance to properly ordained government was something to which he was viscerally opposed.

For all that, the distinction between spiritual and civil power was never as neat and clear-cut as this would suggest. Luther himself intervened ceaselessly in matters that might properly be regarded as political. In Wittenberg he acted as an informal court of appeal for those who had fallen foul of the law or who appealed to Luther to help secure justice. Luther was happy to make representations in such cases to the electoral authorities.[3] Most of these appeals were granted. So numerous indeed were Luther's interventions in such cases that in 1532 the young elector John Frederick was obliged to warn Luther that he might not be able personally to read them all, as had apparently been his father's practice.

In return for such favors Luther was naturally expected to attend to the electors' affairs. Luther was fully aware that imperial politics would determine the course of the Reformation every bit as much as sermons and true teaching. How he chose to reflect this insight in his dealings with his patrons required a subtle balancing of dependence and the evocation of his authority as pastor and prophet. The relationship with his original protector, Frederick the Wise, was one of extraordinary singularity; few in the imperial court could really fathom what motivated Frederick in his protection of Luther. It speaks volumes that in 1522, when Frederick was dealing with the dangerous fallout of his decision to protect Luther from imperial condemnation, he also sent his agents to Venice to purchase more relics for his collection.[4]

Luther owed Frederick his life; but if he recognized the extraordinary skill with which Frederick had protected him, he sometimes chose strange ways to show this. Frederick had shielded Luther by sending him to the Wartburg, and given clear instructions that Luther should remain there until he felt it safe for him to reemerge. Luther decided, nevertheless, to return to Wittenberg, and he announced this extraordinary act of disobedience in a letter of breathtaking rudeness.

> I am going to Wittenberg under a far higher protection than the Elector's. I have no intention of asking Your Electoral Grace for protection. Indeed I think I shall protect Your Electoral Grace more than you are able to protect me. And if I thought that Your Elec-

toral Grace could and would protect me, I should not go. The sword ought not and cannot help a matter of this kind. God alone must do it, and without the solicitude and co-operation of men. Consequently he who believes the most can protect the most. And since I have the impression that Your Electoral Grace is still quite weak in faith, I can by no means regard Your Electoral Grace as the man to protect and save me.[5]

In 1525 Frederick died, to be succeeded by his brother John. In one respect this made life easier for Luther, since Elector John was a firm supporter of the Reformation. His succession allowed the Wittenberg theologians to complete the work of transforming the churches in the electorate for evangelical worship. But the new elector was also po-litically cautious and anxious to remain on reasonable terms with his cousin, Duke George, ruler of Ducal Saxony and Luther's most ardent critic. In the years around 1530, as the relationship between Protestant and Catholic powers in the Empire became ever more strained, John came under heavy pressure to offer the coalescing Protestant forces more forceful leadership. The directing spirit behind this more aggres-sive policy was Landgrave Philip of Hesse, ruler of a substantial territory in central Germany. Philip's decision to convert his lands to the Reforma-tion was very much his own. His first direct contact with Luther was as late as 1526, when the two men exchanged letters.[6] Luther seems not to have warmed to Philip, who had taken a leading role in the brutal sup-pression of the peasant armies in 1525, and now seemed bent on con-frontation with the Catholic states. But it was impossible not to engage with this political agenda, especially when Elector John threw in his lot with Philip.

Luther now had to face the possibility—indeed, the likelihood—that the princes would take up arms against their sovereign lord, the Emperor Charles V. This went against all his instincts, and indeed, his previous pronouncements on the subject of civil authority. In practice, however, he could not put himself at odds with the movement's protectors. The result was a work, the *Warning to His Dear German People,* which, while not explicitly endorsing resistance, nevertheless gave every encouragement to the Protestant leadership with its forthright denunciation of the Catholics and their proceedings. If it came to war then the Catholics would be to blame. Furthermore, Luther would not condemn those who took up arms to defend the righteous cause.

> [S]hould it come to war—which God forbid—I will not have rebuked as rebellious those who offer armed resistance to the murderous and bloodthirsty papists, but rather I will let it go and allow them to call it self-defense, and will thereby direct them to the law and to the jurists. For in such a case, when the murderers and bloodhounds wish to wage war and to murder, it is also in truth no rebellion to oppose them and to defend oneself.[7]

Luther had given the princes what they needed. Without having to repudiate his previous views, he had given his tacit consent to the armed struggle. Not surprisingly the delighted leadership of the new Schmalkaldic League ensured that the *Warning* was widely circulated, both on its first publication in 1531, and again on the outbreak of the Schmalkaldic War in 1546.[8]

Luther had done his duty, but the special pleading in this piece was fairly threadbare. Catholics were quick to exploit his discomfiture, among them the redoubtable and persistent Duke George. For Luther the duke was a formidable foe. In many respects, as Luther acknowledged, he was a thoroughly admirable man, even the model of a Christian prince. He was educated, thoughtful, and moderate, certainly as capable a theologian as the more boisterous Henry VIII of England. He was also a genuine reformer.[9] For all these reasons he had a capacity to needle Luther that many would have envied. His lands were strategically placed to impede the distribution of books from Wittenberg, not least by closing to them the important Leipzig market; his constant complaints about Luther also had an impact on his cousins in Electoral Saxony. In

1531 he took aim against Luther's *Warning,* in a well-reasoned and cleverly argued dissection that exposed the evident contradictions in Luther's position.

> Luther has now recently published a treatise once again which he called "A Warning To His Dear Germans," but which with more justice might be called an enticement and guide to disobedience and rebellion. For in it he basically seeks nothing else but to make us Germans disloyal to the emperor and insubordinate to all authority.

This for the clear-sighted duke was the nub of the matter. The princes' military preparations were clearly at odds with the reformer's teaching, that the Gospel could not be maintained by the sword, but by the power of God, "as Luther himself . . . had often indicated."[10]

Luther's response was a brutal tirade, *Against the Assassin of Dresden.*[11] While purporting not to know the author of the duke's original attack, this was aimed squarely at George, charging the Catholics with responsibility for the impending armed struggle. Luther was sufficiently provoked to send this to the press without having sought the approval of Elector John, who had, in fact, specifically forbidden any further attacks on Duke George. This act of defiance went unpunished; it did, after all, suit the purpose of the Protestant princes that Luther should be drawn ever more openly into defense of their cause.

The succession of John Frederick in 1532 brought a further significant shift. Frederick the Wise and his brother had both been, in their different ways, a restraining influence on Luther. John Frederick was a much younger man (twenty-nine when he began his reign) and a staunch advocate of the Reformation. Rather than restraining Luther he encouraged him to go on the offensive. When Duke George took action against those in Leipzig who surreptitiously followed the evangelical way, Luther took up the cudgels in their defense. His *Vindication Against Duke George's Charge of Rebellion* went through six Wittenberg editions in 1533, all published by Schirlentz; his *Short Answer* to Duke George's response, a further two from Lufft (also the publisher of the *Warning* and *Against the Assassin*).[12] Unseemly it may have been, but it did good business for the printers. It also drew Luther ever more closely into the role of principal propagandist for the Protestant princes.

For this, there would eventually be a price to be paid. It came in 1539, when the personal affairs of Philip of Hesse reached a crisis.[13] Philip was locked into a loveless dynastic marriage. Like many in such a position he took solace in another relationship, with the young Saxon noblewoman Margarethe von der Saale. Troubled in his conscience, he now wished to marry Margarethe, but without divorcing the estranged Christina, the daughter of George of Saxony. He approached the Wittenberg reformers, through Martin Bucer, to ask their blessing for a bigamous marriage. This was an impossibility, condemned by the law of the church and the Empire, and punishable by death. But the consequence that an embittered Philip would abandon the evangelical cause was too awful to contemplate. Somehow Melanchthon's subtle mind offered a way through these impenetrable thickets. The theologians would tolerate in this exceptional case a bigamous marriage, so long as it was kept a secret. They would make no public statement, but offered this counsel only under the seal of the confessional.

Of course, such a secret could not be kept. When the truth leaked out, along with the complicity of the Wittenberg reformers, it did untold damage both to Luther's reputation and to the evangelical cause. Luther remained relatively sanguine, Melanchthon much less so; not for the first time when faced by a crisis Luther's fragile health gave way. For a time his life was despaired of. For a movement that drew much of its moral capital from Luther's reputation for straight dealing and plain speaking, the sordid nature of this episode and Melanchthon's sophistry did great damage. But the reformers had little choice. In giving his name to this squalid bargain, Luther was doing no more than recognizing the essential truth that now shaped the future of his movement:

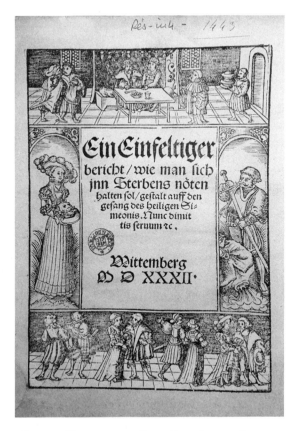

SERMONS HONORING THE DEAD DUKE JOHN OF SAXONY

A beautiful product of the Cranach workshop, but was Salome really appropriate for such a solemn purpose?

that its survival depended on the support and leadership of Germany's Protestant princes. It may have been the cities that had shown the vital early enthusiasm for Luther's teaching; it was certainly in the cities that his printed works found the most readers. But it was the princes who by adhering to the movement could create the territorial churches that gave Luther's movement its stability and political muscle. The price, as Luther and Philip both knew, was that the reformers could not refuse the comfort they offered the landgrave to preserve his leadership of the movement.

SIGNS AND WONDERS

In December 1532 the Leipzig preacher Johann Koss suffered a catastrophic stroke in the pulpit while attacking Martin Luther. He died shortly thereafter. Luther viewed this as a manifest sign of God's judgment—like all his contemporaries, he had no doubt that the Almighty would and did intervene directly to shape affairs according to his will.[14] The end of the same decade brought further decisive signs of God's favor, not least in the fateful resolution of the succession in Ducal Saxony. In 1537 Luther's old adversary Duke George had suffered a critical blow with the death of his son John. Only one son, the mentally handicapped Frederick, now stood between him and the accession of his evangelical brother, Duke Henry. The desperate Duke George somehow contrived a bride for the feeble Frederick, but in February 1539 he, too, died; two months later George also passed away. Luther had no doubt that these family calamities were a judgment on George's sins, the awful cost of resisting God's will. The new Duke Henry swiftly moved Ducal Saxony into the evangelical fold. But the brightening prospects in Saxony were in these years a rare ray of light in a darkening political perspective. All around, the Reformation was assailed, a fragile plant beset by winds and torrents. How were these more ominous events to be interpreted?

Luther and Melanchthon were, like many contemporary theologians, eager students of astrology.[15] Scholars scanned the heavens for intimations of God's purpose; the less cautious offered predictions of future events based on these observations. Both reformers also shared the widespread fascination with human and animal misbirths, what they might mean or portend. As Luther put it in a preface to the prophecies of Johann Lichtenberger, published in 1527:

God also makes His signs in the heavens if a misfortune is to occur and causes shooting stars to appear, or sun and moon to darken, or

some other unusual manifestation to appear, also [when] abomina-
ble horrors are born on earth to both man and animal, all of which
are not done by the angels but only by God Himself. With such
signs He threatens the godless and indicates disasters coming upon
lord and land, in order to warn them.[16]

In 1523 Luther and Melanchthon had an enormous success with a
pamphlet interpreting two such signs, the so-called monk calf (a mis-
shapen calf fetus) and the "Papal Ass," a strange beast washed up in the
Tiber in 1495.[17] This scarcely contemporary event was now interpreted
as a clear foreshadowing of the corruption of the papacy. The pamphlet,
published by Rhau-Grunenberg, was rapidly reprinted all over Germany.[18]
Its success no doubt owed something to Cranach's arresting images, but
it also caught the mood of the moment. In the mid-1520s the turbulence
of the Reformation combined with the general sense of apocalyptic expectation to create a widespread fear of impending catastrophe. It was
forecast that in 1524 Germany would experience a deluge comparable to
the Great Flood. While sharing the general mood of apocalyptic tension,
Luther counseled against too precise an attempt to tie the end-time to a
particular moment. His endorsement of Lichtenberger's prophecies was
careful and measured:

> I think the basis for his astrology is correct, but the science is uncer-
> tain. That is, the signs in the heavens and on earth do not err; they
> are the work of God and of the angels; they warn and threaten the
> godless lords and countries, and they signify something. But to
> found a science upon them and to place it in the stars—there is no
> basis for that.[19]

When in 1533 his friend and protégé Michael Stifel announced a precise time for the end of the world (8 A.M. on October 19), Luther strongly
disapproved. Crowds streamed into Stifel's village of Lochau to share the
moment of rapture. When 8 A.M. came and went without incident, Stifel

THE PAPAL ASS

Luther and Melanchthon had one of their greatest successes with their descriptions of the monk calf and Papal Ass. This version is from an English translation, published more than fifty years later.

was quickly removed to Wittenberg to protect him from the anger of his disappointed followers. He would spend two years of reeducation in Luther's house before being quietly reassigned to a new parish.[20]

Luther reacted with understanding and generosity to Stifel's enthusiasm partly because he shared the fundamental conviction that these were indeed the last days. This apocalyptic vision helps explain both the tone and preoccupations of his late polemics, particularly his late-blossoming engagement with the Turkish threat.

Luther's first reaction to the seemingly invincible Turkish horde was to regard it as God's scourge, a just punishment visited on Christendom for having tolerated the papal Antichrist.[21] This laid him open to the charge, duly made in *Exsurge Domine,* that Luther believed that "to fight against the Turks is to oppose God's visitation on our iniquities." Never one to give ground in such circumstances, Luther reiterated his belief that war against the Turks was futile as long as the papacy remained. But as Turkish armies continued their inexorable march through Christian territory, and particularly after the calamitous slaughter of the Hungarian nobility at Mohács, Luther was forced to a more considered reflection on the clash of civilizations. The siege of Vienna of 1529, a milestone in German resistance to the Ottoman armies, called forth two substantial works, *Concerning War Against the Turks,* and the *Army Sermon Against the Turks.*[22] Here Luther conceded the need for military resistance, though the true solution still lay in spiritual repentance. These works are also notable for Luther's clear identification of the true identities of the papacy and the Turk: the papacy was Antichrist, the Turk the Devil itself.

This revelation, reinforced by Luther's study of the apocalyptic prophecies of the Book of Daniel in 1530, shaped his treatment of the Turkish threat when he returned to the subject in his last years. The respite provided by the relief of Vienna had proved short-lived; the Turkish host was on the march once more. In 1541 Suleiman captured Buda and Pest and invested Hungary. John Frederick called upon Luther to rally the congregations of Saxony for prayer against the Turks. Luther's response, the *Admonition to Prayer Against the Turks,* was dark in tone.[23] Clearly identifying the Turk as the beast of Revelation, Luther called above all for repentance. The German people had received the Word of God; it was their ingratitude that had caused God to send this new plague. This line of argument was developed further in two important short statements published as preface and afterword, one to Brother Riccoldo's *Refutation of the Koran,* and the other to Bibliander's edition of the text. The preface to the Koran edition was Luther's letter to the Basel

Council urging that publication be permitted; it is not clear whether Luther expected to see it printed. Here he made a clear case that it was necessary to know the enemy.

> We must fight everywhere against the armies of the Devil. How many different enemies have we seen in our own time—the defenders of the pope's idols, the Jews, a multitude of Anabaptist monstrosities, the party of Servetus and others. Let us prepare ourselves against Mohammed as well. But what will we be able to say concerning things of which we are ignorant? That is why it is beneficial for learned people to read the writings of their enemies.[24]

In the preface to Riccoldo he warned against concluding that the Ottomans' military success meant that they enjoyed God's favor. "This does not happen because the faith of Mohammed is true and our faith is false, as the blind Turk boasts. Rather, this is the manner in which God rules his people." Most of all, it was a judgment on a people who continued to tolerate the papacy, "our Christian Turks." At least the Mohammedans were ignorant of the truth of God's word. "But our Christian Turks have God's Word and preachers, yet they do not want to hear it."[25] The moral was clear:

> I do not consider Mohammed to be the Antichrist. He acts too crassly and has a recognizable black devil, which is incapable of deceiving either faith or reason. He is like one of the heathen, who persecutes Christendom from without, as the Romans and other heathen have done. . . . But the pope among us is the true Antichrist.[26]

This was the last occasion on which Luther addressed the issue in print. But the Turkish threat was never far from his thoughts in these last days. On January 31, 1546, in one of his last sermons, Luther spoke of the trials of the church, tossed on the sea of tribulation like the apostles on the Sea of Galilee. The Turk was prominent among the Devil's agents.[27]

LAST BATTLES

The Turkish onslaught during Luther's last years was for the reformer just one more confirmation of the truth that had framed his career: that he, and his suffering fellow Christians, were living through the last days plainly foretold in Scripture. Aware that his own days were numbered, Luther was ever more conscious that his bodily failings were mirrored in the threats assailing his young and fragile church: the looming danger of the emperor's revenge; quarrels among the princes; the gathering forces of Antichrist. Ever more clearly he saw his own prophetic role, to call the Christian people to repentance, to nurture the dismally small number who had heeded the call to follow the Gospel.

This mental and physical world was the context in which Luther fought his last battles. Luther saw it as his inescapable duty to parry the Devil's thrusts, by smiting all of his servants: the papists, those false brethren who had betrayed the Gospel, the Turks, and the Jews. This last group had, until this point, occupied very little of Luther's attention. There were at this date relatively few Jews in Germany; Luther's own community in Wittenberg had expelled its Jewish population some ninety years before his arrival. In Wittenberg the memory lived on in the Judengasse, a thoroughfare on the city's northern periphery where many of those employed in the book trade were now settled.

Luther did not aspire to the expertise in Jewish questions of, for instance, his old adversary Johann Eck, who writing in the 1540s would claim firsthand knowledge of a sensational case of ritual child murder that had taken place in Freiburg im Breisgau in 1503. Eck recounted this story in his *Refutation of a Jewish Booklet,* a response to an attempt by the Protestant reformer Andreas Osiander to debunk such claims of ritual murder.[28] Luther's first utterance on the Jewish faith was, in marked contrast to Eck, extremely measured.[29] His treatise from 1523, *That Jesus Christ Was Born a Jew,* was essentially a lament that the current Christian hierarchy impeded any attempts to bring Jews to Christianity:

> For our fools, the popes, bishops, sophists, and monks—the gross asses' heads—have treated the Jews to date in such a fashion that he who would be a good Christian might almost have to become a Jew. And if I had been a Jew and had seen such oafs and numbskulls governing and teaching the Christian faith, I would have rather become a sow than a Christian.[30]

With this Luther turned to other theological concerns, returning to the matter only in 1538 with an open letter *Against the Sabbatarians*.[31] This far more pugnacious text seems to have been partly stimulated by a shadowy meeting in 1536, when three learned Jews called upon Luther in Wittenberg to probe him on his interpretation of certain passages in the Old Testament. The reformer may have got somewhat the worse of this encounter; certainly his rather grumpy reference to his own personal experience of their stubborn refusal to be persuaded suggests that it left rather an acid taste. Even so this small and rather modest work does little to prepare us for the violent and intemperate tone of Luther's most notorious work, *On the Jews and Their Lies*.[32]

This was the first of three writings that Luther devoted to Jewish beliefs and teachings in 1543; they can, in fact, be treated as three parts of one major contribution to the debate, although Luther, characteristically, allocated them to three different Wittenberg printers, Lufft, Rhau, and Schirlentz. The second and third tracts, *On the Ineffable Name* and *On the Last Words of David*, both offer important discussions of teachings in the Old Testament that in Luther's view attested to the truth of Christianity (on the Trinity and the Virgin Birth).[33] The second part of the trio, *On the Ineffable Name*, was by far the most successful in publishing terms, though it is *On the Jews and Their Lies* that has attracted the most attention, not surprisingly, given the violence of its language. Although Luther claimed here that he had reentered the debate with the greatest reluc-

THAT JESUS CHRIST WAS BORN A JEW

Luther's first, very measured pamphlet on the Jewish faith. This edition, despite the addition of Wittenberg to the title page, was published in Augsburg.

tance, his advice to Germany's princes was uncompromising. The Jewish presence in Germany was a plague that should be eradicated; synagogues should be destroyed and Jewish books confiscated. None should suggest that the Jews were indispensable for financial reasons; now was the time to remove them from Germany.

Of all Luther's writings none was more damaging to his later reputation, particularly in modern times, after these passages had been cited with such enthusiasm by the ideologues of National Socialism. Contemporary reaction was also decidedly tepid. Luther's friends were by now wearily familiar with the violent language with which he assailed the church's enemies, and this intemperance would reach new heights in the writings of these last years. But whereas the last tirades against the pope found eager readers, *On the Jews and Their Lies* did not. Published twice in Wittenberg, it was not reprinted elsewhere in the original German.[34] Significantly, the authorities in Strasbourg, which by this date had become the largest Western center for reproductions of Luther's works, intervened to prevent publication, for fear of possible violence. The print history gives a clear indication that, whatever their momentous later consequences, these works were at the time regarded as minor. Certainly Luther, harassed on all sides by political turbulence in Germany and premonitions of his own impending end, had other pressing preoccupations that demanded all of his attention.

Chief among these was the incessant, dangerous squabbling among the German princes. In 1539 the leaders of the Protestant alliance, Elector John Frederick and Philip of Hesse, became embroiled in a trial of strength with Duke Heinrich of Braunschweig-Wolfenbüttel, a devoted Catholic and outspoken critic of Protestantism. Despite these strongly held views, the city of Braunschweig had embraced the Lutheran Reformation, with strong support from Wittenberg: Bugenhagen had drafted its church order, which was published in Wittenberg in 1528.[35] The local imperial city of Goslar was also a source of provocation to the duke. By supporting these demonstrations of independence, the Protestant princes were also engaging in a very obvious struggle for local political supremacy; by 1541 each side had accumulated an impressive quantity of grievances and provocations, and these were extensively ventilated in print.

The quarrel called forth one of the most famous tracts of Luther's last years, *Against Hanswurst*.[36] Hanswurst was a character taken from contemporary theater and farce, a dolt who wore a string of sausages around his neck; the inference for Duke Heinrich was not flattering. Luther, in fact, denied having characterized the duke in this disrespectful

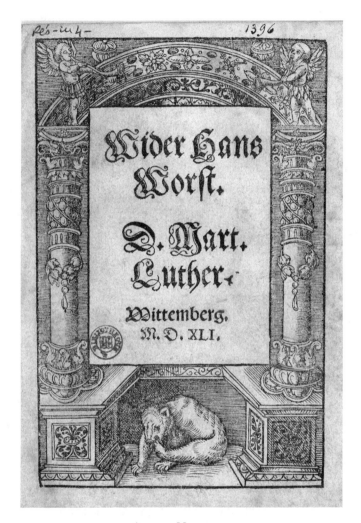

AGAINST HANSWURST

Much of Luther's time in his later years was occupied trumpeting the cause of the Protestant princes. This violently abusive piece was an outraged denial that Luther had called his own prince, the corpulent John Frederick, "John Sausage."

way. His offenses were far more serious: he was a devil, a coward, a murderer, and an adulterer.

The sustained invective of this tract reveals the depth of contempt that Luther felt for a man devoted to stamping out the Gospel in and around his territories. But this work was a solitary and possibly reluctant intervention into a furious print controversy driven forward by the princes themselves. In detailing his grievances, Heinrich was happy to dwell on Philip of Hesse's marital misfortunes; John Frederick he characterized repeatedly as a corpulent drunk. This line of attack was perhaps not prudent as Heinrich also had a complicated love life. Having sired three children by his mistress, Heinrich offered her an elaborate church funeral, only for it later to be discovered that her death was a charade. Eva von Trott had, in fact, been hidden away so that the relationship could continue (as it did, with several more children).

This dirty washing was gleefully aired at the Imperial Diet of 1541, with little regard for the damage such charges and countercharges could do to the reputation of the princely caste as a whole. This pamphlet warfare generated over thirty different publications in 1541 alone, each more vituperative than the last. As so often, the elaborate titles left little to the imagination. Thus John Frederick's *Second Treatise* was answered by Duke Heinrich's *Well-Grounded, Steadfast, Grave, True, Godly, Christian, Nobly-Inclined Duplicae Against the Elector of Saxony's Second Defamatory, Baseless, Fickle, Fabricated, Ungodly, Unchristian, Drunken, God-Detested Treatise.* It was to answer this that Luther had been called to the colors. But the princes also had their say, with the modestly titled *True, Steadfast, Well-Grounded, Christian and Sincere Reply to the Shameless, Calphurnic Book of Infamy and Lies by the Godless Accursed, Execrable Defamer, Evil-Working Barabbas, Also Whore-Addicted Holophernes of Braunschweig, Who Calls Himself Duke Heinrich the Younger.*[37] Evidently delighted with their handiwork, the elector distributed three hundred copies of this work to those attending the Diet, and even had it translated into French so that the incredulous emperor might share in the spectacle. It is easy to think that Luther's rather modest contribution to the debate may have been lost in the noise, though *Against Hanswurst* enjoyed its own success, with translations into Latin, French, and Czech.[38] The whole, distasteful business usefully reminds us that the trenchant tone and flamboyant language of Luther's polemics was by no means unusual in the inflamed atmosphere of 1540s Germany.

Confronting these unseemly and destructive quarrels, the Emperor Charles may have been forgiven for thinking that it would require decisive intervention on his part to bring peace to Germany. But for the moment his hands were tied; only in 1544 would he finally extricate himself from the debilitating warfare with France that had since 1538 consumed much of his attention and vast quantities of money. In the last desperate throes of this conflict, Charles had, in fact, made new concessions to Protestantism, assuring the princes that in return for financial support for his wars, the settlement of religion would await a "general, Christian, free Council in the German nation." The pope, not surprisingly, was appalled at this clear encroachment on his own prerogatives and dispatched a stiff letter of protest. A copy of this private letter was soon in the hands of Martin Luther, most likely with the connivance of imperial officials. The Protestant princes urged Luther to reply, but in truth he needed little bidding. For in this, a defense of his church and the German nation against papal power, Luther had embarked on the last great polemical work of his life.

Against the Papacy at Rome, Founded by the Devil gave Luther the opportunity to return to the themes that had defined his career and encapsulated his life's work.[39] The pope could not be head of the Church:

> Rather [he] is the head of the accursed church of the very worst rascals on earth; vicar of the devil; an enemy of God; an opponent of Christ; and a destroyer of the church of Christ; a teacher of all lies, blasphemy, and idolatries; an arch-church-thief and church-robber of the keys [and] all the goods of both the church and the secular lords; . . . an Antichrist; a man of sin and child of perdition; a true werewolf.[40]

Luther could now explain his concept of a true church, free of papal interference. A long historical excursus reviewed papal claims to primacy, deemed by Luther to be fraudulent. This learned exploration of Protestant historiography and the consideration of the scriptural passages generally taken to support the papal primacy have received less attention than the violence of the language and the earthy vulgarity: a crudity reinforced by a remarkable series of polemical illustrations, specially commissioned from the Cranach workshop.[41] Luther was closely involved in the design, allowing the woodcuts to be carefully aligned to key passages in the text. The penalty for the long history of papal "lies and deceit, blasphemy and idolatry" was that the tongues of the pope and his cardinals should be torn out and nailed to the gallows alongside their bodies. One of the woodcuts shows precisely this.

By this stage in his long career there was little to restrain Luther's natural instinct toward polemical violence, particularly if, as in this case, he was acting with the explicit encouragement of the elector. Philip Melanchthon had long since given up on any attempt to restrain Luther's extravagance of language; here it is given full rein. So, too, is Luther's fondness for scatological abuse. But if we look beyond the steaming turds and farting (graphically represented with all Cranach's customary skill), we should recognize the deadly seriousness of Luther's purpose. This was a last call to arms, in these last days, against the papal Antichrist. This was the revelation that had led Luther outside the church, and this was the still imminent threat to the survival of his new church. If some were too delicate to recognize these truths, then so be it. As he reflected to Amsdorf:

> [Y]ou know my nature, that I am not accustomed to attend to what displeases many provided that it is pious and useful and that it pleases the few good [people]. Nor do I think that those [who are displeased with it] are bad, but they either do not understand . . . the horrifying and horrible monstrosities of the papal abominations . . . or they fear the wrath of kings.[42]

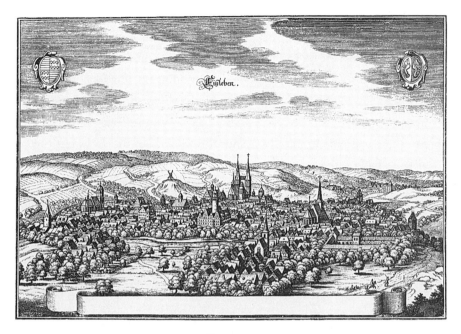

EISLEBEN

When Luther fell mortally ill in 1546 his presence in Eisleben, the town of his birth, was quite coincidental. The reformer seems to have felt it was the call of destiny, and swiftly reconciled himself to death.

In any case, it would soon fall to others to settle these questions without his guiding hand.

EISLEBEN

The demands of Protestant politics did not spare Martin Luther, even in his declining years. With the Peace of Crépy, the Emperor Charles was at last free to settle the matter of Germany. It swiftly became clear that he was determined to enforce his own settlement of the religious question. It was thus even more important that there should be no dissension among the Protestant princes. In the autumn of 1545 Luther was once more called into action, this time to mediate the quarrel between the Count of Mansfeld and his brother Gerhard. Twice he traveled to Eisleben, the town of his birth, to promote reconciliation, an exhausting round trip of some 125 miles. A settlement was promised but was not yet achieved, so on January 23, 1546, he set off again, this time via Halle. Negotiations progressed well, but Luther was forced to absent himself from the final session on February 17 as he was suffering from chest pains. He was able to join his friends for supper, but the pains returned after he had retired to bed; it was quickly clear to Luther that this time there would be no recovery.

Luther's church now faced a critical test. Much would depend on what occurred in the next few hours, and how Luther's departing was represented to grieving followers or exultant foes. Luther had received a taste of what was in store in the previous year, when a false report of the reformer's death had circulated in Italy. A maliciously hostile description of Luther's passing was published as a broadsheet. According to this tendentious text, when Luther realized that he was dying, "he asked that his body should be placed on an altar and worshipped as a God." But in the event:

> No sooner had his corpse been laid in the grave than a terrible roar and noise were heard, as if devil and hell had collapsed. All those present were greatly terrified, frightened and afraid. . . . The following night everybody heard an even greater roaring at the place where Luther's corpse had been buried. . . . When daylight came, they went to Luther's grave and opened it. They saw clearly that there was neither body nor flesh nor bones nor clothes, but a sulfurous odor which sickened all those who stood around.

A copy of this printed broadsheet came into Luther's hands, and he promptly had it published with his own defiant attestation:

> And I, Martin Luther, confess and witness with this statement that I received this furious story of my death on 21 March. I read it

gladly and joyfully indeed, except for the fact that such blasphemy is attributed to divine majesty. Otherwise I do not really care about it that the devil and his followers, pope and papists, are so hostile to me. May God convert them from the evil![43]

Luther had lost none of his flair for exploiting the press, but now the spark was about to be extinguished.

Happily for his posthumous reputation, his followers had also had plentiful opportunity to prepare for the end; it was, after all, over a decade since he had experienced his first critical health episode, and his increasing debilitation had been there for all to see. It was essential that Luther should die well, and his colleagues ensured that it would be so. In the presence of his watching friends the reformer's life slipped peacefully away at three o'clock on the morning of February 18. There was no roaring and no groaning. The Devil did not come to claim him, as his enemies had so gleefully foretold.

News was immediately dispatched to Elector John Frederick and Luther's colleagues on the Wittenberg faculty. It was left to the theologians to bring the sad tidings to a distraught Katharina von Bora. Melanchthon shared the news with his lecture class: "Now has died the charioteer and chariot of Israel who guided the Church in this last age of the world."[44] In Eisleben, meanwhile, Luther's body was laid out in St. Andrew's Church in a simple white smock. A painter, Lukas Furtenagel, was summoned from Halle to sketch a last image of the reformer's face, at rest and at peace. Justus Jonas, Luther's faithful friend and companion, preached a sermon over the body. The following day Michael Coelius delivered a second sermon before Luther's body began its final journey, from the city of his birth and death to his adopted home, Wittenberg.

On February 22, the reformer was laid to rest in the castle church, as the elector had commanded. Bugenhagen preached at the ceremony; Melanchthon followed with his own eulogy. These early reflections of Luther's life and achievement were swiftly circulated in print, and they would play a crucial role in shaping interpretation of Luther's life—and death. Bugenhagen expressed the emotion of those who had lost a father or friend; for the faithful Johannes, Luther was a teacher and prophet sent by God. None should rejoice at his death, since his "powerful, blessed, divine teaching" lived on. Melanchthon, as was his wont, was more studied and forensic. He did not conceal his own intermittent discomfort at Luther's polemical style. But Luther's real legacy would not be this, but the theological insights: justification by faith, the Law and the Gospel, the spiritual and civil spheres. All this, of course, sat alongside the legacy of true teaching, nurturing the Christian people, along with the enduring monument of his Bible translation.

Luther's dying was the last great triumph of his life; and it was, like so much that had made his movement, a collaborative effort. As on so many occasions in the previous three decades, Luther could rely one more time on the talent and forbearance of the exceptionally gifted group of colleagues who had gathered around him. Together, and in their different ways, they shaped the interpretation of an event unprecedented in the history of Christianity: the death of a man who had established a successful and enduring counterchurch within the family of Western Christendom. And as they had done at every stage of Luther's movement, the printers played their part. In the course of 1546 alone, these funeral orations were published in over thirty editions. In Wittenberg, Melanchthon, Bugenhagen, and Justus Jonas all entrusted their work to Georg Rhau (a significant departure from Luther's established practice of spreading the work around). Thereafter there was a flurry of reprints all around Germany. In the case of Melanchthon's oration, editions were published in Augsburg, Frankfurt, Magdeburg, Nuremberg, Strasbourg, and Zwickau, with a Low German translation in Lübeck.[45] Most of these established centers of Protestant printing also sponsored editions of Jonas's and Bugenhagen's sermons, with the significant additions, for Jonas, of Ulm, Regensburg, Wesel, and Hannover. Presumably, in these cases, they very often carried the first news of Luther's death. The publications issued to mark Luther's departure also included a verse lament, the work of Leonhard Kettner, with significant input by Hans

Sachs.[46] The first editions were most likely from Nuremberg, with reprints in Lübeck, Erfurt, and Zwickau.

In this way Luther's supporters, with significant assistance from the printing industry, laid claim to the narrative of Luther's death. Not everybody would be convinced. Luther's opponents were not to be cheated of their quarry, and hostile rumors continued to circulate. In response Philip Melanchthon penned a brief encomium of his friend to accompany a memorial selection of Luther's works; Johannes Cochlaeus, the most dogged of Luther's first detractors, countered with a far longer and predictably skeptical account of Luther's life and career. Thus would be inaugurated the struggle for Luther's legacy, a contest that would play a crucial role in shaping his church in the decades and centuries after his death. At first the debate over Luther would follow predictable, confessional lines. But all too soon, more tragically, the contest for Luther's posthumous approval would embroil former friends in furious disagreement as his movement split into contesting branches. This, too, was a part of Luther's potent, troubled legacy: a spirit too large, too restless, and ultimately too ambiguous to be easily confined within a narrow confessional straitjacket.

12.

LEGACY

O N FRIDAY, OCTOBER 31, 1617, all over Protestant Germany, citizens were called to church for a special service of thanksgiving. This was the day chosen to mark the centenary of the Reformation, one hundred years to the day when, it now suited the church's leaders to recall, Luther was believed to have published his ninety-five theses. The sermons chosen for this day differed from place to place. The city of Ulm chose indulgences; Electoral Saxony, keen to reclaim its special place in the Reformation narrative, chose to place more emphasis on the life and work of Martin Luther. In many places celebrations and special events continued for some weeks, in the case of Strasbourg all the way to Christmas. To the pious population this may have been increasingly burdensome. Although they had flocked to the sermons of October 31 in large numbers—Ulm had laid on extra clergy to hear confessions in the weeks leading up to the great event—the stipulation that inns and taverns remain closed during the festivities may have tested this enthusiasm to the limit.[1]

The careful arrangements made for the jubilee celebrations reveal that this was far from a spontaneous outpouring of popular enthusiasm. The planning, down to the last detail, was exclusively in the hands of the secular and ecclesiastical authorities. The celebrations were conceived both as an opportunity to reinforce community solidarity and as a major pedagogical tool. Plays were written to be performed in public or in the schools, reliving the dramas of the Reformation and the events of Luther's life. Special prayers were printed to be distributed to all the churches; children were to learn them by heart. In return for this dutiful service the children were presented with a specially minted medal: Ulm printed 4,000 copies of the jubilee prayer and distributed 2,250 medals.[2] Many territories had such medals struck, most bearing images of Martin Luther and references to the Reformation drama or its key theological precepts.[3] This medal culture was the innovative cornerstone of a veritable media blitz. Not surprisingly, the printers played their part. In addition to the printed prayers, sermons, and official ordinances prescribing the ceremonies, the year 1617 also produced a notable outpouring of commemorative broadsheets, intended to be exhibited on the walls of public places or in private homes. In woodcuts or utilizing the increasingly popular technique of engraving, these images revived the familiar tropes of the Reformation decade: the pope toppling from his throne, the hapless indulgence seller vanquished by the evangelical light.[4] Above them all towered the figure of Martin Luther, simultaneously the calm patriarch (revisiting one of Cranach's most famous images) and the warrior for Christ. Luther's omnipresence was a reminder of better, more innocent days; in 1617 it was as if he had never been away.

The Reformation Jubilee was a vast act of communal solidarity; it was also an intensely political event. The initiative had come not specifically at the prompting of the evangelical ministers of Saxony, as might have been expected, but as a suggestion of the leader of the Protestant military alliance, the Protestant Union, Frederick V of the Palatinate. The union had been formed in 1608 as a counterweight to the increasing militancy of Catholic forces in the empire. Frederick, a committed Calvinist, was met by considerable suspicion from the major Lutheran princes as he attempted to weld the divided Protestant powers into a coherent force. The Luther commemoration, conceived at a meeting of the union in Heilbronn in April 1617, was a gracious and canny contribution to building this Protestant solidarity. Even the choice of title for the commemoration, "Jubilee," was one freighted with meaning, since this, of course, was the name given to the special years of grace and indulgence celebrated by the Catholic Church every twenty-five years.[5] The distribution of special medals during the Reformation commemoration also mimicked the Catholic custom of jubilee coins, with a nod to the more ancient tradition of pilgrimage tokens. But the Reformation commemoration, as was emphasized in numerous pamphlets and sermons, was no mere echo of such tawdry rituals, but a true evangelical jubilee.

The Reformation Jubilee was a remarkable act of communal remembering, improvised at remarkably short notice and drawing on all the theological and media weapons developed over a long century of confessional division. Its consequence was to canonize 1517 and the posting of the theses as the key date of the Reformation, a status it had never before held, to judge by the numerous alternative dates previously celebrated in Lutheran territories as local days of remembrance. From this point on the posting of the theses would be the acknowledged point of beginning, a point rammed home by one of the most widely produced of all the polemical broadsheets of the year, the so-called dream of Frederick the Wise.[6] In this complex allegory, Luther writes on the door of the castle church with a giant quill. Its elongated stem passed through the ear of an enraged lion (for Pope Leo), before knocking the papal tiara off the pope's head. There is even room in such illustrative woodcuts for the unfortunate Tetzel, once again invoked as the pantomime villain of the movement: quite literally so in Heinrich Kielmann's *Tetzel Peddling,* one of several new plays written for the jubilee celebrations. In other images, and rather in defiance of chronology, sinister Jesuits also make their appearance.[7]

This then was a complicated ceremony of confected memory and genuine theology, of affectionate allusive recollection of the founding father and dogged incantation of familiar foes. As 1617 drew to a close it was hard to deny that the jubilee had been an enormous success, engaging the curiosity and enthusiasm of Protestant communities across the

DREAM OF FREDERICK THE WISE

One of the most widely disseminated of the broadsheets published during the jubilee year 1617, this complex image helped canonize the posting of the theses as the moment the Reformation began.

Empire. This was now an established church; some of those involved would have been the grandchildren of those who had first taken the momentous step outside their historic Catholic allegiance. But as the Lutheran congregations processed, sang, and clinked their newly minted medals, it was easy to forget that this act of commemoration was equally an act of forgetting. Forgetting the storm clouds that loomed over Germany and would within a year plunge it back into a long and destructive war that at times seemed once again to threaten the survival of Luther's church. Conveniently ignoring the fact that the driving force behind these events was not the established leaders of German Lutheranism but the Elector Palatine, a committed Calvinist. Most of all, casting a veil over two generations of poisonous contention within the Lutheran family, of friendships severed, of feverish pamphlet battles, and even of occasions when fellow Lutherans were pursued to their death, all to claim the right to interpret the meaning of Luther's great movement.

This, too, was part of his legacy. It meant that even after Luther's death the battle of the books could not be stilled. The struggle for Luther's posthumous approval continued to consume his followers and provided for Germany's printers a steady stream of work to the end of the century and beyond. In other parts of Europe during these decades, France and the Low Countries for example, wars of religion stimulated a new surge of pamphlet publications reminiscent of Germany in the 1520s. The situation in Luther's homeland was rather different. Here the output of the presses was much more diverse, reflecting the needs of a church still troubled by new challenges, but essentially fixed and settled. Now there were churches to be built, ministers to be trained, a Christian people to be educated, enemies, old and new, to be confuted. All provided work to keep the presses rolling. Print, it transpired, was not just an instrument of agitation and change: now it was equally necessary to win the peace and shape the new churches of the Gospel preaching.

THE WAY OF THE CROSS

On April 24, 1547, fourteen months after Luther's death, the forces of the Schmalkaldic League came face-to-face with Emperor Charles V at Mühlberg. The printer Georg Rhau was also there with his field press, ready to convey to the world the news of the anticipated Protestant victory. Alas for Rhau, alas indeed for the Protestant princes, the battle would take a very different course. The league's forces were routed and Charles emerged triumphant. Among his prisoners were the leaders of the Protestant resistance, Elector John Frederick and Philip of Hesse—along with Rhau and his press. Wittenberg and Electoral Saxony now lay defenseless before the victorious imperial army.

The emperor moved quickly to exploit his triumph. John Frederick was hustled off into captivity, emerging only five years later, condemned, and stripped of his electoral title and much of his territory. From Wittenberg, Lucas Cranach, now an old man in his seventies, journeyed to the imperial camp to plead for the elector's life; he later joined his master in the last stage of his captivity.[8] His workshop was left in the more than capable hands of his son Lucas Junior. Wittenberg was besieged and then occupied. According to tradition, one of the emperor's first actions on entering the occupied city was to visit Luther's grave in the castle church. Twenty-six years earlier Luther had slipped through Charles's fingers at Worms. Now he had evaded him in death.

For all that, some sort of retribution, however symbolic, might have been in order. Luther had died a condemned heretic and outlaw. Custom and legal practice might have suggested that the appropriate penalties should have been visited on his corpse. Ten years later the government of Mary Tudor would do precisely this with the remains of the Strasbourg reformer Martin Bucer, who had died in England; a century later similar indignities were visited on Oliver Cromwell's remains by Charles II. Shrewdly, the emperor denied himself the satisfaction. At Worms he had let Luther depart because he had promised to do so to conciliate the Protestant princes. Now he had similar policy objectives in mind. Why outrage Protestant opinion when he hoped to enforce on his defeated enemies a settlement of religion that at least some of them could accept? His partial success in this endeavor would come close to ripping Luther's church apart.

In the existential crisis after Mühlberg, German Lutheranism looked for leadership to Philip Melanchthon, Luther's closest friend and intellectual companion. This, alas, was a role for which Philip was singularly unsuited. His true vocation was that of the scholar and theologian; as a church politician, or even as the leader of a church (as the months of Luther's absence in the Wartburg had proved long ago), he was totally at sea. Stunned and still grieving from the loss of his friend, Melanchthon was forced into a series of compromises that badly divided and scarred the movement; never was the church more in need of Luther's brutal clarity and stubborn immovability than in these desperate years after his death.

In 1546, as the contending armies approached Saxony, Wittenberg University had been temporarily dissolved. Melanchthon fled with his family to Zerbst. With the war concluded, Wittenberg, now a town under occupation, was passed to Maurice of Saxony along with the electoral title as a part of his reward for allying with the emperor against his cousin and the Schmalkaldic League. Faced with the fallout from this dynastic pragmatism, Maurice was keen to reestablish his Protestant credentials and to woo the absent professors back to a restored Wittenberg University. This faced Philip with a difficult decision. Should he return, and seem to endorse the passage of power to a man who had abandoned his Protestant brethren for short-term gain? Melanchthon was already aware that the three sons of the imprisoned John Frederick were hatching plans for a new alternative university at Jena, in the small residual territory left to the defeated Ernestine line; but it might be many years before anything came of this (and indeed, the university only opened its doors in 1558). Philip, with hesitation and reluctance, opted to return home.

Worse was to come. In 1548 the emperor, as expected, moved to impose a new settlement of religion on German Protestantism. This, the Augsburg Interim, would have involved the reinstatement of many aspects of traditional religion. The Interim was immediately condemned by the Lutherans of northern Germany, safely removed, it must be said, from the conquering imperial army. The Interim was also unpalatable to Maurice, a committed Lutheran when all was said and done. He requested that Melanchthon confer with colleagues to see what could be conceded to the victorious emperor without compromising the essentials of faith. In an exhaustive series of meetings through the summer and autumn of 1548 Melanchthon was gradually brought to moderate his initially emphatic repudiation of the Interim. Comforting himself that he salvaged the principal theological tenet of the church, justification by faith, Melanchthon acknowledged that it was legitimate for the state power to regulate church practice with respect to ceremony and church order—matters of custom and practice, nonessentials or adiaphora. For many Lutherans, the messy document in which Melanchthon articulated this complex formula, which became known as the Leipzig Proposal, was the ultimate betrayal. Could such "trifles" as holy water, censing, the Consecration of the bread, or unction at baptism be regarded as adiaphora, was the sarcastic inquiry of the Berlin theologians.[9] And could the church really tolerate the reimposition of Catholic Church structures, including the authority of bishops?

Melanchthon's acceptance of the Interim, for all his qualifications and mental reservations, was a turning point for the movement. For the first time Wittenberg's leadership of Luther's movement was called into question. While old colleagues like Bugenhagen stayed loyal, others in the inner circle now separated themselves from Melanchthon, including Luther's old companion in arms Nicolas von Amsdorf. These dissidents found a new spiritual home in nearby Magdeburg, the imperial free city that in 1548 had most loudly proclaimed its defiance of the emperor and the Interim. For three long years, until forced to capitulate to the besieging armies of Maurice and his allies, Magdeburg held out, a beacon of resistance to the emperor and his subjugation of Lutheranism.[10]

The energizing spirit of this resistance was a man of a younger generation, Matthias Flacius Illyricus. Flacius was also part of the Wittenberg circle, appointed professor of Hebrew in the university in 1544 at the age of twenty-four. But he was not one of the initial band of brothers, and can only have known Luther in his late, declining years. Having removed to Braunschweig at the suspension of the university in 1546, Flacius had little appetite for an institution living under the Interim, and in 1549 he transferred to Magdeburg. Here he swiftly emerged as one of the most skillful polemicists of defiance. His response to the Interim, and his former Wittenberg colleagues, was brutally simple: the Interim was a deception, little more than a camouflage for the reintroduction of Catholicism. The appeal for unity and order, for obedience to the state power, could not justify a denial of the true faith. As it was succinctly stated in an open letter from the Hamburg ministers to the Wittenberg professors, twice reprinted in Magdeburg, it was most unsafe "to place one's trust in princely courts to the exclusion of God's Word."[11] Behind all of this, and the indignant wounded replies of the Wittenberg faculty, floated the unstated question: What would Luther have said? What would he have done in this situation? There was little doubt that those gathered at Magdeburg and their allies in the north German cities believed that they were the real keepers of the flame.

It was not just in its theologians that Magdeburg sought to inherit the mantle of Wittenberg: the same could be said of its printing industry. The two principal printers of the pamphlet polemic had both cut their teeth in Luther's school for bookmen. Michael Lotter, when he moved to Magdeburg, was already an accomplished printer, having first arrived in Wittenberg to assist his brother, the soon disgraced Melchior, in the early 1520s. Michael lingered for a few years after his brother's departure, before transferring definitively to Magdeburg in 1529, where he built a lucrative line in reprints of Wittenberg editions of Luther's works.[12] In 1539 he was joined by Christian Rödinger, whose Wittenberg apprenticeship had been far more brief. In Magdeburg he, too, built a substantial business through the publication of Luther and his supporters. The presence of these two canny and established operators meant that it was relatively easy to gear up production when Magdeburg enjoyed its brief moment at the eye of the storm: in the five years between 1548 and 1552 the Magdeburg presses turned out 460 works.[13] This output was wholly dominated by the pungent polemical pamphlets of the resistance. As a media campaign they exhibit all the features that we recognize from Wittenberg in the 1520s: clarity of purpose and intellectual coherence, reinforced by a clear if simple design identity. Magdeburg offers a further striking example of the capacities of the printing industry to respond to the rapid fluctuations of demand that followed the great events of the Reformation.

There was little doubt that in this respect the siege of Magdeburg was a true defining moment: the time when in defense of the faith

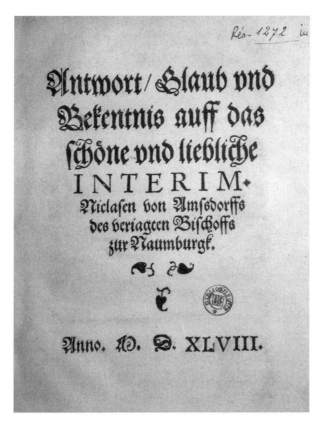

MAGDEBURG RESISTANCE

As Wittenberg was compromised by its stance during the Interim controversy, Magdeburg and Jena emerged as new centers of Lutheran resistance. This attack on the Interim was printed by Michael Lotter, a printer who had started his career in Wittenberg in the workshop of his brother Melchior.

Lutherans turned from theoretical considerations of the right of resistance to open defiance of the emperor's power. Magdeburg's sacrifice, and ultimate vindication in the Peace of Augsburg of 1555, was a sign that the critical mass of Lutheran powers would choose the clarity of orthodoxy rather than the subtle syncretism of Melanchthon. The strength of this feeling was graphically demonstrated when John Calvin, the young reformer of Geneva, attempted rather unwisely to fish in these troubled waters.[14] The ostensible cause was the rough handling of a group of evangelical exiles expelled from England on the death of Edward VI, and denied entry to a succession of north German Lutheran towns in a bitter winter while in search of a new home. Calvin was scandalized by this lack of evangelical fellowship. When he took aim against the spokesman of the Hamburg church, Joachim Westphal, he expected Melanchthon's support. But Melanchthon, bruised and dejected from the violence with which he had been assailed within the Lutheran family, kept silent, and Calvin was further surprised by the vigor with which other Lutherans rallied to Westphal's side. The Genevan beat a swift retreat: he had badly misjudged the temper of German religion after this traumatic decade, and indeed, the extent to which Melanchthon had been humbled by his call for temperance and accommodation.

In due course the political wheel of fortune would turn against the Habsburgs, providing German Lutherans with some relief. Once again the critical figure was Maurice of Saxony. Having abandoned the Protestant princes in 1546, he now turned against Charles. Old, tired, and worsted on the field of battle, the emperor abandoned the project of re-Catholicization, leaving it to his brother Ferdinand to settle the question of religion in Germany. The resulting Peace of Augsburg ostensibly gave Lutherans all they could hope for: freedom of religion under the protection of their local prince. But the festering sores left by the memory of the Interim controversies were laid bare in repeated eruptions of theological feuding, as the contending factions fought for possession of Luther's legacy. At the heart of much of this lay the contentious figure of Matthias Flacius Illyricus.

After the capitulation of Magdeburg, Flacius retreated to Jena. Here in the rump of Ernestine Saxony he found a base from which he could harry the Wittenbergers in a series of theological controversies. These became increasingly abstruse and to many in the movement infuriatingly self-destructive, though most led back in some way to the doubtful accommodations embedded in the Leipzig Proposal, now taking on a canonical status never intended by Melanchthon, who had been trying to make the best of a political emergency.[15] Flacius sought targets where he could find them, first Melanchthon, then the highly respected George Major, even a colleague in Jena. The logical if absurdist consequence was a schism among the Lutheran ultras, leading in 1561 to the expulsion of Flacius and his supporters from Jena.

No sooner was this conflict resolved than a new danger emerged: Calvinism. In the middle years of the sixteenth century, John Calvin was rapidly emerging as one of the most dynamic forces in the international Protestant movement. Although his primary concern was for the conversion of his French homeland, Calvin also had an interest in building the church in Germany (in an earlier stage in his career he had worked for three years in Strasbourg, so was well acquainted with the ecclesiastical politics of the Empire). Calvin's bruising encounter with the Hamburg Lutherans proved to be no more than a temporary rebuff. By the 1560s Calvinism was making serious inroads in the Empire, particularly among the smaller principalities of the German northwest. Most dangerous of all was the growing indications that the electors of the Palatinate intended to convert their lands to Calvinism. The Rhineland Palatinate occupied a sensitive and strategic territory close to the heartlands of the Calvinist resurgence in western Europe. Any shift in its political allegiance was, therefore, a potent threat to the political balance of power, as a potential military ally to the Calvinist insurgency in France and the Netherlands. Any change in religion here also presaged a full-blown constitutional crisis in the Empire. The guiding principle of the Peace of Augsburg, that each prince should choose the religious disposition of his lands, envisaged only a binary choice between the two prevailing orthodoxies, Catholic and Lutheran. There was no room for the distinctly un-German force of Calvinism.

Yet despite this, the prestige of the Palatinate ensured that this unwelcome interloper could not be ignored, particularly as it became increasingly clear that Calvinist theology was not without appeal to the Melanchthonite wing of Lutheranism. Gnesio-Lutherans, as the orthodox were now known, followed these developments with a dogged determination to root out any signs of backsliding or theological equivocation.

Once again Wittenberg and Electoral Saxony lay at the heart of the crisis. The death of Melanchthon in 1560 and his friend Paul Eber in 1569 finally severed the connection with the first generation of reform. The new leaders of the church soon came under suspicion for doctrinal revisionism, forcing the elector to take the extraordinary step of banning German editions of the new Wittenberg catechism. Worse was to follow. Persuaded now that the crypto-Calvinist tendencies of the Melanchthonite wing of his church amounted to a betrayal of public doctrine, Elector Augustus, who had succeeded his brother Maurice in 1553, had four of its leaders arrested; two died in prison.

Things could not continue this way, and Augustus now joined a concerted effort to heal the rifts that had festered since the divisions opened up by the Schmalkaldic War. The result was the Book of Concord, a new statement of Lutheran belief that closed the door to theological equivocation. It was a resounding victory for orthodoxy, and a repudiation of the spirit of Melanchthon or any accommodation of the foreign force of Calvinism. For two generations relations between Lutherans and Calvinists would be almost more poisoned than those with the forces of resurgent Catholicism: better a Catholic than a Calvinist, was the notorious refrain. Such antagonisms bedeviled attempts to find a common Protestant front in an era of increasing confessional conflict; in this, the convivial cross-confessional celebrations of the 1617 Reformation Jubilee were more a brief interlude than a lasting act of healing.

PROPHET, TEACHER, FRIEND

The querulous disputatiousness of the theological controversy casts a somber light on the troubled decades after Luther's death, an era paradoxically often thought of as an interval of relative tranquillity between the showdown with Charles V and the outbreak of the Thirty Years' War in 1618. But there was more to Lutheran church life—and far more to Luther's legacy—than shrill pamphlets and the restless search for theological purity. In the search for this other Lutheranism it is often the parishioners, the men and women in the pews, who set the tone. Beneath the hubbub of theological argument and the corrosive search for the enemy within, we see the emergence of another form of church: the calm unfolding of a new worship tradition slowly embraced by generations of parishioners. This, for Luther, would have been his true legacy, and perhaps his largest gift to the church: a people confident that separated from the Catholic Church they had found a new and vibrant worship tradition, one that bore all the hallmarks of Luther's lifelong vocation to build a new Christian people.

A traveler in Germany in the second half of the sixteenth century would inevitably pass through many different political jurisdictions; and thus, through both Protestant and Catholic states. It would not take long for him to discern the confessional allegiance of each locality, purely from the physical appearance of the church interior and the nature of the worship service. It did not require the radically stripped-down austerity of Reformed worship to be aware of the revolution wrought by Luther, most obviously, of course, when the congregation came together in church. Here the tenor and temper of congregational worship would have been utterly different from the Catholic Mass. The traveler would have been struck especially by the prominence of the sermon in a service built around a liturgy in German, and by the high level of congregational participation, evident not only in the vernacular responses but in congregational singing. Lutheran worship was suffused by singing, a passion of Luther's, and one of his most profound legacies to his church. In the religion of the everyday, this musical heritage was certainly more deeply rooted than any of his leading theological revelations.

For Luther, music was an essential conduit of God's word.[16] So long as it was stripped of its theological monstrosities, he was quite content that the canon of the Mass, the Credo, Gloria, Agnus Dei, should form the framework of the Protestant liturgy. Music was for Luther a multivalent expression of devotion: an articulation of the voice of the Christian community; a comfort to the troubled soul; a powerful teaching tool.

Between 1523 and 1524, a busy and contentious time in his developing movement, he wrote no fewer than forty hymns. Although other ministerial colleagues would eagerly take up the charge, these original compositions of Luther always had a special status in the movement. Many are still sung today. Luther's hymns were the stimulus for a vast outpouring of composition and publication that utterly defined his movement. In the course of the century, Germany's printers turned out over one thousand editions of the German hymnal.[17] The fact that so many of these survive in only one copy suggests that many further editions may have been published that are now altogether lost. One can say with confidence that in the course of the century several million copies would have been in circulation, for use in the church, the classroom, and the pious home.

It was never Luther's intention that singing should be confined to the worship service. Luther's 1524 hymnal was published first and foremost for the Wittenberg town school and its choir. Other hymnbooks were specifically for domestic use, interspersing hymns with prayers appropriate for the family. Luther was careful to ensure that he composed hymns for every part of the catechism. In an age when so much learning was inculcated by rote, song was seen both as a critical aid to memory and as a means of sugaring the pill of endless repetition.

Luther, as we have seen, was both a passionate advocate and an acute philosopher of education. This, along with his musical legacy, was his second major contribution to the development of the Lutheran social community. Luther's catechism was one of the most popular and republished of his books, but there was nothing prescriptive about its use. Here, as in his benignly curious attitude to liturgy, Luther positively encouraged variety.

These two passions, music and education, coincided in the extensive use of music in the Lutheran schoolroom. We have seen already how striking was the concentration on schoolchildren in the jubilee celebrations of 1617: in the performance of plays, the learning of new prayers, the distribution of commemorative medals. This ubiquitous pedagogic instinct had by this time become thoroughly engrained. It was quite common in a church community to teach new hymns or catechismal responses first to the children; their voracious memories could then be a help to the slower minds of their elders. In many German towns, the school, and its choir, became a crucial salient of Lutheran pedagogy. The school choir at Joachimsthal made a biannual singing procession through the town. They sang at funerals and at a special procession in Lent, chasing out the pope. This conscious evocation of the medieval practice of driving out death is a neat example of the appropriation of pre-Reformation ritual for new purposes. All of this had its effect; Joachimsthal instituted an hour of congregational singing preceding the Sunday service that was popular and well attended. The Joachimsthal choir was also sent round the town recruiting new scholars:

> Come with us, dear children,
> And become pious students
> We shall lead you to our school
> Where you will study God's Word.[18]

For Luther and his colleagues the freedom from papal tyranny was only a beginning. The education of the Christian community to a comprehensive understanding of their faith was a necessary part of the process of Reformation. Lutheran pastors would never be content that they had achieved this goal, and regular inspections of parishes by the territorial officials sometimes presented a bleak view of how much still needed to be done.[19] But the result was certainly a vast and sustained increase in school provision. Literacy rates took a large step forward, and crucially the gaping chasm between urban and rural education levels began to be addressed. By the end of the century most habitations of any size in Lutheran Germany had a school.

When schoolchildren confronted a raging master, or their parents sang in the church or workplace, they did not always see Luther's hand at work (perhaps, in the case of the schoolchildren, thankfully so). Their Luther was a different presence: a semimythical figure, a folk memory through which was channeled many different emotional needs. Teacher, prophet, healer, and friend: Luther was all of these things. From beyond the grave, now beyond reproach and beyond criticism, he continued to guide his flock: a benign giant stripped of the foibles of his lifetime.

This mythical Luther took several forms. There was Luther the prophet.[20] The reformers' own attitudes to their prophetic status had, as we have seen, been decidedly cautious. In their writings Luther and his colleagues seemed extremely doubtful whether the role of prophet could be attributed to any living teacher; unless, that was, the prophetic vocation was defined so loosely that it lost all meaning.[21] In Luther's case the awful warning of the false prophets, and their claim to inspired utterance, was a further incentive to reticence. Paradoxically, this reticence was largely abandoned after Luther's death, when he was no longer there to prophesy. Volumes of Luther's prophecies became a popular subculture of the Luther publishing industry.

By the time of his death Luther's was one of the most famous faces in Christendom. Through the efforts of the Cranach workshop, friend and foe alike had been able to track the physical change in Luther through a series of portraits drawn from life. After his death it was only representations of the mature Luther that were disseminated, on medals, mass-produced studio portraits, and in broadsheets. These provided the opportunity to place Luther in a whole series of new illustrative scenarios: standing foursquare alongside his elector or protectively behind his shoulder; the companion of Jan Hus in a genealogy of reform; tilling the Lord's vineyard with his Wittenberg companions.

These were the official images of Luther; folk memory and custom created more. Most powerful were the images of Luther as wonderworker, the chosen one of God. Here Luther is identified as God's special instrument by quasi-miraculous acts or occurrences. Responding to Catholic taunts that if Luther were a true prophet this should be revealed in miracles, in 1576 Johann Lapaeus accompanied the by now familiar list of Luther's prophecies with direct evidence of miracles.[22] The most spectacular proof of Luther's special status was the "incombustible Luther," portraits of Luther thrown into the flames, which nevertheless refused to burn.[23] This was a remarkably early tradition, first found in an account of the burning of Luther's books at Worms, where a portrait of Luther added to the pyre emerged unscathed. It was also remarkably long lasting, with portraits of Luther discovered in the ruins of burned houses through to the eighteenth century.

Through these tales of God's special protection, and Luther's special powers, we are tiptoeing toward an uncomfortable image: that of Luther as saint. This was especially difficult for a movement that had denounced the false honoring of saints in the Catholic world, and even in some parts of Europe inhibited the use of saints' names for children. Two woodcut portraits of Luther with the nimbus of sainthood were a short-lived aberration of the Strasbourg book industry and never officially affirmed. But the association with St. Martin, a popular saint in the Rhineland, was enduring. Father, patron, judge, and friend; members of the congregations made of Luther what they would. It was an extraordinary legacy to a church as frequently in need of comfort and reassurance as of teaching.

WITTENBERG AND JENA

In 1552 John Frederick, the vanquished and deposed elector of Saxony, was released from captivity. Wittenberg was no longer his, so he made his way to Jena, ruled in his absence by his three defiantly loyal sons. This new capital was now nurtured as the true spiritual home of Luther's movement. From 1558 it had the long-promised university; from 1553 its own printing press. This became the fulcrum of a concerted effort to claim the Reformation heritage for the heirs of its original protector, Frederick the Wise. Once again the printing press stood at the heart of the Reformation conflict, although now it was a conflict not between Catholic and Protestant, but between contending factions of Luther's own church. The genesis and development of the press in Jena is one of the most singular examples of the regeneration of the printing industry stimulated by the Reformation.

The Jena printing industry grew from small, and from Luther's point of view somewhat unpromising, beginnings.[24] Between 1523 and 1524 Michael Kramer briefly ran a press exclusively devoted to publications of the works of Andreas von Karlstadt and his supporters—hardly a cause dear to Luther's heart. This was one of the pop-up enterprises typical of these years; having served its purpose, Kramer retreated back to Erfurt, and Jena had no further involvement in the printing industry until after the Schmalkaldic War. But from 1553, when printing returned, until the end of the century, Jena's printers turned out a considerable volume of works: over two thousand in all. Many of these were substantial books. From a standing start Jena had become a major force in the industry.[25]

The confessional purpose of the new press became clear from the identity of the first man recruited to run it: none other than Christian Rödinger, called from Magdeburg to establish a press under the direct protection of the newly released John Frederick. Rödinger was lured by lavish incentives: the provision of a generous workshop in the town's former Carmelite cloister, financial assistance, and, most important of all, the exclusive rights to print Luther's works in John Frederick's (admittedly much diminished) territories.[26] Rödinger's most significant and complex assignment was the Jena edition of Luther's complete works, an unfinished multivolume project passed after his death to his heirs. From 1558 Rödinger's heirs shared the Jena market with Thomas Rebart, a former apprentice who had performed a variety of roles in the book industry before opening his own shop. His business, perhaps reflecting his previous roles in the trade, was very much oriented to the Frankfurt market. He also, in time-honored fashion, married Rödinger's daughter. Donat Richtzenhan, another apprentice of Rödinger, went one better: he married his widow. Jena printing, in fact, continued to be the business of this one extended family until the end of the century. In 1568 Christian Rödinger Junior set up his own shop. When he died his widow married first Günther Hüttich then Ernst von Gera, who successively continued the shop. The establishment of a new shop by Tobias Steinmann was prepared by a strategic marriage to the daughter of Rebart. Salomon Richtzenhan, who carried the tradition into the seventeenth century, was the son of Donat and his wife Margarethe Rödinger. Such marriages were an absolute commonplace means of conserving capital and maintaining market position in the early modern print world, and, for the apprentice, a rare opportunity to become a master tradesman. The Jena example is, however, rather extreme. Wittenberg, as we have seen, tends toward the other end of the spectrum, with growth fueled by the frequent arrival of ambitious new players from outside the city. This undoubtedly contributed, particularly in the early years, to the very high level of product innovation and dynamism of this rapidly expanding industry.

The Jena press, in contrast, was created to perform a precise and limited role. Although a new industry, it proved to be remarkably well capitalized. This it owed to two converging circumstances: the continuing robust market for Luther's own writings, and an ideologically driven publishing program underpinned by direct subsidy. After Luther's death, editions of his works were published quite freely around Germany. In the absence of his commanding presence, and with no chance of newly minted works to encourage compliance with his wishes, there was now little to deter printers from pursuing short-term commercial advantage. Yet even so Jena secured a share of this highly competitive market second only to Wittenberg itself.[27] This would not, however, have been sufficient to create the working capital for so ambitious a project as the Jena edition of Luther's collected works. Here Rödinger relied on the investment of a substantial publisher. With this cash injection the project made rapid progress, despite its size and complexity. Two volumes were published in 1555 and two more in 1556, along with the first volume of a Latin collection; and these were substantial volumes in folio, characteristically close to six hundred leaves each. Rödinger reputedly devoted four presses to the task; he would indeed have needed them all to keep abreast of it.

The struggle between Jena and Wittenberg to appropriate Luther's theological heritage also dictated that the two competing editions of the collected works should adopt radically different organizational structures.[28] The Wittenberg theologians had adopted a thematic approach, grouping together works of the same type or addressing the same issues. Jena adopted a strictly chronological organization. In the atmosphere of distrust that now characterized the relationship between rival keepers of the Lutheran flame, this was intended to legitimize the charge that the Wittenbergers distorted Luther's message by taking his words out of their historical context.

The Jena challenge was direct and serious, the more so as these were difficult years for Wittenberg. Luther's death, depriving the city of its most priceless asset, had been followed within a year by the suspension of the university, conquest and occupation, and the transfer to Maurice. Even when the university was reestablished and the city had settled down under Albertine rule, it was still a difficult decision for pious parents whether to entrust their children to the university in such circumstances. The death of Melanchthon in 1560 deprived it of its most luminous remaining teacher. To add to the difficulties, Wittenberg had to adapt to the fact that it was no longer the only university in Electoral Saxony, since Maurice brought with him into his enhanced territories the venerable university of the Albertine territories, Leipzig.

For all that this new competitive situation posed new challenges, there is no sign that Wittenberg experienced serious economic difficulties or went into any sort of long-term decline. Certainly the city was able to continue to finance significant building projects. In 1570 the town hall built in the first flush of the Reformation was pulled down and replaced by a new, larger building, the impressive edifice that dominates the main square today.[29] A fine, confident monument to the city's wealth and international status, the new five-story structure bears comparison with other new town halls erected in this same era in Antwerp and Emden, two other boomtowns reinvesting the proceeds of international trade.

Certainly Wittenberg's printing industry continued to thrive. None of the established printers working in the city at the time of Luther's

A PROSPEROUS CITY: THE WITTENBERG RATHAUS

Despite the increased competition and political difficulties in the decades after Luther's death, Wittenberg remained the preeminent center of Lutheran education and publishing. This imposing new town hall replaced one built only fifty years before, in the first years of the Reformation.

death had departed as a result of the political turmoil. Unsurprisingly, 1547 was a rough year, with only thirty titles published, but within a decade production had recovered, and then exceeded prewar levels. In the second half of the century Wittenberg could continue to trade very successfully on its reputation as the fountainhead of the Reformation. Religious books continued to dominate output, reinforced by the multiplication of numerous academic dissertations, produced to be distributed as part of the examination process and then sold by the agile printer as bundled collections. Since the student was expected to meet the initial cost of publication, and publication was a required element of supplication for the degree, the only limitation on what could be charged was the customer's poverty, particularly in places where the university required students to make use of the services of one designated printer. That we know this privilege was sometimes abused is clear from protests made to the governing bodies of different European institutions against the prices charged for these small publications. Happily in Wittenberg the work seems to have been spread around, honoring Luther's principles even after his death.

This was a healthy industry, still one of the cornerstones of the Wittenberg economy. The printers' work supported a considerable number operating in ancillary trades, not least a large number of bookbinders, a sure sign that local citizens were themselves beginning to put together extensive collections. Not all would eke out more than a modest living: some of the lesser lights of the industry were frequently found in the city's lowest tax bracket. But among the more established figures the gains to be made were very considerable. Markplatz 3, the impressive four-story building close to the second Cranach house, was from 1564 the home of Samuel Selfisch, titan of the local publishing industry.[30]

Selfisch, who was a major supplier of paper to the local printers' shops, exhibited one other characteristic of this phase of the European printing industry, a pronounced tendency for the controlling interest in the trade to pass from printers to publishers. The term publisher covers a wide variety of individuals involved in the book trade, whose main role was to provide the investment capital to underwrite projects in which they were interested. By and large they did not run their own presses, but would contract out this stage of the production process to one of the city printers. Once the work was printed, they would then take control of the distribution (and much of the profit). In the case of Selfisch and other paper merchants this might involve a simple barter transaction: they would provide the necessary paper in return for a stipulated number of printed sheets (the ratio was normally one printed sheet for every two sheets of paper, reflecting the industry norm that paper made up half the costs of production). This was an arrangement that suited both parties. The printer solved a difficult problem of supply, and eased cash flow, and the partners cut out an additional middleman who would otherwise demand his cut.

Archival records, though fragmentary in this period, provide illuminating hints as to how this market functioned, and its underlying ruthlessness. By 1539 the printer Joseph Klug owed the publisher Moritz Goltz considerable sums of money. To assist him in meeting this obligation Goltz contracted Klug to print a large number of books: two thousand copies of the dialogs of Urbanus Rhegius, three thousand of Melanchthon's grammar, six thousand copies of two different hymnbooks—a total of seventeen thousand books.[31] Goltz loaned Klug the money to enable the work to go ahead, on the expectation that profit from sales, along with the delivery to Goltz, would allow Klug to pay off the debt. But these were strikingly large print runs, and the local sales that would have rescued Klug from his financial difficulties did not materialize. In 1540 Klug's wife appealed to the council, asking for this onerous contract to be set aside. It may be that Klug's difficulties were compounded by illness and he was too sick to attend this hearing in person; certainly he subsequently revived, and printed on until his death in 1555.

Wittenberg, we have often emphasized, was an unlikely hub for a major printing industry. But this obscurity had one countervailing advantage. Because there was no preexisting patrician elite, as was the case in places like Augsburg and Nuremberg, those successful in the book industry could rise very swiftly to the top of the social hierarchy. Cranach, Lufft, Goltz, and Selfisch all occupied positions of eminence on the city council.[32] Here they were able to represent the interests of their trade and ensure that no regulations were introduced that would disadvantage them financially. There were other prizes for those with influence: Goltz was one of three publisher-booksellers who enjoyed an electoral privilege for the distribution of the Luther Bible. This was a substantial business, and it required increasingly intricate regulation to ensure that the profits were distributed equably, in this case between the distributors and the printer, Hans Lufft.[33] But as Luther himself had always recognized, the industry was simply too important to the city for its economic interests to be ignored.

A GERMANICAL NATURE

For the cornerstone of an international movement like the Reformation, Lutheranism was a curiously parochial, German phenomenon. In the first years, fascination with Luther spread across Europe, to England and Spain, Poland and Bohemia. But it was only in Luther's homeland, and in neighboring lands where German cultural influence was strong, that a Lutheran Church could successfully be planted. The reasons for this were often political. Dutch admirers of Luther, at one point numerous, ran into the immovable determination of Charles V not to be worsted again, in these his patrimonial lands, by the heretic monk who had eluded him at Worms. The Reformation in the Low Countries was brutally repressed. Cultural disdain contributed to the failure of the Reformation in Italy. But Luther's own temperament played its part. Although his theological message was couched as an exhortation to all Christian people, his frame of reference, the human experiences on which he drew and his emotional sympathies, were almost entirely German. Luther lived a life almost entirely within the relatively narrow frame of northeastern Germany, and this seemed to content him. His only sortie outside the German lands, to Rome in 1510–1511, was unsettling and unhappy. This would later fuel an antipapal rhetoric that was at one level profoundly anti-Italian. Since most of his subsequent interactions with Italians were with agents of the despised papal power, this served only to confirm these prejudices. In contrast Luther was from the beginning a shrewd reader of German politics, both within his own Augustinian order and in the wider affairs of the Empire. With his appeal *To the Christian Nobility of the German Nation* he allied himself adeptly with long-held grievances against the clerical estate; this work, too, had a powerful xenophobic tinge.

Like other of the reformers and major intellectual figures of the age, Luther maintained an enormous correspondence. But this, again, was far more geographically constrained in scope than, for instance, that of the Swiss reformers Calvin and Bullinger, or Desiderius Erasmus. Whereas Calvin and Bullinger worked systematically to build contacts and friendship networks around Europe, Luther's connections with the movement outside Germany were more theoretical than real. The case of England is instructive. Calvin and Bullinger both corresponded with a wide circle of churchmen and potentially influential councillors, and Erasmus actually lived in England twice. In Luther's case his contact with English affairs was almost entirely limited to those Englishmen who came to study in Wittenberg. His toxic public exchange with King Henry was hardly likely to win his movement friends. But this was not Luther's intention. After 1525 and the sour experience of the Peasants' War, he found it hard to conceive of a Reformation proceeding without the support of state power. When in 1531 a group of evangelicals from the Low Countries sought the reformer's blessing for their plan to establish a separate, secret congregation in Antwerp, Luther offered them no comfort: they were advised, to their surprise and disappointment, to conform and wait for better times.[34]

Luther was a German figure and a German writer. His pleasures—food, music, family, beer—were not especially cerebral, and this was conveyed in an engaging style honed over many years of ministry and preaching to his Wittenberg congregation. Luther was a thoroughly educated man, but he wore this lightly. His sermons were littered with homely examples and improving tales, drawn equally from the fables of Aesop and the follies of life he observed all around him.[35] All of this was integrated into a style of theological writing that Luther had essentially invented.

Luther was a cultured and purposeful theological writer. He wrote fine Latin, and his Latin works measured up well against those of talented adversaries. But it was his German writings that redefined theological debate and reshaped its audience. The decision to make the case against indulgences in German with the 1518 *Sermon on Indulgence and Grace* was, as we have seen, momentous; and this proved to be only the first of several hundred original German compositions, many like this, short, terse, and phrased with a directness and clarity that was a revelation in itself. Luther's innovation as a writer continued with his German Bible, an experiment in style and language that shaped the way German was written and spoken from that day forth. Luther called the German people to engage in serious questions of salvation and Christian responsibility, and they responded in huge numbers. In piquing their interest, the medium—Luther's choice of words and style, the accessibility of ideas briefly put, the visual signals of pamphlets with an increasing design homogeneity—was in many respects as important as the message.

The impact of this extraordinary literary career, the late-blooming talent of a driven man, can be measured in many ways, not least in the thousands of men and women drawn from their old allegiance to follow his teachings. Nowhere was this impact more profound than its consequence for the printing industry. Luther was the most successful author since the invention of printing. His output far outstripped that of any living contemporary, both in the number of his published works and in their success in the marketplace. His sales outstripped all of the ancients, even staples of the school curriculum such as Cicero. In the sixteenth century printers put out almost 5,000 editions of Luther's works; a further 3,000 can be added if one reckons with other projects with which he was involved, such as the Luther Bible.[36] But of these 4,790 editions, almost 90 percent were published in Germany, and almost 80 percent in the German language. For a theological writer, in an age when Latin was still the language of schooling and intellectual debate, these are extraordinary statistics. The contrast with Erasmus, Luther's main publishing rival, is instructive. Erasmus, though comfortably outpublished by Luther, had a far more international appeal. His works circulated in Europe, with especially strong demand in France, the Low Countries, and Germany. Numerous editions were published in all of these places, but since 80 percent of the Erasmus editions were published in Latin, they crossed boundaries with ease. This contrast exposes both the potency and the limitations of Luther's movement. But for German printers and

German readers the intensity and focus of Luther's publishing barrage was gold dust.

Martin Luther had many strokes of good fortune in the early years of the Reformation; we have experienced them most vividly in the reca-pitulation of the Reformation's torrid early years, when a word from Frederick the Wise could have doomed him to a heretic's death. One as-pect of this good fortune is less immediately obvious, but especially per-tinent to this current discussion: and that is the nature and organization of the German printing industry. In contrast to most parts of Europe, Germany had no dominant printing entrepôt, but several competing centers of production. This accident of fate would serve Luther well. The multitude of jurisdictions made it virtually impossible to impose controls over output; the wealth and size of Germany's major cities pro-vided both a well-capitalized publishing industry and a ready audience. Many authors chafed at the ease with which their works were pirated and reprinted, but for Luther this was a great boon, particularly in the early years. Through reprints of Wittenberg editions in Augsburg, Stras-bourg, and elsewhere, Luther's works, and news of his cause, passed eas-ily into the bloodstream of German public life. He, of course, helped by writing works of a length that made it straightforward for publishers to run off a new edition.

Of the six established centers of the German print industry only Co-logne was entirely closed to Reformation publishing. The others all had a slightly different role: Leipzig as the local entrepôt as Wittenberg found its feet, Nuremberg and Augsburg the great commercial centers in the south, Basel as the center of Latin exchange, Strasbourg the gateway to the west. All made a major contribution to printing Luther as well as the works of local supporters of his movement; this endorsement by re-spected local figures across Germany was also crucial to the Reforma-tion's success. The rise of Wittenberg added a seventh major printing center to the roster. The established centers could bring both capital in-vestment (crucial for larger works like the Luther Bible) and design so-phistication to the work of spreading the word. Yet just as striking as the engagement of these major publishing hubs was the foundation, or re-foundation, of printing in numerous smaller towns across the Empire.

This wave of new foundations came in two main periods. In the mid-1520s, a print shop was planted in a number of often quite tiny places: these were often presses established as a branch office for a larger press elsewhere, and often with very specific confessional purposes. This was followed by a great wave of expansion in the middle of the century, when the Reformation was an established fact. Between 1540 and 1544 printing came to Berlin, Bonn, and Dortmund; between 1550 and 1558 to a dozen other towns, including Emden, Bautzen, Düsseldorf, and Jena. Striking is both the density of these new foundations and a perceptible shift in the industry's center of gravity from south to north: to Lübeck on the Baltic coast and Hamburg, to Königsberg, Rostock, and Frankfurt-an-der-Oder in the north and east. Many of these places were in a region that, when Luther came to Wittenberg, he memorably characterized as beyond the boundaries of civilization. At the end of the century they were strongholds of Protestantism.

This gradual reorientation of the Empire's publishing industry northward was mirrored by a similar shift on a wider European scale. In the first age of print Italy had swiftly usurped Germany's early primacy and become the heart of the new industry, producing the best and most elegant books, and making the most substantial contributions of design and form as the printed book emerged as an independent artifact. Italy, especially Venice, also established a dominant role in the export market. By the end of Luther's century this was no longer the case. Here the evidence provided by overall production statistics is dramatic. From the birth of printing to 1517, Italy and the Holy Roman Empire enjoyed virtual parity in terms of overall production, and between them dominated the European printing industry.[37] By the end of the sixteenth century, Germany had forged ahead; and in the first half of the seventeenth century Germany outpublished Italy by a factor of three to one. By this point France, England, and the Low Countries, all key northern zones of the publishing trade, had also begun to eclipse the printers of the Italian peninsula.

Obviously not all of this can be attributed to Luther, though the publication of church orders, Bibles, catechisms, and hymnbooks provided a steady bedrock of demand long after the polemical fires of the 1520s had dimmed. But the influence of Luther's movement was more profound even than this. The Reformation was not simply a towering movement of religious renewal: it was also an astonishing, sensational, and, for a few years at least, all-consuming public event. The drama of the indulgence controversy, Luther's defiance, the confrontations at Augsburg, Leipzig, and Worms, the Peasants' War; these provided an astonishing rolling news event such as Europe had never known. These dramas in Luther's life found echoes in a rippling succession of local confrontations as each German city faced its moment of decision. Luther engaged the nation's attention as few had done before him. He created an appetite for news, for public engagement, every bit as dramatic as the fundamental questions of theology his movement posed.

Once the drama had faded, or at least become more intermittent, the appetite for news remained. Printers who had found a new public through Luther were loath to see this market disappear; so they fed it by offering other sensations, news of battles and the deeds of kings, natural disasters, spectacular crimes, or extraordinary heavenly apparitions.[38] It is no surprise that by far the most lively market for these printed news pamphlets was in Luther's homeland. These news pamphlets were remarkably similar in design and form to the Reformation *Flugschriften:* like the religious pamphlets they were usually in a neat quarto format and four or eight pages long. The developing news market also exploited another format that had developed with the Reformation, the illustrated broadsheet. Like the famous polemical images that had promoted Luther's movement, these broadsheets were able to feed off the highly developed illustrative tradition of the German woodcut industry, the most advanced and sophisticated in Europe. In the seventeenth century these finely drawn woodcuts would gradually be replaced by engravings, as another pan-European news event, the Thirty Years' War, came to dominate the news sheets.[39] It was about this time that a German publisher first conceived the idea of printing his bulletins of news as a regular sequence: thus was born the newspaper, at first as a weekly service, and only gradually transformed into the familiar daily. In the seventeenth century this innovation spread like wildfire through the German cities, and it remained for a long time the news medium of northern Europe.

Thus we return to the paradox with which we began this book: printing was essential to the creation of Martin Luther, but Luther was also a determining, shaping force in the German printing industry. Many things conspired to ensure Luther's unlikely survival through the first years of the Reformation, but one of them was undoubtedly print. Books, circulating with uncontrollable rapidity through the German towns, created at least the appearance of a new consensus: that the settled will of the German people was that Luther should be heard. This intimidated and sometimes silenced opponents, and fortified Luther's far from numerous supporters in the German Estates. But Luther could not have been a force in the German church without his instinctive, towering talent as a writer. This was his most astonishing gift to the Reformation and to the German print industry. After Luther, print and public communication would never be the same again. It was an extraordinary legacy for an extraordinary man.

ACKNOWLEDGMENTS

The idea for this book came from Scott Moyers of Penguin Press; I am grateful to Scott for thinking of me in this context, and for tolerating the adjustment to his concept that allowed me to shift the focus to accommodate my own interest in media and mass communication. This book gave me the opportunity to unite the two abiding passions of my academic life, the Reformation and the early history of printing. The work on the Wittenberg printing industry was undertaken largely in successive trips to Germany, where I made many demands on libraries and received many kindnesses. I am grateful to Martin Treu of the Luther Gesellschaft, Falk Eisermann of the Staatsbibliothek Berlin, and Matthias Müller of the German Historical Museum for their help at all stages of this project. I was also able to consult a variety of relevant texts in Paris, Copenhagen, New York, Washington, London, and Edinburgh; collections of Luther's works are now to be found in many of the world's great libraries. Especial thanks are due to Florence Poinsot of the Library of the Société de l'Histoire du Protestantisme Français for the warm welcome she offered to me and my graduate student, Drew Thomas. I am also grateful to Ulrike Eydinger for a privileged view of the magnificent collection of German illustrated broadsheets in the Forschungsbibliothek Gotha. Work on sixteenth-century books has also been greatly facilitated by the large number of high-quality, full-text editions now available digitally. Here, the work of the Bayerische Staatsbibliothek in making so much of their collection available in this way deserves special praise. Of course, for the book historian the digital image is never a substitute for working book in hand, and I have been privileged to be allowed to do this in so many great collections. But as a means of spreading knowledge of the contents and beauty of so many small and often very rare Reformation pamphlets, digitization has been an enormous benefit.

This text has benefited greatly from being read by a number of friends and colleagues. Scott Dixon, one of the most formidable interpreters of the German Reformation, was kind enough to read the whole text, and saved me from a number of errors. My student Arthur der Weduwen read every chapter as it was written, and Jan Hillgärtner, Saskia Limbach, Nina Lamal, and Drew Thomas all read the first draft of the complete text. Scott Moyers also subjected it to a rigorous workout. The final version is much the better for all of their suggestions and observations. In New York, the staff of Penguin were a model of professionalism, and helpful to me at every stage of the production process. I also owe a particular debt to Jane Cavolina, whose copyediting was a marvel of eagle-eyed clarity. Another student, Amelie Roper, drew my attention to essential literature that I would otherwise have missed. Lucas Kriner drew the maps, and along with his wife, Katie, indulged me in a walking tour of Wittenberg that provided the inspiration for the imagined perambulations in chapter 1.

As these remarks suggest, I have been lucky to be working in an extremely supportive context in St. Andrews, where assembling a community of talented postgraduate students has been one of the great pleasures of my academic career. In addition to the Germanists who examined the text, I thank also colleagues in the Reformation Studies Institute, particularly its director, Bridget Heal, and coworkers in the St. Andrews book historical research group. Together we constructed the Universal Short Title Catalogue (USTC), an indispensable resource for understanding the wider context of Wittenberg print, and much cited here. Particular reference here should be made to Graeme Kemp, the project manager of the USTC and the architect of the wonderful search engine that presents this mass of data to the scholarly community.

One of the main surprises in beginning this work was to find how little scholarly attention had been devoted to the Wittenberg printing industry: all the more astonishing in the light of the settled assumption of the close relationship between print and the Reformation. So I was especially grateful for the opportunity to speak at a conference in Wittenberg devoted to the subject of print, and to meet there members of the archaeological research group who have accomplished some of the most illuminating recent work on sixteenth-century Wittenberg. Especial thanks go to Thomas Lang for helping me keep in touch with their publications. Also present at the conference were Eberhard Nehlsen, the great expert on Reformation musical printing, and Christoph Reske, whose survey of sixteenth-century German printers has been a foundational text for this book. Nehlsen's willingness to share with the St. Andrews group his developing researches reflects a generosity of spirit that equally characterizes Reformation scholars in the Anglo-American research community. This is a good opportunity to thank all those in this group who have been such good friends over the years. Many are students of three great figures who shaped the field when I entered it, Heiko Oberman, Robert Kingdon, and Steven Ozment. The first two have both passed away and are much missed. Their students, along with those of Ozment, continue to be an adornment to the profession. Among those emerging as the new generation of research leaders I owe a particular debt to my former colleague Bruce Gordon, whose insights and deep knowledge of the Reformation have shaped my understanding over many years.

This has been a book long digested but written relatively quickly. Writing always places extra demands on a family, who endure both the absences of research trips and the preoccupied half presence of the writing process. To Jane, Megan, and Sophie, go, as always, my thanks for the greatest happiness of my life.

St. Andrews
October 2015

Abbreviations

Benzing

Josef Benzing and Helmut Claus, eds. *Lutherbibliographie. Verzeichnis der gedruckten Schriften Martin Luthers bis zu dessen Tod.* 2 vols. Baden-Baden: Koerner, 1966–1994.

CE

Peter G. Bietenholz, ed. *Contemporaries of Erasmus. A Biographical Register of the Renaissance and Reformation.* 3 vols. Toronto: Toronto University Press, 1985–1987.

Corr. Eras.

R. A. Mynors et al., eds. *The Correspondence of Erasmus.* 12 vols. Toronto: University of Toronto Press, 1974–2003.

Correspondence

Preserved Smith and Charles M. Jacobs, eds. *Luther's Correspondence and Other Contemporary Letters.* 2 vols. Philadelphia: Lutheran Publication Society, 1913–1918.

Letters

Gottfried G. Krodel, ed. *Letters. Luther's Works,* vols. 48–50. Philadelphia: Fortress Press, 1963–1975.

LW

Jaroslav Pelikan et al., eds. *Luther's Works.* Philadelphia: Fortress Press / St. Louis: Concordia, 1955–.

Prefaces

Christopher Boyd Brown, ed. *Prefaces. Luther's Works,* vols. 59–60. St. Louis: Concordia, 2011–2012.

USTC

The Universal Short Title Catalogue. http://ustc.ac.uk/.

WA

D. Martin Luthers Werke. Kritische Gesammtausgabe. Weimar: Böhlau, 1883–.

WABr

D. Martin Luthers Werke. Kritische Gesammtausgabe. Briefwechsel. 18 vols. Weimar: Böhlau Nachfolger, 1930–1985.

WATR

D. Martin Luthers Werke. Kritische Gesammtausgabe. Tischreden. 18 vols. Weimar: Böhlau Nachfolger, 1912–1921.

Notes

Chapter One: A Small Town in Germany

1. For an evocative selection, see Martin Luther, *Table Talk,* ed. Theodore G. Tappert, LW 54. Over the years, twelve different men were involved in recording Luther's dinnertime utterances, which accounts for the record's somewhat uneven quality.

2. For a speculation as to what might have happened had Charles V followed this advice, see Andrew Pettegree, "The Execution of Martin Luther," *History Review* (March 1996), 20–25, now available online at http://www.historytoday.com/andrew-pettegree/execution-martin-luther.

3. This section draws heavily on Helmar Junghans, *Wittenberg als Lutherstadt* (Berlin: Union Verlag, 1979) and E. G. Schwiebert, *Luther and His Times: The Reformation from a New Perspective* (St. Louis: Concordia, 1950).

4. WATR II, n. 2800b, III, n. 3433. Quoted in Maria Grossmann, *Humanism in Wittenberg, 1485–1517* (Nieuwkoop: De Graaf, 1975), 36.

5. Friedrich Myconius, quoted in C. Scott Dixon, *Protestants* (Chichester: Wiley-Blackwell, 2010), 10.

6. Ernest G. Schwiebert, "The Electoral Town of Wittenberg," *Medievalia et Humanistica* (1945), 99–116, here 108. Cochlaeus was writing in 1524. The sentiment that this was more of a village than a town, and emphasizing the poor state of the local houses, was something of a commonplace, and remarked by friends as well as enemies. See Schwiebert, *Luther* (citing Myconius and Melanchthon).

7. Schwiebert, "Wittenberg," 108–9.

8. Wolfgang Behringer, *Im Zeichen des Merkur: Reichspost und Kommunikationsrevolution in der Frühen Neuzeit* (Göttingen: Vandenhoeck & Ruprecht, 2003).

9. The production of manuscripts seems to have peaked around 1480, thirty years after the invention of printing. Uwe Neddermeyer, *Von der Handschrift zum gedruckten Buch: Schriftlichkeit und Leseinteresse im Mittelalter und in der frühen Neuzeit: quantitative und qualitative Aspekte* (Wiesbaden: Harrassowitz, 1998). On Gutenberg see Albert Kapr, *Johann Gutenberg: The Man and His Invention* (Aldershot: Scolar Press, 1996).

10. Andrew Pettegree, *The Book in the Renaissance* (London and New Haven: Yale University Press, 2010).

11. Augsburg, Nuremberg, Cologne, Strasbourg, Basel, and Leipzig; Rome, Venice, Florence, and Milan; Paris and Lyon. Figures and analysis drawn from the USTC.

12. For this variety of means of conversion, see especially Andrew Pettegree, *Reformation and the Culture of Persuasion* (Cambridge: Cambridge University Press, 2005).

13. Below, chapter 12. Christoph Reske, *Die Buchdrucker des 16. und 17. Jahrhunderts im deutschen Sprachgebiet: auf der Grundlage des gleichnamigen Werkes von Josef Benzing* (Wiesbaden: Harrassowitz, 2007).

14. Erwin Iserloh, *Luthers Thesenanschlag: Tatsache oder Legende?* (Wiesbaden: Steiner, 1962). For an English introduction see Iserloh, *The Theses Were Not Posted: Luther Between Reform and Reformation*, trans. Jared Wicks (Boston: Beacon Press, 1968).

15. Joachim Ott and Martin Treu, eds., *Luthers Thesenanschlag—Faktum oder Fiktion* (Leipzig: Evangelische Verlagsanstalt, 2008).

16. Below, chapter 3.

17. In 1516 Luther enumerated the residents of the house as twenty-two priests and twelve novices: including servants, forty-one persons in all. WABr I, 72–73. *Letters* I, 28.

18. Known as a Portiuncula indulgence after the church near Assisi first granted such a valuable privilege.

19. Paul Kirn, *Friedrich der Weise und die Kirche* (Leipzig: Teubner, 1926; repr., Hildesheim: Gerstenberg, 1972).

20. *Dye Zaigung des Hochlobwirdigen Hailigthums der Stifftkirchen aller Hailigen zu Wittenburg* (Wittenberg: Symphorian Reinhart, 1509). USTC 641851. For a list of the woodcuts see F.W.H. Hollstein, *German Engravings: Etchings and Woodcuts, ca. 1400–1700* (Amsterdam: Hertzberger, 1954–), VI, 72–76.

21. Junghans, *Wittenberg als Lutherstadt*, 51.

22. Since 1720, the Golden Eagle, and still a splendid and atmospheric hotel. See http://www.goldeneradler-wittenberg.de/index.php?link=Hotel.

23. Junghans, *Wittenberg als Lutherstadt*, 107–9.

24. USTC. See also Maria Grossmann, *Wittenberger Drucke 1502–1517: Ein bibliographischer Beitrag zur Geschichte des Humanismus in Deutschland* (Vienna: Krieg, 1971).

25. The surviving books account for only seventy days' work; even allowing for the numerous saints' days, this implies that it was working at around one-third capacity.

26. Vicky Rothe, "Wittenberger Buchgewerbe und -handel im 16. Jahrhundert," in Heiner Lück et al., eds., *Das ernestinische Wittenberg: Stadt und Bewohner.* Wittenberg-Forschungen, 2.1 (Petersberg: Michael Imhof, 2013), 77–90.

27. Grossmann, *Wittenberger Drucke.*

28. The largest books published certainly benefited from the elector's financial support. Below, chapter 2.

29. USTC.

30. USTC. See also, for a survey based on more rudimentary statistical data, Mark U. Edwards, *Printing, Propaganda, and Martin Luther* (Berkeley: University of California Press, 1994).

31. The figures are computed from the USTC.

NOTES

Chapter Two: The Making of a Revolutionary

1. *Scriptorium Insignium Qui in Celeberrimis, Praesertim Lipsiensi, Wittenbergensi, Francofordiana ad Oderam, Academiis a Fundatione Ipsarum usque ad Annum Christi Floruerunt, Centuria.* This document was rediscovered and published at Helmstedt in 1660. See Bernd Moeller, "Das Berühmtwerden Luthers," *Zeitschrift für Historische Forschung* 15 (1988), 65–92, here 67.

2. Luther's very brief reminiscence on the origins of the Reformation, appended as a preface to the 1545 Latin edition of the collected works, is available at LW 34, 323–38.

3. Johannes Cochlaeus, *Commentaria de Actis et Scriptis Martini Lutheri* (Mainz: Beham, 1549). USTC 663508. See Elizabeth Vandiver et al., eds., *Luther's Lives: Two Contemporary Accounts of Martin Luther* (Manchester: Manchester University Press, 2002), which also includes the short biographical sketch of Philip Melanchthon.

4. Some uncertainty persists, with his mother remembering 1484 as the year. Most evidence, however, coalesces around 1483.

5. This sketch of Luther's early life draws mainly on Martin Brecht, *Martin Luther: His Road to Reformation, 1483–1521* (Minneapolis: Fortress Press, 1985), E. G. Schwiebert, *Luther and His Times: The Reformation from a New Perspective* (St. Louis: Concordia, 1950), and Heiko Oberman, *Luther: Man Between God and the Devil* (New Haven: Yale University Press, 1982). See also, most recently, Heinz Schilling, *Martin Luther: Rebell in einer Zeit des Umbruchs* (Munich: Beck, 2012).

6. In 1507 Luther's father owed the considerable sum of one hundred gulden for a mortgage on the family house. Brecht, *Road to Reformation*, 10.

7. Erik H. Erikson, *Young Man Luther* (London: Faber & Faber, 1959). The influence of Erikson's once seminal work is probably now most evident in John Osborne's powerful drama of Luther's life, first performed in 1961.

8. Brecht, *Road to Reformation*, 33–34.

9. Oberman, *Luther*, 125–29.

10. Ibid., 147.

11. Here, most usefully, Maria Grossmann, *Humanism in Wittenberg, 1485–1517* (Nieuwkoop: De Graaf, 1975).

12. Ibid., 41.

13. *Libellus de Laudibus Germaniae et Ducum Saxoniae* (Bologna: Faelli, 1506). USTC 855511.

14. Grossmann, *Humanism in Wittenberg*, 64. F. von Soden and J.K.F. Knaake, eds., *Christoph Scheurl: Briefbuch*, 2 vols. (Potsdam, 1867–72; repr., Aalen: Zeller, 1962), I, 26.

15. Grossmann, *Humanism in Wittenberg*, 55–56.

16. Andreas Meinhardi, *Dialogus Illustrate ac Augustissime Urbis Albiorene Vulgo Vittenberg Dicte Situm Amenitatem ac Illustrationem Docens Tirocinia Nobilium Artiu Iacentibus Editus* (Leipzig: Martin Lansberg, 1508). USTC 636015. Available in translation as Edgar C. Reinke, ed., *The Dialogus of Andreas Meinhardi* (Ann Arbor, MI: University Microfilms, 1976).

17. Irmgard Höss, *Georg Spalatin, 1484–1545: Ein Leben in der Zeit des Humanismus und der Reformation* (Weimar: Böhlau, 1956).

18. On printing, see USTC; Grossmann, *Humanism in Wittenberg*, 86–99; Grossmann, *Wittenberger Drucke 1502–1517: Ein bibliographischer Beitrag zur Geschichte des Humanismus in Deutschland* (Vienna: Krieg, 1971).

19. Erfurt in 1473; Leipzig in 1480. USTC.

20. Grossmann, *Wittenberger Drucke*. Andreas Gössner, "Die Anfänge des Buchdrucks für universitäre Zwecke am Beispiel Wittenbergs," in Enno Bünz, ed., *Bücher, Drucker, Bibliotheken in Mitteldeutschland* (Leipzig: Leipziger Universitätsverlag, 2006), 133–52.

21. *Dye Zaigung des Hochlobwirdigen Hailigthums der Stifftkirchen aller Hailigen zu Wittenburg* (Wittenberg: Symphorian Reinhart, 1509). USTC 641851. A variant in the British Library in London is USTC 641850.

22. He was referred to in the literature as "magister." Christoph Reske, *Die Buchdrucker des 16. und 17. Jahrhunderts im Deutschen Sprachgebiet: Auf der Grundlage des gleichnamigen Werkes von Josef Benzing* (Wiesbaden: Harrassowitz, 2007), 992.

23. WABr I, 56. *Letters* I, 18–19. In fact, the lectures on the Psalms were never published, so Luther seems to have got his way.

24. *Eyn Geystlich edles Buchleynn. von Rechter Underscheyd und Vorstand. Was der Alt und New Mensche Sey.* Benzing 69. USTC 656035.

25. *Oratio Philippi Beroaldi Bononiensis de Summo Bono* (Wittenberg: Johann Rhau-Grunenberg, 1508). USTC 680993.

26. Margaret M. Smith, *The Title-Page: Its Early Development, 1460–1510* (London: British Library, 2000).

27. USTC 672547. Maria Grossmann, "Bibliographie der Werke Christoph Scheurls," *Archiv für Geschichte des Buchwesens* 10 (1969), 373–95.

28. USTC 680833, 681174.

29. USTC 680834. Grossmann, "Bibliographie Scheurls."

30. Grossmann, *Humanism in Wittenberg*, 100–112.

31. Brecht, *Road to Reformation*, 126.

32. The full text is in WA 54, 179–87. Here quoted in Oberman, *Luther*, 165.

33. For the struggles with former friends and followers see below, chapter 9.

34. Benzing 68a; USTC 693439; Grossman, *Wittenberg Drucke*, 90. Luther's copy of this volume survives in the Herzog August Bibliothek, Wolfenbüttel. Illustrated in Oberman, *Luther*, 163.

35. USTC 640335. A page of Luther's personal copy is reproduced in Helmar Junghans, *Wittenberg als Lutherstadt* (Berlin: Union Verlag, 1979), 100.

36. Brecht, *Road to Reformation*, 150–55.

37. Oberman, *Luther*, 169–173. Brecht, *Road to Reformation*, 128–36, 144–50.

38. David H. Price, *Johannes Reuchlin and the Campaign to Destroy Jewish Books* (Oxford: Oxford University Press, 2011).

39. *Epistola ad Athletam de Filiae Educatione Epistola* (Wittenberg: Rhau-Grunenberg, 1515). USTC 689206.

40. WABr I, 41. Grossmann, *Humanism in Wittenberg*, 83.

41. Kurt Aland, "Die theologischen Anfänge Martin Luthers," *Internationale Katholische Zeitschrift* (1983), 556–67.

42. *Ad Subscriptas Conclusiones Respondebit Magister Franciscus Guntherus Nordhusensis pro Biblia* (Wittenberg: Johann Rhau-Grunenberg, 1517). Benzing 84a. Wolfenbüttel: Herzog August Bibliothek, A: 434.11 Theol. 2.

43. Though fragments of a previously unknown Caxton turned up in 1980 in precisely

the same way. Paul Needham, *The Printer and the Pardoner* (Washington: Library of Congress, 1986).

44. For a systematic reconstruction of the publication of theses as broadsheets in Wittenberg see also Bernd Moeller, "Thesenanschläge," in Joachim Ott and Martin Treu, eds., *Luthers Thesenanschlag—Faktum oder Fiktion* (Leipzig: Evangelische Verlagsanstalt, 2008), 9–31.

45. WABr I, 103–7.

Chapter Three: Indulgence

1. Albert Kapr, *Johann Gutenberg: The Man and His Invention* (Aldershot: Scolar Press, 1996), 189–97.

2. Falk Eisermann, "'Hinter Decken versteckt.' Ein weiteres Exemplar des 31 zeiligen Ablassbriefs (GW 6556) und andere Neufunde von Einblattdrucken des 15. Jahrhunderts," *Gutenberg-Jahrbuch* (1999), 58–74.

3. *Türken-Kalender (Eyn Manung der Christenheit Widder die Durken)*. USTC 749528.

4. R. W. Swanson, *Indulgences in Late Medieval England* (Cambridge: Cambridge University Press, 2007), 8–22. Swanson, *Promissory Notes on the Treasury of Merits: Indulgences in Late Medieval Europe* (Leiden: Brill, 2006).

5. See the numerous certificates produced for individual churches in Falk Eisermann, *Verzeichnis der typographischen Einblattdrucke des 15. Jahrhunderts im Heiligen Römischen Reich Deutscher Nation: VE 15*, 3 vols. (Wiesbaden: Reichert, 2004).

6. A particularly generous one: that on specific days visitors received the cardinal's quartum of one hundred days, multiplied by the number of relics in the collection. Harald Meller, *Fundsache Luther: Archäologen auf den Spuren des Reformators* (Stuttgart: Theiss, 2008).

7. Norman Housley, "Indulgences for Crusading, 1417–1517," in Swanson, *Promissory Notes*, 277–308.

8. Nikolaus Paulus, "Raimund Peraudi als Ablasskommissar," *Historisches Jahrbuch* 21 (1900), 645–82.

9. Bernd Moeller, "Die letzten Ablasskampagnen. Luthers Widerspruch gegen den Ablass in seinem geschichtlichen Zusammenhang," in Hartmut Boockmann et al., eds., *Lebenslehren und Weltentwürfe im Übergang vom Mittelalter zur Neuzeit* (Göttingen: Vandenhoeck & Ruprecht, 1989), 539–67, here 560.

10. Wolfgang Undorf, *From Gutenberg to Luther: Transnational Print Cultures in Scandinavia, 1450–1525* (Leiden: Brill, 2014), 293–96.

11. Janus Moller Jensen, *Denmark and the Crusades, 1400–1650* (Leiden: Brill, 2007), 141.

12. Moeller, "Letzten Ablasskampagnen," 557–58. A useful table is in W. E. Winterhager, "Ablasskritik als Indikator historischen Wandels vor 1517: Ein Beitrag zu Voraussetzung und Einordnung der Reformation," *Archiv für Reformationsgeschichte* 90 (1999), 6–71, here 23.

13. "They preach only human doctrine who say that as soon as the money clinks into the money chest, the soul flies out of purgatory." Kurt Aland, *Martin Luther's 95 Theses* (St. Louis: Concordia, 1967), 57.

14. Paul Needham, *The Printer and the Pardoner* (Washington: Library of Congress, 1986), 32–33.

15. See now, especially, Eisermann, *Verzeichnis der Einblattdrucke*. F. Beyer, "Gedrucke

Ablassbriefe und sonstige mit Ablässen in Zusammenhang stehende Druckwerke des Mittelalters," *Gutenberg-Jahrbuch* (1937), 43–54.

16. Falk Eisermann, "The Indulgence as a Media Event: Developments in Communication Through Broadsides in the Fifteenth Century," in Swanson, *Promissory Notes*, 309–30, here 315–17.

17. Kapr, *Gutenberg*, 191.

18. Needham, *Printer and Pardoner*, 31.

19. Eisermann, *Verzeichnis der Einblattdrucke*.

20. Ibid., 62–200.

21. Jensen, *Denmark and the Crusades*, 138.

22. Eisermann, *Verzeichnis der Einblattdrucke*, 10–61.

23. Hans Volz, "Der St. Peters-Ablass und das Deutsche Druckgewerbe," *Gutenberg-Jahrbuch* (1966), 156–72.

24. Moeller, "Letzten Ablasskampagnen," 555.

25. Winterhager, "Ablasskritik," 42.

26. Ibid., 24.

27. Ibid., 42–43.

28. Both published by Friedrich Peypus in Nuremberg: USTC 672544, 645357. The German translation was by Luther's friend Christoph Scheurl.

29. David Bagchi, "Luther's Ninety-five Theses and the Contemporary Criticism of Indulgences," in Swanson, *Promissory Notes*, 331–55, here 347.

30. Philip Robinson Rössner, *Deflation—Devaluation—Rebellion: Geld im Zeitalter der Reformation* (Stuttgart: Franz Steiner Verlag, 2012).

31. G. Mehring, "Kardinal Raimund Peraudi als Ablasskommissar in Deutschland 1500–1504 und sein Verhältnis zu Maximilian I," *Forschungen und Versuche zur Geschichte des Mittelalters und der Neuzeit. Festschrift Dieter Schäfer* (1915), 334–409. Francis Rapp, "Un Contemporain d'Alexandre VI Borgia, le Cardinal Raymond Péraud (1435–1505)," *Comptes Rendus des Séances de l'Academie des Inscriptions et Belles-lettres* 138 (1994), 665–77.

32. For a sequence of pamphlets published by Peraudi in Speyer in 1503 see Mehring, "Peraudi als Ablasskommissar," 408–9.

33. Winterhager, "Ablasskritik," 49.

34. Ibid., 29–30.

35. Ibid., 38–39.

36. Aland, *95 Theses*, 62.

37. Winterhager, "Ablasskritik," 40.

38. Aland, *95 Theses*, 62.

39. Winterhager, "Ablasskritik," 41.

40. Bagchi, "Luther's Ninety-five Theses," 332.

41. WA 56, 417. LW 25, 409.

42. Jüterbog is twenty-four and Zerbst twenty-seven miles from Wittenberg; still a long day's walk away.

43. Cited Heiko Oberman, *Luther: Man Between God and the Devil* (New Haven: Yale University Press, 1982), 188.

44. WA 1, 141. Bagchi, "Luther's Ninety-five Theses," 334.

45. Jared Wicks, "Martin Luther's Treatise on Indulgences," *Theological Studies* 28 (1967), 481–518.

46. Theses 81 and 82. Aland, *95 Theses*, 62.

47. The literature is summarized ibid.

48. Luther to Lang, October 26, 1516. WABr I, 72–73. *Letters* I, 27.

49. Andreas Gössner, "Die Anfänge des Buchdrucks für universitäre Zwecke am Beispiel Wittenbergs," in Enno Bünz, ed., *Bücher, Drucker, Bibliotheken in Mitteldeutschland* (Leipzig: Leipziger Universitätsverlag, 2006), 133–152. Maria Grossmann, *Wittenberger Drucke 1502–1517: Ein bibliographischer Beitrag zur Geschichte des Humanismus in Deutschland* (Vienna: Krieg, 1971).

50. Above, chapter 2. For context, see also Falk Eisermann, "Der Einblattdruck der 95 Theses im Kontext der Mediennutzung seiner Zeit," in Irene Dingel and Henning P. Jürgens, eds., *Meilensteine der Reformation. Schlüsseldokumente der Frühen Wirksamkeit Martin Luthers* (Gütersloh: Gütersloher Verlagshaus, 2014), 100–106.

51. The letter is known from Luther's reply: WABr I, 118.

52. In his treatise *Against Hanswurst* of 1541. Aland, *95 Theses*, 40. USTC 706721–706724.

53. Aland, *95 Theses*, 69.

54. The instructions for the church province of Magdeburg were printed in Leipzig: *Instructio Summaria* (Leipzig: Melchior I Lotter, 1516). USTC 669147. There was also an edition for the Province of Mainz, *Instructiones Confessorum* (Mainz: Johann Schöffer, 1516). USTC 669171.

55. WABr I, 110. Aland, *95 Theses*, 69–71.

56. Wicks, "Martin Luther's Treatise on Indulgences."

57. Aland, *95 Theses*, 116–18; Martin Brecht, *Martin Luther: His Road to Reformation, 1483–1521* (Minneapolis: Fortress Press, 1985), 204–5.

58. Leipzig, Jakob Thanner. Benzing 88. USTC 751650.

59. Benzing 89. USTC 639278. Erasmus to More, March 5, 1518. *Corr. Eras.*, EP 785. Brecht, *Road to Reformation*, 204–5.

60. The translation was said to have been by the Nuremberg Councillor Caspar Nützel. Brecht, *Road to Reformation*, 204.

61. One copy has survived: USTC 751033.

62. Luther to Lang, March 21, 1518. WABr I, 154–56, n. 64.

63. The *Sermon* is available in an accessible English translation in Aland, *95 Theses*, 63–67.

64. Benzing 90–103, with a further nine editions in 1519 and 1520.

65. Against Eck's "Obelisks" of 1518. The title page, confusingly, alludes to 370. USTC 626334.

66. Dewey Weiss Kramer, ed., *Johann Tetzel's Rebuttal Against Luther's Sermon on Indulgences and Grace* (Atlanta: Pitts Theology Library, 2012).

67. Johann Tetzel, *Vorlegung Gemacht von Bruder Johan Tetzel Prediger Ordens Ketzermeister: Wyder eynen Vormessen Sermon von Tzwentzig Irrigen Artickeln Bebstlichen Ablas und Gnade Belangende allen Cristglaubigen Menschen Tzuwissen von Notten* (Leipzig: Melchior I Lotter, 1518). USTC 704278.

68. *Eyn Freiheyt deß Sermons Bebstlichen Ablaß unnd Gnad Belangend*. Benzing 181–90.

Chapter Four: The Eye of the Storm

1. This section leans heavily on Jared Wicks, "Roman Reactions to Luther: The First Year (1518)," *Catholic Historical Review* 69 (1983), 521–62. See also Scott H. Hendrix, *Luther and the Papacy* (Philadelphia: Fortress Press, 1981).

2. Wicks, "Roman Reactions," 529.

3. *In Praesumptiosas Martini Lutheri Conclusiones, de Potestate Papae, Dialogus* (Rome: Marcello Silber, 1518). USTC 841732. The German reprints are USTC 689669, 689670, 689720.

4. Bernhard Alfred R. Felmberg, *Die Ablasstheologie Kardinal Cajetans (1469–1534)* (Leiden: Brill, 1998). David Bagchi, "Luther's Ninety-five Theses and the Contemporary Criticism of Indulgences," in R. W. Swanson, *Promissory Notes on the Treasury of Merits: Indulgences in Late Medieval Europe* (Leiden: Brill, 2006), 347–51.

5. A pamphlet urging the Estates not to agree to the new taxation was circulated in Augsburg: *Exhortatio ad Principes, Ne in Decimae Praestationem Consentient* (*Admonition Directed to the Sovereigns Not to Consent to the Tithe*), attributed to Ulrich von Hutten (Augsburg: Sigmung Grimm & Marx Wirsung, 1518).

6. Luther to Spalatin, March 11, 1518, May 18, 1518. WABr I, 153, 173–74. *Letters* I, 63.

7. Melanchthon arrived in Wittenberg on August 25. His inaugural lecture, four days later, dealt with curriculum reform.

8. *Correspondence* I, 82.

9. Benzing 205–8.

10. Benzing 212–23.

11. On Eck, Edwin Iserloh, ed., *Johannes Eck im Streit der Jahrhunderte* (Münster: 1988). CE I, 416–18.

12. November 5, 1517, Scheurl to Truchsess: "I am sending you and our mutual friends Dr. Eck and Prior Kilian some truly theological and wonderful theses." Kurt Aland, *Martin Luther's 95 Theses* (St. Louis: Concordia, 1967), 116.

13. Luther to Johann Sylvius Egranus, March 24, 1518. WABr I, 278. *Correspondence* I, 75–77. Leif Grane, *Martinus Noster: Luther in the German Reform Movement, 1518–1521* (Mainz: P. von Zabern, 1994), 21. Luther to Eck, May 19, 1519. *Correspondence* I, 85–87.

14. USTC 626334.

15. Benzing 115–24.

16. Luther sets out eloquently the multiple claims on his time in a slightly later letter of March 1519. Luther to Spalatin, March 13, 1519. WABr I, 359–360. *Letters* I, 111–15.

17. Benzing 234–39 (*Acta Augustana*), 240–48 (*Appellatio*).

18. WABr I, 280–81.

19. Benzing 416–30.

20. For the prehistory of the Leipzig Disputation see particularly Martin Brecht, *Martin Luther: His Road to Reformation, 1483–1521* (Minneapolis: Fortress Press, 1985), 299–309.

21. Benzing 392–396 (though some of these were a revised edition published after the debate).

22. For Emser, CE I, 429–30.

23. Brecht, *Road to Reformation*, 313–14.

24. Jerome Emser, *De Disputatione Lipsicensi* (Leipzig: Melchior I Lotter, 1519); Melanchthon, *Epistola de Lipsica Disputatione*. Melanchthon's work was printed four times while Emser's contribution required only a single edition. USTC 629501 (Emser), 651520, 651522–651524 (Melanchthon).

25. Benzing 408–15.

26. Three editions of each work; *Disputatio Adversus D, Martini Lutter,* USTC 638161, 638162, 638164, *Excusatio ad Philippis Melanchton,* USTC 655190–655192.

27. Karlstadt's writings were published in twenty-two editions in these years, Melanchthon's in eighteen, and Eck's in twenty-six.

28. On Augsburg printing in this era see particularly Hans-Jörg Künast, *"Getruckt zu Augspurg": Buchdruck und Buchhandel in Augsburg Zwischen 1468 und 1555* (Tübingen: Niemeyer, 1997).

29. USTC.

30. USTC 639278.

31. USTC 608977, Benzing 2a, 3. In February 1519 Froben informed Luther that he had sent six hundred copies to France and Spain, "where they were read and approved by the Doctors of the Sorbonne." WABr I, 331–35. *Correspondence* I, 161–62.

32. Benzing 4, 5. Older authorities speak of a second Froben edition, but this seems to be a confusion with this Strasbourg work.

33. See Froben in CE II, 60–63, and *Corr. Eras.* EP 904, n. 20, for evidence Erasmus instructed Froben not to print Luther. Below, chapter 9, for Erasmus's complicated relationship with Luther.

34. USTC records 416 editions published in the Holy Roman Empire in 1517; 1103 in 1520; 1332 in 1523. In the same year 1523 Italian presses turned out 327 editions, and France, 329.

35. Below, chapter 6. For an excellent case study see Gerhard Piccard, "Papierzeugung und Buchdruck in Basel bis zum Beginn des 16. Jahrhunderts," *Archiv für Geschichte des Buchwesens* 8 (1967), 26–322.

36. For a marvelously atmospheric vignette of the work of a major merchant publisher see Barbara C. Halporn, *The Correspondence of Johann Amerbach* (Ann Arbor: University of Michigan Press, 2000).

37. Luther to Spalatin, August 28, 1518. WABr I, 190–91. *Letters* I, 75.

38. For instance the reply to Priarias, Benzing 224–26. *Letters* I, 75.

39. For context, Thomas Döring, "Der Leipziger Buchdruck vor der Reformation," in Irene Dingel and Henning P. Jürgens, eds., *Meilensteine der Reformation. Schlüsseldokumente der frühen Wirksamkeit Martin Luthers* (Gütersloh: Gütersloher Verlagshaus, 2014), 87–98. Helmut Claus, *Untersuchungen zur Geschichte des Leipziger Buchdrucks von Luthers Thesenanschlag bis zur Einführung der Reformation in Herzogtum Sachsen* (Berlin: Humboldt-Universität, 1973).

40. Chapter 2.

41. *Instructio Summaria,* USTC 669147. Hans Volz, "Der St. Peters-Ablass und das Deutsche Druckgewerbe," *Gutenberg-Jahrbuch* (1966), n. 3.

42. USTC 704278, 689669, 689670.

43. Benzing 224–226.

44. Luther to Spalatin. May 8, 1519. WABr I, 381–84.

45. WABr I, 425 n. 5.

46. Benzing 416–420, with subsequent reprints and translations, 421–30.

47. Robert Proctor, *An Index of German Books 1501–1520 in the British Museum* (London: Holland Press, 1903/1954), has an index of the printing types; here, 125–28 (Lotter Senior, Leipzig), 162–63 (Lotter Junior, Wittenberg).

Chapter Five: Outlaw

1. E. G. Schwiebert, *Luther and His Times: The Reformation from a New Perspective* (St. Louis: Concordia, 1950), 439.

2. Benzing 591–604, seven editions in Latin, and seven in the German translation of Georg Spalatin. There were also translations into Dutch, French, and English. Benzing 605–608. WA 6, 104–134; LW 42, pp. 117–66.

3. Luther to Spalatin, March 13, 1519. WABr I, 359–60. *Letters* I, 113.

4. WA 6, 202–76. LW 44, 15–114. Also available through the Christian Classics Ethereal Library, http://www.ccel.org/ccel/luther/good_works.html.

5. LW 44, 22.

6. Benzing 633–44 (*Good Works*), 669–79 (*Sermon on the Mass*).

7. Strasbourg, Matthias Schürer, February 1519. Benzing 4. USTC 608979.

8. *Condemnatio Doctrinalis: Responsio Lutheriana* (Wittenberg: Melchior II Lotter, 1520). Benzing 627. USTC 623261. This was reprinted in Leipzig, Augsburg, Schlettstadt, Mainz, Antwerp, and Vienna. Benzing 628–632a.

9. *Correspondence* I, 484.

10. This is not surprising, given that the first edition of Luther's ninety-five theses has also been lost. But in the case of *Exsurge Domine* many more copies would probably have been printed (Eck apparently brought one hundred copies of the bull with him to Germany), and there is a fair chance that at least one presently lurks unnoticed in some church archive.

11. Karl Schottenloher, "Die Druckauflagen der päpstlichen Lutherbulle 'Exsurge Domine.'" *Zeitschrift für Bucherfreunde* 9 (1917), 197–208. The editions are listed in the USTC.

12. USTC 617441 (Prüss), 617438 (Schott), 617364 (Landsberg).

13. USTC 666606 (Ingolstadt), 640786 (Cologne).

14. *Von den Eckischen Bullen und Lügen* (*On Eck's New Bull and Lies*), Benzing 718–23. *Adversus Execrabilem Antichristi Bullam*, Benzing 724–27.

15. *Assertio Omnium Articulorum M. Lutheri per Bullam Leonis X* (*Assertion of All the Articles*), Benzing 779–83.

16. WA 6, 404–69. LW 44, 115–217.

17. LW 44, 153, 154 (in a slightly less vivid translation). This version comes from Schwiebert, *Luther*, 471–2.

18. Benzing 683–96.

19. WA 6, 497–573. LW 36, 3–126.

20. Benzing 734–53 (*Von der Freiheit*), 755–64 (*De Libertate*).

21. Luther to Spalatin, December 10, 1520. WABr II, 234. *Letters* I, 186–87.

22. Andrew Pettegree, *The Book in the Renaissance* (London and New Haven: Yale University Press, 2010), 203, 205. Richard Friedenthal, *Luther* (London: Weidenfeld, 1967), 251.

23. Benzing 1014–24. Gerald Fleming, "On the Origin of the Passional Christi und Antichristi and Lucas Cranach's Contribution to Reformation Polemics," *Gutenberg-Jahrbuch* (1973), 351–368. F.W.H. Hollstein, *German Engravings: Etchings and Woodcuts, ca. 1400–1700* (Amsterdam: Hertzberger, 1954–), VI, 40–41.

24. P. Kalkoff, ed., *Die Depeschen des Nuntius Aleander von Wormser Reichstage 1521* (Halle: Niemeyer, 1897), 166. *Correspondence* I, 521–22.

25. Kalkoff, *Depeschen*, 69 ff. *Correspondence* I, 454–61.

26. The books exhibited are listed in the two contemporary accounts reproduced in LW 32, 101–32. Von der Ecken is not to be confused with Luther's old adversary Johann Eck, though von der Ecken was as determined an opponent, and had organized the burning of Luther's books at Trier.

27. Schwiebert, *Luther,* 504–5.

28. Duke John, Frederick's brother, had apparently discovered Luther's whereabouts by September, having previously been kept in the dark. *Letters* I, 307, 319.

29. Luther to Philip Melanchthon, May 26, 1521. WABr II, 347–49. *Letters* I, 234.

30. Benzing 944–946 (*Rationis Latomianae*), 972–75 (*Ein Urteil der Theologen zu Paris*).

31. Benzing 827–32, 868–71.

32. Although Luther was initially not pleased with Spalatin's intervention, and submitted only after some testy correspondence. *Letters* I, 325, 350, 353.

33. Luther to Lang, January 26, 1520. WABr I, 619. *Letters* I, 150. *Operationes in Psalmos,* 1519–1521, Benzing 516. It is notable that later editions printed in Basel manage to print the work as an integrated whole. Benzing 517–18. The threatened Lotter reprint seems not to have been published.

34. Benzing 947.

35. Luther to Spalatin, August 15, 1521. WABr II, 379–81. *Letters* I, 292–93.

36. Benzing 944–45. USTC 688352, 689876. Benzing 948–49.

37. Benzing 948–49.

38. Luther to Spalatin, August 15, 1521. WABr II, 379–381. *Letters* I, 295.

39. Luther to Spalatin, August 6, 1521. WABr II, 377–78. *Letters* I, 290–91.

40. *Letters* I, 290.

41. And this is exactly what happened, though if Lotter's typefaces were used it was still printed in Rhau-Grunenberg's shop. Benzing 1061, 1064, with continuations and many subsequent editions. Luther to Spalatin, August 15, 1521. WABr II, 379–81. *Letters* I, 296.

42. Luther to Spalatin, July 31, 1521. WABr II, 368–69. *Letters* I, 276.

Chapter Six: Brand Luther

1. William M. Conway, *The Writings of Albrecht Dürer* (London: Peter Owen, 1958), 154–161. Hans J. Hillerbrand, *The Reformation in Its Own Words* (London: SCM Press, 1964), 381.

2. USTC. The estimate of total copies is based on an average edition size of a thousand copies, though we know that some of Luther's works were published in far larger editions.

3. Of the 55,484 editions known for the period 1450 to 1517, 38,973 (70 percent) were in Latin. USTC.

4. USTC 626334.

5. USTC 639728.

6. See, for instance *Ad Dialogum Sylvestri Prieratis Magistri Palatii de Potestate Pape Responsio f. Martini Luther Augustinensis, Vittenberge* (Leipzig: Melchior I Lotter, 1518). USTC 608851.

7. The USTC lists 1,075 German and 860 Latin works for Augsburg in the period to 1517. In contrast Nuremberg published two works in Latin for every book in German, and Venice three works in Latin for every one in Italian.

8. WABr I, 146. *Correspondence* I, 161–62.

9. Chapter 2.

10. Above, chapter 4.

11. Of the 55,484 editions known for the period 1450 to 1517, 13,643 (24.6 percent) were published in folio, and 27,793 (50 percent) in quarto. USTC.

12. Among the copious literature on Cranach see, most recently, Steven Ozment, *The Serpent and the Lamb: Cranach, Luther, and the Making of the Reformation* (New Haven: Yale University Press, 2011). Standard works are Max J. Friedländer and Jakob Rosenberg, *Lucas Cranach* (New York: Tabard, 1978), and Dieter Koepplin and Tilman Falk, *Lukas Cranach*, 2 vols. (Basel: Birkhäuser, 1974). Easier access to the major collections after the reunification of Germany has also stimulated an important new wave of Cranach studies. Claus Grimm et al., eds., *Lucas Cranach: Ein Maler-Unternehmer aus Franken* (Regensburg: Pustet, 1994).

13. This was in no way unusual; Holbein undertook similar assignments at the court of Henry VIII.

14. Ozment, *Serpent*, 63.

15. Arthur M. Hind, *An Introduction to the History of the Woodcut: With a Detailed Survey of Work Done in the Fifteenth Century* (London: Constable, 1935).

16. F.W.H. Hollstein, *German Engravings: Etchings and Woodcuts, ca. 1400–1700* (Amsterdam: Hertzberger, 1954–), VI, 20–22.

17. Ibid., 72–76. USTC 641851.

18. Carl C. Christensen, *Princes and Propaganda: Electoral Saxon Art of the Reformation* (Kirksville, MI: Sixteenth Century Journal Publishers, 1992), 39.

19. Friedländer and Rosenberg, *Cranach*, nn. 187–90, 312–13 (Luther and Katharina), 314–15 (Luther and Melanchthon). Many additional copies of these and other workshop portraits of Luther have reappeared since the compilation of this catalog.

20. On the role of the apothecary as information exchange see especially Evelyn S. Welch, *Making and Marketing Medicine in Renaissance Florence* (Amsterdam and New York: Rodopi, 2011). Filippo de Vivo, "Pharmacies as Centers of Communication in Early Modern Venice," *Renaissance Studies* 21 (2007), 505–21.

21. Andreas Tacke, *Der katholische Cranach* (Mainz: Zabern, 1992). See also the most fundamental study of Albrecht's artistic patronage, Thomas Schauerte and Andreas Tacke, eds., *Der Kardinal: Albrecht von Brandenburg, Renaissancefürst und Mäzen* (Regensburg: Schnell & Steiner, 2006).

22. Ozment, *Serpent*, 125.

23. Hollstein, *German Engravings*, VI, 7.

24. Ibid., VI, 8.

25. Luther to Cranach, Frankfurt, April 28, 1521. WABr II, 305. *Letters* I, 201.

26. Friedländer and Rosenberg, *Cranach*, nn. 148–49. For a woodcut version see Hollstein, *German Engravings*, VI, 107.

27. See below, chapter 9.

28. See Koepplin and Falk, *Cranach*, I, 307–19.

29. WABr II, 305 (where Luther sends greetings to Döring through Cranach), and WABr I, 99 (where Döring is visiting Luther while Luther writes to Lang and sends his regards).

30. The pioneering study of this book art is Tilman Falk, "Cranach-Buchgraphik der Reformationszeit," in Koepplin and Falk, *Cranach*, I, 307–412. See also *Cranach im Detail: Buchschmuck Lucas Cranachs des Älteres und Seiner Werkstatt* (Wittenberg:

Lutherhalle, 1994). A selection of the title pages are also illustrated in Hollstein, *German Engravings*, VI, 163–75.

31. USTC 614281 (Saul), 636595 (Samson), 634675 (David and Goliath). *Cranach im Detail*, 37d, 42b, 42c.

32. The definitive study is now Heimo Reinitzer, *Gesetz und Evangelium*, 2 vols. (Hamburg: Christians Verlag, 2006). For illustrations of the Cranach works, see II, 215–38, 250–52.

33. See USTC 628327, 636548.

34. USTC 646907 (Augsburg), 700131 (Nuremberg), 643615 (Zwickau). *Cranach im Detail*, 21c, 21d, 27b.

35. Martin Luther, *Von der Babylonischen Gefengknuß der Kirchen* (Strasbourg: Johann Schott, 1520). USTC 703376. Michael Stifel, *Von der Christförmigen, rechtgegründten leer Doctoris Martini Luthers* (Strasbourg: Johann Schott, 1522). USTC 617295.

36. *Acta et Res Gestae, D. Martini Lutheri, in Comitiis Principum Wormaciae, Anno MDXXI* (Strasbourg: Schott, 1521). USTC 608615, 608616. Also illustrated in Werner Hofmann, *Köpfe der Lutherzeit* (Munich: Prestel, 1983), 64–65.

Chapter Seven: Luther's Friends

1. Timothy J. Wengert, "Martin Luther's Movement Toward an Apostolic Self-Awareness as Reflected in His Early Letters," *Luther Jahrbuch* 61 (1994), 71–92, here 82.

2. Robert Kolb, *Martin Luther as Prophet, Teacher, and Hero* (Grand Rapids: Baker, 1999), 17–28.

3. R. W. Scribner, *For the Sake of Simple Folk: Popular Propaganda for the German Reformation* (Cambridge: Cambridge University Press, 1981). In context, Werner Hofmann, *Köpfe der Lutherzeit* (Munich: Prestel, 1983).

4. Luther to Spalatin, September 9, 1521: "You will be able to have this passed by the City Council quite easily with the help of Lucas and Christian." WABr II, 387–89. *Letters* I, 309.

5. Below, chapter 8. The considerable literature on this subject is excellently reviewed in C. Scott Dixon, "The Imperial Cities and the Politics of Reformation," in R.J.W. Evans et al., eds., *The Holy Roman Empire, 1495–1806* (Oxford: Oxford University Press, 2011), 139–63.

6. Below, chapter 9.

7. Cochlaeus's life of Luther is conveniently available in Elizabeth Vandiver et al., eds., *Luther's Lives: Two Contemporary Accounts of Martin Luther* (Manchester: Manchester University Press, 2002). For the four evangelists see p. 310.

8. David H. Price, *Johannes Reuchlin and the Campaign to Destroy Jewish Books* (Oxford: Oxford University Press, 2011), 18–19.

9. USTC 683888 (Wittenberg, Rhau-Grunenberg), 683824 (Basel, Froben). For an English text see R. Keen, *A Melanchthon Reader* (New York: Peter Lang, 1988), 47–63.

10. See his account of the lecture in his letter to Spalatin, August 31, 1518. WABr I, 191–2. *Letters* I, 76–79.

11. WA 30, II, 68–69. Quoted in Timothy J. Wengert, "Melanchthon and Luther," *Luther Jahrbuch* 66 (1999), 58. *Prefaces* I, 250 renders the passage slightly differently.

12. Irene Dingel, ed., *Justus Jonas (1493–1555) und seine Bedeutung für die Wittenberger Reformation* (Leipzig: Evangelische Verlagsanstalt, 2009).

13. CE II, 245.

14. CE II, 246.

15. As related by David Chyträus, and recorded by Daniel Cramer in his *Das Grosse Pomrische Kirchen Chronicon* (1603). See Kurt K. Hendel, "Johannes Bugenhagen, Organizer of the Lutheran Reformation," *Lutheran Quarterly* 18 (2004), 43–75, here 48.

16. Johannes Bugenhagen, *In Librum Psaltorum Interpretatio, Wittenbergae Publice Lecta* (Basel: Adam Petri, 1524). USTC 667459, 667604. It was reprinted in the same year at Nuremberg, Strasbourg, and Mainz. The quotation from Luther is taken from *Prefaces* I, 87. Luther uses the term "this Pomeranus" rather than Bugenhagen's name, a common use in their intimate circle.

17. Rainer Postel, *Die Reformation in Hamburg, 1517–1528* (Gütersloh: Mohn, 1986).

18. Above, chapters 4 and 5.

19. Luther to Spalatin, March 7, 1521. WABr II, 283–85. *Correspondence* I, 485.

20. Luther to Melanchthon, July 13, 1521. WABr II, 356–59. *Letters* I, 257.

21. Luther to Amsdorf, July 15, 1521. WABr II, 361–63. *Letters* I, 264–65.

22. *Prefaces* I, 26–36.

23. *Prefaces* I, 20.

24. *Prefaces* I, 45.

25. *Annotationes in Johannem* (Hagenau: Johann Setzer, 1523). USTC 683801.

26. *Prefaces* II, 113–16, 349–51.

27. *Prefaces* II, 136.

28. Johann Brenz, *Homiliae Viginti* (Wittenberg: Johann Weiss, 1532). USTC 663962. *Prefaces* II, 4–6.

29. *Prefaces* II, 286–94. See also below, chapter 11.

30. Luther to Amsdorf, January 13, 1522. WABr II, 422–23. *Letters* I, 363.

31. James Westphal Thompson, *The Frankfort Book Fair. The Francofordiense Emporium of Henri Estienne* (New York: Burt Franklin, 1911).

32. Luther to Melanchthon, August 1, 1521. WABr II, 370–72. *Letters* I, 288.

33. The canonical work is Philipp Schmidt, *Die Illustration der Lutherbibel, 1522–1700* (Basel: Reinhardt, 1977), 93–112.

34. WABr II, 525, n. 1.

35. Luther to Spalatin, September [20], 1522. WABr II, 598. *Letters* II, 15–16.

36. Conveniently listed in Heimo Reinitzer, *Biblia Deutsch: Luthers Bibelübersetzung und ihre Tradition* (Wolfenbüttel: Herzog August Bibliothek, 1983), 116–27.

37. USTC 633799 (Galatians), 641835 (Romans).

38. The trials and tribulations of finishing this project are expertly set out by Martin Brecht in *Martin Luther: Shaping and Defining the Reformation, 1521–1532* (Minneapolis: Fortress Press, 1990), 46–56, and *Martin Luther: The Preservation of the Church, 1532–1546* (Minneapolis: Fortress Press, 1990), 95–113.

39. Reinitzer, *Biblia Deutsch*, 199.

40. Though curiously, Luther approved. Luther to Amsdorf, January 13, 1522. WABr II, 422–23. *Letters* I, 363.

41. Luther to Amsdorf, September 9, 1521. WABr II, 390–91. *Letters* I, 311.

42. In both cases, by the faithful Rhau-Grunenberg. USTC 650579 (*Endschuldigung des Falschen Namens der Auffruer*), USTC 653446 (*Erklerung wie Carlstat Sein Lere von dem Hochwirdigen Sacrament, und Andere Achtet und Geachtet Haben Will*). Luther's two prefaces are in *Prefaces* I, 127–37.

43. Ibid., 130.
44. Martin Luther, *Table Talk*, ed. Theodore G. Tappert, LW 54, 141.
45. USTC 649728.

Chapter Eight: The Reformation in the Cities

1. R. W. Scribner, "Anticlericalism and the German Reformation," in his *Popular Culture and Popular Movements in Reformation Germany* (London: Hambledon, 1987), 243–57.
2. R. W. Scribner, "Erasmians and Reform in Erfurt," *Journal of Religious History* 9 (1976), 3–31. Scribner, "Civic Unity and the Reformation in Erfurt," *Past and Present* 66 (1975), 29–60.
3. Hans J. Hillerbrand, *The Oxford Encyclopedia of the Reformation*, 4 vols. (Oxford and New York: Oxford University Press, 1996), II, 425.
4. CE III, 35–36. Hillerbrand, *Encyclopedia of the Reformation*, III, 183–85.
5. Gerald Strauss, *Nuremberg in the Sixteenth Century* (Bloomington: Indiana University Press, 1966), 165.
6. Rainer Postel, *Die Reformation in Hamburg, 1517–1528* (Gütersloh: Mohn, 1986).
7. Hillerbrand, *Encyclopedia of the Reformation*, IV, 118–19.
8. Ibid., IV, 102–3.
9. D. F. Wright, ed., *Martin Bucer: Reforming Church and Community* (Cambridge: Cambridge University Press, 1994).
10. CE I, 193–94. Hillerbrand, *Encyclopedia of the Reformation*, I, 214–16.
11. CE III, 24–27. Hillerbrand, *Encyclopedia of the Reformation*, III, 169–71.
12. James S. Hirstein, "Wolfgang Capito and the Other Docti in Johann Froben's Basel Print Shop," in Erika Rummel and Milton Kooistra, eds., *Reformation Sources: The Letters of Wolfgang Capito and His Fellow Reformers in Alsace and Switzerland* (Toronto: CRRS, 2007), 19–43.
13. Luther to Capito, January 17, 1522. WABr II, 430–34. *Letters* I, 372–79. Capito's letter of December 4, 1520, is reproduced in WABr II, 222–26, and summarized in Erika Rummel, ed., *The Correspondence of Wolfgang Capito*, 3 vols. (Toronto: University of Toronto Press), I, 110.
14. William S. Stafford, *Domesticating the Clergy: The Inception of the Reformation in Strasbourg, 1522–1524* (Missoula, MT: Scholars Press, 1976). Miriam Usher Chrisman, *Strasbourg and the Reform* (New Haven: Yale University Press, 1967).
15. Hummelberg to Vadian, March 7, 1521. *Correspondence* I, 486.
16. Blaurer to von Botzheim, February 15, 1521. *Correspondence* I, 464.
17. January 25, 1521. Boniface was in Avignon, and Basil in Basel. *Correspondence* I, 448.
18. Hillerbrand, *Encyclopedia of the Reformation*, I, 12.
19. With 101 editions between 1517 and 1525. USTC.
20. A conclusion drawn from analysis of data in the USTC, searching for 1520 to 1525 and filtering for place (Holy Roman Empire), type (religious), and format (quarto).
21. Miriam Usher Chrisman, *Lay Culture, Learned Culture: Books and Social Change in Strasbourg 1480–1599* (New Haven: Yale University Press, 1982), 3–36, 151–69.
22. USTC. Hans-Jörg Künast, *"Getruckt zu Augspurg": Buchdruck und Buchhandel in Augsburg Zwischen 1468 und 1555* (Tübingen: Niemeyer, 1997). Künast, "Martin Luther und der Buchdruck in Augsburg, 1518–1530," in H. Gier and R. Schwarz, eds., *Reformation und Reichsstadt—Luther in Ausgburg* (Augsburg: Dr. Wissner Verlag, 1996), 65–77.

23. The exception was Philip Melanchthon.

24. *Correspondence* I, 422, 429.

25. *Correspondence* I, 456.

26. The imperial press was run by Hans von Erfurt, who came from Augsburg. The Mainz press of Peter Schöffer had also established a branch office in Worms in 1518. Christoph Reske, *Die Buchdrucker des 16. und 17. Jahrhunderts im Deutschen Sprachgebiet: Auf der Grundlage des Gleichnamigen Werkes von Josef Benzing* (Wiesbaden: Harrassowitz, 2007), 1019–20. For the absence of local Reformation printing see USTC.

27. Luther to Spalatin, February 17, 1521. *Correspondence* I, 466.

28. Scribner, "Erasmians," 23.

29. USTC 665548.

30. It still went through four editions.

31. Richard G. Cole, "The Reformation Pamphlet and the Communication Process," in Hans-Joachim Köhler, ed., *Flugschriften als Massenmedium der Reformationszeit* (Stuttgart: Klett-Cotta, 1981), 145.

32. USTC.

33. Geoffrey Dipple, *Antifraternalism and Anticlericalism in the German Reformation: Johann Eberlin von Günzburg and the Campaign Against the Friars* (Aldershot: Scolar Press, 1996), 2.

34. A question much debated; see Bernd Moeller, "What Was Preached in German Towns in the Early Reformation," in C. Scott Dixon, ed., *The German Reformation* (Oxford: Blackwell, 1999), 33–52.

35. Mark U. Edwards, *Printing, Propaganda, and Martin Luther* (Berkeley: University of California Press, 1994), 86.

36. Miriam Usher Chrisman, *Conflicting Visions of Reform: German Lay Propaganda Pamphlets, 1519–1530* (Boston: Humanities Press, 1996). Paul A. Russell, *Lay Theology in the Reformation: Popular Pamphleteers in Southwest Germany, 1521–1525* (Cambridge: Cambridge University Press, 1986).

37. Lazarus Spengler, *Schutzred unnd Christenliche Antwurt ains Erbern Liebhabers Gotlicher Warhayt* (*Why Dr. Martin Luther's Teaching Should Not Be Rejected as Unchristian but Rather Be Regarded as Christian*). USTC 692555. Edwards, *Printing, Propaganda*, 53.

38. David V. N. Bagchi, *Luther's Earliest Opponents: Catholic Controversialists, 1518–1525* (Minneapolis: Fortress Press, 2009), 210–14. Edwards, *Printing, Propaganda*.

39. Thomas Murner, *Von Doctor Martinus Luters Leren und Predigen* (Strasbourg: Johann Grüninger, 1520). USTC 703761. Edwards, *Printing, Propaganda*, 62.

40. *Correspondence* I, 497. *Prefaces* I, 25–26.

41. Allyson F. Creasman, *Censorship and the Civic Order in Reformation Germany, 1517–1648* (Aldershot: Ashgate, 2012).

42. A good example is the anonymous pamphlet posted up in Erfurt in 1520, discussed on pages 211–12.

43. Reske, *Buchdrucker*, 519–20. When Ducal Saxony converted to Protestantism two years later, Wolrab also switched to the publication of Protestant works, to the fury of Cochlaeus.

44. Bagchi, *Luther's Earliest Opponents*, 200.

45. Edwards, *Printing, Propaganda*, 77.

46. Impressum Romas per Jacobum Mazochium. USTC 617363. Illustrated in Karl Schottenloher, "Die Druckauflagen der päpstlichen Lutherbulle 'Exsurge Domine.'" *Zeitschrift für Bucherfreunde* 9 (1917), 197.

47. The USTC lists 542 works for Hans Sachs, of which 407 were published in Nuremberg.

48. USTC, and see Helmut Claus, *Das Leipziger Druckschaften der Jahre 1518–1539* (Gotha: Forschungsbibliothek, 1987).

49. A copy of the edict in Heimo Reinitzer, *Biblia Deutsch: Luthers Bibelübersetzung und ihre Tradition* (Wolfenbüttel: Herzog August Bibliothek, 1983), 194–95.

50. Felician Gess, ed., *Akten und Briefe zur Kirchenpolitik Herzog Georgs von Sachsen, Volume I: 1517–1524* (Leipzig: Teubner, 1905), 641. Quoted in Edwards, *Printing, Propaganda*, 14.

51. Frank Aurich, *Die Anfänge des Buchdrucks in Dresden: Die Emserpresse 1524–1526* (Dresden: SLUB, 2000). Reske, *Buchdrucker*, 162–63.

52. USTC.

53. Reske, *Buchdrucker*, 516–17.

54. Ibid., 517–18.

55. USTC. Reske, *Buchdrucker*, 314.

56. Reske, *Buchdrucker*, 183.

57. He provided ten fonts of type, so the Emser press was especially well supplied for an enterprise of its size. Reske, *Buchdrucker*, 163.

58. Ibid., 163–64, 519.

59. Paul Valkema Blouw, "Augustijn van Hasselt as a Printer in Vianen and Wesel," in his *Dutch Typography in the Sixteenth Century* (Leiden: Brill, 2013), 117–72.

60. Reske, *Buchdrucker*, 11.

Chapter Nine: Partings

1. Melanchthon to Camerarius, June 16, 1525. Heinz Scheible, ed., *Melanchthons Briefwechsel: kritische und kommentierte Gesamtausgabe* (Stuttgart–Bad Cannstatt: Frommann-Holzboog, 1977–), I, 408. Rather charmingly, although clearly furious, Melanchthon was sufficiently in control of himself to clothe his criticism of Luther by writing in Greek.

2. For the polemical context see especially Marjorie Elizabeth Plummer, *From Priest's Whore to Pastor's Wife: Clerical Marriage and the Process of Reform in the Early German Reformation* (Aldershot: Ashgate, 2012).

3. USTC. *Corr. Eras*, EP 492 for the Erasmus Catalog.

4. Spalatin to Erasmus, December 11, 1516. *Corr. Eras.*, EP 501. Melanchthon to Erasmus, January 5, 1519. *Corr. Eras.*, EP 910.

5. Erasmus to Frederick the Wise. *Corr. Eras.*, EP 939.

6. Spalatin to Erasmus, December 11, 1516. *Corr. Eras.*, EP 501.

7. Erasmus to More, March 1518. *Corr. Eras.*, EP 785.

8. Lambert Hollonius to Erasmus, December 1518. *Corr. Eras.*, EP 904.

9. Luther to Erasmus, March 1519. *Corr. Eras.*, EP 933. Erasmus to Luther, May 30, 1519. *Corr. Eras.*, EP 980.

10. Capito to Erasmus, April 1519. *Corr. Eras.*, EP 938.

11. Erasmus to Frederick the Wise, April 14, 1519. *Corr. Eras.*, EP 939.

12. See, for instance, the letters of Aleander.

13. Luther to Lang, March 1, 1517. WABr I, 90. *Letters* I, 40–41.

14. Luther to Lang, January 26, 1520. WABr I, 619. *Letters* I, 150.

15. CE III, 205. Robert H. Murray, *Erasmus & Luther: Their Attitude to Toleration* (London: Society for Promoting Christian Knowledge, 1920), 76.

16. Erasmus to Luther, August 1, 1520. *Corr. Eras.*, EP 1127A. Luther to Lazarus Spengler, November 17, 1520. WABr II, 2172–18. *Letters* I, 184–85. Luther to Spalatin, September 9, 1521. WABr II, 387–89. *Letters* I, 305–6.

17. Erasmus to Richard Pace, July 1521. *Corr. Eras.*, EP 1218.

18. *Corr. Eras.*, EP 1443; Erasmus's reply is EP 1445.

19. USTC: Cologne, Strasbourg, Augsburg, Nuremberg, and Basel, as well as Mainz and Vienna, and outside the Empire at Antwerp and Venice.

20. USTC; Benzing 2201–9; 2210–11 for the German translation. WA 18, 600–787. LW 33.

21. Erasmus to Emser, March 1526. *Corr. Eras.*, EP 1683. The preface to the *Hyperaspistes* printed as *Corr. Eras.*, EP 1667.

22. The USTC records eleven editions in 1526.

23. Peter Rückert, *Der "Arme Konrad" vor Gericht* (Stuttgart: Kohlhammer, 2014).

24. Translation taken from Peter Blickle, *The Revolution of 1525: The German Peasants' War from a New Perspective* (Baltimore: Johns Hopkins, 1977), 197–201.

25. USTC 635723. For a modern facsimile edition, *Thomas Müntzer: Deutsche Evangelisch Messe, 1524*, ed. Siegfried Bräuer (Berlin: Evangelische Verlaganstalt, 1988).

26. Tom Scott, *Freiburg and the Breisgau. Town-Country Relations in the Age of Reformation and Peasants' War* (Oxford: Oxford University Press, 1986).

27. Helmut Claus, *Der Deutsche Bauernkrieg im Druckschaffen der Jahre 1524–1526* (Gotha: Forschungsbibliothek, 1975). Tom Scott and Bob Scribner, eds., *The German Peasants' War: A History in Documents* (Atlantic Highlands, NJ: Humanities Press, 1991), 170–96.

28. Claus, *Bauernkrieg*, nn. 1, 4–28, 48–56. For another important contribution see Gerhard Pfeiffer, "Musik in Bauernkrieg 1525," in Friedhelm Brusniak and Horst Leuchtmann, eds., *Quaestiones in Musica* (Tutzing: Hans Schneider, 1989), 467–78.

29. Benzing 2117–35.

30. John Rühel to Luther, May 26, 1525. WABr III, 510–11, cited in Mark U. Edwards, *Luther and the False Brethren* (Palo Alto: Stanford University Press, 1975), 69.

31. Edwards, *False Brethren*, 41–44, 74. *Against the Heavenly Prophets*, LW 40, 73–223.

32. WA 18, 344–61.

33. Benzing 2137–76. Claus, *Bauernkrieg*, nn. 113–37.

34. Claus, *Bauernkrieg*, nn. 134–37

35. Benzing 2178–85.

36. Scott and Scribner, *German Peasants' War: Documents*, 174–76.

37. Luther to Linck, June 1525. WABr III, 536–37, quoted in Edwards, *False Brethren*, 71.

38. C. Scott Dixon, "The Politics of Law and Gospel: The Protestant Prince and the Holy Roman Empire," in Bridget Heal and Ole Grell, eds., *The Impact of the European Reformation: Princes, Clergy and People* (Aldershot: Ashgate, 2008), 37–62.

39. Edwards, *False Brethren*.

40. The standard study is still G. R. Potter, *Zwingli* (Cambridge: Cambridge University Press, 1976).

41. USTC. Manfred Vischer, *Bibliographie der Zürcher Druckschriften des 15. und 16. Jahrhunderts* (Baden-Baden: Koerner, 1991), C1, 10, 11, 12, 17, 18, 19.

42. *Von Erkiesen und Fryheit der Spysen* (Zurich: Forschauer, 1522). Froschauer printed three editions, and it was reprinted in both Augsburg and Basel.

43. See, for instance, the forty reprints in the German towns of works by Zwingli listed in the USTC.

44. Martin Brecht, *Martin Luther: Shaping and Defining the Reformation, 1521–1532* (Minneapolis: Fortress Press, 1990), 293 ff.

45. *Eyn Sendbrieff Widder den Newen Yrrthumb bey dem Sacrament des Leybs und Blutts Unsers Herrn Jhesu Christi* (Wittenberg: Joseph Klug, 1525). USTC 656438, 656439.

46. Benzing 2313–18. WA 19, 482–523. LW 36, 329–61.

47. Benzing 2416–22. WA 23, 64–283. LW 37, 3–150.

48. For two good accounts of the Marburg Colloquy see Edwards, *False Brethren,* and Brecht, *Shaping the Reformation,* 325–33. A collection of contemporary documents is offered in LW 38, 5–89.

49. The text is in LW 38, 85–89.

50. Edwards, *False Brethren,* 108.

Chapter Ten: The Nation's Pastor

1. Below, chapter 11.

2. "They will never force a wife upon me." Luther to Spalatin, August 6, 1521. WABr II, 377–78. *Letters* I, 290.

3. E. G. Schwiebert, *Luther and His Times: The Reformation from a New Perspective* (St. Louis: Concordia, 1950), 587–89.

4. Martin Treu, *Katharina von Bora, die Lutherin* (Wittenberg: Stiftung Luthergedenkstätten, 1999).

5. See Susan Karant-Nunn and Merry Wiener-Hanks, *Luther on Women: A Sourcebook* (Cambridge: Cambridge University Press, 2003).

6. Luther to his son, Hans, June 19, 1530. WABr V, 377–78. *Letters* II, 321–24.

7. Heiko Oberman, *Luther: Man Between God and the Devil* (New Haven: Yale University Press, 1982).

8. Marjorie Elizabeth Plummer, *From Priest's Whore to Pastor's Wife: Clerical Marriage and the Process of Reform in the Early German Reformation* (Aldershot: Ashgate, 2012).

9. Werner Schade, "Cranachs Bildnisse der Frau Katharina," Angela Günther, "Ein Doppelporträt mit der Darstellung Martin Luthers und Katharina von Boras," in Treu, *Katharina von Bora,* 52–56, 303–5.

10. Above, chapter 5.

11. This follows Timothy J. Wengert, "Wittenberg's Earliest Catechism," *Lutheran Quarterly,* n.s. 7 (1993), 247–60.

12. It also seems to have been the sort of work that could be smuggled past the censors in Catholic Leipzig, where it was published five times in the same period.

13. *Luther's Small Catechism* (St. Louis: Concordia, 2005). This extract is taken from the translation at http://bookofconcord.org/smallcatechismpdf.php.

14. Benzing 2548–88 (*Large Catechism*), 2589–2666 (*Small Catechism*).

15. Ian Green, *The Christian ABC: Catechisms and Catechizing in England, c. 1530–1740* (Oxford: Clarendon Press, 1996). Green, *Print and Protestantism in Early Modern England* (Oxford: Oxford University Press, 2000).

16. Gerald Strauss, "The Social Function of Schools in the Lutheran Reformation in German," *History of Education Quarterly* 28 (1988), 191–206, here 193.

17. Also to the *Instructions for the Visitors of Parish Priests in Electoral Saxony,* WA 26, 195–240. LW 40, 263–320, with the school ordinance at 314–20.

18. Benzing 2821–28.

19. Strauss, "Social Function," 196.

20. Susan Karant-Nunn, "The Reality of Early Lutheran Education," *Lutherjahrbuch* 57 (1990), 128–46.

21. Helmar Junghans, *Wittenberg als Lutherstadt* (Berlin: Union Verlag, 1979), 107–9.

22. Lowell Green, "The Education of Women in the Reformation," *History of Education Quarterly* 19 (1979), 93–116, here 97.

23. Benzing 1875–85. There was also a Latin translation and a later translation into Danish.

24. Karant-Nunn, "Reality," 142. Paul F. Grendler, *Schooling in Renaissance Venice* (Baltimore: John Hopkins University Press, 1989), 44.

25. John L. Flood, "Lucas Cranach as Publisher," *German Life and Letters* 48 (1995), 241–61.

26. Between them they were responsible for 86 percent of the 1,623 books published in Wittenberg between 1530 and 1546.

27. Hans Volz, "Die Arbeitsteilung der Wittenberger Buchdrucker zu Luthers Lebzeiten," *Gutenberg-Jahrbuch* (1957), 146–54.

28. Georg Buchwald, "Kleine Notizen aus Rechnungsbüchern des Thüringischen Staatsarchivs (Weimar)," *Archiv für Reformationsgeschichte* 31 (1934), 209–14.

29. Hans Volz, "Zur Geschichte des Wittenberger Buchdrucks, 1544–47," *Gutenberg-Jahrbuch* (1963), 113–19.

30. Luther to Melanchthon. WABr V, 350-351. *Letters* II, 318, n. 13. Jonas to Luther, June 13, 1530. WABr V, 361.

31. Benzing 2780–87.

32. Caspar Huberinus, *On the Wrath and Mercy of God* (Wittenberg: Rhau, 1534). USTC 702629. *Prefaces* II, 69.

33. *Prefaces* I, 285. The preface, addressed to Brenz, is dated August 26, 1530.

34. Luther to Katharina, August 15, 1530. WABr V, 545–46. *Letters* II, 403.

35. Luther to Katharina, September 8, 1530. WABr V, 608–9. *Letters* II, 418.

36. Benzing 2891.

37. Mark U. Edwards, *Luther and the False Brethren* (Palo Alto: Stanford University Press, 1975), 91–93.

38. Luther to Capito, July 9, 1537. WABr VIII, 99–100. See also *Letters* III, 172 n. 7.

39. Above, chapter 4.

40. *Christlike Ordeninge der Stadt Göttingen* (Wittenberg: Hans Lufft, 1531). USTC 622153. *Prefaces* I, 312.

41. Preface to Justus Menius, *Defense and Thorough Explanation* (Wittenberg: Hans Lufft, 1526). *Prefaces* I, 189.

42. Allyson F. Creasman, *Censorship and the Civic Order in Reformation Germany, 1517–1648* (Aldershot: Ashgate, 2012), for a survey.

43. Wengert, "Wittenberg's Earliest Catechisms," 250–51. USTC 656100.

44. Above, chapter 7.

45. Wengert, "Wittenberg's Earliest Catechisms," 254.

46. Luther to John Frederick, July 9, 1539. WABr VIII, 491. *Letters* III, 186–87.

47. Between 1539 and 1600 Wittenberg published 7,366 editions to Leipzig's 4,660. USTC.
48. The story is told by Luther in the *Tischreden*. WATR IV, no. 4690.
49. Huberinus, *On the Wrath and Mercy of God*. *Prefaces* II, 66–69.
50. Anton Corvinus, *Quatenus Expediat Aeditam Recens Erasmi de Sarcienda Ecclesiae Concordia Rationem Sequi* (Wittenberg: Schirlentz, 1534). USTC 689386. *Prefaces* II, 60.
51. Vicky Rothe, "Wittenberger Buchgewerbe und -handel im 16. Jahrhundert," in Heiner Lück et al., eds., *Das ernestinische Wittenberg: Stadt und Bewohner*. Wittenberg-Forschungen, 2.1 (Petersberg: Michael Imhof, 2013), 77–90.

Chapter Eleven: Endings

1. Benzing 1508–20. WA 11, 245–80. LW 45, 75–129.
2. W.D.J. Cargill Thompson, *The Political Thought of Martin Luther* (Brighton: Harvester, 1984), 1.
3. Examples in Martin Brecht, *Martin Luther: The Preservation of the Church, 1532–1546* (Minneapolis: Fortress Press, 1990), 3.
4. Bernhard Lohse, *Martin Luther* (Edinburgh: T & T Clark, 1986), 43.
5. Quoted in ibid., 111–12.
6. Richard Andrew Cahill, *Philipp of Hesse and the Reformation* (Mainz: Zabern, 2001), 152.
7. Cited in Mark U. Edwards, *Luther's Last Battles: Politics and Polemics, 1531–1546* (Minneapolis: Augsburg Fortress, 2004), 28.
8. Benzing 2908–24.
9. Christoph Volkmar, *Reform Statt Reformation. Die Kirchenpolitik Herzog Georges von Sachsen, 1488–1525* (Tübingen: Mohr Siebeck, 2008).
10. Edwards, *Last Battles*, 47.
11. Benzing 2935–41.
12. Benzing 3063–68, 3074–75.
13. Brecht, *Preservation of the Church*, 205–15.
14. Ibid., 65.
15. Paola Zambelli, ed., *"Astrologi Hallucinati": Stars and the End of the World in Luther's Time* (Berlin: De Gruyter, 1986).
16. *Prefaces* I, 182.
17. Jennifer Spinks, *Monstrous Births and Visual Culture in Sixteenth-Century Germany* (London: Pickering & Chatto, 2009), 59–79.
18. Benzing 1548–57.
19. *Prefaces* I, 183.
20. Brecht, *Preservation of the Church*, 9.
21. On this issue see especially Adam S. Francisco, *Martin Luther and Islam* (Leiden: Brill, 2007). Edwards, *Last Battles*, 97–114.
22. Benzing 2701–10, 2711–23.
23. Benzing 3378–89. WA 51, 585–625. LW 43, 213–41.
24. *Prefaces* II, 294.
25. *Prefaces* II, 255, 260.
26. *Prefaces* II, 264.
27. Francisco, *Luther and Islam*, 217 ff.

28. Johann Eck, *Ains Juden Büechlins Verlegung: Darin Christ Gantzer Christenhait zu Schmach Will es Geschehe den Juden Unrecht in Bezichtigung der Christen Kinder Mordt* (Ingolstadt: Alexander I Weißenhorn, 1541). USTC 610531. David Bagchi, "Catholic Anti-Judaism in Reformation Germany: The Case of Johann Eck," in Diana Wood, ed., *Christianity and Judaism,* Studies in Church History 29 (Oxford: Blackwell, 1992), 253–63. R. Po-chia Hsia, *The Myth of Ritual Murder: Jews and Magic in Reformation Germany* (New Haven: Yale University Press, 1988).

29. There is a copious literature on these writings; for a measured treatment see Edwards, *Last Battles,* and most recently Thomas Kaufmann, *Luthers Judenschriften* (Tübingen, Mohr Siebeck, 2011).

30. Cited in Edwards, *Last Battles,* 121. WA 11, 314–36. LW 45, 195–229. Benzing 1530–42, with a Latin translation by Justus Jonas.

31. Benzing 3293–95.

32. WA 53, 417–552. LW 47, 121–306.

33. Benzing 3436–42, 3428–29.

34. Benzing 3424–25. There is a single edition of a Latin translation by Justus Jonas. Benzing 3426.

35. USTC 633193. The printer was Joseph Klug.

36. Benzing 3369–76. WA 51, 469–572. LW 41, 179–256.

37. Edwards, *Last Battles,* 146–47.

38. Benzing 3373–76.

39. Benzing 3497–3502. WA 54, 206–99, LW 41, 257–376.

40. Quoted in Edwards, *Last Battles,* 183.

41. The illustrations were sometimes also published as a separate pamphlet. See R. W. Scribner, "Demons, Defecation and Monsters: Popular Propaganda for the German Reformation," in his *Popular Culture and Popular Movements in Reformation Germany* (London: Hambledon Press, 1987), 277–99.

42. Edwards, *Last Battles,* 199.

43. Martin Luther, *Ein wälische Lügenschrift von Doctoris Martini Luthers Tod* (Wittenberg: Hans Lufft, 1545). Benzing 3491–93. WA 54, 192–94. LW 34, 363–66. The translation is from Hans J. Hillerbrand, *The Reformation in Its Own Words* (London: SCM Press, 1964), 403–4.

44. Hillerbrand, *Reformation in Its Own Words,* 409.

45. USTC.

46. USTC.

Chapter Twelve: Legacy

1. The definitive study is Ruth Kastner, *Geistliche Rauffhandel: Form und Funktion der illustrierten Flugblätter zum Reformationsjubiläum 1617 in ihrem historischen und publizistischen Kontext* (Bern: Peter Lang, 1982). Also excellent is Charles Zika, "The Reformation Jubilee of 1617: Appropriating the Past Through Centenary Celebration," in his *Exorcizing Our Demons: Magic, Witchcraft and Visual Culture in Early Modern Europe* (Leiden: Brill, 2003), 197–236.

2. Zika, "Reformation Jubilee," 215.

3. Christian Juncker, *Das guldene und silbere Ehren-Gedächtniss des Theuren Gottesleben D.*

Martini Lutheri (Frankfurt and Leipzig: Endner, 1706; repr., Stuttgart: Steinkopf, 1982).

4. John Roger Paas, *The German Political Broadsheet 1600–1700*, vol. 2, *1616–1619* (Wiesbaden: Harrassowitz, 1986), 207–84, 296–98, 301–11, 335–37.

5. Above, chapter 3.

6. Four versions in Paas, *German Political Broadsheet*, 274–77. Hans Volz, "Der Traum Kurfürst Friedrichs des Weisen vom 30./31. Oktober 1517," *Gutenberg-Jahrbuch* (1970), 174–211.

7. For the plays, Robert Kolb, "The Hero of the Reformation: Popular Presentations of Luther in Maturing Lutheranism," in his *Martin Luther as Prophet, Teacher, and Hero* (Grand Rapids: Baker, 1999), 121–34.

8. In consequence he died, not in Wittenberg, but in Weimar.

9. For these meetings see especially Irene Dingel, "The Culture of Conflict in the Controversies Leading to the Formula of Concord (1580)," in Robert Kolb, ed., *Lutheran Ecclesiastical Culture, 1550–1675* (Leiden: Brill, 2008), 15–64. Clyde Leonard Manschreck, *Melanchthon: The Quiet Reformer* (New York: Abingdon Press, 1958).

10. Nathan Rein, *The Chancery of God: Protestant Print, Polemic and Propaganda Against the Empire, Magdeburg 1546–1551* (Aldershot: Ashgate, 2008).

11. Ibid., 117.

12. Christoph Reske, *Die Buchdrucker des 16. und 17. Jahrhunderts im Deutschen Sprachgebiet: Auf der Grundlage des Gleichnamigen Werkes von Josef Benzing* (Wiesbaden: Harrassowitz, 2007), 580. USTC for the Magdeburg Luther editions (seventy-five editions published by Michael Lotter between 1529 and 1554).

13. USTC.

14. Andrew Pettegree, "The London Exile Community and the Second Sacramentarian Controversy, 1553–1560," in his *Marian Protestantism: Six Studies* (Aldershot: Ashgate, 1996), 55–85.

15. Dingel, "Culture of Conflict."

16. On Lutheran music see Christopher Boyd Brown, *Singing the Gospel: Lutheran Hymns and the Success of the Reformation* (Cambridge, MA: Harvard University Press, 2005). Rebecca Wagner Oettinger, *Music as Propaganda in the German Reformation* (Aldershot: Ashgate, 2001).

17. Philipp Wackernagel, *Das Deutsche Kirchenlied von der Ältesten Zeit bis zu Anfang des XVII. Jahrhunderts* (Leipzig: B. G. Teubner, 1864–1877).

18. Brown, *Singing the Gospel*, 71.

19. Famously studied by Gerald Strauss in his *Luther's House of Learning: Indoctrination of the Young in the German Reformation* (Baltimore: Johns Hopkins University Press, 1978). Brown's *Singing the Gospel* takes a very different viewpoint.

20. R. W. Scribner, "Luther Myth: A Popular Historiography of the Reformer," in his *Popular Culture and Popular Movements in Reformation Germany* (London: Hambledon, 1987), 301–22. Robert Kolb, *Martin Luther as Prophet, Teacher, and Hero* (Grand Rapids: Baker, 1999).

21. Jon Balserak, *John Calvin as Sixteenth-Century Prophet* (Oxford: Oxford University Press, 2014).

22. Scribner, "Myth," 310.

23. R. W. Scribner, "Incombustible Luther: The Image of the Reformer in Early Modern Germany," in *Popular Culture and Popular Movements*, 323–53.

24. Reske, *Buchdrucker*, 400 ff.

25. The seventh largest printing industry in Germany, in fact. USTC.

26. Reske, *Buchdrucker*, 400–401.

27. 114 editions to Wittenberg's 234. USTC.

28. Dingel, "Culture of Conflict," 26.

29. Helmar Junghans, *Wittenberg als Lutherstadt* (Berlin: Union Verlag, 1979), 146.

30. Diana Berger-Schmidt et al., "Das Wohn- und Geschäftshaus Markt 3," in *Das ernestinische Wittenberg: Universität und Stadt (1486–1547)* (Petersberg: Imhof, 2011), 180–90.

31. Vicky Rothe, "Wittenberger Buchgewerbe und -handel im 16. Jahrhundert," in Heiner Lück et al., eds., *Das ernestinische Wittenberg: Stadt und Bewohner,* Wittenberg-Forschungen, 2.1 (Petersberg: Michael Imhof, 2013), 77–90.

32. Ibid., 89–90.

33. Ibid., 84.

34. Alastair Duke, *Reformation and Revolt in the Low Countries* (London: Hambledon, 1990), 114.

35. Carl P. E. Springer, *Luther's Aesop* (Kirkville, MO: Truman State University, 2011).

36. USTC.

37. Each of them with approximately 16,000 editions, out of a total of 55,000 published throughout Europe. USTC.

38. Andrew Pettegree, *The Invention of News: How the World Came to Know About Itself* (New Haven: Yale University Press, 2014).

39. Paas, *German Political Broadsheet*.

ILLUSTRATION CREDITS

Via Wikimedia Commons: 7, 15, 31, 33, 38, 40, 45, 63, 65, 76, 90, 111, 134, 138 (photo by Robert Scarth, 2006), 149, 156, 172, 215, 223, 227, 236, 249, 258, 303, 329 (photo by Michael Sander, 2006).

Stiftung Deutsches Historiches Museum, Berlin, Bibliothek: 17 (R 79/724.2), 70 (R 79/724.2), 113 (TOP, BOTTOM) (R 57/8142), 203 (R 55/911.6).

Lucas Kriner: 29, 123, 239.

BPK, Berlin / Staatsbibliothek zu Berlin, Stiftung Preussischer Kulturbesitz / Art Resource, NY: 59, 104.

© Société de l'histoire du Protestantisme Français, Paris: 95, 130 (BOTTOM), 209, 232, 241, 264, 274, 278 (TOP, BOTTOM), 289, 297, 299, 317.

Used by permission of the Folger Shakespeare Library under a Creative Commons Attribution–ShareAlike 4.0 International License: 130 (TOP), 189, 292.

© Trustees of the British Museum: 159, 176, 311.

INDEX